harmon killebrew baseball's superstar

harmon killebrew baseball's superstar

dr. wayne j. anderson

Published by
Deseret Book Company
Salt Lake City, Utah
1971

Library of Congress No. 77-159034
SBN 87747—405—2

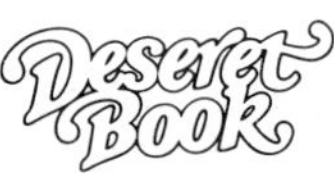

LITHOGRAPHED BY
DESERET NEWS PRESS
IN THE UNITED STATES OF AMERICA

Dedication

This book is affectionately dedicated to people everywhere, who, like Harmon and Elaine, dream the "Impossible Dream," and climb every mountain to find it.

Prologue

On November 7, 1970, Harmon Killebrew was given The Sporting News' annual award as American League Player of the Year for the second season in a row, something which had happened only once previously since the Sporting News' awards were originated in 1948.

The American League players who voted for his selection, also picked him as the third baseman of the 1970 Sporting News' All-Star Team.

The selection of Killebrew shows the high regard in which he is held by other major league baseball players.

In two seasons, the players also honored Harmon by voting for him as a member of the Sporting News' All-Star Team. He was picked as an All-Star outfielder in 1964 and the All-Star first baseman in 1967. In addition, the American League players have selected Harmon on their All-Star Team eleven different seasons.

Harmon Killebrew is also held in high esteem by the baseball writers of America, the men who are keen analysts of a player's worth. To show their respect for him, they selected him as The Most Valuable Player in the American League for 1969.

The third group who have honored Killebrew have been the fans. To show their appreciation for his outstanding abilities, they have sent him thousands of fan letters. And in 1970 when the voting was placed in their hands, they selected Harmon a member of their All-Star Team in the American League.

Harmon Killebrew is indeed a most valuable man.

Author's Note

When I first met Harmon Killebrew, I sensed there was something different about him.

My initial meeting with his wife, Elaine, gave me the same impression of her.

I thought for a long time, trying to decide what this special quality was.

At last, the answers came. Here is a couple who have love in their lives. A deep love for each other. A tender love for their family. And an understanding love for their fellowmen.

They also bear the mark of champions—those individuals who dream, dreams and are willing to climb mountains to make them come true.

The longer I knew the Killebrews, the more strongly I felt that their story must be told. When I approached them with my idea, they modestly said, "We don't like to talk about ourselves, and besides there is not very much to tell."

"I think there is," was my reply.

Finally, they decided to let me try to present the story of their life. Working with them was a delight. They graciously turned over all of their family scrapbooks and photograph albums to me. And with patience and good humor, they taped everything they could remember about their activities. They also gave the names of friends whom they wanted mentioned in the book. There were so many, it was impossible to contact them all. But those whom I did reach, felt it a privilege to be included in the volume.

It took months of research and writing to get the many

events in the Killebrew's lives down on paper, and I wish to express my gratitude to my wife, Elise, for her patient and cheerful cooperation. She has always given me inspiration and backed me in everything I have done. Our children Annette, Cherie, Wayne, Jim, Julie Gay, and Jill also kept me going with their cheerful encouragement.

I want to thank Harmon and Elaine Killebrew for allowing me to tell their life story. I hope the way I have presented it pleases them and their thousands of fans.

Wayne J. Anderson

ACKNOWLEDGMENTS

The author wishes to thank the following for their generosity in furnishing photographs for the book:

Tom Mee, Director of Public Relations, Minnesota Twins

Don Wingfield, Chief Photographer, Edited Sports Personalities

Jim Muncaster of the Orlando Sentinel

And all others as listed on the page "Photograph Credits."

All pictures not otherwise credited are from Harmon Killebrew's private collection.

The author is also grateful to the following for permission to reproduce all or parts of their written materials:

John P. Carmichael, Sports Editor, The Chicago Daily News.

Dick Cullum and Mike Lamey, sportswriters for the Minneapolis Star and Tribune.

Bill Clark and the Orlando Sentinel

Jim Murray, sportswriter of the Los Angeles Times.

Tom Mee, Director of Public Relations, Minnesota Twins

Those sportswriters of past years who could not be located.

The editors of the magazine *Sport*, "How Pitchers Face up to Killebrew," by Jack Zanger.

And all others who graciously granted interviews or responded with letters to help make this volume possible.

Contents

Metropolitan Stadium, the home of the Twins, Bloomington, Minnesota

the impossible dream

Part I

the awards dinner

1

Charlie Johnson, veteran Twin Cities sportswriter, stood before the group to make an award. As he started to talk, every person in the spacious ballroom leaned forward in order to catch every word. An air of happy expectancy swept over the audience seated at the long banquet tables, and each face lighted with a smile as Charlie said, "I've had the privilege of meeting many athletes in my years as a sportswriter, but none I've had greater respect for. He's modest to the nth degree and has done more, in his way, for baseball than anyone else I know. He started every game last year. He scored 106 runs last season and stole 8 bases. He had a batting average of .276 and led the American League in homeruns, with 49. He also led the league in runs-batted-in with 140, had a slugging average of 584, and did something else which few people are aware of. He was the number one fielding first baseman in the American League for 80 games.

"Well, who could it be?"

No one waited for the answer to Charlie's question.

Instead, the 900 people in the hall rose in unison, like one giant person, and applauded loud and long for their favorite —Harmon Killebrew.

As Harmon stood up and waited in his unassuming way to acknowledge his ovation, Charlie continued, "Harmon, your name has been mentioned over and over during this awards banquet and you are richly deserving of everything good that has been said about you. Your 1969 comeback after you had been seriously injured was out of this world. How did you do it?"

One cannot help but wonder what thoughts had been going through Harmon Killebrew's mind before he was called upon to respond to Charlie's question and receive the award in honor of his being the "American League's Most Valuable Player for 1969." Here he was the featured guest at the Mid-Winter Baseball Dinner sponsored by the Twin City Baseball Writers' Chapter.

Despite the frigid, thirty-below-zero January night, made even colder by an icy wind, 900 people had braved the weather and had filled the ballroom of the St. Paul Hilton Hotel to capacity, motivated by their desire to honor Harmon, and their other baseball favorites.

Just what *did* Harmon think about as he looked out over the huge crowd and pondered what he would say when called upon to acknowledge his award?

Did his thoughts go back to the hard knocks of his rookie days and the frustrations he endured while riding the bench for two years, after being signed as the Washington Senators' first bonus player?

Did he remember the critical comment of his first major league manager, Bucky Harris, who once said, "Good grief! The kid throws like a girl!"

The blunt question of his second manager, Charlie Dressen, who complained, "How do they expect me to win with guys like Killebrew?"

Or was his mind occupied with the biting comments of various sports writers, who at different stages of his career had written:

"Killebrew runs like a water buffalo."

"After all, Harmon is no gazelle."

"The program listed Killebrew as 'first baseman' but it was beyond the scope of his capabilities . . ."

Did the repeated needling of the fans still rankle in his memory? Their yoyo-like comments had labeled him as "Killer Killebrew" when he was hitting and "Harmless Harm" when he was in a slump. Or was he preoccupied with the moment when the comments had reached an all-time low, when a fan had suggested, "The way to improve the Twins is to trade Killebrew for the rights to three undetermined little leaguers."

Did such memories flash through Harmon's mind as he waited to speak? Did he see an opportunity to get even with his critics of the past? Suppose Harmon did dismiss these thoughts. One might still conjecture that he would use the opportunity to talk about the trials brought by his past injuries, and he had a natural opportunity to tell of the pain and struggle he endured in recovering from his recent torn hamstring muscle when Charlie Johnson said, "Your 1969 comeback after you had been injured was out of this world. How did you do it?"

He could have told the audience that he could not sit down for nearly a month after suffering the injury. (Doc Lentz said Harm ate his meals standing up that long.) He could have described the torment of either hobbling around on crutches or lying in bed, the long hours spent lifting weights and lying on his back exercising and stretching his leg, or the days spent laboriously hiking in the hills of Oregon. But Harmon did not mention any of these things. When the time came to answer Charlie's question, he replied, "I want to thank Dr. O'Phelan, Dr. Michienzi, and Doc Lentz who made it possible for me to come back."

Charlie interrupted, "The entire medical staff, eh?"

"That's right."

"But what did *you* do?"

Harmon blushed, "They did it. What do you want me to

say?" Then in typical Killebrew fashion he turned the conversation to someone else, looked out over the audience, and said, "I would also like to thank a young lady who helped me come back. Through the years she has put up with a lot of heartaches and has backed me in everything I have done—my wife, Elaine."

As Harmon said this, his lovely, blonde wife stood on her feet and, amid thunderous applause, waved and blew a kiss to her husband.

Those who are acquainted with the Killebrews know that Harmon's tribute to his wife, Elaine, was heartfelt and richly deserved. In all of his struggles to succeed since his rookie days, she has stood by his side, and in his darkest moments has helped him fight his way back closer to the top with her reassuring words, "You can do it, Harm!"

Despite Harmon's effort to turn the topic of conversation to someone else, Charlie Johnson was not about to be put off. He wanted Harmon to say something about himself, so he fired some personal questions that Killebrew could not duck.

The conversation went as follows:

Charlie: "Do you feel a day on the bench would have helped when you were in that last slump?"

Harmon: "It's natural to feel tired during a long season and I suppose we all need some rest."

Charlie: "Didn't you feel a lot of pressure in the last days of the homerun race?"

Harmon: "No! I'm glad my homerun rival, Reggie Jackson, is here. He's a great slugger."

Charlie: "What can you say about Frank Howard?" (Harmon's other rival for homerun honors)

Harmon: "He's fabulous."

Charlie: "Have you learned to hit out to right field when the other team puts on the Killebrew shift?"

Harmon: "I'd like to be able to when the second baseman shifts over to the shortstop's side. Sometimes I can and sometimes I can't. It depends upon the kind of pitches I get."

Charlie: "Which homerun of the 1969 season do you remember the best?"

Harmon: "I suppose the one I hit in Boston that hit the screen and bounced back into the field. The umpire didn't see it and wouldn't allow it. It would have given me fifty this season (a long sought goal of Harmon's).

Charlie: "Are you angry about this?"

Harmon: "Well, I suppose everything evens out in the long run. I hit one in Detroit that was ten feet foul that the umpire called a homerun."

"I suppose the greatest homerun to me was the one I hit in 1968 on the pitch when I had first come back to play after recovering from my ruptured hamstring muscle."

Charlie: "How do you stay in shape?"

Harmon: "I push away from the table and try to stay in good condition."

Charlie: "Well, Harm, we hope you'll have an even greater year in 1970 and in the years to come. The other writers join me in presenting these two gifts to you. We hope you'll be around a long time and good luck."

Harmon: "Thank you very much, Charlie, and the Twin City Writers. I also want to thank all of the players on the squad. You can't win an award by yourself. I'm just glad to be on the same squad with these great players."

During the course of the banquet, other speakers paid tribute to Harmon, and two of them who were from rival teams had the following to say:

Bill Rigney, former manager of the California Angels, who had just been appointed the Twins' new manager, smiled with relief as he said, "Killebrew has scared me to death for the last ten years every time I've seen his number three at the plate. And my pitchers, they can't figure out what to throw to him. I remember one hurler who had struck out the first man up, and then up came Killebrew to bat second. My pitcher signaled to me for help in how to pitch to the "Killer." I said, I wouldn't even worry about him. Just hit him . . . and put him on first base."

Bill Rigney's comment was no idle exaggeration, as those who have watched the Twins play, well know. Every time Killebrew steps to the plate the air is charged with tension. All the spectators lean forward expecting to see the ball either propelled like a rifle shot out of the park or soar like a rocket into the stratosphere and eventually touch down approximately 400 ft. away in either the left or right field stands or beside the center field batting eye.

And the opposing players? What do they do when they

see Killebrew's number three at the bat? Sometimes they put on the Killebrew Shift in an effort to stop the ball, and have the second baseman, shortstop, and third baseman all line up in a row between second and third base like a cordon of policemen trying to encircle a rioter. At other times, they stay in their usual positions with the fatalistic attitude of "whatever will be, will be!"

The opposing pitcher's reaction? This valiant man, being in the direct line of fire, must face the onslaught of the Twins siege-gun head on, so he calmly (Did we say calmly?) hitches up his belt, gives his cap a tug, and throws the ball toward home plate, somewhere along the edge of the strike zone, but very rarely in it. Killebrew, through constant hard work and self-discipline, has overcome his earlier tendency (of his rookie days) to bite at offerings outside the strike zone. Opposing pitchers know this. So they make their pitches as good as they can without courting disaster by putting them over the plate. The result? Killebrew will be fed a low slider that breaks just outside the strike zone, then a high ball that whizzes past his neck, and a pitch inside, thrown in an attempt to jam him and get him to hit the ball with the handle of the bat. If Harmon doesn't go for these pitches, the opposing twirler usually shrugs his shoulders with an air of resignation and throws the fourth ball that puts the "Killer" on first base. Mute evidence of this is the fact that Killebrew usually leads the league in walks. During the 1969 season he, as was previously stated, received 145 bases on balls.

Of course, such a maneuver by the opposing pitcher often works in favor of the Twins. About two weeks before the close of the 1969 season, statistics showed that giving Minnesota's homerun king a base on balls, had backfired 32 times. That number of runs had been scored by Killebrew, or men running for him, after he had been walked.

It's understandably frustrating for a slugger with Killebrew's power to take so many walks, and any player who was not a dedicated team man like Harmon probably would not. When asked about all his walks, Killebrew said, "Walks are important too, even if they are hard to take. They try to force me to swing at bad pitches." But, Harmon does avoid swinging at bad pitches, and consequently has an outstanding record of runs batted in. He does this even though it may cut down the number of runs he might bat in—for the simple reason that he is a team man.

Bill Hengen, Minneapolis Star sportswriter, pointed this out in an article on September 16, 1969. He wrote: "Killebrew has also lost chances to drive in runs by taking walks. Of his walks, 93 have come with runners on base —55 runners in scoring position (34 at second base and 21 at third). Figuring that Harmon hits at least once every four times at bat (he's batting .275) and that his 137 hits average nearly one RBI per hit, walks have cost him 14 RBI's."

Pitchers openly admit that they try to give Harmon bad pitches hoping he will swing at them, and if he does not, they will walk him rather than put the ball over. Oakland battled the Twins for the divisional title most of the 1969 season and Jim Roland, (a former Twin) their ace relief pitcher, made a comment which is typical of pitcher strategy in trying to cope with Harmon. In an interview with Bill Hengen he said, "We had been pitching Harmon outside. But when we got the ball over the plate a little, he would belt it. This time we talked it over and decided to throw all inside pitches—even if it meant walking him."

The other speaker from a rival team who spoke at the banquet was Reggie Jackson, the 23-year old Oakland right fielder who was named the "Slugger of the 70's" at the Baseball Writers' Dinner. Powerfully built and sharply dressed in a mod-tailored suit, Reggie made a tremendous impression when he said, "They named Harm right when they called him the 'Killer'. It's when I see number 3 batting against us that I get scared. Why, he hit 11 homeruns and batted in 34 runs against us. If he did against everybody else what he did against us, he'd have hit 121 homers and had over 350 RBI's. If Killebrew isn't the MVP, I've never seen one. He's bringing people into ballparks all over, not just here. Without Killebrew baseball wouldn't be as attractive. I would hope in a few years to be in the same category. I'm sure Mr. Griffith will show his appreciation for all the nice things he said about Harm. He is worth more than $100,000. They should pay him $200,000."

Reggie said more, but the amazing thing about his speech was the friendly, almost reverent attitude he had toward Killebrew, the man who had just finished beating him out of the league's homerun title.

The Awards Dinner, which turned out to be more like a happy family reunion, was a huge success. Under the skilled direction of Herb Carneal, Twins sportscaster, things moved swiftly and with just the right touch of humor. Consequently, the evening ended all too soon. To inform sports fans who could not attend of what else took place, the program is reproduced at the end of the chapter.

My wife Elise and I had the privilege of attending the event with Elaine Killebrew, Harmon's charming wife. Thus, an opportunity was afforded to observe baseball fans' reactions toward her. Believe it or not, she is just as popular as Harmon. People were converging on her from all sides with a "Hi!" a handshake, or a hug. In turn she was friendly too, and interested in everyone.

Long after the banquet had ended, we observed Elaine still chatting gaily with friends, and Harmon patiently signing autographs.

The next day, Bob Short, owner of the Washington Senators, invited Harmon and Elaine to fly with him in his private jet to Washington, D. C. where Harmon was again honored at the Baseball Writers' Award dinner at the Shoreham Hotel and presented with the Washington Baseball Writers' Award. The presentation was made by veteran American League umpire Hank Soar.

After the banquet was over, Hank approached Killebrew and said, "They wanted me to rib you when I gave you the award, Harm. But I just couldn't. I think too much of you."

After the Washington dinner, Harmon was honored on

successive nights at banquets in Fairfax and Alexandria, Virginia. Subsequent to these appearances he had been requested to attend award dinners and ceremonies in his honor throughout the nation.

—*SCORECARD*—

INVOCATION .... Rev. James Whalen, College of St. Thomas
LEADOFF .... Mike Lamey, BBWAA Chapter Chairman
MASTER OF CEREMONIES Herb Carneal, WCCO Radio
SCHOLARSHIP PROGRAM .... Bill Boni
A FORWARD LOOK BACKWARD AT THE 60s .. Boone and Erickson, WCCO Radio
'GOOD GUY' OF THE YEAR ....? ? ? ? (presented by Arno Goethel)
TWINS PRESIDENT .... Calvin Griffith
MOST IMPROVED TWIN .... Rod Carew
(Chosen and presented by Calvin Griffith)
FORGOTTEN MAN' AWARD ....Jim Kaat (presented by Bill Hengen)
UPPER MIDWEST PLAYER OF THE YEAR ....Jerry Koosman
(presented by Sid Hartman)
TWINS ROOKIE OF THE YEAR . George Mitterwald (presented by Glenn Redmann)
NEW FACE IN THE BULLPEN .... Stan Williams
THE NEW SKIPPER .... Bill Rigney
TWIN PITCHER OF THE YEAR (Joe Haynes Award) .... Jim Perry
(presented by Max Nichols)
MAJOR LEAGUE FIREMAN OF THE YEAR .... Ron Perranoski
(presented by Pat Thompson)
SLUGGER OF THE 70s .... Reggie Jackson (presented by Ken Murphy)
SPECIAL SALUTE TO THE '69 TWINS .... presented to Jim Perry
player representative by Dave Shern, president Mid-America Bank Corporation)
TWINS MOST VALUABLE PLAYER .... Harmon Killebrew
(presented by Charlie Johnson)
A VOICE FROM BROOKLYN .... Comedian Phil Foster
WORLD SERIES FILM

OTHER BASEBALL GUESTS: Twin coach Vern Morgan; John Goryl, manager of Twins' Wisconsin Rapids farm team; trainer George (Doc) Lentz; equipment manager Ray Crump. Twins Bob Allison, Bob Gebhard, Charlie Manuel, Chuck Nieson, Tony Oliva, Rick Peterson, Frank Quilici, Rich Reese, and Charlie Walters. Friendly Foes—Bob Johnson, Oakland; Zoilo Versalles, Washington; Bob Locker, Seattle; Lee Stange, Boston; Joe Schultz, coach at Kansas City.

* * *

OTHER HEADTABLE GUESTS: Jack McLaughlin, president, St. Paul Minutemen; Bill Young, president, Minneapolis Minutemen; Phil Lewenstein, BBWAA scholarship winner; Bob Short, owner of the Washington Senators.

* * *

OTHER CHAPTER MEMBERS: Bob Beebe, Tom Briere, Ben Brown, Jim Byrne, Dick Cullum, George Edmond, Willis Evans, Paul Foss, Bob Fowler, Dick Gordon, Bob Harris, Hank Kehborn, Gene Lahammer, Bob Penick, Don Riley, Jon Roe, Mike Smith, Dan Stoneking, Mark Tierney.

* * *

SPECIAL SALUTES: St. Paul and Minneapolis Minutemen, Norm McGrew, Joe Duffy, Tony Felicetta, Ernie's (Bill Conter), sportscasters of the Twin Cities radio and televison, Coca Cola.

Harmon as a baby,
right, his cousin Jane Jackson

Harmon Killebrew at age seven

clayton killebrew's bay window

2

Ever since Thetis, the mother of Achilles, dipped her son into the river Styx to make him invulnerable to the wounds of battle, parents have been hoping to bear perfect and powerful sons.

Clay and Katherine Killebrew got just that when their son Harmon was born. Although he was destined to future greatness, when young Harmon arrived on June 29, 1936 his coming was not heralded with trumpets, nor did his hometown stage a celebration. Instead, the two thousand plus inhabitants of Payette, a small town on the Idaho-Oregon border, passed the word around that the Killebrew's had another son.

Casual friends said, "Isn't that nice. I wonder if they wanted a girl?"

Close friends brought Harmon the usual blue nightgown and knit suits, and as they watched him lie in his crib said, "Isn't he cute? He looks just like his dad."

But his debut into this world caused no great stir.

Today, thirty-four years later, Harmon Clayton Killebrew, Jr. is known throughout the world as a man of power, an Atlas who bears the fate of the Minnesota Twins on his shoulders. Unlike Hercules, Harmon did not strangle two huge snakes while a child in his cradle, but on the current sports scene he is expected to perform Herculean feats everyday, and if he fails, his fans groan with disappointment.

Harmon has been called "the strongest man in baseball," "the owner of the league's No. 1 pair of biceps," "the most feared long-ball hitter in the major leagues," and "the perfect specimen (by Doc Lentz, Twins trainer, who should know)."

Rival pitchers have been trying for a long time to find Killebrew's Achilles heel. So far it has proven to be an impossible task. "Sudden" Sam McDowell, of the Cleveland Indians, thinks there might be one square inch of the strike zone where Harmon has a weakness, but Sam is not sure. He says, "There's about a one-inch spot high and right where you can work on Killebrew's only weakness—if he has one—with the fast ball. But if you get it out away from him an inch, it's a 'see-you-later' homerun."

What caused Killebrew to become the intelligent, disciplined, mighty man of muscle that he is? Was it fate? Or a combination of factors, such as hereditary endowment, positive environmental influences, and a strong motivation to succeed?

The latter assumption seems more reasonable. Let's look at the combination of things which have produced a superstar.

First, Harmon was given an endowment of strength and athletic skill from two generations of strong men. His grandfather Culver Killebrew was known as "the strongest man in the Union Army from the Illinois brigades." Not only was he the heavyweight wrestling champion of the Northern forces, but he was also known as a dare-devil who would attempt to perform any conceivable athletic feat.

When he was sixty-five, Culver fathered and passed on

his strength to Harmon Clayton Killebrew, Sr. Clay Killebrew also became nationally famous as an athlete. He became a blockbusting fullback at West Virginia Wesleyan in 1915, and was described by his coach Earl (Greasy) Neale as a "bruiser and line-smasher."

"Fuzzy" Sutherd of Decatur, Illinois, a high school teammate of Clay Killebrew, wrote the following on June 2, 1962, in a letter he sent to his friend, Joe Carpe of Boston, Massachusetts, ". . . Clay's father, Culver was a huge muscular man, and Clay told me one time when I was visiting him, that when his father went up to Macomb, Illinois to join the Union Army that they told him he was the best physical specimen they had ever seen. Culver also told Clay that he had never met a man who could do anything that he could not do better—except one thing. Clay's father said, "There was some little shrimp who could run, leap over a horse's back and turn a handspring while doing it. He dared me to try it, and when I did I nearly killed myself."

In 1916, Clay played fullback for the first unbeaten team at Millikin College in Illinois which is now known as Millikin University. He was so good that he received honorable mention on Walter Camp's All-American football team in 1916.

In the one year that Clay Killebrew was at Millikin, he performed athletic feats that have become legendary. Jimmy Ashmore, who had been a Millikin coach, said, "Killebrew was the only man I ever saw who could run 40 yards for a touchdown through the center of the line and knock the tacklers out of the road himself.

"He had lost the sight of one eye, and the hardest jolt a man could take was to tackle Killebrew on his blind side. He ran 80 and 65 yards for touchdowns that season."

Fuzzy (Eugene) Sutherd, who was the captain of the Millikin football team in 1916, and was instrumental in getting Clay Killebrew to come to the school, added this about Clay in his letter to Joe Carpe, "Clay was five feet, 11 inches, weighed 190 pounds stripped, and was as strong as a bull. I also want to say that Killy (Clay Killebrew) was one of the finest, most pleasant friends I ever had. When I think back on some of the fine times we had together, and knowing him like I did, I am sure that my old pal is mighty proud of his son Harm, who is now knocking the horsehide out of the park."

After his college days, Clay played professional football for a number of years, and later used his great athletic skills as a professional wrestler. He was a favorite along the Pacific Coast. Eugene, his oldest son, remembers watching his father wrestle for the Pacific Coast Middleweight Title at Portland in 1924.

After retiring from athletics, Clay took a job as sheriff in Payette, Idaho, and later built a flourishing business as a house painter and decorator.

The above information makes it evident that the hereditary qualities of strength and athletic skill were handed down to Harmon from his father, Clay. However, Clayton Killebrew did much more than this for Harmon and his other sons. As a devoted father he used his skills in teaching his sons, and in addition presented them a fine manly image to pattern after.

Harmon's wife was very fond of Clay and describes her feelings about him in the following way:

"Clay Killebrew was an outstanding athlete and also a good student. He achieved these honors despite the fact that he had just one eye. There was an accident on his family's farm in Nebo, Illinois when he was a young boy, and during the mishap he lost the sight in one eye. It occurred when some type of poison that was used out in the hog pens got into his eye.

"I remember Clay Killebrew because Harm and I were 12 years old when we first met each other, and sometime after that I saw Clay more and more because we would sit together to watch Harm play ball. I recall that I was rather shy and quiet and I wouldn't say anything to him until he spoke to me. Often this would take awhile. If I were sitting on the side where he had no vision, he wouldn't notice that I was there.

"He was a very distinguished looking man and had a beautiful head of salt-and-pepper-gray hair. Also he was a very good-natured sort of person, quiet and easy going. Harm is like his father in this respect, and I don't think either of them has ever had an enemy.

"Harmon's mother, Katherine May, also has been a tremendous influence in his life. She came from a family of sturdy ranchers and farmers who did not know the meaning of the word 'quit.' "

Katherine May Killebrew stands a tall 4 feet, 10 inches, and she uses every inch of herself in accomplishments. She laughingly says, "Clay used to tell me, 'Katie, your legs are so short that when you walk, you bounce up and down and stay in one place.' "

But Katie has always kept walking forward.

At one time in her life, she lost several of her loved ones within a short period of time. First, her father "Pop May" died. Her mother died shortly after. Then her husband, Clay, passed away, and to add to her loneliness her son Bob was then sent overseas to Korea. As if these things were not enough to bear, her daughter Eula's husband died of a heart attack at the age of forty. At that time Eula, who was expecting her third baby within six weeks, came with her family to live with Katie.

Despite these heartaches Katie has never burdened others with her grief and meets each day with a calm and cheerful heart.

Her husband was partially right; Katie does take tiny steps, but she goes places with them. I remember one day when a group of us were visiting a large zoo. Although it was spread out over a broad area, Katie kept right up with the rest of us on our walking tour and never once asked us to slow down.

Another incident that shows her pluck occurred when my wife, Elise, and I were walking down a lengthy airport corridor with Elaine and Katie—after having seen her sister Anne Grace embark for her Idaho home. After a long walk we came to an escalator, and adjoining stairway,

Clay Killebrew holding friend on his shoulders

Harmon's father Clay winning the 220 low hurdles at Illinois College Western High School Track meet, 1914

Harmon and family at dedication of Killebrew Drive in Payette, Idaho

that was necessary to take in order to reach our destination. Without hesitation, Katie said, "You folks take the escalator; I'll climb the stairs. My bifocals make me dizzy when I ride on an escalator. I was sure we would have to wait for Katie at the top of the landing, but to my amazement she kept pace with us, navigating the final step of the stairway at the same time we stepped off the escalator.

Harmon's mother sparkles with vitality and is interested in everything around her. She goes to most of the home games Harmon plays and also finds time to watch her grandsons, Cameron and Kenny, perform. She has a good grasp of religion, politics, and current affairs, and makes a solid contribution to such discussions. At seventy-four her voice is as vibrant as a teen-ager's, and it is easy to mistake her for a sixteen-year-old when she answers the phone.

Yes, Katherine Culver Killebrew has contributed an important ingredient, an example of drive and courage, to the mixture that has made Harmon Killebrew a star. Harmon knows it and loves her for it.

Harmon's boyhood in Payette was a happy one. He was the youngest of four children. His eldest brother, Eugene Ferris, was 20 years his senior. His sister, Eula May, was 15 years older, and Harmon and his brother Robert Culver were only three years apart. He also had a sister, Patricia, who died at the age of four months, in 1931. Naturally, his brother Bob was his closest companion. But the Killebrew family was a closely-knit group. They all loved Harmon, and apparently he was the apple of everyone's eye.

His mother and I were walking behind Harmon and Elaine at one time, and Katie with obvious pride said, "Harmon's built exactly like his father was. When he was six years old and the children were playing baseball and other games, everyone's eyes were on Harmon. They all said, 'He's got it. He'll be a great athlete.'

"He and Bob were great pals, but of course, when Harm was a baby he would get into mischief. I remember when Bob was three and Harm was still crawling. Bob was so neat and particular when he played that he'd pile up his blocks straight and perfect, and then Harmon would come along and knock them all over. Bob would get angry and ask, 'Are we going to keep him all winter?' "

Growing up as he did in a loving family, and among relatives and friends, Harmon had childhood experiences that were both fun and educational. In order to get some first hand accounts of these incidents Elaine arranged a reunion of relatives and friends who recorded their memories of Harmon's childhood days. Their stories reveal the spirit of friendliness and good fellowship that prevailed in the group.

Harmon's grandparents, the Mays, his mother's father and mother, lived with his family; so he also benefited from pleasant associations with them. The two families lived together in harmony, and Clay loved the Mays the same as if they were his own parents. Harmon's mother took good care of her parents, and as they got older and became more feeble and less able to care for themselves, she nursed them right up until they died.

Grandfather May (Pop May as they called him) was a great practical joker. Eugene, the older brother, remembered an incident that took place once when the family was listening to "Inner Sanctum" on the radio. He said, "Mom's dad put an old overcoat over his head and sneaked out the back door and around to the front of the house. Then he rapped on the front door and stepped back into the shadows. My father, Clay, opened the door and grandpa lunged toward my father to frighten him. Dad met him with an uppercut to the jaw and he was laid out flat on the front steps. Needless to say Pop May didn't try that stunt again."

As a child, Harmon had many opportunities to get acquainted with the great outdoors which he grew to love. He spent a lot of time at the C. C. Grace ranch in the summer. Charlie and Ann Grace (Mrs. Killebrew's sister) were uncle and aunt to the Killebrew children. They have two children, Bill and Doris, who are older than Harmon. His Aunt Ann recalls that "When Harmon was six he would climb a little ladder to get on his horse and help with the ranch work." Harmon says that he enjoyed carrying water to the animals and thought it was great to ride the derrick horse when hay was being stored in the barn loft. Harmon has retained his love for horses, and he and Elaine, who are both expert riders, keep some fine saddle horses at their Ontario home.

During his early school years, Harmon began to develop an interest in baseball, but the boys in the neighborhood who were all older wouldn't let him play with them because they thought he was too young and too small.

There was a lot of good-natured kidding among the youngsters, and his brother, Bob, remembered an incident which illustrates the practical jokes the fellows used to play. He said, "Bill Grace and I took the post hole digger and dug a hole nearly 4 feet deep in a small irrigation ditch. Then we asked Harm if he wanted to go wading with us. He said, 'Yes.' So we all waded along in the ditch. When we reached the hole, Bill stepped over it and so did I. But Harm, of course, didn't know it was there so he walked right into it and sank. Wow—What a laugh!"

The Killebrews have many friendly neighbors in Payette, and two of them, who have lived right across the street since Harmon was a child, are Mary and Jess Pederson. The Pedersons watched the two younger Killebrew boys, Bob and Harmon, grow up, and they claim they were the best youngsters they have ever seen. The boys, in turn, admired Mary and Jess, and they always looked out for their flower garden and guarded it from dogs or mischievous kids.

Jess likes to tell about Harmon's first fishing trip. He said: "Mary and I were getting ready to go fishing up to Smoky, a mountain nearby. We knew Harmie had never been fishing because he had said, 'I wish my dad would take me fishing, but mom says he won't. He never fishes or hunts because he just won't kill anything.'

"So we decided it would be a good chance for Harmie to go fishing with us. We went over and asked Kate and Clay if we could take Harm along. Clay said it was all right with him, but Kate said, 'Why he's never slept away from home in his life. He'd get homesick.'

"I said, 'Well, he plays with Gerrie (their niece) so much and we're taking Gerrie.'

"Kate said, 'Well—sure, if you both want to take him. It's fine with me.'

"Mary and I said, 'Of course we want to take him.'

"That evening I said to Harm, 'How would you like to go fishing with us?'

"Harmie said, 'I'd love to, but I couldn't do it because Mom wouldn't let me go.'

"I told him we'd already asked his folks and they said it was all right.

"He said, 'Oh boy, wait until I get my notebook. I'll come back and you tell me what to take.'

"He went home and got his notebook and pencil and back he came. 'Now Mary,' he said, 'you write down what you want me to take.'

"Well, she wrote down toothbrush, toothpaste, and an extra change of clothes, in case he fell in the creek. He got them together, and we went fishing.

"Those kids went fishing with me every day, and I'll tell you if they got a couple of feet away from me, they'd start hollering. We were wading up the middle of the creek, see, but it was shallow, and I knew there wouldn't be any danger of them drowning.

"We just had a ball. We had a little old tent and Mary and I had our bed in the back of it, and we put two cots on each side. Gerrie slept on one and Harmon on the other. We never went to bed before ten or eleven o'clock because we'd play cards and we'd lie there and talk for an hour. One evening, everything in the tent had quieted down, and I thought we were going to get some sleep, when Harmie raised up and said, 'What'll we talk about now?'

"The payoff was when we came back and drove up into our yard. Kate came over and asked, 'Harmon, did you get homesick?'

"Harmie said, 'I never even thought about home.'

"We took him fishing three or four times up there. The last time he was getting pretty big. After that he began going with Jimmy Arment and his wife.

"Harmon used to come over a lot because he liked Mary's huckleberry pies. Mary can tell you about those."

Mary said, "Well, we'd gather huckleberries and make some pies. Then we'd put them in a dutch oven and bake them under the ground. The kids loved them. We also used to take some white beans and cook them with a ham shank. The kids would come from town and gorge themselves with them. Then they'd say, 'We can't eat another bean in our life.' But the next day they'd come back and eat just as many again."

People are often curious about how celebrities were disciplined during childhood.

In every growing family there has to be some kind of discipline, but the Killebrew children needed very little. They were taught by their parents to keep busy and respect other people. This they did, and the boys' great love for sports always provided them with something interesting to do. There were also other pleasant pastimes. Harmon's Aunt Ann Grace remembers how the boys liked to carve things on the big trees with their pocket knives and how Harmon liked to dress up in cowboy clothes and try riding their trick horse. Ann also recalls that no matter what Harmon did at play or work he was always loving and kind and never wanted to hurt anybody's feelings.

Clay Killebrew was so proud of his sons' athletic abilities that when they were younger, and had ball games all the time at home, he never wanted to break up a game and make the boys do their chores.

Kate Killebrew says, "One of the boys' jobs was to bring in coal for the stove. Clay would go out himself many times and get the coal, so he wouldn't break up the ball game. This annoyed me, and I would say, 'Clay you're going to have to enforce the fact that the boys must do their chores.'

"But Clay would always reply, 'Now Katie, there's always time in their lives for them to do these jobs. They're playing a ball game. Just leave them alone.'

"One time, a neighbor was passing by and she stopped to visit with Clay who was in the front yard. She said, 'Clay, you're not going to have a bit of grass or any flowers left the way those boys are playing ball in your yard every day.'

"Clay grinned and said, 'Well, that's all right. We're not raising flowers and grass, we're raising boys.' "

Since Harmon has won acclaim for his achievements, reporters have frequently questioned his mother about his childhood and the type of discipline that was used. The following interview that was made after Harmon was voted "Most Valuable" reveals Mrs. Killebrew's common sense attitude in handling her children:

"Was Harmon an average boy?"

"Yes, he was."

"Did he ever get into mischief?"

"Yes, I think so."

"Did he play ball around the house?"

"Yes, he did. And he broke a lot of windows."

I've been told your boys always looked clean, that they never got dirty."

"They looked clean because I did many a washing to get their dirty clothes clean."

"I understand Harmon practiced throwing a ball in an oatmeal box. Did he use a lot of them?"

"No."

"When did he first play baseball?"

"With the knothole team."

"Were you pretty strict with your youngsters?"

"Well, we always knew where they were and what they were doing."

"Did you spank your children?"

"We never whipped them. Clay never touched them, and I never did much more than touch them."

"Do you think one of the problems today is that parents don't know where their children are and what they are doing?"

"Well, I would say so."
"Has Harmon changed since he became a star?"
"No, he still has the same personality."

Despite all of Harmon's other activities, sports constituted his first love. He first started playing on a baseball team when he was in the third grade—at the age of eight. But even before that, his father Clay saw the prospect of future athletic greatness in his son, and he nurtured Harmon's potential as only a loving father could. He and little Harmon talked almost exclusively about great athletes from the time Harmon was a toddler. Clay told him about the feats of Babe Ruth, Ty Cobb, Tris Speaker and other major league greats. He described in glowing terms the accomplishments of Jim Thorpe, the great all-around athlete, and Red Grange, the football star. So by the time little Harmon was seven years old he knew more about the lives of great athletes than did many sportswriters. As an outstanding athlete, himself, Clay knew that if his son acquired a knowledge of the possibilities to do great things in sports, and became dedicated to setting his life in that direction, that his abundant natural talents would be used systematically and not in sporadic outbursts of achievement.

After steeping young Harmon in the traditions and glories of the sports world, Clay set about to teach his son the skills needed to excel. His father was a good teacher. He taught Harmon how to hold and swing a bat in such a way that his strength went into each blow—to always keep his eyes on the ball and adjust his movements according to where the ball was and what was being done with it during each moment of the game. Clay was such a good teacher that by the time Harmon was just a kid in grade school, he not only knew the fine points of baseball but also knew how to run with a football. He learned how to "time his steps to cross his legs at just the instant that would make it almost impossible for a tackler to nail him. He also knew how to drop his shoulder and roll into a tackler to avoid injury." (Don Lynch—The Argus Observer, June 21, 1954.)

Above all, Clay taught Harmon that the key to athletic accomplishment was constant concentration on the game and complete dedication to everything he did.

Harmon was an apt pupil, and he spent long hours putting his father's instructions into practice. When he was in grade school, he fastened an oatmeal box above the door and pitched a tennis ball into it hour after hour. And he was always swinging a bat at imaginary pitches. The story is told that he once got a spanking for shattering a favorite family rose bush with a mighty swing of his bat. I asked him about that, and he grinned and said, "I don't remember that, but I do remember swinging at things of different heights to perfect my timing. Sometimes it would be a lilac bush, forsythia leaves, or anything that gave me a chance to adjust my swing to different levels."

There was always a game going on in the Killebrew yard, and stray baseballs kept Clay repairing broken windows. When the gang chose up sides for a game, Harmon was always picked first because he was recognized as a good hitter. His constant practicing paid off early, as he made the American Legion baseball team when he was eleven years old.

His proud father, Clay, was always in the background patiently encouraging and coaching Harmon.

The Killebrew boys got together at the time this book was being written and recalled some of the things their father did to encourage them in athletic achievement.

Harmon said: "I can remember back when we were quite young and Dad used to encourage us along the line of athletics. He bought a punching bag to help us develop coordination. Boy, he could really use that thing, couldn't he? He punched that bag with his elbows and everything.

"He used to play ball with us. He'd play catch, hit ground balls and fly balls. He did this even though it was difficult for him to play baseball because his depth perception, with just one eye, made it kind of tough.

"I remember the first pair of football shoes he bought Bob, and he bought me a pair later on, too. He encouraged Bob more along the lines of football and boxing.

"It was great when a carnival or circus came to town. They'd bring a champion wrestler with them, and the people in town would get Dad to wrestle with him, and Dad would always beat him.

"Dad used to take us to movies, and he'd race us home. Of course he'd always beat us because he was a good runner. I understand he held a lot of track records in Illinois, and some of them possibly still haven't been broken. He ran the short sprints, the low and high hurdles, and also threw the shot. He has won all kinds of medals in these events."

Bob recalled: "I'll never forget what Dad told me about running with a football. He said, 'When you're running with the ball and the tackler comes at you, just lower that shoulder and hit him as he's starting to tackle you. You can do just as much damage to the tackler as he can to you.' In that same respect, he said to give them that limp. I never got it quite perfected, but the moment that tackler hits you, you can stiffen your hip or that side of your body and then relax.

"Dad and I would put on boxing gloves and spar around. I was always in fast for the kill and would fling my fists all over. But Dad would just wait until I wore myself out. Then he'd hit me a good one on the side of the face and say, 'See now, you're going to have to stop and think what you're doing. Don't ever lose your head and go in there throwing your fists around. Once you lose your head, you're going to lose the fight—every time. Play it real cool and stay calm and collected.'

"One reason I think Harm has done so well in sports is not only because Dad taught us all to keep calm, but also because Harm was always playing with me and kids my age who were older and he had to do his best to compete with us."

The oldest Killebrew son, Eugene, former editor of the Payette Valley Sentinel at New Plymouth, gives his memories of his father in an article that is reprinted here with his permission. He calls it: Dad's Bay Window.

Dad's Bay Window

"I seldom think of my father without also remembering his bay window. We call it dad's bay window because he seemed always to be putting a new window pane in it. The window was a large one on the south side of our old house in Payette, Idaho, and it overlooked a good-sized lawn which was just right for an athletic field for small boys.

"I was the first to break dad's window, when I was four years old, in 1921. And from then on it really took a beating. All types of balls went through that window in the next thirty-five years, footballs, baseballs, snowballs, golf balls, and numerous rocks of assorted sizes.

"Each time the window was broken, dad quietly went to town and got another pane and put it in. He never once told us kids that we couldn't play ball in the yard. Lots of times when there was a game in progress and dad came home from work, he joined in, and several times he broke the window himself by batting a baseball or kicking a football through it.

"Dad always took the breaking of the window as a matter of course and showed no reaction except to replace it. But with mother, it was different. She always urged dad to do something about the situation each time the window was broken, but she never got very far. One winter, things concerning the constant breakage of the window reached a crucial point. The temperature was near the zero mark when a frozen snowball blasted through the window. Dad went to town to get a new pane, but it turned out that a piece of glass that size wasn't to be found in town. I guess dad had used them all up in previous mishaps. Anyway, one had to be ordered, and in the meantime a canvas was tacked over the empty window to keep out the cold. Mother had what is known in polite terms as a fit. It took dad several days to get her calmed down, but things were all right again as soon as the new window arrived and was installed.

"I recall one time when Harmon crashed a baseball

through the window and mother told dad that he just had to do something to stop the needless window breakage. Dad said, 'Now Katie, don't get excited, we can always get another window, but where are we going to get another boy like that?'

"At one time, things got so bad with brothers Harmon and Bob growing up that the bay window was just about out as much as it was in. So dad finally worked out a new plan. He had the large window replaced with a French type window made up of a lot of small panes. Then he purchased some extra small panes for the new window and sat back to wait. It wasn't long before a ball came sailing through the window right into the lap of grandfather who was sitting in a chair by the window. But this time it was only a few minutes' work and a lot less expensive to replace a small square of glass in the window.

"Dad is gone now, and all the Killebrew kids are grown. Our widowed sister, Eula, is living with mother in the old house. She has two small boys who are just beginning to throw balls around. I predict that the destruction of dad's old bay window will continue for several years to come. I'm sure that dad would be happy if he knew that his grandchildren were carrying on the Killebrew tradition of window breaking."

Clayton Killebrew passed away at the age of 59 as the result of a heart attack. At that time Harmon was a junior in high school. It was a tragic blow to the Killebrew family, and it ended a unique father and son relationship. Clay didn't live to see his dream come true, that of worldwide athletic greatness for his son Harmon. But Harmon Clayton Killebrew Sr. had done his work superbly well before he left. He had taught his son Harmon the skills and had inculcated in him the temperament and incentive necessary to become a superstar.

When talking about his late father, Harmon said, "You know, after people are gone, they usually leave a lot of material things around, but this wasn't the case with dad. There was nothing left."

Elaine interjected, "There were his paintings."

"That's true," said Harmon, "but I mean personal possessions. Nothing tangible he really owned that he had collected."

"He left his personality," said Elaine.

Yes, that was it. Clayton Killebrew left the influence of his personality with his family. What greater gift could they have asked for?

along came elaine

3

We were waiting to be served in the attractive *Steak N' Ale* Restaurant in Maitland, near Orlando, Florida. As we sat in the charming old English surroundings, it was easy to perceive the affection Harmon and Elaine Killebrew have for each other. Even in the subdued light given out by the ornate lanterns the signs were unmistakable.

Elaine's proud glances at her husband and Harmon's gentle teasing of his pretty blonde wife portrayed a relationship that contained the necessary ingredients for a happy marriage—mutual love and respect.

I looked at this handsome couple who seemed as right for each other as apple pie and vanilla ice cream and asked, "How did you two get acquainted? Who made the first advances?"

Harmon grinned and said, "Well, I suppose I was first attracted to Elaine because she was always out in front doing things when we were in high school. She was a yell leader and a majorette. She was great at twirling two batons.

She was also on the tumbling team, and in addition played softball and basketball. I couldn't help but notice her blonde hair and her good figure; so naturally I wanted to meet her."

"It was Harm's pretty legs that first attracted me," said Elaine with a smile. "Harm was a real good-looking kid, the cutest boy in the junior high. I used to notice his nice looking legs when he played basketball. I was a yell leader at the time, and I had my eyes on him every minute when I was at the game.

"I was fairly quiet and shy and he was pretty shy too. So it was some time before we really spoke to each other.

"I had a good school-days friend named Meridell Cooper who is now Mrs. Len Mohler. She lived just a few blocks from Harm over on the West side, so sometimes I would walk over to her house after school. We would walk behind Harm, and she would try to talk me into going up and walking beside him, because she knew that I liked him. She was always a flirt, cute and outgoing. I was more reserved, so I always admired her and watched to see how she flirted. Meridell finally instigated things; so Harm and I began walking together.

"Harm and I felt comfortable with each other, so we gradually became good friends."

"That's right." said Harmon. "From that time on, it just seemed natural to be together, and we would not change a thing if we had it to do over again."

Just what kind of woman is Elaine Roberts Killebrew —the lifetime companion and constant inspiration of superstar Harmon?

Elaine is a striking 5 feet 7½ inches in height and has the figure and poise of a professional model. Her features are a combination of classic beauty and the wholesome look of the girl-next-door. They include a well-formed nose, which tilts a tiny bit upward, giving her a slightly saucy look—calm blue eyes which change expression with her moods, sometimes displaying tender compassion and at other instances the challenging look of a Viking goddess.

Sensitive lips complete the composition of a lovely and expressive face. Framing her countenance is soft, wavy hair which reminds you of the finespun, liquid gold, with which the Italian painter Botticelli adorned his female subjects.

Classical painters would depict her as a goddess—while today's pre-teen set would say she looks like a Barbie Doll.

Elaine has a multi-faceted personality made up of traits which often seem to be at odds with each other.

She can be a gay and delightful companion, sparkling with wit and congeniality. At one banquet, I remember a male admirer saying, "Elaine—You're an All-American girl, a regular Doris Day!"

"I don't sing," was Elaine's good-natured comeback.

"Doll, you don't need to," was the admirer's rejoinder.

She can also use the same good humor mixed with genuine concern when disturbed by the habits of her friends.

"Charlie," she will say, "you've got to cut down on your smoking. I'm worried about you."

Or, she will cheerfully remark, "Bill! That liquor isn't doing you any good. I'll let you drink this instead. How about it?"

She is the only person in history who has talked me out of a cold glass of orangeade on a hot day. She fixed her blue eyes upon me and said, "That stuff is just loaded with sugar."

Feeling like a criminal, I handed it untouched to someone else.

The serious part of her nature comes to light when she defends her convictions. She will write to her Congressman and criticize his stand on air pollution, or engage in debate with all comers on controversial issues. She has her feet planted firmly on the ground, and the strength of her convictions enables her to engage in dialogue with the most articulate academicians.

Elaine, like Harmon, is the soul of generosity. "Here is some lotion," she will say. "It should help your skin irritation." Or she and Harmon will give expensive toys to the children of a young couple, with the comment, "Our children are too big for these. We'd like you to have them."

Despite her generosity to her friends, Elaine is frugal in her own spending. She makes most of her own clothes and hunts for bargains to meet the family's needs. Her hands are always busy making things, such as knitting a sweater or crocheting a scarf. If you comment and say you like it, she will happily say, "I already have three orders for this pattern."

Dramatic evidence of her thrifty nature was revealed one time when I accompanied her to the airport. After she had purchased her ticket, we placed three pieces of her luggage on the scales. The clerk looked at them and said, "We can only put those two suitcases in the baggage compartment. If you want to include the overnight case it will cost you four dollars for excess baggage."

"I'll carry it on the plane myself then," said Elaine as she promptly picked up the case.

I did not see how she could possibly carry the case, as she was already loaded down with several other assorted bags.

She put my mind at ease, however, as she said with eyes flashing, "I've carried this much before and I can do it again. Imagine wanting to charge four dollars for that little thing."

For a moment I thought it a bit unusual for a woman of her means to be so concerned over four dollars. But then I remembered Elaine's childhood and how she had mowed lawns around the neighborhood and worked in the orchards picking peaches or thinning strawberries in order to help her family meet expenses, and I realized why she acted as she did. Elaine had been taught the virtue of hard work as a child and had learned that money is not easy to come by. Thus, her philosophy is that it should be spent wisely.

Despite her dynamic personality and the beautiful image she presents to the world at large, Elaine is basically a modest and shy person. At one time, when she was our house guest, I asked her if she would favor us with some selections on the piano, and she modestly said she did not play well enough to entertain others. However, later in the quiet of the evening, when the others had gone, she sat at the piano and played semi-classics with skill and beauty.

Elaine is also a deeply spiritual person. She believes in God and feels that her greatest mission in life is to be a loving companion to Harmon, care for their children, and thus build a harmonious and loving family unit that will endure forever.

I asked her once how she felt about women striving for equal rights with men.

Her answer was brief and to the point. "A woman can do and be what she wants. It's her decision. Of course, I believe in individual growth and freedom of expression, but I see no reason why being a good companion to her husband and a homemaker for her children should deprive her of either opportunity."

I teach courses in marriage and family living at the University of Minnesota, and a short time ago I invited Elaine to visit my classes. After giving brief introductory remarks about the topic for the day, I asked Elaine, without a moment's advance notice, to stand before two different classes and express her thoughts on marriage. Now, university students are a sophisticated group, and I suspected there might be some adverse reaction to her thinking. But there was none. On the contrary, I could see that the students, male and coeds alike, were impressed by her sincerity and her logic. In fact, she covered the entire spectrum of premarital and marital adjustments with such wisdom that not one voice was raised in dissent.

It is impossible to recapture the mood and impact of her talk on paper, so I shall list the topics she discussed and tell how she answered the students' questions.

Do you believe in sexual intercourse before marriage?

No! Don't engage in it. Save yourself for your husband. Your husband would like to know you belong completely to him, and it's great to belong to one guy.

How do you feel about early marriage?

Harm and I were attracted to each other at 12 and were going steady at 16. So naturally, we were seeing too much of each other and it was hard to hold off. My mother objected to our steady dating and I said, "Well, I'll see him away from home, then." I didn't, but you know how it is. You can't think of anyone except your boyfriend or girlfriend.

Yes, we did get married early. We were both just nineteen. Maybe we did get married too soon, but we had things going for us. Harm had a bonus and a $10,000 dollar-a-year major league contract, and we were ready to get married, and we knew where we were going. For goodness sakes, don't you get married that young if you don't know what you're going to do or where you're going.

Did you have marriage adjustments to make?

When you first start out in marriage, you think love will conquer everything. It doesn't.

First, you have to adjust to your husband's job. Harm was signed as a bonus player by the Washington Senators, and then he had to sit on the bench for two years. It's frustrating to see your husband do this and not be able to do anything about it, especially when you've seen him perform as a high school star.

Then you have to understand your husband's way of life, and it's more difficult when you have different religions. My husband's and my religious beliefs were different, and it took about 8 years before we felt the same way religiously. You need guidelines for your family, and religion can give them.

But isn't it easy to be the wife of a superstar?

You've got to remember you don't start at the top. It takes hard work to get there. Harm says success is one percent talent and ninety-nine percent desire, and you have to set your goals high and pay a hard price to be a winning ball player.

When Harm was playing in the minor leagues, we never knew when and where we would have to move. Once, when we were sent to Chattanooga, we couldn't find a place to live, and had to move in with another ballplayer and his family. At another time when I was expecting our second baby in 10 days, I was flying to Indianapolis to be with Harm, and I heard over the radio that he was being transferred to Chattanooga. So you see, you have to learn to adjust.

But now that Harmon has made it, it must be easy.

It's easier in some ways and harder in others. After he was elected "Most Valuable," it seemed like thousands of people wanted him to speak at dinners, so he was away from home most of the winter. Then during spring training the kids and I don't see him for three months at a time.

Can Harmon be a good father when he is away so much?

He makes up for it when he's home. He's one hundred percent. He's helped feed and change the children. He'll get up at night and give their milk to them, and he also helps do the laundry.

Do your boys idolize their dad?

Secretly, yes. But they don't want any publicity because of him. When Cameron, our oldest son, was 13, they wanted Harm to do a TV show at Cam's Junior High. Cam said, "Mom, do you know what it would do to me if they come and do that. The kids will razz me." It took me a long time to help Cam see it would be an honor.

How do you feel about having five children?

It's wonderful! But you've got to teach them what's right and discipline them, or you can raise little monsters.

Don't you ever feel neglected?

Of course, especially when I have all five children coming at me at once and Harm's not around to help cope with them.

Don't you ever get jealous when you're husband's away so much and he has so many admirers?

Jealous? No! I love Harm and I know he loves me, so I trust him completely.

The students' reaction to Elaine's talk was great. Typical of their comments were, "Isn't she gorgeous!" by the coeds, and, "She's really something," by a male student who added, "Now I can understand why Harmon says she has been a constant inspiration to him."

Elaine's childhood experiences present the key to understanding her unique personality, and there is no better way to hear the account than from her own lips. Here is the way she remembers her life as a small girl.

"My twin brother, Duane, and I were born in Emmett, Idaho, on March 10, 1936. We have a sister six years older who was born on March 19, 1930, so for 16 years we three children lived together in the family. We lived in Emmett until Duane and I were about three years old. Then our family moved to northern Idaho to a small town called Shupe which is located up near the Salmon River.

"Times were very hard when we were small children

and our father worked at many different kinds of jobs. He worked in a grocery store in Emmett and also sold sewing machines for the Singer Sewing Machine Company. When we moved to Shupe, he worked in the mines.

"Living conditions were pretty rugged up there in the north country. We had no running water in the house, so we had to carry our water from a spring. Our house was small and it was necessary for my twin brother and me and our older sister to sleep in one bed. It was crowded, but we did keep warm. Despite these experiences, I still remember how much fun it was to live there. It was a beautiful country. In the winter the deep, deep snow covered the ground like a white blanket, and we could look across the Salmon River and see the deer and elk standing there like sentinels on the horizon.

"We stayed in Shupe about two years. Then we moved down to Payette, Idaho. I remained there with my family until I got married.

"About the time we moved to Payette my brother and I were old enough to go to school, so our parents enrolled us in the East Side grade school which was about two blocks away from our house. At that time Harm was attending the West Side grade school, so we hadn't met.

"My mother, Fern Smith Roberts, is a real homemaker. She prepared nutritious meals for us, and arranged things so she was always there to greet us when we came home from school. She is tall and slender and also was a blonde in her younger years. Mom's whole life centered around her family.

"She is very religious. Her great grandparents joined the Mormon Church in Denmark. After joining, they left their home and made the long trip to Utah, where they settled so they could live in the center of the Church. Consequently, mom was brought up in a devout Mormon family. So it was she who saw to our religious training.

"She has always been devoted to dad. She nursed him back to health after three heart attacks, and after he had a stroke and became partially paralyzed on the left side, she became his left hand and worked right alongside him in the shop.

"Mom liked Harm from the start and had complete confidence in us regarding our dating relationships and our desire to get married.

"She really showed us children the kind of devotion and help a loving wife should give her husband.

"My father, Kelly Roberts, was a hard worker. It seemed he was working most of the time. I really believe that he got most of his enjoyment out of his job. He often would eat dinner and then go back to work until 10:30 or 11:00 at night. Dad had taken correspondence courses so he could become an electrical repairman, and he took one room of our home and made it into a shop. A few years later he built a shop out behind the house and continued his business there.

"Dad was a tall, good-looking man and very sociable. People would come to his shop to have something repaired and would chat and visit with him by the hour. He often would wind up by inviting them to dinner, and would simply bring someone to the house and say, 'Fern, put some more water in the soup! Bill Green is staying for dinner.' Because dad socialized so much in his shop, we had very little social life as a family.

"Some people called dad a hard-headed Englishman. I like to be more diplomatic and say he had a very strong will. He was a student of Indian history and politics, and he would fight to defend his principles. He would often take the family to visit places of historic interest.

"He had an interesting family background. One of his grandfathers left his job as a newspaper man in New York City and became the first stone mason in the west. His father and others in the family were pioneers in homesteading farm lands around Boise and Emmett, Idaho.

"I loved to be with dad, and when I was twelve, I worked in his shop rebristling brushes.

"Dad was also very fond of Harm, and the three of us spent many good times together watching television.

"Despite his long hours of work, dad, who had a great sense of humor, found time to play practical jokes. One stands out especially in my mind. He had fastened a rack on the back of his car so he could haul things that he repaired, and to have some fun he had rigged a hidden shocking device on it. One day when we were visiting grandma in Emmett, dad maneuvered things around so that grandma casually sat down on the rack. Then he pressed his secret switch and gave her a shock. Grandma leaped up high in the air and then surprised us all by saying, 'My, that really felt good.'

"That was one time when dad didn't know what to say.

"I really felt close to dad. He knew this book was being done, and even though he was in pain, he told me as much as he could about his life.

"My father wasn't a member of the Mormon Church, and the rest of us in the family were. He almost never went to church with us. But I remember one special time when he did. It was when I got married in the Church in Payette. Then, dad was there dressed in his finest clothes. Before the ceremony began, he held me and gave me an affectionate hug, and then he gave me away to Harm. I shall always treasure that memory.

"My father passed away just a few weeks ago from a heart attack. Before his funeral service our family gathered at the church, and Harm said a beautiful prayer. We were all left with a feeling of peace. I know it's going to be hard on mom to be alone, and I hope she can keep busy with interesting things.

My twin brother and I were very close during grade school, and I played more with his group of boys than I did with girls. So I was quite a tomboy. Living in town we didn't get much chance to go out in the country and do any of the fun things you do on a farm. Our grandfather, Orson Smith, lived on a farm in Emmett, Idaho. We would occasionally go there to visit. He didn't have any horses, so I didn't have the opportunity to ride horses and work on the farm in the summer as Harm did. I was crazy about horses, and wished to earn some money so I could get to ride them. I remember mom having said, 'If you can earn your own money to do it, it's all right with me.'

"But mom," I protested, "what can I do to get money?" "Look around," she said, "maybe you can earn some from the neighbors."

"I was quite small, but I decided I could mow lawns. I took our mower and asked our neighbors for jobs. I was received in different ways. Some would say, 'Do you think you're strong enough to do it?' or others, 'What does a little girl like you need money for?'

"But they hired me anyway. I would spend the week working at any job I could find, and then go out to the riding academy on a Saturday or Sunday and spend all my money.

"During my grade school years, I met Meridell Cooper, who was a good friend to me. She quit school and got married when she was about sixteen.

"When I went into junior high, I first met Harm. From that time on it seemed that life was not quite complete unless he was around."

Harmon, a freshman—and his brother Bob, a senior—both stars on the Payette High School varsity football team

happy high school days

4

"Harm, now that you're starting Payette High School, you've got a chance to participate in all kinds of sports," said his fond father, Clay.

"Well, I could try out for baseball, dad," replied Harm. "I like it real well."

Clay looked at his young son with fatherly kindness and said, "Harm, try out for football and basketball too. That way you will learn what you can do best. In addition, you'll get some good coaching and make a lot of friends."

Harmon followed his father's advice, and as soon as he enrolled in high school in the fall of 1950, he tried out for the backfield on the football team and made it. He played on the varsity team alongside his older brother Bob, who was already a star halfback. The same year he made the school varsity basketball team, again joining his brother Bob. When the baseball season came around, Bob played left field, and Harmon held the shortstop position on the varsity team.

From that time on, Harmon performed athletic feats

that have become legendary in the North Country. Before he finished high school, he had won a letter every year in each of the three varsity sports.

You who have grown up and attended high school in a small town, can appreciate the impact that Harmon's achievements had upon the people of Payette and southwestern Idaho. For those who have not had this experience, you should know that the high school is the activity center of the community. Everyone who can make it, attends the sports events, the school plays, the programs, the debates, and even the PTA meetings. Football, baseball, basketball, swimming, and track stars become home town heroes, and their fans cheer them on to victory with the zeal of crusaders. If an athlete suffers an injury, his condition becomes the chief topic of barber-shop conversation, or if he wins a game, he is the current home-town idol.

Nearly as much adulation is accorded to those who play the leads in the school play, the school debaters, or the young people who participate in school programs. Proud relatives will say, "Molly is prettier and a much better actress than most of those Hollywood stars," and the crowd at the town drug store who stops for a malt after a game will agree that their favorite Joe "Could teach all those 'pros' a thing or two," about baseball, or football, or whatever the current sport may be.

Such involvement on the part of all age groups is good for the community, in that it eliminates age-ism and causes old and young alike to enjoy the associations that come from being united in a common cause.

In looking back, it's easy to see how Harmon became the town idol. The people of Payette took him into their hearts, and they followed his post-high-school achievements with the fervor that only home-town admirers can feel.

Elaine also won the plaudits of the townspeople and her fellow students with her talents and charm. She was a cheerleader who could get the crowd to shout loud enough to shake the rafters. When she marched around as a majorette twirling two batons in perfect rhythm, her blonde hair glistening in the sun, many a head turned to drink in her beauty. She also displayed her talents in many other ways by holding several student offices and working on the school yearbook staff. To crown her achievements, she performed in two school plays, "Night of January Sixteenth," in her junior year, and "My Friend Irma," when she was a senior, in which she played the title role. A number of people in the audience who watched her performances nudged the person seated next to them and said, "Look at that Elaine Roberts. Isn't she a beauty? Some Hollywood talent scout is bound to sign her up."

The following summary of the high school extra-curricular activities of Harmon and Elaine discloses how active and talented they both were. Here it is as it appeared in the school yearbook at the end of their senior year.

Harmon Killebrew
- Football 4 yrs—(Captain Sr. yr)
- Basketball 4 yrs
- Baseball 4 yrs
- Key Club 2, 3, 4 yrs (Pres. Sr. yr)
- Glee Club 4 yrs
- Student Council 2, 3 yrs
- Class President 2, 3 yrs

Elaine Roberts
- Girl's Athletics 4 yrs
- Future Homemakers of America 4 yrs
- Majorette 4 yrs
- Thespians 4 yrs (Pres. 3, 4, yrs)
- Forum Club 3 yrs (Treas. 3 yr)
- Office Assistant 3, 4 yrs.
- Yearbook staff Sr. year
- Choir Jr. yr.
- Tumbling Sr. yr.
- School plays—Jr. yr. "Night of January Sixteenth"
  Sr. yr. "My Friend Irma" (lead)

Those high school days were happy ones for Harmon and Elaine, but everything did not always come up roses.

They also had their share of hardships and heartaches.

Harmon had become known for his talents even before he went to high school, so naturally the coaches had their eyes on him. The Payette High school football coach, Walter Buettgenbach, recalls, "I became aware of Harmon when he was in junior high school. I had a junior high physical education class, of which Harmon was a member. I soon found that Harmon could do everything a little better than the other boys. I remember he could "jump and reach" 23 inches, which is phenomenal for a junior high boy. I began planning on how I would use Harmon when he reached the ninth grade.

"The fall of 1950 found Harmon in his freshman year; and, of course he was out for football, then basketball, and baseball. He was the only boy I ever coached who made the starting lineup in the three major sports as a freshman."

In his freshman year, Harmon made the varsity football team and played in the Payette Pirates' backfield, both at halfback and at fullback. At that time he was five feet six inches tall and weighed around 155 pounds. Bob was already a star halfback and he advised and helped Harmon to be an effective back. The local press had the following to say about Bob:

"Bob Killebrew, a small and fast Pirate halfback, is a senior playing his fourth year with the local gridders. Seventeen years old, Bob weighs 140 pounds and is five feet six inches in height.

"All around athlete Bob won a letter in boxing during his freshman year; has two letters for football, one for basketball and two for baseball.

"He plans to enter college next fall to line up pre-med studies."

Bob made the Snake River Valley Conference All Star football team and was also presented the Ed Parsons Achievement Award. The news account read:

"Bob Killebrew, Payette high school senior, was presented the Annual Ed Parsons Athletic Achievement award as the outstanding Pirate football star for the year 1950, during a special assembly held at the high school last Friday morning.

"M. T. Dixon, city school superintendent, presented the award to Killebrew in recognition of outstanding athletic ability as halfback on the Pirate squad; leadership, citizenship, and scholastic standing."

During his freshman year in basketball, Harmon again joined his brother Bob on the team. He immediately became a regular and was a standout because of his consistent rebounding and accurate shooting.

In the spring he played shortshop in the varsity baseball team, and his brother Bob played left field. He showed the results of his father's tutoring in baseball, just as he had in football. His almost instinctive play making and powerful long ball hitting caused the coaches and spectators alike to sense that he would some day be a great star.

During the summer of 1952, Harmon played on Coach Jack Dailey's Junior American Legion team. Excerpts from news reports show Harmon's value to the team. A few representative ones were:

> Payette swamps Weiser by the score of 15 to 2. . . . Top thrill of the game was the 5th inning when Harmon Killebrew hit a grand slam homerun.
>
> Payette trounces Caldwell 6 to 3. . . . Harmon Killebrew slammed out a homerun with two on to account for the three run margin.
>
> Payette Legions even score with Boise, 5-3. . . . Killebrew garnered two doubles in four at bats for Payette to lead the attack.

The Junior Legion team went on to win the Idaho State title at Lewiston, and they were welcomed home by an admiring crowd.

The Payette Independent Enterprise reported:

> Conquering Heroes Hailed as They Return Home as Champs.
>
> . . . Screaming sirens led the returning heroes into the city to a welcome of which they were justly proud. The baseball team rode down the main street in a truck with banners streaming, proclaiming a welcome to the state champions led by the sirens of the police department's and sheriff's prowl cars.
>
> There were no individual heroes on the team, although several players stood out for their individual play. They won because they played like a team.

> Jim Davis was able to record two doubles in four trips to the plate, and Harmon Killebrew garnered three hits in five times up with a three bagger that brought in the winning run. Ray Looney hit the fence with a two bagger with three on to tie the score in the eighth inning, and every other player on the team played his heart out to win the state championship for Payette.

Harmon had a phenomenal batting average of .538 for the four tournament games with 7 hits in 13 times at bat. His average for the entire season was .472.

At the beginning of the 1951 football season, Harmon started playing like an experienced veteran. He displayed his talents when the Payette Pirates played the Caldwell Cougars, a Big Six Conference team in a non-league game. Although the Pirates were 40 point underdogs, Harmon made the game a close one with several long passes and the Cougars won by a close 26-19 margin.

Despite this encouraging start, the team suffered a serious setback because Harmon incurred a serious knee injury in the game and was able to play only periodically throughout the season.

Coach Walter Buettgenbach was upset. He considered Harmon his best prospect and a great "clutch" player.

Harmon recovered sufficiently to lead the Pirates to a victory in the final game of the season against the Nyssa Bulldogs by a 26-0 score. In reporting the game, the Payette sports reporter wrote:

". . . Pre-game dope had the teams even, but they forgot to tell Harmon Killebrew about it, and the first time the Pirates got the ball, Mr. Killebrew tore through and around the line for a touchdown."

During the game Harmon's passing and running so overwhelmed the Bulldogs that the sportswriter also commented, ". . . Killebrew showed that he could have been the big difference needed in the Vale game and those two tie games with Emmett and Ontario if he had been in condition to play."

That winter Harmon underwent an operation on his knee at a Boise hospital. His mother was deeply concerned and said, "Harmon is very anxious to get back into sports and has high hopes of being as good as new when he recovers. His doctor, Dr. Shaw, of Boise, assured him that he would never know he had been injured by football time."

That was Harmon's first knee operation, and it was not to be his last, but he has never let the problem stop him from excelling as an athlete.

Even though he was not up to par during that winter's basketball season, Harmon was the team's spark plug and the leading scorer in the conference. His constant ball hawking and desire to win caused coach Millard Reynolds to comment, "I wish we had a few more Killebrews."

In the spring, Harmon again turned to baseball and became the team's top hitter. His consistent long-ball hitting sparked the others, and the Payette Pirates won the Snake River Valley Conference title. He was already being talked about as a potential "pro" prospect.

It was during the 1952 football season that Harmon starred as a triple threat man. The new coach, Jack Dailey, moved him to quarterback, and his great all-around ability became obvious. He was a smart signal caller, and Jack Dailey recalls, "The kids just looked to Harm as a leader, and he was smart. I installed a new formation, the Oklahoma T. I showed Harmon the new move just once, and he executed it perfectly.

"Harm could pass with the best of them. His accurate passes made Jim Davis, his receiver, an All-American end. He was a blockbusting plunger and an elusive open-field runner, and could he punt! He had an average of about 46 yards!"

Press reports of two of the games showed Harmon's value to the team.

In one of them, Payette handed the powerful Vale Vikings their first defeat in two years.

". . . Payette's passing game was the deciding factor in the 13-12 win. Coach Jack Dailey said that Jim Davis proved he could catch passes standing on his head.

Other pass receivers were Arnold, Frost, and Smith. All of Payette's passes were thrown by Killebrew.

". . . Killebrew passed as he has never passed before, and his field generalship was outstanding. . . . Once Killebrew threw a pass inside his own 10 yard line, then attempted to pass again, but his receivers were covered, so he ran the ball himself and got to the 30 yard line. . . . At the end of the game the hilarious Pirates carried Coaches Dailey, Reynolds, and White off the field on their backs."

A write-up in the Argus Observer showed how important Harmon was to the football team. In a game which the Pirates lost to the Ontario Tigers, the report read:

"The Ontario Tigers won over the Payette Pirates, which consisted namely of Harmon Killebrew, the passer —Harmon Killebrew, the runner—Harmon Killebrew, the kicker, and Harmon Killebrew the play caller. . . . For Payette, Killebrew stuck out like icicles in August. He attempted 30 passes and completed 13 for 126 yards. He ran for most of the Pirate yardage, took care of the kicking chores, and called the plays."

In the key game of the season in which Payette defeated the Nyssa Bulldogs from Oregon, to win the Snake River Class A Conference Championship, Harmon again starred. The game was a tough defensive battle, and Harmon, finding that his team couldn't gain on the ground, decided to take to the air in the second quarter. He lobbed a pass to Jim Davis, who went all the way for the six points. The kick for one point was missed.

The Bulldogs knotted the game at 6-6 in the third quarter. In the waning moments of the fourth quarter, the Pirates got a break, recovering the ball when the Bulldogs fumbled on their own one yard line. Harmon handed off to his backs in an attempt to penetrate the center of the line, but the Bulldogs didn't give an inch. Finally, on the fourth down, he took matters into his own hands, pulled a quarterback sneak, and smashed through for a touchdown. The Pirates won 13 to 6 and with the win, became conference champions.

Payette High School now had won a place in the sun. The teams by winning the conference title in both baseball and football had become the talk of the town—and the state. Consequently, every other high school began gunning for them. Coach Millard Reynolds hoped to add the basketball title to the collection, and during the 1952-53 season the team came close. They qualified for the District Tournament at Boise and played three games before being eliminated.

In their final game against Meridian, which Payette lost 49-48, the press reports showed Harmon's ability and determined drive to win.

". . . Harmon Killebrew gathered 24 points . . . dropping in two free throws near the end of the game to narrow Meridian's victory margin to one. . . . During the final quarter Killebrew dumped in 12 points, and his teammates added 9 more."

During the tournament Killebrew led his team in scoring with 49 points for the three games. Harmon also finished second in the Snake River Valley Class A league scoring race with a total of 189 points in 12 games and a 15.75 average.

In the spring of 1953, when Harmon was a junior, he again starred on a baseball team, and his powerful hitting led the Pirates baseball team to another Snake River Valley title.

The 1953 football season did not turn out as well. Harmon suffered a pre-season leg injury and was out of action for two weeks. In the final game of the season, however, he ran wild. The Pirates defeated the Nyssa Bulldogs 60-32, and all Harmon did was score five of the touchdowns, pass for three more, and kick for six extra points after touchdowns. The statistics showed that he carried the ball 21 times with an average of 9.5 yards per play. He completed 7 passes out of 13 for 204 yards.

When I met Harmon's coach, Jack Dailey, I asked him what the team's favorite scoring play was. He promptly answered, "A play with which we scored on the first play in seven out of eight games."

Harmon and Elaine, two popular high school students

Leonard Walsh, high school faculty member *who with his wife, June, helped Harmon and Elaine during their high school days*

Harmon's high school football coach, *Walter Buettgenbach*

Harmon as high school senior, Payette team captain and all-American, with his coach Jack Dailey

Harmon as captain of the Payette baseball team and all-conference baseball star in his senior year in high school

Harmon as all-conference basketball star in his junior year in Payette High School

Harmon and Elaine at the Sweetheart Ball

Harmon and Elaine on graduation day at Payette High School

"What kind of play would be that effective?" I asked.

Jack grinned, "Our favorite pass play. Killebrew would pass, Dailey would pray, and Davis would catch."

Harmon's outstanding play on the football field won him national recognition. He won All-American honors as a member of the All-American high school football squad.

The 1953-54 basketball season was a disappointing one; the Pirates finished near the cellar. Despite the team's dismal record, Harmon was voted by coaches and officials as the most valuable player in the conference. He also received the most votes for the Conference All-Star Team.

During the spring of 1954, Harmon played his final high school baseball season before graduating, and he put everything he had into it. He had improved every year under coach Jack Dailey's patient tutoring. He rained hits all over the field, compiled a hitting average of .375, and was the team's leading slugger. The Pirates again won the conference championship. Press reports were filled with accounts of Harmon's hitting.

In a game against Ontario, the report went:

"Killebrew pounded the ball ferociously, slapping out two scorching singles and running the legs off the Tiger outfielders all night."

Against Caldwell:

"Killebrew and Keller swatted over the fence homeruns in the second inning to highlight the attack."

Against Meridian:

"Killebrew added a punch with a first inning triple and two singles in five times at bat."

The foregoing brief account contains just a few of the highlights of Harmon's incredible athletic achievements in high school. The following article appeared in the Payette Independent Enterprise, his hometown newspaper, when he concluded his high school career:

"Killebrew Cited as Greatest Athlete During Annual Awards Assembly. Harmon Killebrew was described by Payette High School coach Jack Dailey as 'the greatest athlete I have ever coached,' during award ceremonies

Friday at the high school. Killebrew received letter awards for varsity football, basketball and baseball, and his official commendation from the Wigwam Wisemen of America, who chose Killebrew for the All-American high school football team.

"His football jersey, No. 12, was retired and will be placed on permanent display in the high school trophy case. Dailey announced that Killebrew also received a lifetime pass to all Payette high school activities."

Coach Walter Buettgenbach, in reflecting upon Harmon's high school achievements, had this to say.

"I can best summarize Harmon's athletic endeavors by saying he was among the few athletes I coached in a rather long coaching experience in high school, college, and university, who always seemed to know what to do in the clutch, and had the ability to do it.

"I not only coached Harmon but I also had him in classes. In his academic work he was never satisfied with anything but his best effort. He was a top student as well as an outstanding athlete. I have often said that one could always trust Harmon to do the right thing in all situations. This, in my book, is the highest compliment anyone can give."

In discussing his sports activities in high school, Harmon remembered several friends who helped shape his life. He also lauded all of his coaches for their interest and concern for their players.

"Don Dibble," he said, "helped me in my younger years. He was a fine student of hitting and got a professional offer from Cincinnati. Don died from Bright's Disease at the age of twenty-seven.

"Then there was Roy Arnold who was great in running back kickoffs. He went on a mission for the LDS Church. I saw him in Anaheim recently.

"Jim Davis was always pleasant to be with, and he'd catch any pass that I placed near him.

"Ray Looney was another great guy. He was an outstanding pitcher on our Legion team. They used to kid him by saying that he learned to pitch by throwing rocks at squirrels.

"Other good friends were Clayton Comish, a member of the Legion team, Neil Fredricksen, an outstanding hitter on the Legion team, and Mac Schmidt, who later played professional baseball in the Pioneer and Northwestern Leagues.

"I felt fortunate in having these fellows as friends because they were all ambitious and had high standards."

Harmon also worked at any available job to earn needed money. He worked on a milk truck for the Farmer's Co-op, did maintenance work for the school system, and other things.

Then there was his social life, mostly with Elaine Roberts.

When I asked Elaine about her high school days, she looked thoughtful and said, "Well, I was really busy and didn't have time to chase all over the country looking for something to do."

After reviewing school records, reading newsclippings, poring over scrapbooks and listening to Elaine's own recollections, I found that to be an understatement. In fact, I'm amazed that Elaine even found time to get any sleep. Because she has always been ambitious, she also worked part-time during all of her years in high school.

When asked about her jobs, she said, "Yes, I worked through high school, too. I worked in the orchards a lot of times, mainly because we could earn more money there. We could earn a dollar an hour thinning peaches, whereas they only paid seventy-five cents an hour for working in the stores.

"In my junior year, I worked for the Fitch Insurance Company after school and on week-ends. When I was a senior, I worked at Glover's Jewelry store in Payette after school and on Saturdays. That job closed at 6:00 p.m.; I went from there over to a drive-in restaurant and car-hopped until late at night."

Elaine continued. "We had many other friends who were

honestly watching out for us and trying to show us how to remain good kids. Harm's father and mother were good to us, and after Clay passed away, I used to go over and spend some evenings with his mother. We became good friends, so by the time we were married I knew her pretty well.

"Another friend who looked out for us was Melvin Debbin. He drove a school bus and worked at the school and post office. I don't think he ever missed a ball game that Harm played in. He was always around, and if we needed a ride somewhere he often took us.

"Some other friends, Reba and Duane Comish, had a restaurant in town named the Bluebird Cafe. They had a son, Clayton, a teammate and close friend of Harm's. They were very close to us and tried to give us guidance and counsel. It seems sometimes that teen-agers turn their own parents off and accept counsel more readily from friends. Reba and Duane helped us, and we are still close to them.

"Jim and Florence Hayden were also good friends. Jim called all of the games, and he was really a Killebrew fan. He was very disappointed when Harm chose baseball as a career, because he thought Harm was such a great football player.

"Jim had a way about him that could build you up so you felt you could just do anything. He was this way with Harm and me. He talked me into entering the Miss Payette County Contest. I did, and finished third.

"Two friends whom Harm and I shall always remember were Leonard and June Walsh. Leonard was our eighth grade social science teacher and also a coach. He could see that Harm and I were together a lot, and he talked to us as a father would about waiting for marriage before we became too deeply involved. He spent a lot of time helping school kids, and he organized us into a square dancing group so we would have a wholesome outlet for our energies. I remember that we used to go several nights a week over to the school to do square dancing. His wife, June, was just as kind and as interested in us, and encouraged us in everything we did. After they left Payette, Leonard was killed in a plane crash in Colorado, and his passing made us very sad."

Elaine's recollections of her dating experiences with Harmon show how much they have always cared for each other. It is easy to sense the mutual respect and affection they have had for each other from their teens on.

Elaine talked about their experiences in an unusually interesting and candid manner. She said:

"When I was in the eighth grade, I remember a dance that was coming up, and I waited and waited for Harm to ask me, but it was finally too late and I couldn't wait any longer. I had received an invitation to go from a high school fellow, so I decided to go with him. I went that night and we dated with another couple. The girl who dated the other fellow lived in the next block down from me.

"After the dance, they parked in front of the other girl's house. The two in the back started necking, so I told the fellow I was dating that we could walk on down to my house if he would take me home. We got down to my house, and he wanted to kiss me. I told him no, he couldn't because I didn't kiss anybody I didn't love. He surely left quickly, and he didn't ask me out again.

"It was some time during the 8th grade, I think, that Harm and I started seeing each other. I remember we went to Saturday afternoon movies meeting there. As time went on, he walked me home at night after school. We would shoot a few baskets out in my yard if he didn't have to stay at school for some kind of practice.

"We just began to get better acquainted and as time went on we sort of paired off. I tried to date other boys after we got into high school, but they just didn't interest me. My mind was on Harm all the time I was with someone else, so I finally just quit trying. I just felt it was a waste of time and I didn't enjoy myself, so why bother.

"Our relationship meant a lot to me. It was really important. I can remember telling my sister one time how I felt. I spent quite a bit of time with my sister. Incidentally, she was six years older and got married when she was 19. She had her own home and lived in Ontario just seven miles from us, so many times I spent weekends with her, babysitting for her or just visiting. I told her that the best friend I had was Harm, and I really felt that way.

"By the time we got into the Junior and Senior years, I wasn't too interested in running around with girls. I was so active with things in school that I simply didn't have time to go around with the girls much. However, the relationship that I had with Harm continued to grow deeper and deeper as time went on, and I felt that our relationship was important to him too.

"When his father died, we were sixteen years old, and Juniors. The night he passed away, Harm and I had been on a date and it was quite late when Harm left me at my home. He had walked me home and then walked all the way from my place over across the tracks to his house. He arrived there, and was just getting into bed about 1:30 a.m., when his mother gave a loud scream. Harm went rushing to the bedroom and saw that his father was dying. He and his mother did everything they could, but it was just a matter of minutes and he was gone. This was a very, very difficult experience for Harm because he and his father had a close relationship. He had helped Harm in all of his athletic endeavors and given him counsel whenever he needed it. His father was close to his entire family, and we all felt great sorrow and missed him deeply.

"Harm and I attended all the school activities together. We went as partners to all of the dances and we pretty much filled in our dance cards with each other's names. We did try to exchange dances with one or two other couples but we still stayed mostly with each other.

"Because we both were so busy, Harm and I didn't get too many opportunities to be together, but I can remember we tried to see each other on Sundays. We knew that that day, at least, we could have to ourselves. We would do something on Sunday afternoon and then go to my house for dinner. We'd turn on the radio every Sunday night and listen to Jack Benny."

Harmon and Elaine are human, of course, and occasionally they would have a disagreement. Elaine remembers one that broke up their steady relationship—temporarily. She said, "I worried continually when Harm played football. I was always afraid he'd get hurt. I would be on pins and needles and worry myself to tears during the football season. I just couldn't stand it because I thought it was so brutal.

"Harm's mother didn't like it either, and everytime he got hurt we both went through agony. One day his mother said to me, 'Why don't you try to get Harm to quit playing football?'

"I thought this over and decided to just put it to him. 'I'll tell him that I'm not going to go steady anymore unless he quits that game.' I gave him the word one day at school, and it backfired. He didn't respond just the way I thought he would. He said, 'Okay, then I guess we'll just have to quit going steady.'

"I recall several nights later, (by this time we were ignoring each other) that I was really feeling terrible. I had gone home after school and was sitting on the couch doing my studies. My brother and one of his boyfriends were sitting there in the room. All of a sudden I leaned over on the couch and started sobbing my heart out.

"My mother came into the room and asked, 'What in the world is the matter with you?' I told her, between sobs, that I had told Harm I wouldn't go steady with him anymore if he was going to play football.

"Mom said, 'You silly thing. You get right on that phone and tell him right now that you didn't mean what you said.'

"I couldn't do it—I was just too proud. Finally Harm came around to my way of thinking. He quit.

"Some time later he was watching a football game at night, and some sort of accident took place in the stands. As I recall it, one of the stands collapsed. It was not the one Harm was sitting in, but Harm decided that he would be just as safe out on the playing field. Jack Dailey, the coach, had brought Harm's jersey along, so he went to the dressing room and suited up during half time and played the second half of the game.

"When I heard what he had done, I was hurt, but by that time I was so happy to be back in his good graces that I was willing to let him play football if that was necessary.

The Payette Independent Enterprise reported the incident this way:

"Harmon Killebrew returned to the local Snake River Valley Conference football wars Friday night against Meridian after reconsidering his resignation from the Payette squad. And his appearance sparked the locals to two touchdowns in the second half."

". . . Killebrew watched the first half of the game from the grandstand, and then asked to suit up for the second half. He played only on offense in the final half and scored both Payette touchdowns. When Killebrew rejoined the squad, it was a new team which took the field for the second half. Killebrew's appearance seemed to inspire them."

When I met Jack Dailey in Minneapolis, on the day the American Legion honored Harmon, I asked him if he remembered the incident. He grinned and said, "You bet! Harm was running around at the top of the bleachers. A section of them wasn't tied down and it collapsed. I just happened to have Harm's football uniform in the team bus, and we got him into it and into the game in a hurry."

After this temporary setback, both Harmon and Elaine felt an even greater need to be together, and Elaine remembers, "As time went on, through high school, it became more and more difficult for us to be apart. As early as our junior year we began talking about 'when we are married. . . .' By this time Harm was, I think, entertaining ideas of playing professional baseball. But he had arranged things academically so he could go to college, and had been accepted and given a scholarship at the University of Oregon. He had a sister living in Portland at the time, so Harm and I, his mother and oldest brother, and Don Dibble paid her a visit and also looked over both colleges while we were there. Harm decided that he wanted to attend the University of Oregon."

In recalling the same incident, Harmon said, "When we went to Portland, Gene and Don Dibble took me over to the University of Oregon and introduced me to Len Casanova, their football coach, and Don Kirsch, their baseball coach. They were both fine men. They showed me their athletic plant, explained the sports program, and arranged football and baseball scholarships for me. I thought it would be great to attend school. I wanted to major in physical therapy and also play football and baseball for them."

Harmon's and Elaine's high school achievements had paid off. Harmon had won a scholarship to see him through the university, and Elaine had developed into a girl who would make an ideal partner for him.

Then Harmon made a decision that shattered the entire picture and changed their lives overnight.

the decision

5

What caused him to change his mind? First, he was still dreaming the impossible dream—that of striking out into the unknown and becoming a major league baseball star.

Since the dawn of history, young men and women have dared to dream impossible dreams. Such young people have not been afraid to break with the status quo and explore the unknown. They have all had three things in common—a dream, the courage to pursue it, and the willingness to work at mastering the difficult things along the way.

The popular Jack Benny, who dreamed of becoming a great comedian, put it another way when he divulged one of the keys to his success. He said, "My father told me, 'Benny, (Jack's name is Benny Kubelsky) if you're going to be a good violinist or a success in anything, you must set a goal, and then practice the hard parts.' "

The field of sports has always had youngsters who have dreamed the impossible dream and have been willing to practice the hard parts to realize it.

But there were immediate factors which influenced Harmon's decision. He could move toward his dream and also solve a family problem. His father's death had left the family without financial support. The small amount of life insurance received had barely paid for the funeral expenses. His oldest brother, Gene, was in the newspaper business in the nearby town of Plymouth, and Bob, another brother was in the army in Korea. The only money coming in was the social security income, and the allowance for Harmon, as a dependent, would stop when he was eighteen.

Don Lynch wrote the following comment about this on June 2, 1954. (The Argus Observer)

> When Gene told Harmon the amount the Senators had offered, the young ball player staggered back a step and almost fell over. At first he couldn't believe it—thought Gene was kidding.
>
> ". . . Clay, the father, would have been immensely proud of his 'big leaguer' for reasons other than athletic talent, if he could have been here this Father's Day.
>
> The money didn't mean anything to the youngster for himself.
>
> His comment was, 'That means I can take good care of mom, and help Bob go to college and maybe even help Gene get ahead faster in the newspaper business.'
>
> That sentiment was in line with an old piece of family fun.
>
> Father Clay used to say to the family, 'We'll all have a big time when Harmon gets in the big leagues.'

The final factor that erased all doubt in Harmon's mind about pursuing his dream was the influence of Ossie Bluege. Ossie, a former star third baseman for the Washington Senators, and at that time their farm director, had flown to Payette to watch Harmon play ball with his semi-pro team, the Payette Packers, a member of the Idaho-Oregon Border League.

There is an interesting story behind Ossie's trip. The late Senator from Idaho, Herman Welker, also from Payette, had known Harmon since he was a boy of six. He had watched the Killebrew lad develop into a star high school athlete, and when Harmon graduated from high school, the Senator could not wait to tell his friend Clark Griffith about him.

At that time, Griffith, the eighty-four-year-old President of the Washington Senators, found his club hopelessly bogged down in the second division, and was hoping a miracle would give him some winning ball players.

One day, when Griffith had decided the situation was almost hopeless, Welker walked into his office and said, "Griff, I've found a ball player who will give your club the spark it needs. In fact, I think he's the best ball player in the world."

Griffith, who had heard such claims before, was a bit skeptical, but he knew Senator Welker was a good judge of baseball talent, so he said, "I suppose this lad's from Idaho and just as great as Walter Johnson was."

"Right on both counts," replied Welker. "Only the fellow's an infielder and he can hit the ball out of sight."

"Can he hit like Mickey Mantle?" asked Griffith.

Welker's eyes sparkled. "Yes he can, and he's only seventeen."

"How's he built?" asked Griffith.

"As strong as an ox, and he weighs nearly two hundred pounds."

"All right! All right! Herm, you've got me interested; where can we see him?" asked Griffith.

"You'll have to go to Payette, Idaho. He's playing semipro ball there," said Welker. "His name is Harmon Killebrew."

Subsequently, Griffith called in Ossie Bluege and told him to fly out to scout Harmon.

When Bluege arrived in Payette, it was raining. In fact, it rained so much for three days that the baseball games had to be postponed. But Bluege didn't waste his time. He asked everyone he met questions about Killebrew, and he learned some amazing things. They all praised Harmon. He learned that in his last three games he had banged out nine hits in nine times at bat with the majority of them going for extra bases.

He talked to Don Dibble, manager of the Payette Packers, and was told that Harmon had compiled a batting average of .500 during his four years in high school. Harmon starred for the Junior Legion team for 5 years since beginning in the sixth grade, had been the Captain of the high school football, basketball, and baseball teams during his senior year, and at present had an incredible batting average of 1,000 in the fast semi-pro league.

Naturally, Bluege hoped the rain would stop. He felt he must see Killebrew play—he sounded too good to be true.

Harmon, in recalling the incident said, "Ossie was a person who lifted you up, and you went away feeling better.

"Before it quit raining, he told me he had to hurry back to Washington, and that he wanted me to come back and work out with the Senators, so he could watch me play there.

"I told him I had already accepted a scholarship at the University of Oregon and I'd probably better keep on with school.

"Finally it quit raining, and he said, 'Now, Harmon, just relax and play your game. Don't worry about me.'

"I thanked him and went out on the field, hoping to do my best."

The muddy infield made it difficult for Ossie to assess Harmon's fielding skill, but he did notice that Killebrew handled a couple of bad hop grounders well. However, his hitting was something to behold. The hit that caused Ossie to shake his head in disbelief was a 435 foot homerun that cleared the left center-field fence, the first to ever go out at that spot. The wallop caused Ossie's eyes to bulge. Turning to the man next to him he asked, "How far away is that left field fence?"

"They say it's about 400 feet," replied the man.

Bluege, hardly able to contain himself, said "Why that ball must have landed nearly 450 feet away."

"Why not?" said the man, "That's the way Killebrew hits them."

Just to be sure of the distance, Bluege got up early the

next morning and tramped through the beet field beyond the left field fence. Carefully pacing the distance, he decided that Harmon's homerun had indeed traveled 450 feet. He hurried to the phone and called Clark Griffith.

"Griff," he said, "This Killebrew kid is even better than Herman claimed. He looks as powerful as Lou Gehrig and he does hit them like Mantle. And he's got the finest wrist action I've ever seen.

"Griff, someone else will get him if we don't hurry and sign him up."

"Calm down, calm down!" replied Griffith. "You're sure getting quick on the draw in your old age. All right, sign him up. Give him a bonus of $30,000, if you have to. Just sign him."

Bluege's enthusiasm for Killebrew's hitting that night was shared by others. In fact, the homerun he hit has become almost an historical landmark in the world of sports, and has been talked about almost as much as "the shot heard 'round the world."

Harmon's mother said, "That homerun is something he's hoped for all his life. Ever since he's been a youngster playing in that old park, he's hoped he could hit one over the fence. It came in his last game."

Lynn Mohler, right-handed fast-ball pitcher who opposed Harmon in the game, remembers his hitting that night this way:

"I only pitched in one game in which Harm was a participant. It was a day in May, 1954, a cold and rainy day. I was in the Air Force at the time, being stationed at Mountain Home AFB, Mountain Home, Idaho. Our team had a couple of games cancelled, so to stay competitive, I pitched two games for a team at Emmett, Idaho.

"Prior to this particular game, Harm had been at bat nine times and had nine hits, this information being given to me before the game. The first time at bat, with two men on in the first inning via errors, he hit an inside fast-ball —so hard I never bothered to follow its flight, knowing it was over the fence. That fence was over 400 feet, and I was told it went out halfway up the light tower. That was the only ball hit off me in my pitching career that I never kept my eyes on.

"The second time up, I had Harm fooled with a change-up curve ball, catching him flat-footed—but he still hit a line drive triple to right field. This made it 11 hits in 11 at bats!

"The third time at bat, he hit a sharp ground ball to the short stop, but he booted it for an error. Harm, his fourth time up, hit another ground ball to the short stop which he handled and threw him out. That gave him 2 for 4 for the game.

"The AFB team on which I pitched had a coach that told me about Harm. He said that Harm was a good hitter; it took me but one game to believe it.

"Harm didn't appear to me to be nervous before or during the game, even though he knew Bluege was there to watch him. The things that impressed me about Harm were his power, quick hands, and he laid off the bad pitches.

"I met my wife because of that one ball game, so because of my good fortune I never asked Harm for any part of his bonus! (a chuckle here)"

That same morning when Bluege was talking to Griffith, Harmon was talking to his mother over the breakfast table.

Mrs. Killebrew, sensing that Harm seemed a little down, said, "I was really happy when you hit that homerun last night. You've been trying to hit one over that wall for years, and it was nice that you could do it when Mr. Bluege was watching. What did he say to you afterward?"

"He didn't even talk to me," said Harmon.

"That's strange," said his mother.

Harmon paused for a moment, thinking, "Oh, well! I'd better get going, I've got to start painting the high school gym. It needs paint badly."

Mrs. Killebrew watched her son walk toward the school building, and she hoped Mr. Bluege would talk to Harmon. Otherwise he'd be disappointed.

Mrs. Killebrew didn't need to worry. Mr. Bluege was getting ready to do a lot of talking, as he had been busy making up an offer for Harmon.

After Harmon had left, Bluege went to the Killebrew home and introduced himself to Mrs. Killebrew. She showed him to a comfortable chair, and he got right to the point.

"Harmon looked good in the game last night," he said. "We're interested in signing him to play for the Washington Senators."

"Yes, I was proud of him," said Mrs. Killebrew. You say you want him to sign with the Senators?"

"That's right," replied Ossie.

"Well, you'll have to talk to his older brother, Gene about that. He works in New Plymouth, about twenty-five miles from here."

So Ossie, not to be put off, drove over and expressed his interest in signing Harmon.

"I don't know whether you have heard," said Gene, "but Harmon's already been offered a scholarship at the University of Oregon, so he can get a college education. I know he's been dreaming about playing baseball in the majors, but he can always do that after he gets his degree."

"I know how you feel," said Ossie patiently, "I'd never wean a boy away from college. But Harmon can get his college education during the off-season. That's what I did, and it worked out fine. We're willing to pay Harmon $30,000 dollars if he'll sign with us now."

"It sounds like a good offer to me," said Gene, "but Harmon will have to decide for himself what he wants to do, and of course he should have Verne Daniel, our family lawyer, look it over in case he decides to sign."

"Fine," said Bluege, "I'll leave the contract with Mr. Daniel. I hope Harmon will accept it."

After Bluege left, Gene got Don Dibble, coach of the Payette Packers, to go with him to tell Harmon the news. Harmon was still painting the gym when they arrived, but he climbed down when he saw Gene and Don.

"Harm, Mr. Bluege made you an offer for the Senators."

"No kidding," said Harmon, looking surprised.

"It's not a very good one, though," teased Gene. "Just thirty thousand dollars for three years."

Harmon staggered back a step. Here was the impossible dream coming true. He had visions of associating with the star players he had idolized and sitting in a box with them, watching his first World Series. He thought of how he could help his mother and the rest of the family financially and of having enough money to get married. But then a previous commitment interrupted his train of thought.

"That's great," he said, "It was kind of Mr. Bluege to recommend me so highly, but there are two things I've got to do before I can sign."

"What?" asked Gene.

"Well, I've got to phone Earl Johnson of the Boston Red Sox. I promised to tell him if I got an offer from someone else. I also want to talk it over with Elaine."

Harmon got on the phone and told Earl Johnson about his offer. Mr. Johnson said it sounded like a good offer, and he knew that the Red Sox could not match it; so he released Harmon from any commitment to him and wished him luck.

Harmon's signing with the Senators was publicized throughout the Sports world. Jim Grant, columnist for the *Idaho Daily Statesman* reported: "Ossie convinced Griffith that Washington needed Killebrew like a man lost in a desert needs a glass of water.

"And Vern Daniel, Senator Welker's law partner and the man who actually signed Killebrew after getting the authorization from Bluege, said Ossie told him 'Killebrew's got the greatest potential I've ever seen in my life. When he bats, he's got the finest wrist action I've ever seen. He looks like the most powerful of any newcomer since Lou Gehrig. He seems to have no weak spots, and can hit fast-balls, curves and all kinds of pitches.' "

The Washington Club flew a photographer to Payette to take pictures of Harmon, and many press services throughout the country played up the signing. However, amidst all the fanfare, very little was said about the feelings of Elaine Roberts, Harmon's sweetheart, whose entire future hung in the balance.

I have discussed this with Elaine, and have sensed that she had some feelings of ambivalence about Harmon signing to play professional baseball at that time. Because of her great faith in Harmon, she did not question his ability to make the grade, but like many other young girls she also had entertained happy thoughts about a future life on the University campus. She had dreamed about eventually living in the married students' housing area and of being known as the wife of the campus football and baseball star, and perhaps of taking part in college dramatics and other activities. When Harmon came to her and said, "I've got a contract to sign with the Washington Senators," Elaine said, "Who are the Washington Senators?"

"When Harm finally signed and left, I felt like my world had come to an end."

So, there was the decision—a momentous one made by a seventeen-year-old boy. When he went to Senator Welker's Payette law office and signed the contract, he accepted a challenge that started him on the road to fulfill the impossible dream—that of becoming a major league baseball star. Even then, Harmon was thinking of others. Roy Arnold, a high school friend, remembers, "Harmon woke me up the next morning, and said, 'Do you want my job with the school board? I've just signed with the Senators.'"

It would have been easier and less risky for Harmon to have taken the scholarship at the University of Oregon. The coaches there, Don Kirsch and Len Casanova, were aware of his talents and were undoubtedly willing to have used all of their resources to help him have a successful athletic career, acquire a college degree, and then perhaps sign for an even greater bonus later. And the chances are that Harmon turned all of these things over in his mind before making his decision.

A skeptic might say, "What kid at seventeen wouldn't

jump at making thirty thousand?" Still, this was not the primary factor that influenced Harmon's decision. Of course, he knew the money would enable him to take good care of his mother, but neither is the kind who folds under pressure.

In the final analysis, Harmon signed at seventeen because he and his father, Clay, had dreamed for years of the day when he would become a major league player. Harmon knew in his heart he could realize that dream and felt that the Senators, who were struggling in the second division, would give him an opportunity to play right away. In addition he had abiding faith in Elaine—she would stand by him.

After signing, Harmon was honored at a farewell dinner given by his friends in Payette.

Jim Grant, Boise columnist, had this to say about the event:

> Payette likes this lad. Meet him and you'll understand why. No false modesty about the old college try; just a mature alertness of the problems he's going to be facing in the big time.
>
> A star athlete, an honor student, winner of the Good Citizenship award offered by his school, and a personable young gentleman, Harmon Killebrew will be starting on a glorious adventure. Payette, and the whole state of Idaho wish him Godspeed."

the bonus baby

6

Harmon's instructions were to take the plane to Chicago where the Washington Senators were playing. So his family drove him to the Boise municipal airport and bade him a fond farewell.

Elaine's voice trembled as she said, "Golly, Harm, it's going to be so lonely without you, I don't know what I'll do with myself."

"I'm kind of scared, myself," said Harmon, "to think of not having you or anyone else from home around. But I'll get you back to Washington to see me as soon as I can."

As the plane soared above the clouds, Harmon had many thoughts go through his mind. "I wonder if they'll expect me to hit pitchers like Bob Feller, Allie Reynolds and Eddie Lopat," he mused.

Then he thought "Maybe, I won't get to play much. Boy, it will be tough if I have to ride the bench."

But he felt better when he suddenly remembered what Ossie Bluege had told him. Bluege had said, "Now Harmon, don't worry about not hitting major league pitchers. They just put their pants on in a dressing room the same as you do."

He chuckled inwardly as he remembered Ossie's comment, and then feeling drowsy, he closed his eyes and fell asleep.

"Fasten your seat belts, we'll be at the Chicago airport in ten minutes," announced the stewardess.

Harmon awakened with a start. "In Chicago already," he thought. "It's a big city. I hope I can find my way around." Then he remembered that Mr. Bluege's brother Otto was going to meet him, and he relaxed.

"Are you Harmon Killebrew?" a friendly man asked, as Harmon reached the bottom of the plane's steps.

"Yes sir."

"I'm Otto Bluege. That cab over there will take us to the hotel. Do you have to check out your luggage first?"

Harmon shook his head. "It's all here in my bag."

Noises that he had never heard before encircled Harmon as the cab sped to the hotel in Chicago's loop. Buses, elevated trains, and automobiles made up a cacophony of sound that had his ears ringing.

"Boy, this is sure different from Payette," he thought as he observed people of every description hurrying in all directions.

At the hotel, Harmon was taken into a room where Clark Griffith, President of the Washington club, and it's manager Stanley Raymond (Bucky Harris) were waiting to greet him. They were so friendly that he felt right at home. But his momentary tranquility was upset when a group of reporters crowded around him.

"What can I say to them?" he asked Bluege. "Why, I haven't even played a league game yet."

"Don't worry," grinned Bluege, "They'll ask plenty of questions. You're Washington's first bonus player. So every baseball fan in the town is interested in you."

The questions came hot and heavy.

"How do you feel about joining the Senators?"

"I'm scared to death, but I'm walking on air, also."

"What position did you play back home?"

"Usually shortstop or third base."

"Do you have a major league hero?"

"There are a lot of great players. I suppose I like Al Rosen of the Cleveland Indians because he hits the ball hard and used to play third base."

Other questions asked Harmon were more difficult, but his willingness in trying to answer them and his friendly manner made a favorable impression on the reporters.

Bob Addie, a sports writer who was at the interview, had some interesting comments to make in his evening column.

Chicago, June 22, 1954

"Harmon Killebrew, the bonus kid walked into the lobby of the Del Prado Hotel this morning keeping close to Otto Bluege . . ."

Bucky Harris stuck out a gnarled hand and said: "I'm Bucky Harris, welcome, youngster."

"Yes sir," the boy said. "I know."

I shook hands with him in turn. He has a powerful grip reminiscent of that of Dr. George Resta, the Nats' club physician, and the irrelevant thought struck me that there would be some bone-cracking when these two powerful specimens meet.

The first glance at Harmon Killebrew was slightly disappointing until I got a better look at him. He didn't look quite six feet tall and 195 pounds, but he is."

Inevitably the picture came back that I had seen many times in Clark Griffith's office . . . That of Walter Johnson when he first reported to the Washington club in 1907. . . He had pants which hugged his legs from fright, a celluloid collar and a 'stick-on bow tie' . . . a too short jacket with the narrow lapel . . . and all this was topped by a derby."

Although Killebrew and Johnson are from the same locale, Payette and Weiser, Idaho, just 15 miles apart, Killebrew, unlike Walter was sartorially perfect. He wore a blue coat with gray slacks, brown shoes, blue and white socks, and an expensive-looking white shirt with button-down collar and a scarlet tie with a fleur de les clip. He has sandy brown hair which ripples in tight curls and white, even teeth. . . He has a nervous giggle and is properly awed by this sudden turn in his life.

. . . Killebrew's athletic accomplishments had to be dragged out of him. Yes, he was an All-American quarterback on the National Scholastic team. He 'had heard' that he had made it in baseball and basketball, too.

. . . When asked what was his favorite big league team and who was his favorite player, he squirmed like a small boy forced to tell the truth about stealing apples.

> . . . "I always admired Walter Johnson, too" he volunteered. I've played on "his" field and now I'm with his team. It's still a dream. Harmon Killebrew and Walter Johnson. Silly, isn't it?"
> Nobody really thought so.

After the interview, Bucky Harris, the Senators' manager, had a chat with Killebrew. Bucky was once known as baseball's 'boy manager', so he understood how the young man felt in his new surroundings.

"Ossie says you've got good wrist action, Harmon," Bucky said in a fatherly way. "In fact, he thinks you have the potential to be a great power hitter like Mickey Mantle."

"That was really kind of Mr. Bluege to say that," said Harmon modestly. "I guess I inherited my strength from my dad, and he spent an awful lot of time teaching me how to swing right. I hope I can hit big league pitching."

Bucky smiled, "Don't worry, we're not going to put you under pressure right away. You'll get plenty of time to watch and learn. There are a lot of players on this team who will help you all they can.

"Did Ossie explain the bonus rule to you?"

"Yes."

"Then you know that we can't farm you out to the minors during the first two years to get daily experience. So we'll use you in spots here. It may be that you'll have to sit on the bench quite a bit."

"I understand," said Harmon, "and I'll do whatever you want me to do."

Bucky introduced Killebrew to a few players who were lounging in the hotel lobby, and told him he would meet the others when he got to Comiskey Park.

A major league baseball stadium is a fascinating place. It almost seems like a fortress enclosing an emerald green spot where players can perform and spectators can watch, oblivious to the cares of the outside world. The average fan delights in booing the umpires, riding certain players, and getting a stomach-ache from wolfing hot dogs and washing them down with cold drinks. He often turns his glances wistfully toward the home dugout and hopes that someday

ASSOCIATED PRESS PHOTO

'You're in the Big League now, son'

*Washington Senators manager, Bucky Harris, right, gets acquainted with the club's first Bonus Baby, Harmon Killebrew, at Chicago's Comiskey Park June 22. The 17-year-old infielder from Payette, Idaho, signed for a reported $50,000. He joined the Senators in time to witness his first Major League contest, which his new teammates dropped to the White Sox, 7-5.**

he will get the chance to walk through its connecting tunnel and invade the inner sanctum—the players' quarters.

It must have been almost overwhelming for young Harmon to view famed Comiskey Park, the largest sports arena he had ever seen, and then to be led by Bluege down the connecting tunnel right past the door and into the player's clubhouse. Of course he had been in men's dressing rooms before, but this was different. Here were stars he had read and dreamed about, and he was associating with them.

Bluege guided Harmon to the manager's office and Bucky, after a warm greeting, introduced Killebrew to his roommate Johnny Pesky.

"Johnny, this is Harmon Killebrew. You fellows will room together on the road, and Johnny, I want you to explain our plays to him, and give him the benefit of your experience."

"Glad to," Pesky said with a grin.

Harmon met most of the other players including Mickey Vernon, the American League batting champion, Camilo Pascal, curve ball artist, Eddie Yost, fancy-fielding third baseman, and sluggers Roy Sievers and Pete Runnels.

After putting on a uniform, he walked out onto the playing field wondering what he should do next.

"Grab a bat, Harmon, and come on," yelled Eddie Yost pleasantly.

Batting practice was about to get under way. Several players helped Killebrew feel that it was the most natural thing in the world for him to take his turn.

"What a difference, what a difference," Bucky Harris told Burton Hawkins, a nearby reporter, "Our fellows are going out of their way to be nice to the kid. They can't do enough for him. That's the way it should be, but it wasn't that way when I broke in.

"When I reported to the Tigers for spring training in 1916, you'd have thought I was bringing the plague with me. Those ball players of that era gave you the cold water treatment. They viewed you as a threat to their jobs. When they spoke to you, it was only to swear at you."

Apparently Harmon remembers the friendly treatment he got on that first day and what it meant to him, because when I asked George Brophy, Farm Director of the Minnesota Twins, to give his impressions of Harmon, he said:

"The thing that always sticks in my mind concerning Harmon is his cooperation. He is always the first . . . to greet a young rookie ballplayer when we bring him into the Twins' clubhouse for the first time. These young boys, highly nervous, are always relaxed by Harmon's greeting and manner with them. He is the first to offer a suggestion if he feels it will help the boy in his play. His very manner sets such an example for the other members in the playing ranks that we have a happy situation throughout the organization."

Harmon didn't set the world on fire in his first batting practice. According to sportswriter Burton Hawkins' report the following happened:

> Killebrew, in a half dozen swings against Dean Stone, didn't pump any drives into the stands. A right-handed hitter, he stroked everything unconvincingly to right field, but Harris wasn't disappointed.
>
> "I know how he feels," Bucky said, "He's shaking in his boots. This is the first major league park he has seen and Stone is showing him better pitching than he has seen. He'll look better tomorrow, when some of the nervousness wears off, and in a week or so he'll start catching up with the pitching."
>
> Killebrew gave no outward evidence of being jittery, but if his tummy was turning flip flops it was understandable.
>
> . . . In his first drill with the Senators last night he was fielding grounders slapped to him at second base by Coach Heinie Manush."

The story is told that once when Killebrew whipped a throw to first. Harris turned to Coach Heinie (Henry) Manush and said, "Good grief! The kid throws like a girl."

So that was Harmon's debut with the Senators. He had done nothing to make them "wildly enthusiastic or solidly skeptical."

The jury was still out on Harmon. But there were three things going for him that presaged a favorable verdict. He was still clinging to his dream; Bucky Harris was an understanding and patient manager, and Ossie Bluege had taken a fatherly interest in him.

That night, Killebrew sat on the bench and watched his first major league game.

Although Harmon did nothing but sit and watch, the Washington papers still managed to keep his name in the news. The Washington Daily News for Tuesday, June 22, 1954, carried a banner headline "Nats' $50,000 Baby Won't Play Tonight, and Probably Not for a Long Time."

In the body of the column, the writer Dave Reque said, "The Nats won't use their new $50,000 bonus baby against the White Sox in Chicago tonight, except maybe if they grab a big lead and let him pinch-hit. Maybe they won't use him for a long time. Harmon Killebrew may be a diamond, but today he's as rough as a gem freshly fished out of a mine, and the Nats expect to do a long job of polishing.

"If you think there's an incongruity between the positions he's been playing and his hitting and physical qualifications, the Nats agree with you.

" 'This kid sounds more like an outfielder to me' Clark Griffith, President of the club says.

" 'Right now, he's just raw material. We're going to give him lots of schooling. Before games, we'll try him out in various positions. We'll have balls hit to him and the coaches and older players will watch how he does and give him instruction. But right now we don't know what his true position is!' "

If Harmon was a little uncertain about his ability to make it in the majors, the press did a good job in reinforcing such doubts. Nevertheless, he kept his head, soaked up instructions, and kept his eyes on his goal.

The second day after joining the team, he got in the game as a pinch runner.

"Killebrew," barked Bucky Harris, "go in and run for Vollmer."

Harmon jumped to his feet and relieved Clyde Vollmer at first base. If he was frightened, he didn't show it. There he was with the giant Walt Dropo, White Sox first baseman on one side of him and the pugnacious Nellie Fox glaring at him from second. Somehow he was supposed to match wits with the Sox pitcher Jack Harshman and negotiate the distance between the two infielders and advance to second. The challenge never materialized. He reached second on a wild pitch and was left stranded there when Johnny Pesky lined out to end the inning.

Thus ended Harmon's first appearance in the big leagues.

Naturally, the Washington fans were eager to see Killebrew perform, and the pressure began to mount to have Harris start him in the game at Griffith Stadium. Reporters were interviewing Harmon via long distance telephone so they could scatter tidbits about him among the Senators rooters.

Typical of the reports was the one which appeared in Sharon Doran's "Teen Scene" in the *Evening Star* on Friday, June 25, 1954.

> Sharon titled her piece, "Harmon Killebrew, 17 Is Baseball's Most Famous Teen-Ager of the Day.
>
> Among other things Sharon said, "Probably the most famous teen-ager in the United States at the moment, is 17-year-old Harmon Killebrew, the brilliant baseball boy who received $30,000 (WOW) to become a player for the Washington Senators.
>
> This teen is only the greatest! I talked long-distance to Harmon in Chicago. . ."I'm pretty excited about it all: gosh, I can hardly believe it!" he exclaimed about this claim to fame.
>
> . . . Really in true western style this teen is neat. He's due to arrive in D.C. shortly after the Fourth of July. . . Sorry girls he's obviously going steady. But men, for true slugger form you'd best keep the ole eye peeled for Harm.

Despite all of the fanfare and the public attention Harmon received when the team returned to Washington, Clark Griffith and Bucky Harris still brought Killebrew along carefully and slowly on the playing field. Harris had only used him twice as a pinch runner in the month he had been with the team.

Finally, a rumor got around that Killebrew was going to start at second base in a Sunday game against Detroit. The Senators were hitting a seasonal low in attendance and such a maneuver would have brought thousands of additional fans into the stands, but Griffith squelched the story when he announced, "I have no intention of using our bonus rookie Harmon Killebrew as a sideshow attraction to bring fans to the stadium. I simply will not take the chance of jeopardizing his career by playing him too quickly."

The fans moaned in protest, so Griffith partially placated them by coming up with a new gimmick and announcing: "Tonight is family night. Dad pays the regular admission rate tonight, but mom and the kids get in for a half a buck apiece."

Despite all of the ballyhoo about him and the protective manner of Clark Griffith and Bucky Harris, Harmon was lonesome his first season away from home.

Ray Crump, present Equipment Manager for the Minnesota Twins, (who was then a bat boy with the Washington club, and the same age as Killebrew) recalls those days as follows:

"At seventeen, Harm was one of the shyest rookies I have ever met in my twenty-two years in baseball. When he joined the Senators he was truly a farm boy coming to the big city. He didn't talk too much and would sit at the end of the bench taking everything in. As I remember, when he did talk, it was more about football than baseball.

"You could sense how important it was for him to make it big in the major leagues for his family's sake.

"Despite his shyness, I could tell that Harmon was, as a country boy would say, 'high, high class.' "

Many times when Harmon felt down he would turn to Ossie Bluege for counsel and Ossie was never too busy to listen, encourage, and advise, and to this day he still has his watchful eyes on Killebrew.

After Harmon had been assigned to room on the road with Johnny Pesky, the Senators shortstop did everything he could to encourage and help the young rookie.

I had the opportunity of talking to Johnny Pesky when he was in Minneapolis with the Red Sox on August 27, 1970. I asked him if he remembered Killebrew as a rookie.

"I'll say I do," he replied. "Harmon seemed very young

Ossie Bluege, Killebrew's scout and long-time friend, 1966

to me at the time Bucky Harris told me how green he was and asked me to show him a couple of things. Don Kirsch had known me as a kid playing baseball in Oregon, and he was also interested in having me meet Harm.

"We roomed together, ate together, and often went to movies. He was chubby then, but he gradually lost his baby fat. Harm was never cocky and was always asking questions such as, 'Why do you do this?'

"He's never changed a bit since he has become a superstar. To me, he's the kind of guy you'd like to take home to your kid sister."

One thing Johnny did that has added spice, support and brought an interesting friend into Harmon's life was to take him to live in the home of Russell Tuckey in Washington, D.C.

Russ remembered it this way:

"Harmon joined the baseball team in Chicago and roomed with Johnny, a personal friend of mine. Moving back into Washington, the home field, John, who was married, brought Harmon to my home and introduced him to me as 'my new roommate and boarder.' "

Ever since that meeting Russ Tuckey has been a staunch supporter and loyal friend to Harmon and his family.

Russell Tuckey is a short, wiry, ageless Irishman, and his eyes twinkle like those of a mischievous teen-ager. He was working as a pullman conductor when Harmon first lived in his home. Later he became transportation manager for the Shipstad and Johnson Ice Follies and also skated in their shows for five years.

Russ went on to say:

"I had associated with baseball players for years and had learned that their favorite food was steak for every meal. So naturally, I served Harmon steak for breakfast.

"He questioned this and said, 'I don't need steak for breakfast.'

" 'Oh yes you do' I said. 'That's the food that ballplayers need to eat if they want to hit homeruns.'

"To prove it to Harm, I took him to Paul Daube's place in New York City which was called The Dutchman's Steakhouse. It was a favorite eating spot for ballplayers because Dutch served the biggest steaks in town. And it was common knowledge that Babe Ruth used to come there and eat three steaks at one sitting. The best Lou Gehrig could do was two.

"So Harm tried to follow their example, but he had to give up halfway through the second steak."

Ever since those early days in Washington, Russ Tuckey has been a devoted friend to Harmon and Elaine and their children.

I met him during spring training in Orlando in 1970, and he was watching over the entire Killebrew family.

He liked to be with the family so much that Elaine once asked him why he had never married. (He is a bachelor at 67.)

Russ grinned and replied, "There was a lady who owned an orange grove that wanted me. But what can you do with oranges?"

One evening he sent Harmon and Elaine off to a movie with us, speeding our departure by saying, "Go out and relax. I'll take care of these kids."

As we looked back, he was sitting like a tired housewife wringing his hands in mock despair—the ever-present twinkle in his eyes.

He picked the boys up and took them to the ballpark every day.

One day, noticing me hurrying to catch a bus, he pulled over and told me to hop into his shiny new Opel Kadet. The Killebrew boys, Cameron and Kenny, and Bob Allison's son, Mark, were sitting in back. On the way to town the fellows in back were raising quite a commotion, and Russ repeatedly said, "Knock it off you guys or I'll belt you one."

Watching the exchange between Russ and the kids was a delight; because beneath their bantering you could sense the mutual affection between them.

Recently, when I was visiting the Killebrew's in their Minneapolis home, a birthday gift in the form of a beautiful wrist watch arrived for Cameron with best wishes from

***Harmon with Russell Tuckey, a long-time friend who invited Killebrew to live** in his home in his first year as a rookie in Washington, D.C.*

Russ. Cam looked at it and seemed somewhat overcome.

Harmon shook his head as he adjusted the watch on Cam's wrist.

Elaine said, "Russ has enriched our lives in so many ways."

"Yes," added Harm. "He also taught me that you can't hit homeruns on ginger snaps and ice water."

Russ also remembered something that happened in those early Washington days that gives insight into Harmon's state of mind at the time.

He said, "When I received the first telephone bill, after Harm had been boarding with me for a month, it was so high that I had to call the phone company to verify it. The records proved it was correct.

"When I had been in the house before and after work, I had seen Harm on the telephone a lot, and I assumed he was talking locally. But, when I showed him the bill, he said he didn't phone anyone in town. When he phoned it was long distance to Elaine in Idaho. Despite everything we could do, he was lonesome for his sweetheart."

Elaine also felt lost without Harmon.

In recalling those days, she said: "When Harm left to join the Washington Senators, I really felt that I ought to go with him as his wife, but he thought he needed to establish himself and see what he was going to do in professional baseball before he took on the responsibility of marriage. Even at seventeen he was showing signs of being sensible and mature.

"It was difficult for me when he left; it really was. I kept busy working at Glover's Jewelry Company. Still it was a miserable summer, but Harm helped me through it by phoning quite often, something which Russ Tuckey well remembers. . . ."

News clippings show that Bucky Harris finally started Harmon in a game on August 23, 1954, about two months after he had joined the team. Harris made sure that the start would be under as little pressure as possible. The Senators seemed to be out of the running for fourth place, a money spot, and a small crowd was expected for the game against Philadelphia in Connie Mack Stadium. Actually, only 2094 spectators turned out for the contest.

Harmon played second base in the last game of a doubleheader and did well. He connected for a pair of singles and a double to drive in two Washington runs.

The newspapers headlined their report of the game with "Killebrew Slams Three Hits to Aid Washington in Twin Win over A's."

Dave Reque in the Washington Daily News, August 24, 1954 reported:

> Clark Griffith was as pleased as a small boy with a new pair of roller skates after his lone bonus baby smashed a double and two singles in his first major league start.
>
> "After what the kid did yesterday, I'd sure start him if I were the manager," Griff chuckled happily today.
>
> "Killebrew can swing that bat, don't think different" the 84 year-old club president added.

After that first full game, Bucky Harris told Burton Hawkins, Washington reporter, "Killebrew's in the lineup until he shows he can't do the job and that day might not arrive. He has a lot to learn, but he's learning every day. If he makes a few mistakes here and there, I'm sure the fans will string along with him. He's just a baby in the baseball sense, but a darned cute baby and maybe it will be fun to watch him grow up."

Despite Harmon's good start, he did not show enough ability to permanently displace an established veteran during the rest of the season.

Consequently, his final record for the season showed that he appeared in nine games, was at bat thirteen times, made four hits (no homeruns) and scored one run.

The Senators had a disappointing season—finishing sixth. Bucky Harris allowed Harmon to return home before the season ended so he could attend the College of Idaho.

Elaine, his family and friends greeted him like a hero when he arrived in Payette. But Harmon was downcast. "Why all the fuss?" he said, "I only played in nine games."

the nats' forgotten man

7

Harmon wasn't idle long after returning home. He enrolled in the College of Idaho for the fall semester and got a taste of the campus life which he had passed up. He had to study hard, as he had enrolled for courses in English, zoology, sociology, and algebra. It is easy to conjecture that he undoubtedly made comparisons between his rookie season with the Senators and what might have happened had he taken his university scholarship. But for Harmon there was no turning back. He had chosen his goal and was committed to reaching it.

The most important event that took place that winter was his engagement to Elaine. Naturally, Elaine was looking forward to becoming engaged and receiving a ring, but Harmon kept her guessing. Never given to much discussion of his personal affairs, he went quietly about pricing rings and turning over in his mind just what kind to buy.

One can imagine him going into a jewelry store and asking a clerk for assistance.

"I'd like to look at some of your diamond rings."

"Did you have any special design or color in mind?"

"Not really. Just something extra special."

"With your reputation, you of course want the best. Now, here are some that would delight any girl's heart. Let me slip one on and show you. Isn't it beautiful?"

"Yes, that is nice."

"Would you like me to tell you the different ways we can set up your payments?"

"Not right now, thank you. I'll look awhile first."

Harmon did look around and came up with a beauty.

Elaine remembers every detail vividly.

"We became engaged in the winter after Harm's first season with the Senators. Although he didn't say a word about it, I knew he had been looking at diamonds. I was still working in the jewelry store, and the other clerks would say, 'Guess who came in today?'

" 'How should I know,' I would reply.

" 'Why, Harmon of course, and he was looking at rings.'

" 'Well, what do you know,' I would say.

"I took a lot of good-natured kidding, but Harm hadn't said anything to me, so I tried not to talk about it. However, I felt sure he was going to give me a ring, but I didn't know when.

"One night, he took me out to a special place for dinner, and I thought, 'This is it. I'm going to get the ring.' Well, he ordered a delicious meal and ate his calmly, and meanwhile, talked about everything but us. He was talking about his classes at school and the Senators' prospects for the next year, while I was miserable. I was sure he had the ring with him, and I thought, 'Why doesn't he make the evening beautiful by giving it to me now?'

"He even looked at me once and said, 'Do you feel all right, Honey?'

"'Of course,' I said curtly. 'You seem to be awfully talkative tonight.'

"So, I suffered through dinner and then we went out and got into the car. As soon as we got in, he opened the glove compartment, took out my ring and gave it to me.

Naturally I was thrilled, but I said, 'Harm, don't you know you ruined my meal by not giving me the ring before we went into dinner?'

"He grinned and said, 'I thought you would be more likely to accept after you had eaten.'

"The ring was so gorgeous that I couldn't stay angry very long. He had picked out a beautiful stone, a perfect diamond. I looked at its brilliance, and thought of the old superstition that the sparkle of the diamond is supposed to have originated in the fires of love. As we sat there, I realized fully for the first time that we were going to become man and wife, have babies, and live a life of love and happiness. Harm didn't say too much, but I could tell that he was as thrilled as I was."

During December Elaine wrote a letter to Mr. and Mrs. Leonard Walsh expressing her joy in her engagement to Harmon and their future plans.

Dec. 28, 1954

Dear Mrs. Walsh and Family,

I've been thinking about you a lot lately so decided to drop a line and see how you are.

I know you've read about Harm's signing so I won't go into that, but I do want to tell you that he is doing all right, and of course his fans love him. In spite of all the publicity he is still my same Harm. Nothing will ever change him.

I am writing to thank you and tell you we sincerely appreciate all you've done for Harm. Without your help the operation wouldn't have been a realization, and without it I don't think Harm could have made it. In just this short time baseball has done much for us. Harm is in college, his mother is being taken care of and me—well I'm just plain happy.

Harm plans to major in physical therapy and is at the College of Idaho at present. He has a 1954 Belaire, and I have a beautiful diamond ring. We are planning on marriage next fall when Harm returns, then we will both attend college, possibly at the U. of I.

We are really happy and feel fortunate that this happened to us. Harm's dream is realized and next fall mine will be, so all in all life is good and the friends who have helped us in so many ways are appreciated and certainly not forgotten.

We have heard a little bit about your accomplishments from Father Walsh, but please write and let us know these things; after all, we are interested in our *old history teacher*, you know.

I've just about got everything off my chest for now, so will close, but please write, give your family my regards and thanks again.

As ever,
Elaine Roberts

Mr. Walsh and his wife, June, had taken a personal interest in Harmon and Elaine when Leonard was teaching in Payette High School. They had subsequently moved to Colorado, and Mr. Walsh had been killed in a plane accident.

When I wrote to Mrs. Walsh asking her if she could recall some experiences with Harmon and Elaine, she graciously responded and said:

I have been down in the basement this afternoon looking through scrapbooks to see what I could come up with. I came across the enclosed letter from Elaine, written nearly sixteen years ago. I'm sure you can come to your own conclusions why I'm sending it. Not many individuals can look back on this span of years and still be able to say the very same things today, as were said then.

My deceased husband thought of Harmon as being the greatest. He was always so proud—proud to be able to say to some individual that Harmon Killebrew had been his student and friend.

We always felt very close to Harmon and Elaine while at Payette, as they dated steady all during the junior and senior high school years, as did my husband and I. It is very gratifying to see these marriages be so successful.

I can only say, in closing, this man, Harm, knows how to live.

Please thank Harm and Elaine for being so thoughtful in remembering us.

Sincerely,
June O. Walsh

As winter lingered on in Idaho, Harmon became impatient to start spring training in Florida. During the winter, Clark Griffith and his nephew Calvin, who had been made vice-president of the club, had made a change in managers. Bucky Harris' sixth place finish the year before had been disappointing, so they had hired Charlie Dressen as their new pilot. Dressen, a peppery personality with the reputation of being a tough disciplinarian, was expected to improve the team's standing.

Harmon had heard about the change in managers, but reasoned that anyone who could help him play his best would be good.

Killebrew's rooters in Idaho were again solidly behind him, and as he left for his second season with the Senators. Local sportswriter Dick Barrett commented:

> Payette's best wishes were draped around Harmon Killebrew's shoulders early yesterday morning when he boarded a train bound for spring training in Florida . . . The popular favorite, just one year out of high school, is still the same kid who won the hearts of Payette fans as a high school flash.
>
> But Killebrew's popularity does not stem only from his athletic feats. He is easily one of the best friends a Payette grade school youth could have had in recent years. His teammates remembered how Killebrew always had time to play catch with a grade school student even while setting records as a high school star.
>
> His coaches remember that while in high school, he was one of the first to be dressed for a game, never assuming the prima-donna role so often associated with top athletes.
>
> It's the same set of traits which have made him popular with the Washington club. Reports indicated at first that some players held the usual resentment toward Killebrew because of the bonus contract he received. But he earned respect with his sincerity and eagerness to learn.
>
> This may be the opening year of a great career for Killebrew. We all hope so.

Elaine remembers the time:

"When Harm left for spring training, I was disappointed when he didn't ask me to go with him. I began feeling sorry for myself and was extremely lonesome. I really felt that he was being unfair and that there was no real reason to postpone getting married. But Harmon just wouldn't consider it until he was better established. He seemed almost too sensible to me.

Harmon reported to Tinker Field, the Senators spring training camp in Orlando, Florida, and immediately came under Dressen's scrutiny. The Senators manager was toying with the idea of shifting third baseman Eddie Yost to the outfield and stationing Killebrew at the hot corner. Consequently, Dressen had his eyes on Killebrew everytime he took batting practice or participated in fielding drill.

Charlie (Chuck) Dressen, Harmon's second manager, Washington, 1955

The skipper came to the tentative conclusion that Harmon had some potential as a hitter, but was too awkward with the glove.

One day, after Harmon had bobbled a grounder and had not got into position fast enough to field another, the outspoken Dressen erupted with "How do they expect me to win with guys like Killebrew?"

Such statements do nothing to build a positive self-image, and Harmon's self-confidence suffered. At one time during spring training he said to Johnny Pesky, "I guess I just don't have what it takes. I might have been better off if I had taken that scholarship."

"Knock it off," retorted Pesky. "You can't expect to make the major leagues overnight. Just keep plugging away. You'll make it."

First, Dressen gave Ellis Clary, a Senators coach, the assignment of working with Killebrew on his fielding. Subsequently, Clary and Killebrew spent many extra hours in fielding drills. Harmon stationed himself at third and working under the hot sun tried to handle everything the coach hit at him, from easy rollers to scorching line drives. Clary drove Harmon relentlessly and spared no criticism in teaching him how to make the different plays. One thing he drilled into the young ballplayer was, "You play the ball. Never let the ball play you."

Watching Killebrew field today either at first or third, it is apparent that the lesson has stayed with him. He always plays the ball.

Although the many sessions gradually improved Harmon's fielding, Dressen never commented on it and despite all the extra work, Harmon was not impressive during spring training.

As usual, some of the sportswriters, who might be accused of writing gossip columns, contributed their bit to undermine Killebrew's confidence. Some of their caustic comments were:

> The bonus business seems to have the Nats "over the barrel." It seems the Nats must carry Harmon Killebrew on the roster this year

> and the young man promises to contribute nothing except a healthy appetite.
>
> The forgotten man of the Nats' spring training period is Harmon "Killer" Killebrew, rookie infielder. Late last season the Nats reportedly paid him a bonus of $30,000 to sign out of the semi-pro ranks in Idaho. In Florida this spring, he has made only brief appearances at third base, is batting .111."

Chuck Dressen finally broke down and expressed a revised appraisal of Killebrew's abilities to Bob Addie, sportswriter, which was hardly the kind to make Harmon's fans stand up and cheer.

"I don't blame the kid," Dressen said. "He's just turned 18, and he's strong as a bull. I think he is going to be a real good hitter, but his fielding needs a lot of polish. He's not going to learn with Washington because he won't get to play enough. He should be playing every day in some Class B or A ball where he can get his confidence. He's got to stay with us under the bonus rule, then maybe he gets grabbed by the military and by the time he comes up and we can send him down, he's 22 or 23 and we lose those good years."

As spring training was drawing to a close, Dressen made a move that he thought might help Killebrew.

"I'm changing your roommate," he said one day.

Harmon just stared and said nothing. He liked Johnny Pesky as a roommate, and hated to lose him.

"I'm putting Cookie Lavagetto with you," Dressen continued. "He thinks you've got a lot of ability, and I feel that he can help you."

"Thanks, whatever you say," said Killebrew.

Lavagetto, a coach with the Senators, shared Bluege's enthusiasm about Killebrew's great potential. On their first night together, when he saw Harmon pick up a book to read, Cookie handed him a different one and said, "Here's a better one."

To Harmon's surprise it was a baseball rule book.

Lavagetto sprawled in a chair and grinned when Killebrew said dryly, "It looks exciting."

"I still read it," said the older man. "Guys who know the

rules have more self-confidence and are more likely to make the right plays. The other fellows can teach you the mechanics of the game; my assignment is to teach you to be a thinking player."

"It looks like you got the toughest job," grinned Harmon.

While Harmon was fighting to make the team during spring training, Elaine was fighting the lonesome feeling that their second separation had brought about.

"I felt the need to go somewhere myself, and I had the opportunity early that summer. My Uncle Charlie and Aunt Ruth from Baldwin Park, California, came to Payette for a visit and then asked me to go back to California with them. I thought this would be an interesting experience, so I went back with them and found a job in West Covina, a town close to Baldwin Park. My position was in a bank working as a typist and switchboard operator. I was still lonesome and missed Harm terribly, but at least I had some new things to tell him about."

Of course, Harmon went north to Washington with the team after spring training. The bonus rule made this necessary. And although both he and the management would have been happier if he could have played every day in a lesser league, they were stuck with each other for the season.

Killebrew's 1955 season with the Senators was not anything to write home about; nevertheless, there were three high spots which should be mentioned.

First, he experienced the thrill of opening day in Washington, D. C. This is always a colorful event and is highlighted by the President of the United States throwing out the first ball from a flag-draped box.

President Dwight Eisenhower was the performer that day, and Harmon remembers how excited he was to see Eisenhower in person. However, there was not much excitement for him during the rest of the season. Dressen called on Killebrew to pinch hit occasionally or play third base when the score was lopsided for or against the Senators, but that was all.

Lavagetto continued to do his best to keep Harmon thinking about the strategies of the game, but nevertheless the bench became mighty hard for Harmon to endure.

The second high spot of the season occurred when Harmon hit his first major league homerun. This came on June 24, 1955, after Dressen, who had decided the Senators weren't going anywhere, finally put Harmon into the lineup. The club was in seventh place and had lost fourteen out of fifteen games. Evidently, Dressen felt things couldn't get any worse; so he started Harmon at third.

The team lost to Detroit 18 to 7, but Harmon showed his power with a tape measure homerun. It came in the fifth inning after the Senators had gone twenty-four innings without scoring, and finally gave the fans and the team something to cheer about.

Billy Hoeft, a smart pitcher, was on the mound and had worked the count to two-and-two on Killebrew. Finally, deciding to get the rookie out of there, Hoeft tried for a strikeout with a fast ball. Killebrew murdered it, and the ball sailed 475 feet into the top rows of the leftfield bleachers.

The crowd roared, the players extended their hands in congratulations, and Dressen grinned and slapped Harmon on the seat of the pants.

Harmon kept a straight face as he crossed home plate, but inside he was quivering with happiness. His dream of becoming an established major league player seemed a bit closer to fulfillment.

The third high spot during the season was Elaine's visit to Washington. Harmon and Elaine had kept the telephone wires hot keeping in touch with each other, and Elaine was always talking about California. It's possible that Harmon began to worry a little, and wondered if his attractive fiancé would be surrounded by too many admirers out there. Whether this was true or not, only Harmon knows, and he's not talking.

Elaine said:

"I was always telling Harmon how I liked California, and

I really think he got a bit worried about the distance between us. Anyway, he wanted me to fly back and visit him in Washington, D. C. He made it sound logical, because his mother and brother were driving back there, and he said I could go back to Idaho with them after and get ready for our wedding in the fall. Of course, he also wanted to see how I would like living in Washington.

"I hated to tell my boss I was quitting the job because they had trained me. I had only been there two months, and had assured them I wouldn't be leaving. The manager was very understanding when I explained the situation, and wished me well.

"The people in the bank kidded me, and they seemed to have a terrible time remembering and pronouncing the name Killebrew.

"One joker said, 'Why don't you get your boyfriend to shorten his name to Brew. That would be easier to remember.'

" 'That will be the day,' I said. Then I continued, 'Now listen you people! You're going to be hearing plenty about that name in the next few years. It's spelled K-I-L-L-E-B-R-E-W—so memorize it.'

"I got on the plane in Los Angeles. It was my first trip by air, and it was a thrill. I was nervous at first and leaned forward to help the plane get off the ground, but once we were in the air, It was glorious.

"I began to read some magazines, and before I had finished reading everything I wanted to, we were in Washington, D. C. It seemed almost fantastic that we had covered so much distance in so short a time.

"Harm was waiting at the airport.

"I rushed into his arms, and we both knew that time and space had not affected our love for each other.

"Washington, D. C. is a beautiful and an exciting city to visit. Harm took me sightseeing and I saw one fabulous thing after another. We went up to the top of the Washington Monument and viewed the vast panorama of scenic beauty surrounding it.

Harmon with Elaine, his brother Bob and his mother on steps of the Nation's Capitol Building in Washington, D. C. 1955.

"When I saw the Lincoln Memorial, it was hard to hold back the tears. Lincoln's image in stone portrayed him just like I think he was, human, kind, and understanding.

"Harm also took me out to the Maryland side of the city and showed me the ball players' apartments, and I began to think of how much fun it would be to live there.

"It was really educational to visit the capitol building, and we spent some time there with Senator Welker and Jim Hayden from Payette, who was the senator's top assistant.

"Senator Welker was so gracious, and he invited us to his home for dinner one day. While we were there, he phoned his neighbor, Vice-President Richard Nixon, and invited him over. Mr. Nixon is a real baseball fan, and he knew all about Harm's career. He was very friendly and kind, and we were thrilled to meet him.

"We were grateful that we had the opportunity to visit in the home of Senator Welker at that time, because soon after that he passed away.

"Finally, we had to draw our visit to a close. It wasn't easy. Harm's mother, brother, and I had been staying at a hotel, so Harm came over to help us load the car and to bid us good-bye. We decided then to set our wedding date for October first, and it seemed a long way off at the time. The final minutes with Harm were difficult, as it seemed almost like I was walking away from a beautiful dream world.

"As Harm waved good-bye, he looked so lonely that I felt like jumping out of the car and running back to him."

Just as one swallow does not make it summer, one homerun doesn't make a career. Harmon hit three more before the season ended, but Dressen still used him sparingly, and when the season closed he had played in only 38 games. His season's batting average was only .200 with 16 hits in 80 appearances at the plate.

It had been a dismal year, and the Senators finished in last place.

Harmon again wondered if his dream of becoming an established major leaguer would ever come true, and he became a bit despondent. Then a ray of hope, like sunshine, boosted his spirits as he remembered that his pretty blonde sweetheart, Elaine, was home preparing to marry him, on October first. He smiled to himself as he boarded the plane for Idaho, because he knew in his heart that once Elaine became his wife and was constantly at his side, urging him on, that nothing could stop him from realizing his impossible dream.

from wedding bells to tortillas

8

Elaine was working in the orchards earning a dollar an hour thinning peaches. It was hot, and she was lonely. She had a difficult time concentrating on her work, because she was thinking about Harmon. Although she was making preparations for the wedding, it seemed that the summer would drag on forever.

In recalling that summer she said:

"It was such a difficult summer for me. I hated the separation, and I missed Harm terribly. Sometimes I felt the summer would never end."

But it did, and one night when she was lying in bed with the cool night breeze of September stealing softly through the window, the phone rang. "Honey," said Harmon from Washington, "everything's wound up here. I can fly home tomorrow. Will you have time to meet me at the airport?"

"Will I have time?" said Elaine, her voice trembling. "Oh, Harm, it will be so good to see you that I'll probably be at the airport hours ahead of time, waiting."

When Harmon got off the plane he was carrying a box, a huge box. In fact, it was so big he had to set it down while they hugged each other.

Bursting with curiosity Elaine asked, "Harm, what in the world do you have in that box? Is it something for me?"

"It could be," Harm said.

"Well let's open it then."

"Sure, you can in five days, on October first, after we're married," said Harm firmly.

"Well, what can you do with a man like that? I just had to wait."

"Our wedding took place on the first day of October in the year 1955. It seemed like I had waited forever for that day to come. Then when it did, I was so excited I could hardly breathe. It was a beautiful Saturday afternoon the day we were married. All of our relatives and friends gathered together with us in the chapel of The Church of Jesus Christ of Latter-day Saints in Payette. Ours was the first wedding that was performed in the chapel.

"Bishop Dean McDonald performed the marriage ceremony. When we had both said 'I do,' and Harm had placed the wedding band on my finger, I felt the most peaceful feeling come over me, and I knew we had both joined with God in the beginning of a new and more abundant life. I had never doubted that Harm loved me, but when he took me in his arms and kissed me, I knew then we would be one person in spirit from that moment on.

"After that, Harm let me open the big box he had brought from Washington. It contained a beautiful nightgown and peignoir set. I thought it was so sweet of him."

Pictures of the wedding ceremony show Harmon looking at Elaine with an unmistakable expression of pride, contentment, and love.

Elaine looked beautiful in shimmering white. Her wedding dress had a lace bodice and peplum with long lacy sleeves, and a full satin skirt with a sheer net overlay.

Harmon presented a distinguished and handsome appearance in his tuxedo.

Weddings held in small town churches are happy affairs, and Harmon's and Elaine's was no exception. To the townspeople it was a gratifying experience to see two outstanding young people, whom everyone had grown to love, united in the holy bonds of matrimony. Harmon and Elaine are modest in describing their reception, but undoubtedly it was a high spot in Payette history. In addition to the congratulations of the people of Idaho, a congratulatory telegram was received from Clark Griffith and a letter and autographed photograph from Vice-President Richard Nixon.

It is easy to imagine how many warm friends embraced them both, gave them gifts, and wished them well.

After the reception, the newlyweds went to the Killebrew home, where the entire family was assembled, to enjoy some time together with them before they left for their honeymoon.

When the happy couple went to their automobile to depart, they discovered that pranksters had jacked their car up on blocks and written. "Suckers never learn." "Mexico or bust," "Caution! Newlyweds."

But undaunted, the new Mr. and Mrs. Killebrew put things in order and left.

Their first night was spent in Boise, and then the Killebrews drove down toward the Texas border to cross over into Mexico, where Harmon had signed to play winter ball with the Cordoba Coffee Pickers in Cordoba, Veracruz, Mexico.

Elaine and Harmon gave us a very interesting account of their trip down and their stay in Mexico. "We drove down to Laredo, Texas, which is right on the Mexican border, and then proceeded to drive across the Rio Grande River to Nuevo Laredo, which is the Mexican town on the other side. But we did not know what was in store for us. The regular bridge crossing the Rio Grande had been washed out by floods, so we had to creep at ten miles an hour over a temporary swinging bridge that was swaying like a clothesline full of washing, flapping in the breeze.

There are toll stations where you pay for crossing on both sides of the Rio Grande, and neither side looks very friendly. The American point of entry is bordered by a high fence trimmed with barbed wire, and the Mexican side has a high stone wall, and of course the customs officers of both nations are stationed there to check you through. It looked like illegal entry would be extremely difficult.

"When we went to enter Mexico, we discovered that the papers which were supposed to be there to let us in had not arrived."

Harmon said: "It was rough trying to explain our plight to anyone, because none of the Mexicans spoke more than two or three words of English. Finally, after a lot of gesturing with our hands, we found our way to the Mexican Consul, and through him were able to reach Señor Pinagos, who said he would arrange for the ball club's general manager to come and help us get into the country. The general manager went to Mexico City to get the papers necessary for me to work in Mexico.

"Meanwhile, we got better acquainted with Laredo. We learned that even though it was in Texas, the city officials, waitresses, clerks and other workers were Mexican, and very few spoke English. Many worked in Laredo and lived in Nuevo Laredo, because living was less expensive in Mexico.

"One thing that bothered us in Laredo was the great number of crickets. They were horrible looking, big, black insects, crawling all over the sidewalks. We had heard before about hordes of grasshoppers devouring farmers' crops, and we almost felt like this big horde of crickets would devour us.

"The general manager finally returned to Laredo, and after six days of haggling over money and papers, he got us into Mexico on a worker's permit. Most of the fellows didn't bother to get a worker's permit and took their chances of staying there and playing on a tourist card, but we wanted to do it the right way.

"The Mexican consul said it couldn't be done in less than five weeks. If it had taken that long, Elaine and I would have long since been back in Idaho."

Elaine continued, "Even though we got our permits, I can't say we were very happy, because things were bleak, and we both felt in the mood to head back home. But our homeward bound ideas were shattered when our friend Garcia Rivera, a lawyer, who had made the arrangements said, 'I come with and drive you to Cordoba.'

" 'You're tired from traveling,' Harm said, 'Just sit back and relax. I can drive. I'll follow the map.'

"That drive was so rough that riding a wild horse bareback could not have been worse.

"Hurricane Janet had just swept over the mountainous area, and everything was a mess. Trees had been uprooted, roads torn up, and lakes made of the highways. Every road we traveled on was the same; so we decided that Janet had been everywhere.

"By the time Harm had driven from the border to Monterrey, it was dark, so we stopped there for the night, dead tired from the long and dangerous drive.

"The next morning our little friend Garcia said, 'Now, I drive.'

"We were too tired to argue, so he took the wheel. First, he drove to Victoria where money was waiting for us. Then he took off for Mexico City. When I say took off, I mean it literally. Garcia drove at break-neck speed over holes, ruts, pools of water, and what have you. We had to strain our eyes watching those horrible roads, and we took turns warning our driver of pitfalls ahead.

" 'Take it easy!' Harm would say, 'there's a big hole ahead.'

" 'Watch out,' I shouted once. 'The entire road is under water up there.'

"The result? Garcia stepped on the accelerator and shot through the water like a Marine's landing craft approaching a beachhead.

"This reckless driving went on clear through the day and all night, until we finally reached Mexico City.

"We were so exhausted that we almost fell into bed—at seven o'clock in the morning.

"A short time later, there was a loud banging on our door, 'Mr. Killebrew, get up,' a voice said.

" 'Go away,' Harm groaned as he rolled over deep in sleep.

" 'But Mr. Killebrew, you're wanted at the ballpark, the voice persisted.

"This last statement roused us both enough to cause us to look at the clock. It was 11:00 a.m.

"So after driving all night over rough roads, Harm got up and went to the ballpark. Not to play, of course, but they wanted him there just the same."

Harmon's account follows: "My team was in Mexico City for a series with the Reds, and I played one game there and got one single off Early Wynn.

"We met an American in Mexico City named James Shindler. He was a companion in our misery, and we became good friends.

"When it came time to drive on to Cordoba, our friend Garcia put in an appearance and insisted that he was going to continue riding with us. I told him, 'Thanks, we'll find our way.'

" 'Yes, and we'll arrive in one piece too,' Elaine couldn't resist adding.

"'But you need me,' Garcia protested. 'And I must also go there.'

"Thank goodness I remained firm. There were a few more fast words, and we departed, Jim Shindler, Elaine and I—without Garcia Rivera.

"The seven hour trip to Cordoba was really bad. I am a careful driver, but it still took all of my energy to negotiate the hairpin curves in the mountain roads. To make things worse, there was a thick fog to fight. There was also a sheer drop-off on one side of the road, and the only guide lines were occasional rocks painted white to remind you that you were skirting the edge of a precipice.

"Finally, we got out of the mountains, began to see tropical plants along the way, went through a town named

Orizaba, and reached Cordoba (population 32,733) at two o'clock in the morning.

"It began raining the next morning, and the water came down in bucketfulls for three days. When it finally cleared up, the sun was shining beautifully and everything looked bright—everything but our room. My, what a damp, dark hole in the wall that place was. The cold went right through to our bones, and we finally bought a heater to take the chill out of them.

"When it finally stopped raining, we went out to see the ballpark, and there was the most beautiful (and at the same time unusual) little ballpark you would ever hope to see. There were sheep, donkeys, and horses grazing in the outfield, rocks strewn around the infield, and to keep things confused, there were no decent stands for the spectators to sit in.

"They had their own special way of dragging the infield in their ballpark. They did it with a long stick that had ropes of different lengths tied on both sides of the stick. It worked quite well, considering everything.

"The ballpark is surrounded by mountains covered with very thick foliage. We were told that they hunt lions among those craggy peaks, and one day while the team was practicing, I could hear guns and see puffs of smoke up there.

"We didn't see any animal life that was different, but the things that did give us an eerie feeling were the vultures. They could be seen hovering in the sky all day long, and you had the feeling that they were ready to swoop down and pick you apart. Once in a while, if you approached quietly, you would come across a flock of them eating some dead animal."

Elaine added, "You could name Cordoba, the donkey town. I saw more donkeys there than I have in all the rest of my life put together. I still remember when I was a little girl and saw a donkey for the first time. 'Dad,' I asked, 'what's that funny looking thing?'

"'That's just a jack rabbit, Honey,' dad said laughing.

"To this day, I still think donkeys look like sleepy-eyed jack rabbits.

"The town of Cordoba in Veracruz, Mexico, is in a beautiful area about 1500 miles south of the border and quite a ways from the coast. The country has a tropical climate, and there are lush fields of coffee beans and corn and trees loaded with bananas. The corn is so plentiful that they sell it outside the ballpark. As you are about to enter, you encounter women taking cobs of corn out of huge pots of hot water and offering it for sale.

"The mountains in the background are beautiful, and the most famous one, Orizaba, lends a majestic air to the countryside.

"We did find a better place to live, because we left our hole-in-the wall apartment and moved to nicer rooms in a hotel in town. We also learned that there was a tourist motel outside of town that had a beautiful pool of gardenias. We went there often to swim and chat with the tourists who spoke English.

"Traveling in Mexico was slow but interesting. The ballplayers did all their traveling by bus, and I made all of the trips so I could be with Harm, and also because I was the only wife who had come down from the states.

"Our frequent traveling gave us the opportunity to see many interesting things, especially how the people lived. The poverty we saw at that time in Mexico made us sad. In Costa Rica we saw many homeless individuals sleeping in the streets, with their only protection being a piece of paper over their heads. We also saw many grass-roofed huts with dirt floors.

"Nearly all of the people we saw approached us and tried to sell us something, and some of the young boys and girls would not let us get away unless we purchased something.

"Modern appliances were unknown in some of the rural areas, and we stopped one time to watch some women wash their clothes in a stream. They would pound them with rocks to get them clean, and then lay them out on the ground to dry.

"Another time, we watched an old man plow with his oxen, and then we gave him a peso to pose for us.

"Religious rites are practiced widely in Mexico. We saw people worshiping at roadside altars, and the Catholic church across the street from us had a bell in its tower that was rung every morning. Once a week, fireworks were thrown from the roof of the church to a tile roof below.

"Baseball has become a popular sport in Mexico, and the people take the game very seriously. We read an account in the paper stating that some fans whose team had lost had overturned the players' bus and attempted to stone the players.

"The ballplayers who rode in the bus with us didn't try very hard to win friends. They knew we were newlyweds because we sat together in the front of the bus. They sat behind us and constantly snickered and teased us. Inasmuch as we couldn't speak their language and they didn't understand us, their joking about us got pretty tiresome."

Harmon offered the following viewpoint:

"Elaine went with me on the road trips. She was the only woman down there, so I didn't feel she should be left alone. The fellows made fun of our just having been married and on the road trips and all.

"Some of the ball parks in Mexico were good. I remember in Mexico City, if you would hit a ball and run, you'd be out of breath because the altitude is so high. The manager of that ball club was Preston Gomez who now manages the San Diego Padres, a real fine man and a real fine manager. I played third base down there. I don't remember what my record was, but it wasn't anything exceptional.

"I should say something about the food we ate while in Mexico. Incidentally, the flies tried to eat everything we did, and we often used one hand for eating while batting the flies away with the other.

"I suppose tortillas are the most widely known of Mexican foods. They are made with the patting of palms on dough. These handclapped tortillas which often become pancakes as big as dinner plates are prepared in many different ways by Mexican cooks. They are made of coarse meal and are the basic ingredient for a variety of dishes.

"Unless you had a pretty good Spanish vocabulary when you asked for tortillas, you were in for some surprises. For example:

"Tortillas rolled over a mixture of beef, pork, chicken or cheese become tacos.

"Tortillas served with tomato sauce are known as enchiladas.

"Tortillas fried and stuffed with chicken, meat or salad are called tostados or chapulas.

"Tortillas made into fried turnovers filled with beans, meat and potatoes are labelled quesadillas.

"Tortilla dough filled with chicken or pork or sweets, then wrapped and steamed in a cornhusk is called a tamale.

"So much for tortillas.

"We became very good at ordering ham and eggs and learned how to say 'Queremos huevos y jamón, por favor.'

"We also learned quickly that it is important to know how to ask, 'How much does it cost?' So we learned to say '¿Cuanto cuesta?' ('la comida'—food—'los huevos'—eggs—'el poncho'—the poncho—'la sopa'—the soup).

"Other phrases that were a must were: '¿Dónde está el hotel?' (Where's the hotel?) '¿Cuánto cuesta un cuarto para dos personas?' (How much does a room for two cost?) '¿Dónde está el parque de béisbol?' (Where's the ballpark?)"

Elaine concluded, "Well, we stuck it out for six weeks in Mexico. While we were there the weather was fairly good, being warm most of the time with a few cold spells. Despite this, we were homesick. Although there were a few Americans on the teams, most of the players were Mexicans, so we had very little social life.

"One day we got a telegram informing us that Harm's brother-in-law in Payette, Glenn Cheese, who was married to Harm's sister, Eula, had passed away, so we decided to head for home. Harm's brother-in-law was an architect, and at age 39, had a heart attack at his drawing board and died.

"This ended our stay below the border. We have not been back to Mexico since."

down to the minor leagues

9

Harmon and Elaine arrived in Payette too late for the funeral, and although they did all they could to comfort Harm's bereaved sister Eula, they also had a problem of their own—that of finding a place to live until they left for spring training. Like any young bride, Elaine yearned for their own little love nest, but circumstances made such a move nearly impossible. No one was willing to rent them a house, and in addition they were short of funds. Harmon had sent most of their Mexican earnings back to Payette to help his mother, and they were in between pay periods with the Senators. Consequently, the only practical thing to do was to move into the Killebrew family home. Eula and her two children had already moved in with Harmon's mother, so the group spent a snug winter together.

When the time came to leave for spring training, Elaine was expecting their first baby.

"We really had quite a debate over when we should plan to have our first child. One day, when we were talking about leaving for spring training, I said, 'Harm, I want to have a baby!'

" 'So do I honey, but we've got lots of time to have a baby. We're not even twenty yet. We'll probably be traveling around a lot . . . planning exciting trips together during our vacations the next few years. . .'

" 'But Harm, I can't stand being alone so much. I hate it when you're on the road with the team.'

" 'Can't you talk to the other player's wives when I'm away?'

" 'Of course, but that gets tiresome, and no matter how nice they are they can't move in and sleep with me so I won't be lonely and scared at night.'

" 'I can't see how having a little baby would make you less frightened. Anyway, I phone you every night when I'm away.'

" 'I know, but it's not very exciting to sleep with a telephone.'

" 'You women,' Harm said helplessly.

"The only things I remember about that first spring training in Orlando were being proud of Harm's progress, the excitement of living in Florida, and meeting the ballplayer's wives—and morning sickness."

While Elaine was fighting the miseries of her first pregnancy, Harmon was fighting to stay with the Washington Club. Clark Griffith, one of Killebrew's staunchest supporters, had passed away on October 27, 1955, just a few weeks before his eighty-sixth birthday—without living to see Harmon pay off on his $30,000 bonus gamble. Calvin Griffith, Clark's nephew, became the club president, and naturally Harmon had some feelings of anxiety regarding the change. However, as things worked out later, Calvin showed as much faith in Harmon as Clark Griffith had, and they developed a lasting mutual respect for each other.

Harmon knew the 1956 season would be a crucial one for him. He had now spent two years with the Senators and was eligible to be sent down to the minors anytime the club officials felt it was best.

During spring training in 1956 Dressen experimented in

different ways to find Harmon a place in the line-up. He even played him at second base. When questioned about this by sportswriter Shirley Povich, Dressen said, "I want to let Killebrew hit against all the pitching I can. I'm not serious about developing him as a second baseman, but I am serious about developing him as a hitter and trying to find a place for him in our lineup."

It was evident during spring training that Dressen was trying to find a slot for the soft-spoken Killebrew as he was also stationed at first base during the early drills. This was undoubtedly due to Harmon's display of long-ball hitting which was sorely needed by the Senators. Press reports out of Orlando were dwelling heavily on Harmon's hitting powers and Dressen knew that he should not overlook any possible way of installing Killebrew in the lineup. Kent Chetlain, sportswriter, commented:

> Killebrew seems destined to play some part in Washington's 56 plans because of his consistent long ball hitting. In fact, the Payette, Idaho, third and first baseman is the club's leading homerun hitter in five exhibition games with two, both hit in the last three days.

Dressen finally decided that Killebrew just wasn't ready to displace Eddie Yost at third base; so his hope was that Harmon could move in at Roy Sievers' first base spot and release Sievers for outfield duty. This, the manager felt, would be possible if Killebrew could hit big league pitching and play adequate defense as a first baseman.

As the spring training drew to a close, Dressen felt that Killebrew still lacked the polish to take over at first or third; so Harmon was still a player without a position when he went north to Washington with the club.

When the team arrived in the capital city, Harmon and Elaine moved into one of the attractive apartments in Maryland that Harmon had pointed out on Elaine's first visit to Washington.

Elaine was thinking:

"Isn't it great to be settled in our own home at last. We can look forward to having our baby and meanwhile

Harm and I can enjoy all of the fabulous things in this beautiful city. I know Harm can play major league ball. All he needs is a fair chance."

As Harmon tossed in his sleep at night, the thoughts which kept running through his mind were:

"It's no fun sitting on the bench, and if I have to keep doing it, my big league career will be over before it starts. I know it would be hard on Elaine, but I'd rather be sent to a team where I can play every day. I wonder what Mr. Dressen will do when my bonus status is up on June eighteenth? I know he can send me down to the minors then without asking waivers on me."

Despite the uncertainty of being sent down hanging over their heads like the Sword of Damocles, the young couple went about the activities of living day by day.

Elaine began to sew tiny nightgowns for their expected baby, and Harmon did everything he could to keep his pretty young wife happy and content. But at the ballpark he was still riding the bench. His fielding had improved remarkably and his hitting, while infrequent, was lusty. During April and May he played in a few games, mostly in a pinch-hitting role or replacing an injured player.

In a game against Baltimore on May 29, 1956, Harmon replaced the injured Pete Runnels at second and slammed a pair of homeruns that led the Senators to a 6 to 5 victory. Pete then became a Killebrew fan and predicted that Killebrew, not Mantle, would eventually break Babe Ruth's record of 60 homeruns in one season. He said, "Yep, I can see the headline about seven years from now—'Killebrew hits 62.' "

As the season went into June, Harmon had only played in a handful of games and his batting average was a weak .176. But an indication of his power was that four of his six hits were homers and one a double.

Dressen, whose two year managerial contract was due to expire in the fall, was desperately short of utility players and wanted to keep Harmon on the club for pinch-hitting and utility duty. But Calvin Griffith of the Washington

Senators vetoed Dressen's request. Griffith wanted to build for the future. Keeping Harmon on the bench would be contrary to his building-for-the-future philosophy.

He said, "The position for Killebrew is someplace where he can play regularly, look at more pitching, and find the spot where his talents are best suited. He figures strongly in our future plans, so we will have to get along without him for awhile."

On a day in early June the Sword of Damocles fell. The Senators had just completed a series in Cleveland and were boarding a bus for the airport. Howie Fox, the club's traveling secretary overtook Harmon as he went to climb into the bus and said, "Harm, I hate to tell you this, but you're going to be sent to Charlotte. We'll have to take your bags off the bus."

Killebrew didn't say a word but turned around and began searching for his bags. As he got off with them, Fox handed him a ticket saying, "Here's a train ticket back east. The depot's about one-half mile from here, and the train leaves in an hour."

Ray Crump, the bat boy, approached Killebrew and said, "Harm, this is a sad day for me. You're the best friend I've got."

Harmon still felt like he was having a nightmare, but he was too much the gentleman to show his disappointment. As he turned to walk toward the depot, it began to rain, and Eddie Yost called out, "You'll get drenched, Harm. Wait! We'll call you a cab."

"Thanks just the same, Eddie," Killebrew replied, "I'd like to walk."

As Harmon walked away, Pete Runnels said, "The kid's got what it takes. He'll be back."

Charley Dressen added, "Damn it! He seems so young to go off alone like that. I almost feel like I'd kicked one of my own kids out of the house."

Harmon had other things on his mind. What would he tell Elaine? She loved their little apartment. And how about her having their baby? Could they find a doctor she liked in Charleston? And how would she feel about having her baby among strangers?" The long train ride home helped him get his thinking sorted out, and when he rang the bell of their apartment he had decided what to do.

"Why darling! What are you doing home? Did you get hurt in Cleveland," asked Elaine anxiously.

"No! No! I'm all right. Don't worry," said Harmon as he managed a grin. "I just got my wish. They're sending me to a club where I can play every day."

"Where?"

"Charlotte."

"Charlotte, North Carolina. Oh, no!"

"Come on. Cheer up, honey. It's a nice town. I'll have to get ready to go though, because I'm supposed to report right away."

"I do hate to leave this apartment, said Elaine, wistfully. "I hope we can find a nice one in Charlotte."

Harmon hesitated and then said, "Honey, I don't think you should go to Charlotte. We don't know anyone there, and you might have our baby while I'm on a road trip. I just couldn't stand to think of you having it there with not a single friend around."

Elaine hugged Harmon, "You're almost too considerate, Harm. I suppose you're right, but I'd rather take my chances and go with you."

"We'll have plenty of time together in our married life," Harmon said and added with a twinkle in his eye, "You might even get tired of me."

"Fat chance," said Elaine, trying to smile through her tears.

The young couple stood close, struggling to say a cheery good-bye to each other before the plane's departure was announced.

"Oh, Harm," Elaine whispered, "Good luck! You'll be back with the Senators soon, I know. You can do it. I'll be praying for you every night, darling. But it's going to be so lonesome without you."

"Everything will turn out all right, sweetheart," Harmon

said with the assurance of a confident nineteen-year-old husband. "Take good care of yourself, and don't worry about me. I'll be all right. The time will go by quickly and we'll soon be together again."

So the lovers parted. Harmon, to Charlotte to face a new challenge—making good with a different ball club, Elaine, to fly back to her parents in Payette and face her new challenge of successfully bringing their first baby into the world.

As the plane cruised above the clouds, Elaine sat with tears rolling down her cheeks.

Harmon with Rollie Hemsley, his manager, at Charlotte in 1956

the nice people of charlotte

10

Although Harmon was despondent when he was sent down to Charlotte, the friendly people there soon perked up his spirits. And by the time the season ended, he was able to say, "Mr. Griffith sure picked the right town to send me to. I've never seen nicer people in my life than these Charlotte folks."

The warm welcome started with Killebrew's arrival. Sandy Grady, Charlotte sportswriter, reported it in this manner: Wednesday, June 27, 1956,

"This is the way the Bonus Baby came to town.

"About one o'clock yesterday, a black Chevrolet with Idaho license plates slid to a stop at Griffith Park. A little dust swirled up and out stepped Harmon Clayton Killebrew.

"He had driven during the night from Washington, listening on the car radio to the Hornet game, but now he was freshly-shaved and curious after a few hours sleep at the Hotel Charlotte.

"A big, chunky 19-year-old with a polite air, Harmon shook a few hands. 'How's the team doing,' he asked, 'Who's pitching tonight?'

"Rollie Hemsley, beaming like an oil man who had just hit a gusher, helped Killebrew unload the car trunk. The kid took out a box with ten new bats in it (Bobby Doer, D-2 models) and a traveling bag with 'Washington Baseball Club' stenciled on its blue sides.

"As they carried Killebrew's gear across the sun-blistered parking lot, Mrs. Hemsley and the two Hemsley lads drove up. Rollie introduced his wife to the Bonus Baby.

" 'I certainly hope you can help us,' said Mrs. Hemsley.

" 'I hope so too, ma'm.'

"Mrs. Hemsley asked her husband if Killebrew would play his first night in town. Rollie almost choked. 'If he doesn't play tonight, I'll get lynched by the whole town!' "

Harmon was eager to get ready for the game so he went to the locker room to be fitted with a uniform. Buck Chamberlain, the Hornet trainer, asked his size.

"I'll need a size 44," said Killebrew, and with a grin he added, "Could you please find me number 12? It's been a lucky number for me."

Reporters were still crowding around Harmon as he arranged for his playing equipment, and although he was a bit shy, he answered their questions in a courteous and direct manner.

"How do you feel about coming down to Charlotte," he was asked.

"I'm not exactly unhappy about coming to Charlotte. I know I need a lot of playing experience, and I hope to go back to the Senators in the fall and get another chance to stick."

After he had been questioned in more detail about his career, Garland Shifflet, Hornet pitcher who had known Killebrew in the Senators spring training camp, came into the locker room. They greeted each other with friendly warmth.

"Harmon, you look older," said Garland.

"Yes, I know, I'm getting along," replied Killebrew. "I'll be twenty next Friday. Elaine is back in Payette expecting our first baby. I sure hope I can help out here in Charlotte."

So Harmon had been warmly welcomed to Charlotte. Word was spread by the news media that the young slugger would play for the Hornets that night.

Five hours later, he appeared before a crowd of rabid baseball fans who had come to see the player whom they expected to spark their team to the pennant. But there was general disappointment as they saw little that night to boost their hopes.

"Killebrew's minor league debut was sensational—in reverse," reported sportswriter Sandy Grady. "Pressing too hard against Columbus pitching, Killebrew struck out three times. In the ninth, with the tying run on base, he popped to centerfield."

As Harmon made his way to the dressing room, one fan shouted in a voice tinged with sarcasm, "We're not so bush down here after all, are we slugger?"

Killebrew lowered his head and continued to his locker. Wearily he sat down on the bench, took off his shoes, and stared into space.

"Charley Dressen told me the Sally League is a pitcher's league," he thought. "But I've got to keep swinging."

His thoughts were interrupted by reporters and photographers who crowded around him. He politely answered their questions and posed for a picture. Then, getting dressed, he went back to the hotel and placed a phone call to Elaine.

The next day, Thursday, things went better. Harmon began to show the Charlotte fans why Washington had paid him a $30,000 bonus to sign. In a game against Columbus, he hit a first inning grandslam homer off the first pitch that the opposing hurler, Mike Burack, threw him. As he crossed the plate, the other Hornets swarmed out to shake his hand and the fans went wild. Ignited by Killebrew's blast, the Charlotte players sprayed hits all over the field and went on to clobber Columbus 14 to 2.

There was little doubt that the spectators liked what they saw that day.

TOM FRANKLIN, JR.

***Harmon is a picture of dejection after his first game with the Charlotte Hornets** in 1956. He went hitless in four times at bat, striking out in three of them*

"The crack of Killebrew's big yellow bat sounded as sweet as a Guy Lombardo sax section to Rollie Hemsley," wrote Sandy Grady.

Sportswriter Herman Helms said, "Harmon Killebrew thumped a grandslam homerun in the first inning to start the Hornets on the way to a landslide 14-2 victory over the Columbus Foxes at Griffith Park Thursday night.

"The tremendous shot by the $30,000 'Bonus Baby' whizzed out of the park just a shade to the left of the score board in left-center field and was actually all that right-hander Bobby Brown needed to coast to his fourth victory of the season."

Harmon felt elated that day. Brady said he was "wearing a grin like a half-slice of watermelon."

The following day, Friday, June 29, 1956, was Harmon's twentieth birthday, and in celebration he walloped another ball out of the park. He had given the team its needed spark. Sportswriter Bob Quincy enthusiastically reported:

"It was the Charlotte arsenal 5, Knoxville 2 at Griffith Park last night.

"The combination of fancy rifleman Ken Wood, Glenn Zimmerman for defense, the booming cannon of Harm Killebrew's bat, and the darting machine-gun like pitching of Garland Shifflett simply cut the Smokies to ribbons."

Manager Rollie Hemsley was elated. He said, "If we keep up this kind of playing, I don't believe any club in the league will stop us.

"We needed a spark badly and I think Killebrew has come along to ignite us."

Harmon's spirits soared. Not only had he hit his second homerun in two days, Elaine had also phoned to congratulate him on his birthday. She told him that she was feeling fine and the doctor said everything for their blessed event in August was progressing well.

When he told her of his second homerun, she exclaimed, "That's great, Harm! I knew you could do it. It won't be long before you'll be back with the Senators."

Just after he finished talking to Elaine, someone knocked

Birthday cake sent to Harmon on his 20th birthday in June at Charlotte—with best wishes from his former manager, Charley Dressen, in Washington

at his door, and opening it he saw a messenger holding a large box. He signed for it and opened the lid to stare in surprise at a beautiful birthday cake sent by Charley Dressen, Washington manager.

"Things are bound to work out," he thought. "At least Charley Dressen hasn't forgotten me."

Things did work out in Charlotte. Harmon and the other players caught fire and drove steadily toward the top of the league.

The people of Charlotte appreciated the team's winning drive because they themselves are winners. The town's heritage is one of winning and never bowing to defeat. History bears this out. Despite the fact that Charlotte had been named for the wife of George III of England, a handful of Charlotte patriots signed the Mecklenburg Declaration of Independence protesting British rule in 1775, a full year before the American Declaration of Independence. Succeeding generations of Charlotteites have caught the same spirit of independence and individual enterprise and have made the city of Charlotte, which is located on North Carolina's Piedmont Plateau, one of the most beautiful and important manufacturing centers in America.

In the team's surge toward first place, Killebrew blasted four homeruns in his first eight games, and then went on to hit in 15 straight. At that time he had played in 17 games, hit 6 homeruns (one in every 11 times at bat), and had a batting average of .364.

Pitchers began exchanging notes on how to stop Killebrew. A righthanded hurler said, "Hit the outside corner with the hook and he's dead."

"Put the ball in on the fists with a curve," countered a lefthander. Other pitchers suggested that the way to stop Killebrew was by shifting three infielders to the left side of second base and moving the outfielders drastically to the left on the theory that Killebrew's natural swing or inexperience would keep him from hitting the ball to the right.

But nothing seemed to stop Harmon's barrage of hits.

When asked if Harmon could hit a curve ball, Hornet manager Rollie Hemsley grinned, "I don't know if Killebrew can hit the curve, but he's sure hitting something. Let them shift on him," he continued. "They've been shifting on Ted Williams for ten years, and what's his lifetime batting average—.350?"

"The pitchers are stupid if they think Killebrew can't hit the curve," commented Pappa Joe Cambria, shrewd Washington scout. "Harmon learns fast, and if they give him the curve twice he'll get a good piece of it the second time."

The pitchers finally found out how to stop Killebrew.

During one game when he was sitting in the dugout, Glen Zimmerman fouled a twister in that direction.

"Duck!" yelled someone.

"I ducked," said Harmon, "and when I twisted my head something snapped. Luckily, the ball hit a couple of feet away."

The resulting crick in his neck, not the pitcher's hurling, stopped his hitting streak at fifteen games.

In reviewing Harmon's later career, it is interesting to note that his hitting streaks have been stopped more frequently by injuries such as pulled muscles, dislocations, and sprains than by pitchers.

Harmon's hitting feats at Charlotte caused sportswriters to begin comparing him with Mickey Mantle.

"The similarity in the physical characteristics, personalities, behavior, and boyhood backgrounds of New York's Mickey Mantle and Charlotte's (via Washington) Harm Killebrew is remarkable," wrote Bob Quincy, Charlotte News Sports Editor. "Put the two on second base and a fan sitting in a box behind home plate could hardly discern where Mantle leaves off and Killebrew begins. Their height is within one-half inch, Harm holding the edge there at an even six feet. Both scale 195 pounds. Their weight consists of thick, hardened muscle, and their necks have weight lifter's bulges. Their arms, legs and shoulders dwarf those of their teammates. When they connect with the ball the fans heave a sigh that would befit a Jayne Mansfield appearance in an army barracks. . . . If Harm ever makes the grade to become a Washington regular, watch for an all-time homer mark going his way."

The Senator's management in Washington kept track of Killebrew's hitting, and club manager Dressen said, "Harm Killebrew will be back in the big time before too many seasons." Calvin Griffith also gave indications that he was toying with the idea of trading Eddie Yost and installing Killebrew at third base.

Harmon was happy in Charlotte with one exception. His wife Elaine was not with him, but was in Idaho expecting their first baby in August, waiting for Harmon to join her there at the end of the season.

On August 26, 1956, the blessed event took place. The Killebrew's first child, a son whom they named Cameron, was born in an Ontario, Oregon hospital.

In recalling the event Elaine said: "It was really an exciting time for me. I don't know if there is anything that ever happens that gives you the same feeling that you have when you wait for your first child and then give birth to it.

"I was in labor 36 hours, so by the time Cam was born I was really relieved to have the whole thing over with. But when I held him in my arms, saw that he was healthy and everything was normal, I was filled with joy. I put my cheek against his soft, pink skin, forgot all the pain I had endured, and began to think of the wonderful times he and Harm and I would have together.

"Of course Harm phoned me right away. I was still sleepy from the anesthetic, but I said, 'Harm, we have a son!' I can't remember what Harm said, but I do remember that he hit a homerun in the game that day, something he has done every time we have had a new baby.

"Cam weighed eight and one-half pounds, and I was so excited that I could hardly wait to get home so I could get my hands on him. It was so much fun taking care of Cam, and I was thrilled that I was able to nurse him. However, after a few days it became apparent that he had colic, and it seemed that he wanted to eat most of the time.

"Our families and friends all gave him lovely gifts. I still remember the one Jim Hayden brought. Jim was so excited when Cam was born that he was the first one to bring a gift. And sure enough, it was a tiny football. Jim was always disappointed that Harm didn't go into professional football; so he said, 'I'm going to start Cam out right because I decided long ago your first baby would become a football star.'

" 'But what if Cam had been a girl?" I asked.

"Jim grinned, 'Then he would have become the first female football star.' "

Harmon did much more than hit a homerun after Cameron was born. He rained hits all over the field.

Bob Quincy, Charlotte sportswriter, wrote under the headlines, "Killebrew Really Crowing. Harm Passes Hits for Cigars."

"Ever since the baby came, Harm Killebrew has been crowing with his bat. Learning his wife had presented him with an eight-and-one-half pound boy, he slashed a triple and a single Monday. Last night, he rocketed a triple, an opposite field homer and a single—not to mention the intentional walk he drew. Instead of passing out cigars, Killebrew has been distributing hits much to the dismay of Macon which lost a game last night to a Charlotte squad that is playing the best ball of the season."

Fatherhood seemed to give Harmon Killebrew added confidence, and the fan's shared in his enthusiasm over this new-born son by presenting him with a baby stroller when they held an appreciation night for the team.

The season ended with the Hornets in a deadlock with Columbus for second place. Thus they qualified for the playoffs. Calvin Griffith, although eager to call Killebrew up and see what he could do with the Senators, graciously left him with Charlotte to help them in the playoffs.

Harmon finished the season with a .325 average in his 70 games with the Hornets. His slugging barrage included 15 homeruns, 7 triples, and 16 doubles.

When Harmon was called up to the Senators for the remainder of their season, he went with renewed confidence in his ability to make the "Big Team."

Cookie Lavagetto also felt that the "Bonus Baby" might now be ready to win a regular spot with the Senators; so the Washington skipper put Killebrew into the lineup in 44 games, tried him in different infield positions, and studied his every move.

Lavagetto noticed some improvement in the young slugger, but again came to the conclusion that Killebrew needed more seasoning in the minors.

Harmon did his utmost to show his major league bosses that he was ready for a starting spot on the team, but during the period he went into a hitting slump and wound up with a dismal .222 batting average, and swatted only 5 homeruns.

Some observers felt Killebrew's hitting suffered because he was pressing to make good, but when Harmon was asked about it he gave no alibis. His honest reply was, "Major league pitchers have better control than those in the minors. The way they work the corners and their pinpoint control makes it tough to hit them. I've got to learn the strike zone better and quit swinging at bad balls."

When the season ended, Harmon packed his belongings and began the long drive back to Ontario where Elaine was staying with her sister. As he drove, a nagging thought kept coming into his mind. "Is my dream of becoming a regular major leaguer impossible? Maybe it would be better if I found a different kind of job, especially now that we have Cam in our family."

No matter how hard he tried to brush the thought from his consciousness, it kept coming back like an unpaid debt to haunt him.

"Just how can I get the right answer?" he mused. As he was lost in thought, he unconsciously pressed harder on the accelerator intuitively sensing that the answer would come at the end of his journey. So, although the sun sank below the horizon and the road ahead became cloaked with the blackness of the night, Harmon kept driving at a steady speed—mile after mile. He felt that he must get home as soon as possible because he knew within himself that when he arrived in Ontario and talked to Elaine he would know what he should do.

Finally, he reached his destination just as dusk began to fall the next day. After he had fumbled sleepily with the latch and stepped out of the car door, Elaine carrying Cam in her right arm burst out of the house and hugged him with all the encompassing force of a tidal wave. "Oh Harm! It's been so long," she said, as they melted into each other's arms.

"You can say that again," replied Harmon as he drew her closer.

Just then a scream split the air, and they realized they were pressing too hard on Cam who had slipped from Elaine's right arm and was caught between them. Harmon looked at his son, cradled him tenderly in his arms, and said, "Thanks Elaine! To come home to you and our son is a real thrill. You know, I think he looks a little like me."

"He's surely got your broad shoulders and your winning smile," said Elaine. "And I can tell already that he'll be an athlete. Come in and say hello to Sis. Then I'm going to drive you right over to our new apartment and put you to bed before you fall asleep standing up."

The next morning when Harmon opened his eyes and saw his lovely wife smiling at him and heard their son cooing softly in his crib, he thought to himself, "How lucky can a guy be?" Then like an aching tooth the thought that had nagged him all through his trip came back into his mind, and he looked into Elaine's eyes and said, "You know, darling, I was kind of embarrassed to come home after hitting like I did when I went back to the Senators. I'm beginning to wonder if I can hit major league pitching."

Elaine fixed her clear blue eyes upon him and said simply, without a moment's hesitation, "You've always been a good hitter, Harm, and you'll hit in the majors too. Come on! Let's get going; I've got a lot of surprises to show you."

boarding the chattanooga choo-choo

11

When spring training time rolled around in 1957, Harmon was ready to go. And he was delighted that Elaine and their baby son Cameron could go to Florida with him.

While playing for the Senators in the Grapefruit League that spring he did several things that impressed observers. First, he showed them that he was the second fastest sprinter on the squad. Manager Charlie Dressen tried something new in the workouts—clocked 50 yard wind-sprints. Top man was Pedro Ramos, the Cuban pitcher who sprinted the distance in a fast 5.8 seconds. Harmon who was timed at 5.9 seconds was a close second. Third place went to towering rookie outfielder Bob Allison who was clocked at an even six seconds.

In addition to making an impression with his speed, Killebrew again showed the dynamite that was in his bat. In a game which the Senators lost to the Phillies in Clearwater, Florida, Harmon hit a tape measure homerun, a 440-foot blast over the left center field fence which was 400 feet away from the plate and 40 feet high at the point the ball cleared.

The young slugger also proved he could deliver in a pinch. In a game against Kansas City, with the Senators trailing by a 6-2 count in the sixth, Killebrew clouted a grandslam homerun that knotted the score and sparked the Washington club to a victory.

Despite these impressive heroics the top brass of the Washington club decided that Killebrew was not quite ready for major league status.

Coach Cookie Lavagetto explained their reasoning this way:

"Harmon still swings up at a ball too much. He has yet to overcome the habit of dipping his right knee. He learns fast; so when he forgets what he has been shown, it's probably due to not playing regularly.

"He has the power and the guts to become a noted slugger. He also can hit the ball a mile, and he isn't afraid. But he still needs to get out and play and profit from experience."

"Killebrew must learn to ignore pitches outside his strike zone," added manager Chuck Dressen. "Sure he's a threat every time he swings, but only when he's going after good pitches. Right now, the Yankee pitchers, for instance, are fooling him with slow curves. Only with experience and day to day play will he get smarter."

So once again Harmon was sent down, this time to the Chattanooga Lookouts in the Class AA Southern League.

Something happened, however, during that spring training that has enriched Harmon's life to this day. He became good friends with Bob Allison. Through the years the two stars have developed a brotherly affection for each other and have spent many enjoyable years as roommates while playing with the Minnesota Twins.

Harmon and Elaine have vivid memories of the trip to Chattanooga.

"We had become good friends during spring training with young outfielder Ernie Oravetz and his wife Rosemarie. They were our age, had been married on the same day that we were, and also had a baby two months old. We had a lot in common. Ernie and I had both been sent to Chattanooga, so the four of us drove down there.

Elaine recalls that the trip was really something. "We had the babies in porta-cribs in the back of each of our cars and they both got sick. I remember how we would all stop and get Cam cleaned up and then just get going again when Ernie would honk for us to stop because their baby needed attention. When this goes on all night—two babies taking turns erupting like geysers—you get pretty tense. Harm tried to make a game of it and would say, 'Now it's Cam's turn. Let's keep score and see who throws up more times.'

"Some day when I have time, I'm going to invent an air-conditioned-non-bounceable-porta-crib. I know I'll make a fortune.

"By the time we reached Chattanooga we were worn out, and then to our dismay, good apartments were scarce. Most of them were in terrible condition, and expensive. Finally, after we had decided it would be just about as practical for us to move back to Idaho and have Harm commute daily by plane to Chattanooga, we found one that was fairly decent. We fixed it up as attractively as we could and got settled for the summer."

Chattanooga, which is located in southeastern Tennessee, is one of the chief industrial cities of the South. It lies in a picturesque setting with the winding Tennessee River and surrounding wooded hills giving it an appearance similar to a postcard scene. Southwest of the city is Lookout Mountain, from which vantage point one can view seven states. The town derived its name from the mountain, Chattanooga being an Indian name which means "rock coming to a point."

Inasmuch as Chattanooga was a key city during the Civil War, many fierce battles were fought around it; consequently the area is rich in historic interest.

Harmon and Elaine received a warm welcome in Chattanooga. The Chattanooga Lookouts (who take their name from Lookout Mountain) had undergone some tough sledding the year before, and fan interest had dropped. Consequently, it was being noised about town that the Lookouts might lose their franchise if their fortune did not improve.

Killebrew was one of the new players who was expected to give the team the shot in the arm needed to help them win and revive fan interest. Bob Allison was another.

Cal Ermer, the team's manager and a true southern gentleman, greeted Killebrew and Allison with enthusiasm.

"Well, we can sure use some husky players like you," he said. "I understand you both hit the long-ball."

"We try to," replied Allison.

"Yes," added Harmon, "but I don't seem to hit it often enough."

"I'm sure you'll both hit for distance often down here," said the genial Ermer.

Ermer developed a fatherly interest in both players, and after a few games gave his assessment of Killebrew. "The boy's a good student of the game," he said, "and he's improving each time out. His hitting is something else. He hits balls out of the park like shots and I'm sure he has power he's never used."

Beginning with the first games of the season, Harmon began to stimulate fan interest with his powerful bat. In one game he swung and didn't get "good wood" on the ball, but the pellet still hit the right-field fence for a triple. His first three homeruns included one grand-slammer, and he blasted a ball over the left-field bleachers in Birmingham that drew raves for weeks from the Birmingham fans.

Sportswriters started to praise Killebrew's hitting feats, and one said:

"The fan-drawing problem of this club may be a race between Lookout pitchers coming around and Killebrew clearing some of those light towers with his hits."

In interviews with sportswriters, Harmon played down his hitting and said, "You all have to work together and have good pitching with good hitting to have a winning team. I hope we can all do our share and win for the great Chattanooga people."

The Lookout pitchers had rough going during early season play, and the hitters seemed to be carrying most of the burden. In a game against the Nashville Volunteers, Killebrew led the hitters with two homeruns, a double and a single; still his team lost 13 to 10.

In another contest the Birmingham Barons were edged 12 to 11 when Harmon singled, scored on Allison's hit and then hit a grandslam homerun.

Gradually the pitchers became more effective, and with the continued slugging of Killebrew, Allison, Vern Morgan, Waldo Gonzales and Jesse Levan, the Lookouts put together an eight game winning streak.

Harmon's swing was once more in the groove and he became the Southern Association batting leader. The press reported: "Hitting safely in all but two games and with eight extra base hits, Harmon Killebrew, Chattanooga's sensational third baseman, moved out in front of the Southern Association leaders.

"Killebrew tops the field in runs batted in with 17, in total bases with 35, in hits with 20, in runs with 13, and shares the homerun lead with Ken Walters of Birmingham and Tom Nerard of Memphis."

While Harmon was burning up the league with his hitting, Elaine was also keeping the home fires burning brightly. The change in climate seemed to upset Cameron and he was ill most of the summer. In addition, Elaine had some bouts of her own with illness, but she remained cheerful and kept busy.

The Chattanooga fans considered her "lovely, and friendly," and she was the first "Lookout wife" to be interviewed and written about by the press. Writer, Margaret Morris had the following to say:

"A versatile person, Elaine Killebrew can cook, sew (makes a good deal of her own clothes) crochet, does embroidery and art work. . . .

"She makes a number of things during the summer months, and then when the family returns to Payette in the fall, she exhibits them at the county fair. Last year, her crocheted afghan won a blue ribbon. Her work is beautiful,

BILL YOUNG

Harmon on a rainy day in Chattanooga during the 1957 play-off

BILL TRUEX

Killebrew with Vern Morgan and the Chattanooga Lookouts, 1957

and recently she completed a large cross-stitched picture of mallards in flight.

"Moving is the only part of baseball life that Elaine isn't fond of. She said, 'It's 3300 miles from home to spring training, and by the time you make that trip twice a year, it gets awfully long. We like to take a few of the basic things that we can call our own with us and of course it all has to be portable—portable crib, portable sewing machine, portable TV, portable everything. . . . We feel that Harmon has a future in baseball, and we will stay with it as long as we can.' "

Harmon's play with the Lookouts led him to be named on the Southern Association's All-Star team. And his consistent hitting helped the Lookouts make a challenge for the pennant. At season's end he had a batting average of .279, led the league with 29 homeruns and batted in 101 runs.

Again he was called north to finish the season with the Senators, and Elaine prepared to go back to Payette. It was decided that Elaine's sister, Dolly, should fly back to Chattanooga so she could help drive on the long trip to Idaho.

Elaine's recollection is:

"That was quite a trip. We were taking all our belongings with us; so I was hauling them in a trailer. I can't remember why, but we had started out without a spare tire for the trailer.

"We had driven several hours and were just outside Nashville, and although it was ten o'clock at night we were getting along fine. We decided to keep going. Cam was sleeping peacefully in his crib and Dolly had just said to me, 'Look at that big star in the sky', when a loud explosion just about frightened us out of our wits.

" 'Golly! What was that?' asked Dolly.

" 'Maybe they're blasting around here,' I replied. But I was wrong. We drove a few feet farther and the trailer began to sway like a drunken sailor. We knew then that we had a flat tire. The noise had awakened Cam, and he started crying. Can you imagine anything more frightening for two young women than being stalled at night on a lonely road with a flat tire—no spare, and a crying baby?

" 'What in the world can we do?' asked Dolly.

" 'There's nothing else to do but for me to hitch a ride to Nashville. You stay with Cam, and I'll hurry back as fast as I can,' I replied.

"Thumbing a ride is an interesting experience. The first three cars whizzed past me like I was a gangster's moll. Finally, a lone man slowed down.

" 'You got trouble, lady?' he asked.

" 'You can say that again,' I replied. 'We've got a flat tire on our trailer and no spare.'

" 'Well, hop in. I'll take you in to Nashville. I know a garage where you can get a tire.'

"It was with some trepidation that I stepped into the car and sat beside him. But he was a fine gentleman and did everything he could to help us. He took me to town, helped me get a tire, drove me back to our car and then helped us change the tire; so we got things back in order and resumed driving.

"Several days later, and after more tire problems, we arrived home. I stayed with my folks until Harm returned at the end of the season."

When Harmon was called back up to the Senators, he also parted company with Bob Allison. Bob's record had not been as good as Harmon's. He had played in 125 games for the Lookouts and had hit .246, batting in 38 runs and hitting two homers.

"I knew you'd get called back," said Bob. "Good luck up there with the big boys."

"You'll get your chance too," smiled Harmon. "I hope we'll both be with the Senators next year."

And with a warm handshake, the two future stars parted.

Harmon played in nine games while finishing the season with the Washington club, and he did well. He got 9 hits in 31 times at bat for a .290 average. He also hit two home-runs. Naturally, such a brief period of play didn't prove he was ready to play regularly, but there were indications that he was moving closer to his goal. In addition to retaining his ability to hit the long-ball, his fielding had also improved.

Sportswriter Burton Hawkins commented on this in the Washington Evening Star, September 26, 1957.

"Those reports out of the South which pictured Harmon Killebrew as about as likely a third baseman as John Foster Dulles must be labeled as libelous thus far. The young man had a couple of fierce ones smashed in his direction yesterday as the Senators dropped a 7 to 6 decision to the Red Sox in 11 innings, and he handled them in scintillating style.

"There's nothing wrong either, with Harmon's .316 hitting, which includes a couple of well-kissed homers, in his brief test since being promoted from Chattanooga."

The questions being asked by Washington fans were: "Is young Killebrew ready?" "Do the cellar-dwelling Senators actually have their hands on another power hitter with great homerun potential?"

The administrators of the Washington club gave no answers. Cookie Lavagetto said, "Killebrew's improved all the way around." Calvin Griffith made no definite statement but did show a reluctance to trade Harmon to anyone else.

So Harmon went back home to Payette after the 1957 season with no assurance that he was ready to step into the Senators' lineup.

His good season with Chattanooga had given him more confidence, and his friends in Payette were predicting major league status for him in 1958. But when approached on the subject, Harmon, never one to boast, would say, "You never know what will happen in baseball."

However, deep down within himself he felt that his impossible dream was much closer to fulfillment. And if he had any doubts, he was always reassured by Elaine's "You can do it, Harm."

While waiting for the 1958 season to roll around, he spent the winter again working for the Gas company in Payette. And Elaine, although they were expecting their second baby, worked during the Christmas season in one of the town's department stores.

indianapolis here we come ---and away we go

12

Came the spring of 1958, and the Harmon Killebrews once again started their long drive to Florida. Enroute they visited their friends in Las Vegas, the Jack Daileys and the Don Haydens, both of the men being principals in the school system there.

Harmon had high hopes of getting a good shot at the Senators' third base job. He reasoned that if he couldn't win the position from Eddie Yost, he could at least make the grade as a utility infielder. Press reports from Orlando showed that Killebrew was being scrutinized for the third base job.

John F. Steadman, Sports Editor stated: "Much attention is being shown Harmon Killebrew at third base. He takes a good riffle with the bat but is remiss in the field. Lavagetto and Ellis Clary are trying to mold him into a reasonable facsimile of a third baseman. . . . 'The kid is still tight and we are trying to loosen him up,' says Lavagetto, who played fourteen years as one of the National League's premier third basemen."

Despite continuous coaching help Harmon couldn't seem to get going during spring training. He usually had difficulty making a fast start, and this spring he was also slowed down by a knee injury.

Lavagetto stated openly that Killebrew was having a bad spring, and he did little to bolster Harmon's confidence by making such statements as:

"He needs a year in Triple A.

"Maybe he'd be a better outfielder. Of course he throws like he's passing a football, but we can work that out of him.

"Of course if Harmon keeps learning, stays eager, and watches his weight, he's going to make a fine big league ball player in a year or two."

Harmon took all of the criticism with good grace and worked hard to improve his play. When interviewed he said:

"I know I haven't been doing too well, but I'm going to go all out to stay with the Senators. I've cut 10 pounds off my weight, and I'm willing to try to play any position they want me to."

Basically, Lavagetto's problem was to decide whether Killebrew's greater potential as a slugger would help the team more than Eddie Yost's more polished defensive play.

The decision was hanging in the balance until something happened one day that tipped the scales in Eddie Yost's favor. Harmon was playing with the Senators' B team against Kansas City's B squad in West Palm Beach. The game was hard-fought, and Killebrew had hit a homerun late in the game that tied the score and sent the contest into extra innings. Then fate dealt him a body blow. In the tenth inning, Kansas City had men on second and third with two out. The batter knocked a slow hopper to Killebrew at third. Harmon fielded the ball easily and cocked his arm to throw the hitter out at first. Just then, Hal Smith of Kansas City started running from second to third, and Rocky Bridges, Senators shortstop, yelled, "Tag him!" to Killebrew. Momentarily confused, Harmon held his throw and then made a late and futile attempt to tag Smith. In the meantime, the winning run scored.

Bridges approached Harmon in the clubhouse after the game and said, "I'm sorry, Harm. You were set to make the right play, and I confused you. It was my fault."

"Forget it, Rocky," Harmon replied. "I just goofed."

Such an incident should have little bearing on a player's future, but a Washington sportswriter siezed upon it with sadistic glee, blew it out of proportion, and headlined his account of the game with: "Eddie Yost won the third base job for the Senators today, while sitting in a hotel in Orlando, Florida."

Harmon subsequently went north with the Senators to open the American league season, but Eddie Yost was still stationed at third and Killebrew warmed the bench.

When Harmon went north, Elaine put Cameron in his porta-crib, packed all of their belongings, and drove to Washington. The Killebrews found an apartment in Alexandria, Virginia, attractively arranged their belongings in it, and looked forward to spending the season there together.

For some unknown reason, Lavagetto didn't give Killebrew any chance to show what he could do during the early season games, and in an entire month his total playing time consisted of pinch-hitting twice. Nevertheless, with the eternal optimism of youth, Harmon and Elaine assumed they would stay in Washington, made plans for the future, and began making arrangements for their coming baby. Elaine employed her art talents to paint clever animal figures and interesting pictures and arranged them attractively for a nursery setting. Harmon inquired from other players about available baby foods, laundry facilities and other services necessary in the care of a newlyborn baby.

One night Elaine said, "Oh Harm, I know *now* that dreams do come true! Here we are in our own home with Cam, and another baby ready to join us soon, and you're a big league ballplayer. I knew all the time you could do it."

"It is real nice," Harmon said modestly, "but I just can't understand why Cookie Lavagetto doesn't let me play more."

"Don't worry about it," said Elaine, "things are too wonderful right now to let anything interfere with our happiness."

"You're quite a girl. Do you know that?" said Harmon, taking his lovely wife in his arms. "I was sure lucky to find you."

"Oh that wasn't hard," grinned Elaine. "I've had designs on you ever since I was twelve."

Harmon smiled and turned out the light. The happy couple fell asleep, dreaming of exciting days ahead in the nation's capital city.

The next morning while the team was working out, Lavagetto called Killebrew into his office.

"Harmon," he said, with an apologetic look, "I'm sorry to tell you this, but we're shipping you down to Indianapolis."

Harmon was stunned. Groping for words he stammered, "I was hoping I could—could stay with the Senators this year. I thought I did all right with Chattanooga last season."

"Yes I know! I know you did, Harm. But, well, I don't think you're ready for big league play yet. Indianapolis is Triple A. You'll be in faster company than in Chattanooga and then next year. . . ."

Harmon was too much the gentleman to argue with Lavagetto, but he thought plenty. "Next year! Next year! It's always next year. If I can't make the grade now, maybe I should quit and get some other kind of job."

Lavagetto's comments upset Killebrew so much that he went for advice to a man who had befriended and encouraged him ever since he had left Payette at 17 to join the Washington Club—Ossie Bluege.

Ossie remembers that meeting ". . . like it took place yesterday," as I learned when I made an appointment to discuss it with him. I arrived a bit early, and as my eyes roamed over his well-appointed suite of offices, my attention became fixed on a handsomely framed, colored photograph hanging on one of the walls. It was a large picture showing Harmon Killebrew hitting a homerun. Below it was the caption, "Harmon Killebrew unloads historic 520 ft. homerun off California's Lew Burdette, 4th inning, June 3, 1967. First ball ever to be hit into second deck of leftfield stands at Metropolitan Stadium."

Ossie greeted me with a pleasant smile. He is a handsome man. He was dressed immaculately, and his athletic figure was set off by an ensemble consisting of a dark blue sportscoat with harmonizing slacks and attractive accessories. His hair is what might be described as golden silver and his clear blue eyes bespeak a compassionate nature.

"Harmon was heartsick when he came into my office," Ossie said. "And there were tears in his eyes as he mumbled, 'Ossie, I guess I don't have what it takes. It looks like I'm just wasting my time playing baseball. It would probably be better if I quit and got a different kind of job.'

" 'Now Harmon,' I replied, 'I never expected *you* to throw in the sponge.'

" 'Well, I'm not just thinking of myself,' Harmon said with some embarrassment. 'Elaine's expecting our second baby any day now, and I want to be with her. I don't know whether she can stand the trip from Washington to Indianapolis, and I'm afraid she'll be all broken up when she learns I have to go.'

"I talked to Harmon like a father then," continued Ossie, "and said, 'What does your doctor say about Elaine's condition?'

" 'He says she's fine right now.'

" 'All right then, ask him his opinion about Elaine's traveling. He can tell you what's best.'

" 'I can do that,' said Harmon, 'But there's another side to this thing, too. I thought I had a pretty good season with Chattanooga last year, and they haven't given me a chance to do anything up here except sit on the bench.'

" 'Yes, I know Harm,' I said. 'I don't like that either, but that's the way the breaks go sometimes. You've got the potential to be a great ballplayer, but you've got to learn to be patient and give yourself a chance. You go to Indianapolis; play regularly and things will work out. And I want you to know I'll always be in your corner.' "

Ossie paused and stared silently at me for a few moments. Then he went on. "As you know, Harmon did go down to Indianapolis and made arrangements for Elaine to come later. I wrote to him from time to time wherever he was and tried to help keep his morale up. I would tell him to relax, be natural, learn to feel comfortable in the field and at the plate and to learn his strike zone.

"He's been a joy to me, and I am so happy about his tremendous success. He and Elaine and their children are such a fine young family. And I am just as proud of him as if he were my own son."

Elaine heard about Harmon's transfer to Indianapolis while she was listening to the ball game on the radio; so like a good trooper she began packing even before Harmon got home. But despite her efforts to get ready to move, she was very upset.

"I was just ten days away from having our second baby. I felt so alone when Cam was born, and I was looking forward to Harm's being with me for the birth of this one. When Harm came in I could see how depressed he was and it made me angry to see what the transfer had done to his spirits.

" 'Harm, they can't do this to you,' I said. 'I'd like to give that Lavagetto a piece of my mind. Here, he keeps you sitting on the bench for a month, doesn't even give you a chance to show what you can do, and then ships you to Indianapolis without any advance notice.'

" 'That's the way it goes with a young ball player,' said Harm brokenly. 'I wish I knew what is wrong. Sometimes I think Cookie doesn't like me.'

" 'Anyone who doesn't like you should have his head examined,' I said bursting into tears. Then between sobs, I continued, 'You know Harm, I just don't know whether I can take having another baby if you're not with me.'

" 'Things will work out, Honey,' Harm said. And then tears began to roll down his cheeks. So we both sat down close to each other and cried a few tears.

"Finally, Harm got up and continued packing and I lay on the bed, fighting my tears. But I just couldn't stop, and the farther we got into our packing, the sicker I became. I have a sciatic nerve problem which seems to be aggravated by emotional tension, and at that time the pain ran down from my hips and became so intense in one of my legs that I couldn't stand on it.

"As I lay on the bed and Harm forced himself to keep packing, I recalled the interesting things that had already taken place in our little Belleview apartment. I particularly remembered the time when I had left Cam lying on the bed after changing his pants. I had gone into the bathroom to rinse out his diaper, and when I came back he was gone. 'Harm,' I screamed, 'Cam has disappeared!

" 'You sure he hasn't rolled under the bed?' Harm asked with anxiety in his voice.

" 'I've already looked there!' I shouted. 'He must have gone outside.'

"As we both rushed outdoors to begin our search, a cold rain spattered our faces, and I was becoming almost hysterical. Suddenly, Harm shouted, 'There he is!' Although I was heavy with child, I ran nearly as fast as Harm to catch up with our little fugitive. And do you know when we caught up with him, he was still going at full speed with his unsnapped pants flapping in the breeze. We still don't know where he was going, but he certainly displayed the Killebrew trait of setting a goal and then moving toward it.

"I also remembered the fun things we had planned to do in Washington, and I felt horrible. I closed my eyes and fell asleep.

"Well, we finally got packed, with Harm doing most of it. We also checked with my doctor to see if it would be safe for me to drive down to Indianapolis.

"He said, 'Mrs. Killebrew, don't you even consider it. You're so close to delivering now that you might have your baby in the car.'

" 'I wouldn't care as long as Harm was with me,' I replied.

" 'Well, I would,' he said in Marcus Welby fashion. 'I want you to get on a plane and go to your folks. Have your baby there, and you can join your husband in Indianapolis just as soon as you are strong enough.'

"So again we re-enacted the same old scene. Harm came to the airport and put Cam and me on the plane and then drove alone to Indianapolis. Of course there were parting tears once more, and even though I was pregnant, I felt hollow inside when Harm waved good-bye. As I'm telling this, our life story almost begins to sound like a soap opera, so lest you think I'm over dramatizing things, I'll skip the other details of our parting."

Harmon reported to Walker Cooper, manager of the Indianapolis Indians in the Triple A American Association. He was immediately publicized as a member of one of the strongest infields in the league. But although he got good press notices at first, things did not work out as they should have. He was still handicapped with a serious knee injury which affected his timing at the plate. In addition, he was worried about being away from Elaine when she was about to give birth to their second baby. These factors, combined with a let-down feeling regarding his chances to make it in the majors, caused him to perform below par at the plate and in the field. Nevertheless, he kept plugging away knowing that in time he would get back into the groove.

Meanwhile Elaine, who was home in Payette, spent some time learning more about Indianapolis. She obtained an encyclopedia from the library and was interested to read that Indianapolis is often called "the Crossroads of America," because so many lines of nationwide traffic intersect in the city. And she was delighted to learn that Indianapolis is the home of the famous Motor Speedway, and secretly hoped she might rejoin Harmon in time to see its 500 mile Memorial Day auto race.

The rich cultural life of Indianapolis interested her, and she made plans to visit the city's art institutes and museums. Like Harmon, she had reconciled herself to the thought that his playing in Indianapolis meant taking a step closer to their goal; so she was happy that Harmon had been sent to one of the great cities of the nation.

On May 23, 1958, the Killebrew's second son, Kenny, was born.

Elaine felt great after his birth.

"I got out of bed and walked down the hospital hall to phone Harm and tell him the good news. 'Harm, we've got a battery now, a pitcher, and a catcher.'

" 'You mean another boy? That's great!' Harm said, his voice filled with joy. Then, as always, his first concern was for me. 'Are *you* all right, honey?' he asked anxiously.

" 'This time it was a breeze,' I replied. 'Why it was so easy I could have a dozen more.'

" 'Whoa! Remember now, we're trying for a baseball team not a football squad,' Harm chuckled. 'I can hardly wait to see him,' he added. 'How soon can you all join me?'

" 'The doctor says in about three weeks.'

" 'That's wonderful, I'll get busy and find us a nice apartment. You'll like Indianapolis. It's an exciting city. Take care, darling! Goodbye.'

"I felt lonesome again after talking to my wonderful husband, but I dutifully went back to bed and tried to be a good and patient patient so I would hurry and get strong enough to travel back to Harm.

"Meanwhile, Harm went out and hit another homerun to celebrate. I can just imagine how proud he was when he told the other players, and I would have liked being with him because he has always been such a proud father.

"Cam came down with the red measles while I was away in the hospital and was just beginning to get over them when I brought Kenny home with me. I was concerned about Kenny getting them, but the doctors told me that babies are immune to such diseases during the first six months of life, and their prediction was correct, Kenny didn't get them.

"When Kenny was three weeks old, I went to rejoin Harm in Indianapolis. My dad fixed a wicker clothes basket with a big rubber handle on it so I could carry the baby more easily. At that time the handy little baby seat carriers with handles that mothers have now had not been developed. I packed all of Kenny's diapers in the bottom of the basket and then put Kenny in on top of them. My folks took us to the airport and we boarded the plane for Indianapolis.

"It was really something trying to care for my two boys on the plane. While I was feeding Kenny, Cam got sick, and if it hadn't been for a kind stewardess I would have had a rough time of it. Since then I have become a veteran in anticipating and handling our children's stomach upsets when traveling, and have realized that such things happen to youngsters."

While Elaine was flying with the boys toward Indianapolis, Harmon was on a train with the rest of the Indianapolis team speeding back from Minneapolis to Indianapolis. The team had been on a week's road trip and he had hit a homerun the day before; so he was feeling quite happy.

He was sitting beside a teammate, Al Facchini, and they were engaging in a quiet discussion, when team manager Walker Cooper, walked up the aisle, sat down beside them and said, "Harm, I suppose now is as good a time as any to tell you. We're sending you back to Chattanooga and bringing up Stan Roseboro in your place."

Harmon was stunned, "But Mr. Cooper," he said, "in the last few games, I've been hitting better. I thought I was doing okay."

"Sorry Harm," Cooper said with an air of finality. "You'll be better off with Chattanooga where you can play regularly."

This was chilling news to Killebrew, and the next night when he said good-bye to his teammates in the Tribe locker room at Victory Field, he expressed his personal feelings more openly than usual. Tev Laudeman, sportswriter for the Indianapolis Times, was present and reported the conversation in his column:

" 'I didn't expect it,' said Killebrew.

" 'The last few games I felt like I was starting to swing right. I thought I was going to be okay.

" 'This is the third or fourth time it has happened to me. Somehow you never really expect it. You never get used to it.

" 'I think I would have been all right up here. It just took me a long time to get used to swinging against good pitching. I didn't play much that month I was with Washington. That hurt me . . . I just needed time to get started.

" 'This really messed up my plans. I've just found a house in Indianapolis, and my wife and our two children are on the way here. Now, we'll have to drive down to Chattanooga.' "

" 'I'm taking over the house he rented,' said pitcher Don Rudolph. 'Nobody ever found a house as easy as that.' "

Harmon drove with heavy heart to the airport the next day to meet Elaine and their two sons, but when he met his family his spirits soared.

"Hello darling," he said, hugging Elaine. "And this is Kenny!" Isn't *he* something. And Cam's grown so much just in a few weeks. It's great to be together again."

Elaine remembers that reunion well:

"It was the first time Harm had seen Kenny, and it was like a tonic for me to see how excited and thrilled he was. He bundled us into the car and drove us to the place he had rented. He had pulled our trailer to the house, unpacked all of our belongings and moved in. Everything was arranged so attractively. Gently, he put his arm around me, 'Elaine, I have bad news. They've sent me back to Chattanooga. We've got to pack and leave tomorrow.'

"'Oh No! Not again!'

"Harm was saying, 'I tried so hard to make it here. I just don't know . . . maybe I should quit baseball. It's not fair to you and the boys to have to travel around the country like this.'

"I was ashamed of my outburst, and said, 'Harm, of course I'm disappointed, but that's not what is most important. All that matters is that we can be together somewhere. I don't care if you play triple A or double A or single A as long as I can be with you.' "

Harm added gently, "Being with you and the boys is the most important thing in the world to me, too. Things are completely different when you are around."

Elaine snuggled close to him. "Life has been good to us, Harm. Aren't our two boys handsome?"

"They're great! Just great! They're almost as pretty as you are," Harm said with a grin.

"Of course you still remember you're a major leaguer, Harm, even if some of these hard-headed managers are tough to convince. I know you'll make it soon."

"Darling! With you at my side I can't help but make it. Get your coat on. I'm going to take you and the boys out to dinner. Tomorrow we'll pack for Chattanooga."

Elaine recalled the following: "The next day we packed, got into our car and off we went; the car, the trailer, the two boys, Harm and I, bound for Chattanooga.

"When we arrived, we couldn't find a place to live; so we finally moved in to live with Rosemarie and Ernie Oravetz. Ernie hadn't been moved north to the Senators when Harm was; so they had managed to find an apartment in a nice four-plex. We stayed with them until another ballplayer who lived in the same four-plex was sent down to Charlotte, leaving his apartment available to us.

"That summer was a pleasant one. Our two little roughnecks ran around outside most of the time and became as brown as bears.

"Rosemarie Oravetz had a second child too, and she was expecting her third; so we spent a lot of time together discussing proper methods of raising children.

"Elaine became interested in sewing that summer. I purchased a Singer portable and she was kept very busy taking care of the apartment, watching the boys, and sewing."

One of the first persons to greet the Killebrews when they arrived in Chattanooga was Bob Allison.

"I didn't expect to see you down here again, Harm," he said, extending his hand.

"That makes two of us," replied Harmon. "But I can see their point. I only hit .215 with two homeruns in 38 games in Indianapolis. I can understand their thinking that I need more seasoning. But I can tell you something, Bob. This is it! If I don't do well down here, starting right now, I can forget about playing with the Senators."

"You can say that for me too," said Allison.

The team and fans in Chattanooga were delighted to have Killebrew back with them. As soon as he appeared at the ballpark, his teammates and local sportswriters gave him a warm welcome.

Sportswriter George Short, who was present, wrote:

"Killebrew refreshing addition to Lookouts.

"As exuberant as kids flocking in the direction of the tinkling bell of the ice cream or snowball man, Lookouts swarmed around Harmon Killebrew when he reported to the Chattanooga Club Thursday afternoon.

"The fans took an excited view that Killebrew, like the vendor of summer coolouts, adds a refreshing touch to a Chattanooga Club that is alternately hot and cold.

"It is pretty well agreed that Killebrew will give a lift to the Club.

"What does Killebrew himself think about being back.

" 'Right now I'm too tired from traveling to think,' he sighed wearily, 'But I am ready to play ball and I hope I can help.'

" 'Was it disturbing to be sent down a notch or two during the season?' Killebrew was asked.

" 'Of course. No player likes to go down if he can help it, but he can't; that's part of the game,' Harmon replied. 'But it's not too bad, especially to come back here where a lot of the fellows I played with last year are back, too.'

"Killebrew was sent by Washington to Indianapolis last month; and after 28 games there, he's here.

"Yet he says it's 'not too bad.' Such spirit is commendable."

Red Marion, the new manager of the Lookouts, put Killebrew into the lineup immediately, and Harmon responded in his first game by doubling 385 feet on a liner to right center, and then smashing a homerun over the left field wall, the first one to leave the park at that spot since his own drive the year before.

The Lookouts went on to defeat New Orleans 10 to 2, and the fans were elated. Harmon's slugging was again sparking the Lookouts as it had the previous season, and they began driving toward the top of the league.

Later in the season, on August 21, 1958, he hit the longest homerun of the year at Sulphur Dell against Nashville. The herculean shot cleared the giant center field scoreboard some 450 feet from home plate. Natives of Sulphur Dell began arguing about whether the homerun was the longest in the town's history. They couldn't agree. But no one doubted that it was one of the mightiest blows ever struck in that community.

A week later Harmon blasted a triple and a "mile high bomb that cleared Engel Stadium's scoreboard to left with plenty to spare." The blow helped Chattanooga win a thriller over Nashville 6 to 5.

Bob Allison got Harmon aside after one of his clouts and said, "You hit that ball like you're mad at someone."

"Maybe I'll stay mad all season," replied Harmon with a smile.

Killebrew continued his hitting at a pace that drew comments from everyone around. In the meantime the team edged closer to a playoff spot.

By the end of the season, Harmon had played in 86 games and reached a batting average of .308 which included 17 homeruns and 54 runs-batted-in, and in so doing had helped spark the Lookouts. Again the Washington Senators called Killebrew and Allison back for a late season tryout.

Harmon hit .194 for Washington and Bob .200 in eleven games. However, such records made playing in eleven games have little significance and both players knew that the 1959 spring training would be the decisive one of their baseball careers.

Elaine stayed in Chattanooga until the season ended. Then Harmon drove back down accompanied by Jim Lemon to pick her and the children up.

The Killebrews made the long drive back to Idaho and moved in with Elaine's family until they could find a home of their own. They decided at this time that they must have some kind of permanent dwelling place for their family, so they purchased a house in Payette and spent the winter there. Harm kept busy, again working for the Gas Company.

WORLD WIDE PHOTOS

A handshake from President Eisenhower before the start of the Boston-Washington game, 1959. Calvin Griffith, president of the Washington Ball club is looking on.

the toast of washington

13

While the Killebrews were waiting for spring training of 1959 to roll around, all kinds of rumors were coming out of Washington. The most persistent was the one that the Senators' franchise might be moved to another town. The Washington club owners, like others who had been losing money, were looking for greener pastures. Several clubs had already made moves. The St. Louis Browns had gone to Baltimore; the Boston Braves had moved to Milwaukee, and the Philadelphia Athletics had found a new home in Kansas City. Finally, the Brooklyn Dodgers and New York Giants had stimulated club owners' dreams of greater profits elsewhere by jumping clear across the continent and settling down in Los Angeles and San Francisco.

When these last moves took place, Calvin Griffith, who had been having a rough time financially for years, began dickering with Minneapolis and then its twin city, St. Paul, both of which were beating the drums to obtain major league baseball.

Such negotiations brought protests from Washington

fans who with government officials right up to President Dwight D. Eisenhower stated firmly that the nation's capital should never be without a representative in the Great American Game.

Calvin Griffith seemed almost on the verge of committing himself to a change when he was notified by American League officials that they would not grant him permission to move the franchise. Consequently, Griffith, knowing that the Senators would definitely remain in Washington another season, turned his energies to building up his club that had wound up in the cellar the year before.

During the winter, he made a deal with Detroit which had a definite effect on Killebrew's future. He sent them third baseman Eddie Yost, shortstop Rocky Bridges, and outfielder Neil Chrisley in exchange for infielders Reno Bertoia, and Ron Samford, and outfielder Jim Delsing. At the time he said, "Bertoia is young and can play second or third base."

Subsequently, manager Cookie Lavagetto made plans to have Bertoia replace Eddie Yost at third base.

Harmon had kept abreast of all this news, at home in Payette, and was secretly hoping for two things. He wanted the Senators to stay in Washington so he could prove to the fans there that he was a major leaguer. And he wanted a fair shot at the third base job. As things turned out, both of his desires were realized.

When the Killebrews left for spring training in 1959, they took Harmon's mother along so she could enjoy Florida and visit with them in Washington.

They recalled that drive as one of their most difficult.

"The trip took 9 days," Harmon said. "We always went through Las Vegas, and down through Texas and Mississippi to Florida to avoid the snow and icy roads. But this time things really hit us, and we seemed to be traveling through blinding blizzards or sand storms most of the way. In addition to this, our two boys got sick. By the time we reached Florida we had just about had it. Nevertheless, we were fortunate because we managed to rent a house in Florida and everything started out well."

When Harmon reported for spring training, he immediately had a fight on his hands to win the third base spot. Eddie Yost's departure had left the position wide open, and Bertoia and several rookies were ready, willing, and able to make a play for it. For some strange reason, manager Cookie Lavagetto gave everyone and his dog a chance to play third base ahead of Killebrew. There has been much conjecture about Lavagetto's behavior toward Harmon at this time. Some observers say that Lavagetto was trying to get rid of Harmon and that only Ossie Bluege's intervention kept him with the club. A more plausible explanation was given by one writer who said, "Cheerfulness is not a trade-mark of Lavagetto, who looks more the unctious undertaker. Because Killebrew is such a nice, quiet kid, even Cookie, his ex-roommate, may have underestimated his courage."

However, even if Lavagetto did underestimate Harmon's courage and fail to perceive his total commitment to succeed, Calvin Griffith did not go along with his thinking; and after Lavagetto had tried nine other candidates at third base, Griffith ordered his manager to play Killebrew at third.

Lavagetto asked, "What's wrong with Bertoia at third?"

Griffith replied, "He can play either second or shortstop. Put Killebrew at third."

Lavagetto protested, "Sure, Killebrew is a nice kid, but he's a butcher in the field. He'll never make it."

"I'll admit that Killebrew may cost you a few games with his fielding, but he'll also win some with his hitting," said Cal. Then Griffith got tough and added, "Killebrew's got a chance to become a great player, a spectacular star. He's been put off too long. Let's give him a break—now!"

After this conversation took place, a peculiar thing happened. Because of extra practice, Killebrew became more adept on defense, but his bat seemed to become lifeless, and in the entire twenty-four-game pre-season exhibition schedule he did not hit one homerun.

Worried, he sought help. "What am I doing wrong?" he

asked coaches, the manager, and several teammates. Lavagetto was quick with a sharp answer, "You're lunging at the ball and not watching the strike zone," he said. "Better cut it out, Harm, or you'll wind up in Chattanooga again."

Bob Allison was more understanding. "You're trying too hard, Harm," he said. "Relax!"

Allison's advice was difficult for Killebrew to understand as his temperament is such that he always puts everything he has into every play. So he thought to himself, "The only way I can succeed is by trying hard."

Finally, the veteran Jim Lemon, a noted power hitter in his own right, and Ossie Bluege, a star third baseman in his playing days, combined to give Harmon counsel that helped him at that time and has become a part of his playing pattern.

Lemon said, "The trick is to study each pitcher, Harm. Get to know what he throws and the favorite pitch he uses when in a tight spot. This way you can set yourself for his delivery and develop confidence that you can hit him.

Bluege also helped Harmon with a bit of philosophy that Killebrew has made part of his playing style. "Don't worry about slumps," Ossie said. "Everyone has them and there's no patented solution to avoid them. What you must do is just stand up there and keep swinging, and suddenly the hits start to come again and it's all over."

The slump sent Killebrew into the opening game of the season in an apprehensive mood. He knew that many fans would be there to evaluate his performance, and if he failed to hit, the word might get around that he was "a flash in the pan."

As the team lined up for pre-game ceremonies, Harmon watched Vice-President Richard Nixon throw out the opening ball and also noticed that more than 25,000 spectators were in the stands. They had come to see their widely-heralded, power-packed team which included four long-ball hitters, Harmon Killebrew, Bob Allison, Jim Lemon, and Roy Sievers.

When Killebrew went to his spot at third base, the pressure began to mount within him. This was the first year he had begun the season in a starting spot, and the fact that he also knew this was his final test made it difficult for him to relax.

Right after the umpire called "Play Ball," the Orioles' first batter hit the ball toward Killebrew. It didn't hop as Harmon expected, but hugged the ground and then darted away from his eager grasp, and the batter reached first safely.

His error on the game's first play really shook up Harmon. He felt he could hear Lavagetto moaning in the dugout. The misplay didn't cost the team a run, but when Harmon walked to the dugout at the end of the inning, he wished he could "sink down out of sight into the ground." But Killebrew's great desire to overcome bad breaks and succeed was not to be denied, and the second time at bat he made up for his error and took himself and Calvin Griffith off the hook by blasting one of Baltimore pitcher Hoyt Wilhelm's knuckle balls far into the left field seats of Griffith Stadium. The homerun ignited the Senators and they waltzed to a 9 to 2 victory over the Baltimore Orioles.

In the clubhouse after the game, the happy players congratulated Killebrew. Pedro Ramos, the game's pitcher, said, "Forget the error, Harm. Thanks for the homer."

The comments of the players that day made Killebrew happy, but something else made him happier still. He had started and finished the game at third base. He thought to himself then and there, "From now on I'm the Senator's third baseman, and no one is going to take the job away from me."

He showered and dressed hurriedly, and as he walked out of the player's entrance Elaine stood waiting, her face wreathed in a smile. "Harm! You were just great," she said. "Now 25,000 fans know what you can do."

Harmon chuckled and said, "Well, at least I hit the ball, even if I couldn't catch it."

Harmon's mother, Katie, said, "Don't worry about

missing that grounder. It wasn't your fault the ball scooted the way it did."

The happy threesome climbed into the Killebrew car and drove home to see the two boys.

During the month of April Harmon hit consistently, but not sensationally, and he and Elaine began to wonder if he would be sent down again; so they held off on completely furnishing their Alexandria apartment.

On the first day of May, however, Harmon found his power again and walloped two homeruns off the pitching of Jim Bunning of the Detroit Tigers. The second broke up a ten-inning tie game which the Senators won. The next day, Killebrew hit two more homers to help the team again down the Tigers 15 to 3. From that time on, Killebrew continued his long-ball hitting; his slugging began to attract people's attention like a twinkling neon light, and he became the talk of the town.

Someone learned from an interview with Elaine that the Killebrews had not completely furnished their apartment because, "Harmon and I don't know if we'll stay more than a month or so."

The result? A few days later the doorbell rang, and when Elaine opened the door a delivery man asked, "Is this the Killebrew residence?"

"Yes it is. Why?" asked Elaine in a questioning tone.

"We have some furniture to deliver here," said the man.

"But we didn't order anything," protested Elaine.

"Well someone sure did," grinned the man. "We'll bring it in and you tell us where to put it."

So while Elaine directed them, thinking all the while she must be dreaming, the man and his partner brought in a load of furnishings, all sent free by local dealers who were baseball fans.

When Harmon got home, he looked around and asked, "What happened?"

Elaine grinned and said mischievously, "Oh, I thought I'd buy some new furniture to celebrate all the homeruns you've been hitting."

"You didn't! You wouldn't!" said Harm incredulously.

"Of course not, silly," said Elaine. "Your fans sent all this—with their compliments. And do you know something else? Our new telephone has been ringing all day, and our number isn't even in the directory yet. I suppose you'll soon be so famous we'll have to have an unlisted phone number."

Harmon blushed, "I've just been getting some lucky hits. Who knows how long they'll keep falling in." Then he added drily, "I think all this stuff was sent because some of the guys saw you at the ballpark, and wanted to impress you."

Elaine grabbed a pillow and threw it at Harmon. Then the young couple sat down together in their new love seat, courtesy of the Associated Furniture Dealers of Washington D.C., and had a good laugh for the first time in months.

Harmon kept up his torrid hitting and by May 9, 1959, he was leading the league in homeruns with eight, and was among the top five with runs-batted-in. He had 19.

Ten days later, on May 19th, he led the American League with 14 homeruns and was also first in runs scored and runs-batted-in.

By now, Killebrew was being recognized all over the league as a dangerous new hitter. And opposing pitchers exchanged notes trying to detect his batting weaknesses.

"Throw him curves," said one.

"Forget it!" replied another. "He hit my best curve out of sight."

"How about a fast-ball?" asked a pitcher who hadn't faced him yet.

"He hit mine a mile," said yet another victim.

Finally, the question that had been in everyone's mind came out into the open. Why was Killebrew showing this sudden burst of batting power?

The answer was not difficult to find. Killebrew had been knocking at the door of batting stardom for several years, and finally his self-discipline and perseverance to excel had paid off when he had regular day after day opportunities to bat. The motivation and the ability had always been there; but he had needed regular major league play in order to build his confidence and perfect his timing.

"We thought we had a 'book' on Killebrew," confessed Tiger Coach, Tommy Heinrich. "Last year, we felt that Killebrew had a blind spot. But this year we can't find it, so help me."

Heinrich was in a position to know what he was talking about. In the first four games against Detroit, Killebrew batted in more runs against Detroit (13) than the Tigers' total score (11). And his batting average against their pitching was an incredible .533. This was compiled from eight hits in fifteen times at bat which included six homers, and one double.

The baseball wise said that Killebrew's slugging against the Tigers had as much to do with the early-season firing of Detroit's Manager, Bill Norman, as the efforts of any other opposing player.

Failing to stop Harmon's hitting, rival clubs sought other ways to curb him. The Baltimore Orioles tried to drive him out of the league by bunting on him. In one game, they did place three bunts for hits and someone said, "That's Killebrew's weakness. He can't handle a bunt."

When Ossie Bluege heard this, he became red with anger and retorted, "The bunts Baltimore turned into hits were perfectly placed. No other third baseman in the majors could have played them for outs."

Killebrew's sensational hitting soon attracted the attention of the press, and after he had hit two homers in each of five games, within a period of seventeen days, from May 1 to May 17, the producers of national magazines and newsreels were hot on his trail. His nickname became firmly established as "Killer" Killebrew; and sportswriters couched the alliteration in many different phrases. Consequently, his career became a Washington baseball success story.

One writer said, "Harmon Killebrew is being called the greatest gate attraction since Walter Johnson. The real pros may generate more admiration for the flawless, no-frills swing of his teammate Roy Sievers, but the fans have taken Ugly Duckling Killebrew to their bosom. To them Killebrew represents the perpetual underdog. Without Pepper Martin's color he plays third base about the same way, stopping hard drives with his chest and digging up the ball to complete the play. He'll throw it away on occasion, being no Pie Traynor or Ossie Bluege, but his misplays are indulged."

While Harmon's star was shining brightly in the baseball sky, a series of events had brought some problems at home. They began in Florida. One day, Kenny, the Killebrew's baby boy, got out of the house and toddled over to a brick wall which dropped off into the lake that bordered the Killebrew residence. He stood on its edge and then toppled over into the deep waters. A neighbor lady saw the lad and pulled him out just as he was going down for the third time.

In recalling the incident, Elaine said, "Harm and I were terribly frightened and also terribly grateful to the lady. If she had not seen Kenny, there is no doubt that he would have drowned."

During this same period of time, Elaine was pregnant. "I was trying again for a girl," she said. "I was bothered by morning sickness, and I felt kind of miserable in general. Naturally, I wanted Harm near me. But when spring training was over, he had to travel north with the team; so his mother and I drove up together with the boys. She made the trip pleasant for me, and we got to know each other even better. After we had been in our apartment in Virginia for a while, Harm's mother felt she needed to go back to Payette; so we put her on a plane.

"I was thrilled with Harm's success, but at the same time I felt the need to have him with me a lot, and when he got ready to leave for a road trip to New York the evening of the same day his mother had left, I really felt down.

" 'Harm,' I said, 'Here you are hitting homeruns all over the place and getting famous and everything, and you still can't be with me when I'm miserable and need you most.'

"Harm gave me a hurt look and said, 'Golly, darling you know how much I love you, but what else can I do?'

" 'Oh, don't pay any attention to me. I'm just feeling sorry for myself,' I told him. 'Now, go on and have a good trip and hit a lot of homeruns, I'll be all right.'

"But I felt scared. The next morning I had some odd pains in my abdomen. I dismissed them as being caused by worry. But they recurred and got so bad that I called my doctor. He prescribed some medication and told me to stay off my feet. Now how can a mother who is alone with two small boys do that?

"Two days later and just three after Harm had left, I went to the hospital. I had a miscarriage. This was a devastating experience for me, because I had just passed over the hump of morning sickness and felt quite well.

"Our neighbors in the apartment building were very kind and helpful. They took care of our two boys and did everything they could to cheer me up. But I was deeply disappointed over losing our baby because I had so been looking forward to it.

"I began to dwell on the thought that Harm was never around during a crisis. And when he phoned me from New York, I'm sure I sounded bitter.

" 'How are you, honey?' he asked.

" 'Miserable and alone as usual,' I replied. 'It seems a darn shame that you are hardly ever around when I need you—like right now when I've just lost our child.'

"Harm's voice sounded hollow over the phone. 'Darling' he said, 'you and our baby have been in my mind every minute since I have been away. I love you so much that I'll leave the team and come back right now, if you want me to.'

"Suddenly, I realized what I was doing and I sobbed, 'Oh, Harm, I didn't mean what I said. 'Just come back as soon as you can. I know I'll feel all right when you are with me.'

"Harm came to the hospital as soon as he reached town, and I could see how badly he felt. He took me into his arms and said, 'You know, Elaine. You're too fine a person to be deprived of bearing your baby unless there was a good reason. I feel that your miscarriage might have been nature's way of telling you that something was wrong with your child and it was better for it not to be born.'

"When he said this, I realized that my husband was a man whose kind, patient, humble personality would bring us through such trying times in marriage. I'm a bit more impulsive by nature and sometimes say things that might rock the boat, but I can always count on Harm to patiently get it back on its proper course again."

Harmon's career continued to blossom during the summer of 1959 and his duels with opposing pitchers became more intense. Failing to stop his slugging with sharp-breaking curves and torrid fast balls, the hurlers tried to brush him back from the plate with tight pitches. Frank Lary, ace of the Detroit staff, tried it in a series played in Washington, D.C. He whipped a high, hard one inside, and Killebrew sprawled in the dirt. On the next pitch he delivered a fast ball that he thought would overpower the supposedly shaken Killebrew. With unruffled calmness, Harmon met the ball squarely and parked it in the left field seats 420 feet away.

During the same month, two other Tiger hurlers hit Killebrew, and each time he walloped a homer the next time he had an opportunity to swing. Bob Turley, Yankee ace, and other pitchers tried the brush-off and met the same results.

"You knock him down and you get a guy who's doubly dangerous," an American League coach said.

"Hell, there's no more percentage in flattening Killebrew than brushing back Williams, Mantle, or Sievers. He'll get up—as will the others—and he'll be at you."

Despite all of the efforts to stop him, Harmon kept up his barrage of hits and in the first three months of the season smashed 28 homeruns. Three other Washington sluggers, Bob Allison, Jim Lemon, and Roy Sievers, joined with Killebrew in rattling the fences with their hits, and the quartet became known throughout the league as "The Fearsome Foursome."

One sportswriter wrote, "The quartet have converted the Griffith Stadium left field bleachers into their personal homerun alley."

The 1959 Senators was an unusual team. Opposing pitchers knew of their power and quaked in their boots when they had to face them. Batting wise, the Washington players didn't have to take second place to any team in the league, but unfortunately they were unable to put everything else together, and their no better than average pitching and shaky fielding combined to keep them deep in the second division.

Despite the club's low position in the standing, the fans still swarmed around Killebrew, and for many and various reasons he became their idol.

The optimists looked upon Harmon as a Moses whose hitting could lead the team out of the wilderness of defeat to the promised land of victory—maybe even to a pennant. The Washington Senators had been a tail-ender team for so many years that it had become commonplace around the league to say, "Washington is first in war, first in peace, and last in the American League."

So these enthusiasts thought it was time to change such thinking, and Killebrew was the one to do it.

Those who were less optimistic came just to see Killebrew in action. They liked his youthful boy-next-door appearance and it thrilled them to watch his mighty swing. Everytime he lashed out with fury at the ball, a shudder would run through the stands. If he missed, the crowd would moan like a bride left waiting at the church. If he connected and the ball sailed in a majestic arc over the fence, pandemonium would break loose. Washington fans felt it was exciting to watch Killebrew even when his bat met thin air.

Sportswriters and sports announcers were caught up

in the aura of excitement surrounding the sensational slugger, and the public was flooded with stories about his prodigious homeruns. The publicity also brought Harmon an avalanche of requests for personal appearances. Club groups, ranging from the Kiwanis Club through the Boy Scouts to the Happy Grandmothers, sought his services as a guest speaker. Supermarkets and movie theaters competed for his personal appearances, and he was asked to endorse everything from shaving soap to babies' diapers.

To say that Killebrew was amazed at all this adulation is putting it mildly. Although he had been a sports hero in Idaho during his high school days, he had never been forced to respond to such a barrage of sportswriters' questions. Nor had he been expected to deliver speeches in public gatherings. Nevertheless, Harmon won the hearts of the crowds wherever he went with his unassuming and natural way of expressing himself.

Sportswriters agreed that his modesty was refreshing even though he gave them very few words to work with. For example, if he hit two homeruns in one game and a reporter would ask Harm to comment on his achievement, a typical answer would be, "I was lucky enough to get a hold of a couple."

The big problem that arose from the flood of requests for Harmon's services was that he had difficulty saying no to any request whether it be to attend a banquet, a meeting, or make a personal appearance. It is necessary to understand Harmon Killebrew's personality to realize why this was, and still is, so. And it is not because he likes to be in the limelight. It is simply because he feels that he owes it to the fans.

When he was nearly snowed under with requests during that 1959 season in Washington, he discussed the problem with Elaine. Her answer was clear and to the point. "Harm," she said, "You can't go everywhere people ask you to. It's too much. You'll ruin your health."

"But," Harmon protested, "I'm being paid a good salary because of the fans. I feel it is part of my job to appear when they want me."

Despite Killebrew's sincere intentions to serve the fans, the demands became too great, and he finally gave in to the suggestion of the Washington Club officials and changed his home telephone to an unlisted number. Although this gave him some time to relax with his family, he still was hounded at the ball park by photographers, sportswriters, autograph seekers, and fans who were lifted into ecstatic heights if they could just touch their hero.

In those hectic days, Killebrew gradually learned to budget his time and energies and give of himself when it would serve the greatest good. But then and now, he has always done it in a friendly way and with such a cooperative attitude that he has always had cordial relations with the press and his many admirers.

A letter that Ossie Bluege sent him when he suddenly became a national sports idol has helped Harmon set up guidelines for his behavior. He has kept it in his personal files for years and to show his appreciation he obtained Ossie's permission to reproduce it here.

On May 29, 1959, Harmon Killebrew had an experience that he will always treasure. While he was waiting his turn to take pre-game batting practice, Lavagetto touched him on the shoulder and said, "A fellow over in the box seats wants to see you."

"Who is it?" asked Killebrew as he turned around.

"No one special," grinned Cookie, "it's just President Eisenhower.

"You're kidding!" said Harmon, his voice shaking.

"Look for yourself. He's over there in the Presidential Box."

Sure enough there was President Eisenhower, with government officials and Secret Service men clustered about him.

When Harmon reached the box, Ike flashed his famous grin and shook Harmon's hand.

"It's a real privilege to meet you, Mr. President."

"I'm delighted to meet you," said President Eisenhower. "I wonder if you would do me a favor, Harmon, and auto-

Dear Harmon:

Just a brief note.......

With the exception of your own family and loved ones no one is as proud and happy as I am over your success.... Just a word of caution.. Everybody and his Uncle are Killebrew fans now, and they are all jumping on your band wagon......that's the way it goes in this business.....A hero to-day and a bum to-morrow.... I know that you will keep your feet on the ground and accept all this acclaim with modesty and humility.....

You will have all kinds of demands made upon your time....Sport writers, magazine writers, radio and TV shows, etc., Perhaps some agent - a smart cookie - will come along seeking to act as your personal public relations agent.....

Now, what I wish to say is this.....YOU HAVE TO CONSERVE YOUR ENERGIES AND IT'S JUST IMPOSSIBLE TO BE RUNNING AROUND ALL OVER TOWN AND PLEASING EVERYONE THAT COMES DOWN THE PIKE ....WHO WANT TO MEET AND SEE KILLEBREW.....TO A LIMITED DEGREE, FINE...... BUT DONT BE HESITANT ABOUT TURNING DOWN SOME OF THESE INVITATIONS.. YOU HAVE A JOB TO DO OUT THERE ON THE FIELD, AND THAT COMES FIRST...DONT EVER FORGET THAT.....MY FATHER ONCE TOLD ME "SON, YOU HAVE LOTS OF FRIENDS NOW, BUT I WONDER HOW MANY YOU WILL HAVE AFTER ALL THIS BLOWS OVER... JUST DONT WEAR YOURSELF OUT MAKING A LOT OF PUBLIC APPEARANCES...THERE'S A LIMIT TO EVERYTHING, AND YOU'LL BE GETTING THESE REQUESTS... TELL YOURWIFE WHEN SHE ANSWERS THE PHONE THAT YOU ARE NOT AVAILABLE AND HAVE GONE SOME PLACE. USE YOUR GOOD SENSE, DIPLOMATICALLY.....

I am sure you will continue, perhaps not at XXXXXXXXXX record pace you are setting...but, regardless, it will be a great year for you....

Should you appear on TV shows get the CASH, just as all the others have done and are doing.....

The time may not be to far away that your name will be wanted in connection with sponsoring certain products - dont go into anything which commits you for a long period.....These Royalties can add up to a tidy sum....So, in that connection, as you see how the ball is bouncing....set up a personal corporation for yourself, to which all income over and above your salary will be made payable to the corporation.... You have an older brother who no doubt knows his way around and he could inquire about such a set up....If you so desire, I will look into it for you and try to assist you.. I am thinking along the lines that Bob Feller pursued when he was drawing down handsome dividends...Before, you act on any such approaches I should like to talk with you - in the meantime should anything come along at this time ---THINK BEFORE YOU LEAP....

Just want to see you get ahead...not asking anything for myself.....

KEEP UP THE GOOD WORK...THERE WILL BE BAD AND GOOD DAYS...DONT LET ANYTHING GET YOU DOWN AND MAKE THESE BIRDS THAT KNOCK YOU DOWN, LIKE IT TO THEIR REGRET... WITH YOUR DETERMINATION AND CONFIDENCE AND MY FAITH IN YOU * YOUR FUTURE IS BRIGHT....

OSSIE

Ossie

graph a ball for my grandson, David? He's a great fan of yours."

"I'd be real happy to Mr. President, if you'll autograph one for me," replied Harmon with a courageous smile.

The President threw back his head, laughed, and said, "Why, of course!"

After the exchange of autographs, Killebrew went into the game and hit his seventeenth homerun of the season plus two singles in four times at bat to lead the Senators to a 7 to 6 win over Boston.

Looking back, Harmon recalls:

"It was a great thrill because President Eisenhower was so friendly and enthusiastic. His grandson, David, was just a small boy then. I met David over eleven years later, in January, 1970, at a Baseball Writers' Award Dinner in Washington, D.C., and he told me he still had the ball I had autographed."

Harmon continued his barrage of homeruns and in mid-June, Vice-President Richard M. Nixon, whom Harmon and Elaine had met before, came to the ballpark to see Killebrew perform. Naturally, Harmon was pleased to see the Vice-President, but despite an all-out effort he couldn't hit a homerun that day.

Another honor came to Killebrew in the 1959 season. He was chosen on the American League All-Star team. He was delighted.

"It's a real honor," he told his wife, Elaine, "but I don't know whether I'm that good."

"Now, Harm," Elaine said with conviction, "I've always known you'd be a star, and they couldn't keep you off the team the way you've been hitting homeruns."

Perhaps one thing that pleased Harmon as much as anything else during mid-season was Lavagetto's changed attitude toward him. The Senators manager said, "The kid's got guts. He's going to become a real star. He's willing to work to improve his fielding, and his hitting is sensational."

In addition to fan adulation, press publicity, and All-

DON WINGFIELD

Harmon with Vice-President Richard M. Nixon, Roy Sievers, Secretary of State William P. Rogers embarking for all-star game, 1959

Star selection another thing happened about midway in the 1959 season that put pressure on Killebrew. Sportswriters began to compare him with Babe Ruth. Now, every baseball fan who can read the sports-page remembers Ruth; his closed stance at the plate; his mighty swing; his dog trot around the bases and his record of sixty homeruns in a season. It seemed a bit unfair to expect a rookie who was playing his first regular season of major league ball to even approach the great Bambino's record. But sportswriters, who are always looking for a gimmick, began to play the possibility up.

Ruth's and Harmon's comparative records were printed in newspapers, and calculations were made comparing Killebrew's rate of hitting homeruns with the Babe's. Of course, the whole bit was not just wishful thinking on the part of propagandists, because on July 11th, Killebrew did hit his thirtieth homerun in his eighty-second game; whereas Ruth, in his record year had not hit his thirtieth four-bagger until his eighty-third game. And by July 16th, when Harmon hit his thirty-first homer in his eighty-fifth game he was nine games ahead of Ruth's record.

The papers picked this record up and publicized it with the headline, "Killebrew is nine games ahead of Ruth's record."

Shirley Povich, Washington sports columnist, who has always been provocative and discerning in his writing, sensed what all the ballyhoo might do to Killebrew, so he wrote:

"It is not necessary to measure Killebrew in terms of a threat to Babe Ruth's record of sixty homeruns. If he fails that goal, he will still be a considerable personality. This lad has been an exciting ballplayer. Those muscles have been exciting. He doesn't have to hit the ball on the nose to get a homerun. Just a piece of it is often sufficient. It may be said simply that Harmon gives Washington fans a lot to look forward to."

Harmon did not go on to break Ruth's record. He went into a hitting slump during the second half of the season and only hit fourteen circuit clouts after the All-Star game. However, it became increasingly apparent that the Senators went as Killebrew went. While he was in a slump, the Senators also had a late season slump and lost eighteen straight games which landed them in the cellar.

Critical speculation reached Cal Griffith's ears, and he indignantly snapped back with a logical explanation of Killebrew's drop-off in hitting. "Blast it!" he said, "Killebrew's been under tremendous pressure. Being the kind of kid he is, he's tried to cooperate with everyone in giving his time for personal appearances and everything else. He doesn't want to let anyone down, not even you guys who have built up his reputation as a great hitter. As a result he's begun to press in order to live up to his image. This has made him tense and has affected his hitting."

Of course Calvin was right. But in addition, there was another possible contributing factor that was not made public. Harmon was concerned about Elaine's health. It had taken her some time to bounce back from the emotional and physical effects of her miscarriage. Then, once she had almost recovered, her doctor made further examination and discovered that she had an internal condition that needed to be surgically corrected before she would be able to have any more babies.

In discussing the problem, Harmon said, "Elaine, you know I want more babies just as much as you do. But you're the most important thing in the world to me, and if there is any danger to you in such surgery, let's forget it."

"Now don't worry, Harm," Elaine said with a brave smile. "The doctor said it's just a simple repair job, and you know we've got to keep working on that baseball team and have a few girls besides for cheerleaders."

"You're impossible," said Harmon affectionately. "All right go ahead. But let's schedule the surgery while I'm in town. I just can't be away from you when its done."

Elaine went back to the hospital and underwent successful corrective surgery. Harmon was tense and anxious during this period of time, but not being one to air his troubles, he kept quiet about it and did his best to come out of his slump at the plate.

Despite the pressures surrounding Harmon, he still battled Cleveland's Rocky Colavito down the final stretch of the season for the American League homerun title.

He was often asked, "Can you beat Colavito?"

"I don't know," was his standard answer. "I'll just keep swinging."

When the last game of the season arrived, Rocky had 42 homeruns and Harmon 41. But on this final day of the year, Harmon showed his competitive spirit by blasting number 42 in the fifth inning of a game the Senators lost 6 to 2 to the Boston Red Sox. The wallop was a soaring drive hit off Red Sox pitcher Jerry Casale. As a result, Killebrew wound up in a deadlock for the title with Colavito. Harmon really hit 43 homeruns that season, but one he hit against Cleveland's Herb Score didn't count because rain stopped the game before five innings had been completed.

Thus ended Killebrew's first season as a regular in the majors—a year in which his batting statistics were phenomenal. Although his second-half slump pulled down his batting average to .242, he nevertheless led his team in homeruns with 42, doubles with 20, runs batted in, 105, runs scored, 98, total bases, 282, and walks with 90. He also was second in the league with total bases and in slugging with a percentage of .516. In addition, he handled 495 chances at third base, the second highest total in the league.

When the Killebrew's drove back to Payette at the end of the season, Harmon was recognized as an established major league player.

In discussing the year, Elaine said modestly, "Harm had a good season with Washington, and it looks as if he is going to have a fine career."

The people of Payette were more lavish in their praise. They celebrated Harmon's homecoming by designating October 3, 1959, as Harmon Killebrew Day. During the celebration they renamed one of the most beautiful streets in town Killebrew Drive.

The proclamation by the Payette Board of County Commissioners appears below.

OFFICE OF

BOARD OF COUNTY COMMISSIONERS

PAYETTE COUNTY

PAYETTE, IDAHO

RALPH SHAMBERGER, CHAIRMAN, PAYETTE, IDAHO
S. L. POMEROY, COMMISSIONER, NEW PLYMOUTH, IDAHO
ED B. PATTON, COMMISSIONER, STAR RT., PAYETTE, IDAHO

ALICE I. SNOOK, CLERK

WHEREAS, Harmon Killebrew has made an outstanding record as a member of The Washington Senators of the American League, and has by his ability as an athlete; his fine sportsmanship; and his exemplary conduct, on and off the playing field, brought great credit to the Payette Community, and

WHEREAS, The Payette Chamber of Commerce has designated October 3, 1959, as Killebrew Day, at which time the people will celebrate Harmon's homecoming, and

WHEREAS, Sports Inc. has requested the Board of County Commissioners to designate that road, heretofore known as The Country Club Road, as Killebrew Drive, as a lasting record of the esteem in which he is held, and has presented a petition signed by the residents whose homes and land lie adjacent to this road endorsing the proposed renaming of this road,

THEREFORE, BE IT RESOLVED, That on and after October 3, 1959, that County road beginning just north of the Payette River Bridge, on Highway 30, and running east 3.3 miles to a junction with Highway 52, shall be known and designated as Killebrew Drive.

BOARD OF COUNTY COMMISSIONERS

Ralph Shamberger, Chairman

Ed B. Patton, Commissioner

S. L. Pomeroy, Commissioner

Killebrew with the great hitter Ted Williams, 1960

"not for half a million dollars"

14

While Harmon was working during the winter of 1959-60 as a salesman for the Inter-Mountain Gas Company of Payette, Idaho, Calvin Griffith was trying to strengthen the Washington Club with trades. The Senators Fearsome Foursome of Jim Lemon, Bob Allison, Harmon Killebrew and Roy Sievers had thrown fear into the hearts of the rival teams with their power hitting during the 1959 season, and several clubs were negotiating for individual members of the group. And small wonder. During 1959, Killebrew had tied for the league homerun title with 42. Lanky Jim Lemon had walloped 33 out of the parks. Rookie-of-the-Year Bob Allison had kissed 30 lusty drives good-bye. And Roy Sievers, despite part-time service due to injuries, had added 21 homeruns to the grand total.

These mighty men of muscle had also boomed fan interest in the Nation's Capital, and other club owners wanted a piece of the action.

Trading interest reached the pinnacle one day when Gabe Paul, general manager of the Cincinnati Reds, phoned Griffith regarding Harmon.

"I'm interested in Killebrew," he said.

"Show me someone who isn't," retorted Calvin.

"I'll make it worth your while," continued Paul. "I'll give you half a million dollars right now for his contract."

Griffith didn't hesitate a second in refusing. His club wasn't rolling in money, and the sum would have gone a long way toward straightening out the Washington owners' financial situation, but he said, "No deal. I'm hanging on to Killebrew."

When Harmon heard later about the offer and Cal's refusal, he said, "Golly! It shakes me up to know that Mr. Griffith turned down that much money for my contract."

Elaine laughed and said, "I've always told you that you are my million dollar baby!"

Griffith also showed his high regard for Harmon by raising his contract considerably for the 1960 season. A New York sportswriter took pot-shots at Calvin over the sum, and said if Harmon were playing with the Yankees he would be paid twice as much.

"In a pig's eye," or words to that effect, said Griffith. "I know about the Yankee salary structure. Harmon is financially better off with us."

Harmon was grateful for the raise, and he followed the same pattern he had for years of never quibbling with Mr. Griffith over salary terms. And what's more, he went to spring training camp determined to improve in every way in order to justify Cal's confidence in him.

While he was sweating and straining under the hot Florida sun in an effort to improve his skills, Elaine was home expending a comparative amount of energy under the Idaho sun to landscape their new home.

When asked about that spring she said, "Harm and I decided that it would be more profitable for me to do this than accompany him to spring training; so I stayed home and planted grass and did all the landscaping myself."

Reporters again cornered Harmon during pre-season training in Florida and asked him how he felt about the coming season and the possibility of breaking Babe Ruth's homerun record.

Killebrew was candid with his answers. "I'm not thinking about breaking Ruth's record of 60 homeruns." he said, "but I really hope to hit at least 45 homers this year because I'm anxious to prove I wasn't just a one-year wonder in 1959."

When asked if he knew what caused his hitting to tail off during the second half of the 1959 season, he answered, "I just got into a slump. I lost my strike zone, then I started pressing and hit at bad pitches."

Regarding his fielding he said, "Last year I made a lot of little mistakes that hurt my fielding. I hurried throws, was too anxious on ground balls, and made bad plays that I won't make if I can just relax a little."

Despite his efforts to improve, Harmon's play during spring training of 1960 was nothing extraordinary. Nevertheless, his fielding improved to the extent that Lavagetto felt no qualms about starting him at third base when the season opened.

The Senators of 1960 again presented a lineup of power hitters. Killebrew, Allison, and Lemon were back, and catcher Earl Battey, who had come to Washington from the Chicago White Sox in exchange for Roy Sievers, also swung a powerful bat. Other players who were hitting threats were Don Mincher at first, and Lennie Green in center field.

Harmon opened the season, confident that he could do a good job at third. And he felt happy because Elaine and the boys had joined him. They were all settled in their attractive apartment, and everything seemed right with the world. Elaine was pulling for him to hit at least 45 homeruns, and they had worked out a little deal between them to give Harmon added incentive to rocket the ball out of the park. The deal was, as Elaine told me, "Harm is crazy about pizza and I had a thing going with him that whenever he hit a homerun when the team was playing in town, I would have a pizza ready for him when he got home."

Despite all of the things that Killebrew had going for

him, he couldn't quite get off the ground with his hitting, once the season started. His hits seemed to go directly to the opposing fielders and he was unable to find his home-run swing. Then, just when he seemed to be getting his timing back, the roof fell in. He pulled a hamstring muscle. This injury of the large tendon in back of the knee slows an individual down to less than a walk. The knee can't be bent enough to even sit down without pain; and at best the injured person must hobble around on crutches.

At the time this injury put Harmon on the bench, he had been hitting .256 and had hit only four homeruns. He was out of the game for a month. When I asked Harmon and Elaine about this mishap, they both seemed reticent to discuss it—almost acting like talking about an injury would be an alibi for non-performance on the field. Nevertheless, it is easy to imagine the thoughts and conversations the Killebrews had. Harmon was undoubtedly thinking, "I wonder if I'm jinxed. Everytime things start breaking right, something happens. Reno Bertoia looks good on third base, maybe Cookie will keep him there and send me down again."

When he would express such doubts to Elaine, it is easy to picture her saying, "Now, Harm! You're still the team's best homerun hitter, even if you are on the bench. Doc Lentz will fix you up, and you'll be playing again before long."

With Elaine's encouragement, Harmon went faithfully for treatment of the leg until it healed, and then underwent a rigorous regimen of exercises to get back into playing shape.

Finally, when Killebrew had despaired of ever getting back into the lineup, Lavagetto played him against Cleveland in a Fourth of July double-header and installed him at the unfamiliar position of first base. Harmon collected a scratch single in eight times at bat. By the time he had hit weakly in succeeding games to the tune of two singles in nineteen at bats, Lavagetto pulled him out of the lineup again. Lavagetto only benched him one game, however, and instead of predicting dire things for him, Cookie patiently guided Harmon back to his natural swing. He repeatedly told Harmon to keep swinging naturally and the hits would come.

It got so that when Killebrew stood at the plate he was repeating phrases almost like a Boy Scout does when he takes the Scout oath, but intead of saying, "On my honor, I will do my best," and so forth, Harmon kept repeating to himself, "Stay loose; watch the strike zone; keep swinging."

His efforts paid off, and he hit two homeruns and a single to lead the Senators to a 7 to 2 victory in a game against Baltimore. This first two-homerun game of the year which came in the last half of the season got Harmon back in the homerun groove.

While Killebrew had been fighting his hitting slump, Jim Lemon had been sparking the team, and his long-ball hitting and the twenty homeruns he hit by July 10th had won him a place on the American League All-Star team.

Lemon is 6 feet, 4 inches tall, and his silent manner and easy way of swinging, plus a casual, deceptively fast stride often gave the impression that he was loafing. However, this was never the case. He could be called a Gary Cooper in baseball uniform—a man of steel who makes difficult things look easy.

Harmon took a great liking to Jim Lemon and the pair became almost inseparable. In the process, Killebrew absorbed much baseball wisdom from his older friend who was then thirty-two.

When Lemon won the All-Star award, Harmon told him, "Jim, you sure deserved it. I'm glad they finally recognized your abilities."

"Harm," Jim returned, "a guy as conscientious as you are is bound to be a winner. Just keep plugging away and you'll get your share of glory."

Killebrew did keep plugging away and his hitting improved, so did his play at first base. However, just when he was beginning to feel comfortable around the initial sack, Lavagetto shifted him back to third, and Julio

Becquer, a new addition to the club, was stationed at first.

Harmon didn't complain, adjusted to the move, and kept hitting.

Now that he appeared to be back in the homerun groove, he was again flooded with fans' requests for autographs and personal appearances. Some of the Washington stores put up what they called "Killer-Meters" in conspicuous places to chart Killebrew's homerun production. The large placards featured a thermometer whose temperature would rise as each additional homerun was hit, as well as tabulating slots comparing Babe Ruth's and Harmon's homerun rates.

Jimmy and Billy Robertson, genial Vice-Presidents of the Twins, recall that during this season in Washington a day was held at Griffith Stadium on which long white tapes designating the direction and traveling distance of Killebrew's homeruns were laid out all over the ball park.

Harmon's relationships with his fellow players were a bit unusual. His teammates found him to be an exciting figure on the diamond, but were not very successful in getting him to join in what they thought was exciting off-field activity. When the team was home in Washington, their slugging teammate spent all of his free time with Elaine and the two boys, Cameron and Kenneth.

And when on the road, Harmon almost became an off-the-diamond recluse. For example, someone would say, "How about a game of cards, Harm?"

"I think I'll go to my room and watch TV," was the oft-repeated answer by Harmon, who didn't care for card playing.

The following night an exuberant player would burst in upon the group and say, "I've got some free tickets for the floor show over at the 'Silver Slipper!' They say the chicks there are out of this world. Who wants to go?" All hands would reach out except Harmon's.

"Aren't you coming along, Harm?" someone would ask.

"No thanks," Harmon would reply, "I have a good book I want to finish tonight."

So the gang would take off, and Killebrew would go to his room and read, or watch television or phone Elaine and the boys.

Bob Allison, who has roomed with Killebrew for years, says with affection, "Harm is the greatest TV watcher I've ever seen."

The impression should not be conveyed that Harmon did nothing but watch television and read books in his free time. It is just that he has never been a night club man. He has, on the other hand, always been actively engaged in civic services and in enjoying other types of activities.

National politics has always been one of his interests, and in 1960 when Vice-President Richard M. Nixon was campaigning for the Presidency, Harmon Killebrew, on invitation, joined the "Dick Nixon Sports Committee." The forming of such a committee gave Nixon's campaign managers the opportunity to publicize their leader as "The Nation's Number One Sports fan."

Early in the campaign, the Vice-President was taken to Walter Reed General Hospital in Washington to undergo treatment for a knee infection. Chafing under his enforced idleness, Richard Nixon decided to make the hospital stay more endurable by holding a reception for the nation's prominent athletes. When Harmon was invited, he said he felt honored to go.

The reception was a memorable affair, and some of the sports stars Killebrew met there were his pal Jim Lemon; his former teammate, Roy Sievers of the White Sox; star halfback Frank Gifford of the New York Giants; swimmer Florence Chadwick; and golf stars Wiffi Smith and Marilyn Smith. Harmon said, "Vice-President Nixon greeted us warmly and was very friendly. He seemed to enjoy our company and spent a lot of time talking to us. His manner was in direct contrast to some national figures I have met who seemed more concerned with getting photographers to take their pictures posing with us than enjoying us as individuals."

The 1960 season turned out to be a good one for Kille-

WORLD WIDE PHOTOS

Prior to the Washington-Chicago night game in Washington, June 10, Harmon Killebrew, the Senators' league-leading home run hitter, was honored by the Idaho State Society, Killebrew poses with his mother, who arrived as a surprise from her home in Payette, Idaho, and his wife, Elaine.

brew. One of his outstanding achievements was hitting three homeruns on September 11th in a doubleheader played with the Detroit Tigers in Briggs Stadium.

Although missing nearly two months of play, Harmon finished the season with 31 homeruns, drove in 80 runs, and compiled a respectable batting average of .276. In addition, he fielded at a solid .978 average, committing only 17 errors.

The Washington Senators delighted their fans by finishing fifth, ahead of Detroit, Boston, and Kansas City.

And the Washington fans? The "Bonus Baby" from Idaho had lifted their spirits, and the cynics no longer chanted. "Washington is first in war, first in peace, and last in the American League."

minnesotans welcome the twins

15

Killebrew in '72

The small sign startled me as I walked through the door of the Minneapolis Star and Tribune research library. But there it was, securely taped to the top tier of a filing basket. Behind the same desk, an attractive young lady was seated filling picture requests.

"May I help you, sir?" she said with a pleasant smile.

"I'm not sure," I replied. "But first will you tell me what that sign is all about? What political office is Harmon Killebrew running for?"

"For President, or anything he wants," she said enthusiastically. "He's the greatest guy in the sports world, as far as I'm concerned."

"That's taking in a lot of territory," I said, "Just what makes him so great?"

"He's not only a superstar, but a real gentleman," she said. "He helps the entire Twins club, with his play on the field and his actions off. Everyone I know feels the same way about him. Take my dad, for instance. He was in the hospital for surgery a few weeks ago, and when he was in intensive care I put a big 'Killebrew in '72' banner in his room to cheer him up, and it helped him get well faster. And everyone who saw it thought it was great."

"You're kidding," I chuckled.

"It's the plain truth," she said seriously. "If you're a friend of Harmon's, you tell him that Elaine Jenson said so."

After that, Elaine, who is a senior secretary, and says she acts as a "Girl Friday" in the library and photo department, gave me the other information I was seeking.

Such adulation for Killebrew seems to be present throughout the entire state of Minnesota. Dave Moore, popular WCCO newscaster, reported another incident which illustrates the various ways in which it is expressed. One of Dave's fans, Lorraine Olson, wrote him on July 21, 1970, describing an incident regarding Harmon which took place in a small town in northwestern Minnesota. She wrote:

"One of the local businessmen hung his flag out, and soon the other merchants followed suit, one by one, not knowing the particular occasion, but not wanting to be remiss or unpatriotic. One of the merchants finally found the courage to admit his ignorance and asked the first 'flag-waver' what was the special day.

"Harmon Killebrew's birthday!"

When I corresponded with Dave Moore about the letter, he added his own thinking about Killebrew. He wrote: "Harmon is a rare gem in his field, almost nobility I would say."

It is evident that in the ten-year span since the Twins and Harmon Killebrew have been in Minnesota, the fans throughout the state have adopted Harmon as a favorite son. There are a number of reasons for this. One could be that they associate Harmon, with his stocky build, his powerful bat and the wide swath that it makes in baseball, with their legendary lumberjack hero, Paul Bunyan, who was known for his great size and strength. Bunyan wielded his axe with the same vigor that Harmon swings his bat, and was said to swing it in a circle and cut all the trees around him at one sweep.

Unlike Bunyan, Killebrew does not have a problem with his cooking. It is said that to grease his large pancake griddle, Bunyan had boys skate on it with slabs of bacon fastened on their feet. Harmon's wife takes care of all of Killebrew's griddles with a constant eye on his waistline.

It is probable that the ethnic composition of Minnesota's population also has a bearing on Killebrew's popularity. There are great numbers of Scandinavians in Minnesota and the surrounding states. These people from the northern shores of Europe are friendly, down-to-earth, slow to anger, and not garrulous in their speech. Consequently, Killebrew's similar personality traits cause them to identify with him.

Another likely underlying reason is the upper midwest fans were hungry for big-league baseball, and when the Washington Senators moved to Minnesota their long struggle to obtain a team was successful. So Killebrew, who had been highly publicized as the favorite of Washington fans, immediately became their idol.

The story behind the moving of the Washington franchise to Minnesota is a story of a few individuals who had a dream and were willing to work and sacrifice to make it come true. It started back in 1953 when Gerald (Jerry) Moore, then president of the Minneapolis Chamber of Commerce, asked Charlie Johnson, sports editor of the Minneapolis Star and Tribune, to meet him for lunch one day at the Athletic Club.

"Charlie, what we need in this area is a major league baseball team," Jerry said. Then without waiting for Johnson's comment, he asked, "How do we start? Let's get the ball rolling."

Charlie, in recalling the meeting said: "No one would

have dared offer this man a discouraging word. It would have been like holding down a freight train with a band aid."

Moore's fervor stirred the community to action, and the campaign began with the organization of a committee, including men like Moore, Lyman Wakefield, E. William Boyer, Kenneth Dayton, Hugh Barber and Charlie Johnson.

During the uphill fight, the group went through several periods of bitter disappointment. They were repeatedly told, "Get yourself an adequate stadium, and you'll get a major league ball club."

This statement immediately set off a battle regarding where the stadium should be built. Like human twins, the twin cities of Minneapolis and St. Paul have their rivalries, and at this time both communities wanted a big league team to play in their city; so there was conflict. It was finally settled. Both factions agreed on a site for the ball park in suburban Bloomington, a beautiful and fast-growing town south of the Twin Cities and about equidistant from the two.

To spearhead the drive to raise the millions of dollars necessary to construct the stadium, a group called the Minute Men was formed. And these 200 participants from the Twin Cities area worked diligently until the financial goal was achieved.

When the sports stadium was completed, overtures were made to entice a major league club to move to the area. The New York Giants were wooed and lost to rival suitor San Francisco. For a time it appeared that the Cleveland Indians might make the move. Then they lost interest.

Finally, victory day came on October 26, 1960 when the major leagues decided to expand and the Washington Senators agreed to move to Minnesota.

By mutual agreement, so that the Minneapolis and St. Paul fans would feel that neither city was favored, the Senators were named the Minnesota Twins—the first big league team to be named after a state instead of a city.

Harmon heard of the move while at home in Payette. Although he was fond of Washington, he had visited the Twin Cities area enough to be fairly well acquainted with it, and he liked the more open country which afforded opportunities for fishing and hunting. So he discussed the move with Elaine.

"Golly, Harm!" she said. "It seems we're always moving."

"But I know you'll like the Twin Cities area," he said. "Minneapolis and St. Paul are both big cities, but they also have almost a rural charm about them. Both cities have all kinds of beautiful parks and lakes. And the University of Minnesota, one of the greatest schools in the world, is there."

Elaine smiled and looked at their two boys, Cameron, four, and Kenny, two and a half. "Cam is nearly old enough for school. Maybe we could move to the Twin Cities and the boys could go to school there.

"The University?" grinned Harmon.

"Don't be silly! Oh! I know they're smart enough, but a little too small. Minneapolis is an unusual name for a city. Where did it come from?"

Harmon chuckled, "I looked that up because I knew you'd ask." They say "minne" is an Indian word meaning water and "polis" is Greek and means city. So they named it water city (Minneapolis) because it has twenty-two lakes in it.

"Wow!" said Elaine, "They must have some nice beaches there. I just love to swim. I'll have to move there with you."

"What if there were no beaches?" Harmon asked drily.

"I suppose I'd have to go anyway," teased Elaine. "Now that I'm the mother of your two children, I'm stuck with you."

Lavagetto told Killebrew to bring a first baseman's mitt and a third baseman's glove to spring training in 1961, saying "We'll try you at both places, and you ought to wind up at one of them."

Despite his uncertainty regarding his defensive position, Harmon had a good training period. He hit consistently and garnered six homeruns. His long-ball hitting once more attracted the attention of sportswriters, and there was again conjecture about his breaking Babe Ruth's 1927 record of sixty homeruns.

Harmon gave his opinion of the matter in a typical interview with Tom Briere, sportswriter for the Minneapolis Tribune.

"Harmon," he said, "you've been hitting them out this spring—six homeruns already. This is your best spring record, isn't it?"

"I don't remember doing any better," replied Killebrew.

"Now that you're in the homerun niche so early, do you think you can beat Ruth's record this year?" asked Briere.

"I haven't thought much about it."

"Surely it's been mentioned to you," persisted Briere.

"Yes, quite a few times," said Harmon, "but that's not my chief concern."

"What is it, then?" asked Briere.

"To learn how to place the ball and cut down on my strikeouts, so I can improve as a hitter."

Sensing that Killebrew did not want to pursue the Babe Ruth record topic, Briere shifted to another subject and asked, "Do you know where you'll play yet? At first, or third?"

"No, I don't," said Harmon. "I like first, but I'll play wherever Lavagetto decides to place me."

Before spring training ended, Lavagetto, who had come to realize Killebrew's great potential, made Harmon team captain.

This may have seemed a strange move to outsiders, but those who understood Lavagetto's personality saw that it made sense. Cookie Lavagetto is a soft-spoken, matter-of-fact gentleman who lives within himself. He feels that ballplayers are paid to do their best, and that a team would be led more effectively by a man like Killebrew who always

Harmon gets some batting tips from Manager Cookie Lavagetto and Calvin Griffith 1961

did his best rather than by the loud-mouth, gushy type of personality.

After making the appointment, Lavagetto said, "Sure, Killebrew is quiet, but he's a great kid. He's already a leader in deeds, and this will make it necessary for him to talk more and take charge. I'm sure his calm manner will help settle the pitchers, and the umpires all respect him."

Harmon accepted the honor modestly and said, "I've always thought that the best way for any person to provide leadership is to do the very best job he possibly can do. That's what I try to do in baseball, and will continue doing whether I'm in the field or at bat."

When the Twins started the season, Killebrew was stationed at first base, and a new shortstop, Zoilo Versalles, was expected to strengthen the infield defense.

The Twins opened the season in New York against the Yankees, and they won their first game handily 6 to 0. Pedro Ramos pitched beautifully, and Allison and Bertoia both hit homers to lead the Twins to victory. Killebrew hit a single and drove in Versalles with a sacrifice fly.

The next game was rained out, and the following day the Twins moved to Baltimore to play a series. In the ninth inning of the first game, with Minnesota trailing 8 to 0, Killebrew came to bat with no one out and sent a slow roller to third baseman Brooks Robinson. Harmon pushed himself to the limit to beat the throw to first base, and when he was a step away, calamity struck again. His right leg buckled under him, and as he toppled forward his toe caught on the bag, causing him to fall flat on the ground several feet beyond first base.

As Harmon lay in agony on the ground, his right leg felt as if it had been torn apart. Doc Lentz rushed out to minister to him. Lavagetto and Elmer Valo also hurried over, and together they aided Killebrew as he limped painfully to the dugout.

An examination revealed that he had suffered a pulled hamstring muscle in his right leg. An injury much like the one that had sidelined him in 1960.

When the doctors told Harmon he would be out of action for three weeks, he groaned in protest. "I'd sure like to play in our opening game in Minneapolis," he said.

"I hope you can," said Lavagetto. "Follow Doc Lentz's orders, and we'll see what we can do. Doc and Harmon, who have developed a relationship like father and son through the years, met every day, and they both did everything possible to get the leg back to normal. Sitting on the bench was a nightmare for Harmon. He felt he wasn't earning his salary, and in addition he desperately wanted to help his teammates win more games. After a week, he went to Lavagetto and asked if he could help as a pinch-hitter.

"We'll watch for a chance to use you," said Lavagetto, who was determined to keep Harmon off the playing field until the torn muscle was fully healed.

Harmon kept nagging Doc Lentz every day to okay him as fit to play. Lentz remembers his saying, "Now let's talk this thing over, Doc," and then go on with all the eloquence of a college debater to prove that he was ready to get back into action.

While Harmon was aching to get back into the lineup, Elaine and the boys had moved to the Twin Cities and rented a house in a quiet, wooded area south of the ballpark near Old Shakopee Road and Cedar Ave. The boys loved to play in the woods, and the family was rapidly making new friends.

Harmon phoned his wife every night while he was on the road, and her constant reassurance that he would soon be able to play helped him as much as did Doc Lentz's daily therapy.

"Don't worry, Harm," she said. "You'll soon be all right. Then you'll show the people out here what you can do. Cam, Kenny and I are all pulling for you every minute."

On the afternoon of April the 20th, the Twins arrived at their new home in the Twin Cities. A huge throng crowded around them at the airport, and the same evening hundreds of enthusiastic fans jammed the ballroom of the Radisson Hotel in Minneapolis to give them a warm welcome. The

"Meet the Twins" Banquet was arranged jointly by the Minneapolis and St. Paul Chambers of Commerce Governing officials, as well as interested residents from all over the area, were present.

The team appreciated the warm and sincere reception, and they realized at once that the Minnesotans had adopted them as their very own.

Harmon made a good impression on the speaker's platform that led to an off-the-field activity that he still enjoys. After the banquet, Joe Duffy the stadium manager, took him to meet Art Swift, manager of Minneapolis station WTCN TV. Swift was favorably impressed by Killebrew's personality and he immediately offered him a job. "Harmon," he said, "how would you like to do a show for us on television?"

Harmon blushed, hesitated, and then said, "I don't really know, Mr. Swift. That's something I've never done. What would I have to do?"

"The most natural thing in the world for you," answered Swift, cheerfully. "You would interview other ball players—Twins and opposing players. You know the game inside out, and the players would probably feel more comfortable talking to you than they would to a reporter. All of us at the station feel it would be an outstanding program."

"I suppose I could try it," said Harmon.

"Good!" commented Swift. "We'll get busy and work out the details and contact you again later."

Harmon remembers well that first meeting with Art Swift, and when discussing it he said, "I want you to be sure to mention how kind Art Swift was to give me a start in television, and how helpful he has been along the way."

Today, Killebrew is one of the most popular interviewers in baseball, and other players repeatedly say that they enjoy being on his program because he is so friendly and natural. In addition to this he knows how to talk about baseball in their language.

C. J. LARSON

MDAA—Muscular Dystrophy Association of America

A typical comment was made by Mickey Mantle, who said, "I like to talk about hitting with Harmon on his show because, being a great hitter himself, Killebrew knows what it is all about."

On April 21, 1961 the Twins played their first home game in Metropolitan Stadium in Bloomington. The "Met," as it is called, looked new and inviting, and it was well-designed with the grandstands containing gaily-colored, comfortable seats, housed in three arc-shaped decks. Being of cantilever construction, supporting pillars were eliminated, thus affording each spectator an unobstructed view of the field. The players liked the well-kept grass and the entire efficient layout. Also Calvin Griffith had seen to it that the baseball field's dimensions were proportioned to be of greatest benefit to Killebrew and his other homerun hitters; so it was natural that Twins players felt pleased.

To this day, ten years later, the Met is a picturesque place to visit. It is pleasant to sit there and watch the game with a cool breeze fanning your brow and the beauty of the setting delighting your eyes. The entire structure is set in an area of natural beauty, and the stadium is framed by green fields, gently sloping knolls and a great variety of trees. You can relax at the Met and indulge your own tastes —cooling off with an icy drink or appeasing your hunger with a hot dog—cracking peanuts when you get nervous.

Harmon's leg was too stiff to enable him to play in the opening game; so he sat on the bench and suffered while his teammates lost to the Washington Senators by a score of 5 to 3.

The Twins bounced back, however, and compiled a 9 to 4 record before Killebrew returned to the lineup. In his first few games, Harmon hit at a .360 pace and once more set his sights on the fences and began swatting homeruns.

In early May, while playing at first base he made two errors in a game against the Yankees. Two days later he was shifted back to third when Reno Bertoia pulled a muscle in one of his legs.

Despite the shift to third, Harmon continued hitting

and helped lead the Twins to victory with his powerful smashes.

A three-run homer off Wes Stock of Cleveland and a go-ahead homerun-hit against the Los Angeles Angels, when he connected with the fast-ball of Ryne Duren, were typical of his winning wallops.

After this game, Bertoia was put back in at third base and Harmon returned to first.

Killebrew, while discussing his switches in position with Bob Allison, his roommate, said, "I suppose being used as a utility infielder will give me more chances to play."

"Don't talk that way," said Allison. "You just keep hitting the way you are and you'll never miss a game."

Naturally, it was impossible for Harmon to always deliver in the pinch, and occasionally he would strike out or hit into a double play in a crucial situation with men on the bases. This happened on May 18th, in a game against the Kansas City Athletics. With two men on, one out in the eighth inning, and the Twins trailing 4 to 3, he slammed a grounder that the Athletics turned into a double play, ending the inning.

As he returned with his head down to the dugout, Lavagetto slapped him on the seat of the pants, and said, "Forget it. No one can do it every time."

By the end of May, Killebrew had hit twelve homeruns in twenty-seven games and had won a spot in the hearts of the fans. The spectators chanted and stamped when he came to bat, shrieked every time he swung, roared when he connected and moaned when he missed.

He was swamped with requests to do commercials, and he subsequently signed to represent several businesses including a clothing store, a breakfast cereal firm, and a safety razor company.

He came home one night and said to Elaine, "It's fantastic! These people seem to think if I endorse their products, they'll sell a lot more of them. It's hard to understand why."

"That's because you're the 'Killer,' " said Elaine with an affectionate hug. "You just bowl them all over.

"When you eat cereal, the kids want to, so they can have muscles like yours.

"And suits—young men like to wear clothes like yours, because you're such a sharp dresser.

"And when you appear on a shaving commercial, wow! Are you a lady-killer! The gals nearly swoon and say to their husbands, 'Dear, why don't you try that kind of razor?' "

"You little tease," said Harmon, "I should put you over my knee and give you a good spanking."

"Try it," said Elaine dancing out of range. "You'd have to catch me first and you know, even though you are a 'killer,' they say you aren't very fast."

It was understandable that Griffith and Lavagetto wanted to please the fans by doing well their first season in Minnesota, so when the club went into a slump and skidded to seventh place, by the end of May, they took action to strengthen their personnel. The club obtained second baseman Billy Martin from the Milwaukee Braves in exchange for infielder Billy Consolo and a pile of dollars; and they sent pitcher Paul Giel and third baseman Reno Bertoia to the Kansas City Athletics in a trade for outfielder, Bill Tuttle.

A day later, on June 2nd, they brought first baseman-outfielder Julio Becquer up from Buffalo in the International League.

Despite the trades, the club continued to lose and dropped to eighth place. Rumors of more trades made the players feel insecure, and finally Calvin Griffith made the most drastic move of all when he replaced Cookie Lavagetto with a former Twins coach, Same Mele.

It was a strange arrangement. Griffith insisted that Lavagetto had not been fired and had just been given a week's "furlough" to rest up. This happened on June 6th at 3:30 p.m., and that same evening the Twins made baseball history in a game with the Yankees. Mele was thrown out of the game for protesting Twins player Ron Henry being called out on strikes by umpire Bob Stewart. So, when Sam was banished, pitching coach Ed Lopat took over. Thus the Twins set some kind of record having had three managers, Lavagetto, Mele and Lopat during a five hour period from 3:30 to 8:30 p.m.

In an effort to win, Griffith still continued to shuffle things around, bringing Lavagetto back after a week. And then on June 23rd, he changed his mind again and made Cookie's firing and Mele's managership permanent.

Mele decided to go with Becquer at first and Killebrew at third. Nevertheless, Harmon, determined not to be upset by his frequent shifts, continued his hitting. He did so well that Mickey Mantle told a sportswriter, "Killebrew, with his beautiful swing, is one of the best hitters in baseball."

On July 1st Frank Lane, general manager of the Kansas City Club, after seeing Harmon hit a grandslam homer (Killebrew's twenty-third homerun of the season) against his team said, "That Killebrew is really something! He knows the strike zone, and with his sweet swing, he's worth a half million right now."

Apparently a number of other opposing players had the same high regard for Killebrew because they voted to put him on the All-Star Team, and he played in the All-Star game that July at Candlestick Park in San Francisco.

Killebrew got into the game in the sixth inning as a pinch-hitter, and in this one appearance at the plate he sent opposing pitcher Mike McCormick's delivery high into the stands for a homerun.

In the meantime Mele had shifted Harmon back to first base saying, "I've decided first base is Harmon's best position, and unless something unexpected happens, he'll stay there."

Just for variety, Killebrew hit his first inside-the-park homerun on the Fourth of July at the Met against the Chicago White Sox. He knocked in two men, and when Jim Landis crashed against the fence trying to catch his drive, he raced all the way home and hit the plate with a beautiful slide.

The Twins finally finished the season in seventh place, which didn't please anyone except the opposing teams.

However, Killebrew's record pleased everyone. He batted .288, drove in 122 runs and hit 46 homeruns.

At the season's end, he went home to Payette with Elaine and the boys, feeling that he had won a place on the team and the friendship of the Twins fans, but he still had not won a set position in the lineup.

building a pennant winning club

16

The winter preceding the 1962 season was a busy one for the Killebrews.

First, a writer from a national magazine visited them to do an article on Harmon. After he had made several futile attempts to get Killebrew to overcome his modesty and talk freely about himself, he gave him a question that he felt sure would get an answer, "What was your greatest thrill in baseball?"

Harmon grinned and said, "Wait a minute and I'll tell you." He left the room and came back holding the baseball autographed by President Eisenhower and said, "My biggest thrill was when I got this."

The writer concluded that Harmon simply would not talk about himself and so bade the Killebrews a friendly good-bye.

The birth of their third baby, and first girl, was the high spot that winter for Harmon and Elaine. She made her debut on February 18, 1962, and immediately won their hearts.

Harmon and Elaine remember the event in great detail. She said, "This was the first birth Harm had been home for, and it was quite an experience. I had been having contractions for hours, and about 4:00 a.m., when they became close together and regular, I woke up Harm and said, 'Honey! I can't wait any longer. I have to go to the hospital.'

"It was really a riot to watch him. He jumped out of bed like a volunteer responding to a fire alarm and managed to say, 'Golly, darling don't have it yet. Hold on! Hold on!'

"He was 'shook up' because he was sure I was going to have the baby any minute, and he was so nervous I thought maybe I'd better drive the car; but he calmed down enough to get me to the hospital. When we got there, he said, 'Doc! do something quick! She's going to have her baby any minute.' "

Harmon remembers the incident like this:

"The doctor smiled patiently and told a nurse to make necessary preparations for Elaine. When she went into the delivery room, I sat in the waiting room right outside the door. The birth really gave her a difficult time. Recent corrective surgery had tightened the surrounding tissues so much that she couldn't dilate. So she spent five hours of torture, struggling to push hard enough so the baby could be presented. But she just couldn't get things going. Finally, those attending her decided they would have to do something to help the baby along. So one of the little Sisters, who was the head of the maternity floor in the hospital, found a box and stood on it beside her. This made it possible to push directly down on her abdomen every time she had a contraction.

"Well, the Sister and Elaine made a good team, and Elaine eventually got our baby delivered. The difficult labor had made us afraid that our child might have some brain damage, but she was a beautiful, bright, perfect little girl. We named her Shawn.

"The day after Shawn was born, I signed a new contract at about $34,000 a year, so the family also had something else to celebrate."

Elaine continued, "I was so grateful to have Harm with me for once; and he made some financial sacrifices so he *could* be there. He was supposed to host a trip to some foreign country, and he called it off while we waited for Shawn, who was three weeks overdue. As a result of her delayed birth, he had to leave for spring training two days after I got home from the hospital.

"I forgot to mention that we had been hunting for a larger home before I went to the hospital. We decided on one which was about eight miles away in Ontario, Oregon.

"The final papers were signed while I was in the hospital, and we moved into our new home on April 1st.

"We were thrilled and excited about the new house. It was out in the country but still within walking distance of a grade school. We had an acre of pasture and a beautifully-landscaped yard. The former owners ran a feed and seed store and had planted flower gardens all over the place; so I nearly killed myself trying to care for all of them. I began right away to draw up plans because we needed additional space, and I just couldn't wait to remodel."

While Elaine was busy dreaming up ideas to redecorate their new home, Harmon found himself in an unusual situation during spring training at Tinker Field. He was the highest paid player Cal Griffith had ever signed, the top salaried man on the team, and still he had no set position in the lineup. Mele was tentatively planning to play him at third base and Griffith had been suggesting that he might do well in the outfield.

As spring training progressed, a red-headed school teacher named Rich Rollins, who had played only 13 games the season before, won the third base spot with his aggressive play. And Bernie Allen, a former star Purdue quarterback, took over at second base. Killebrew would have liked to play first base, but Mele was still experimenting with his lineup. One of the big reasons that Harmon was not assigned a permanent position right from the start was his versatility. He had performed satisfactorily in tryouts at first base, third base, and left field; so the management figured he could fill in where he was needed most.

CHIC PHOTOS

Killebrew and teammates talk to Halsey Hall, popular Twins sportscaster

Two days before the season started, Griffith traded Pedro Ramos to Cleveland for first-baseman, Vic Power, and pitcher Dick Stigman. This trade jelled the Twins' infield alignment. Power, a strong hitter and perhaps the top defensive first baseman in the majors, was installed at first with Zoilo Versalles rounding out the inner defense at shortstop.

So Harmon was placed permanently in left field with Lennie Green in center and Bob Allison in right.

Killebrew got off to a slow start in 1962, and by early June was hitting at a low .171 average. Despite his weak batting, the team did well. Rich Rollins had caught fire at the plate and sparked the team until June 20th with a .351 average.

The four starting pitchers Camilo Pascual, Jack Kralick, Jim Kaat and Dick Stigman were hurling well and receiving plenty of help from relievers Frank Sullivan, Lee Stange, and Ray Moore. And Earl Battey, the catcher, gave them all added confidence with his abilities.

Rollins and Power added considerable color to the team with their unusual mannerisms.

Every time Rich approached the plate he would adjust his glasses, straighten his cap, and take three compulsive practice swings before entering the batter's box.

Vic Power entertained the fans with his antics on the field; as graceful as a ballet dancer, he made almost impossible defensive plays look easy. Every time he caught a pop-fly he would do it nonchalantly with one hand, a habit that made hometown fans nervous. As a result he frequently was accused of "showboating", but gloving the ball with one hand was his style of play. He rarely made an error.

Versalles, at short, also had his moments of brilliance, and he ranged deep and wide to cut off hard hit balls. Allen, at second, gave the outward impression that he was loafing; but he always got the job done in a workman-like manner.

It finally appeared that Griffith had put everything together—had assembled a team that was solid at every position. In the outfield Harmon was a dependable and steady left fielder, and his natural baseball instincts helped him to always be in the right spot to get the ball. Lennie Green covered center field like glue, and Bob Allison made several sensational game-saving catches in right field.

On the 7th of June, Mele pulled Killebrew out of the lineup in a game against Kansas City.

"I think you need a rest, Harm," he said. "You haven't had one hit in thirteen times at bat."

Killebrew felt a great deal of frustration about being removed, but he accepted the benching without an argument.

About the same time Harmon was benched, Jim Lemon was sent to the Philadelphia Phillies. Harmon missed his lanky friend and the opportunity to talk about baseball strategy with him.

Mele put Killebrew back into the lineup after four games, and Harmon resumed his efforts to master outfield play. But just as he was beginning to feel comfortable in the position, he was sent back to first base for a brief time when Vic Power was injured.

Beginning about the middle of June, Harmon got back his hitting rhythm and began to belt homeruns with increasing frequency. Very few opposing pitchers seemed able to stop him. He hit them against the best in the league —Whitey Ford of the New York Yankees, Jim Perry of the Cleveland Indians, and Chuck Estrada of the Baltimore Orioles.

Some of his hits were sensational. In a game against the Cleveland Indians, he and Bob Allison hit grandslam homers in the same inning, the first time it had been done in major league history. During this stretch of long-ball hitting he slugged seven homers in seven games.

A reporter cornered him and asked, "Do you have a new swing? Hitting seven homers in seven games?"

"No!" answered Harmon. "I'm swinging the same way. It's just luck I guess."

"But you must have some new technique to be on such a streak," persisted the reporter.

"No, I guess it just happens that way," said Killebrew.

The reporter went away talking to himself. Getting a story from Killebrew was like pumping water from a deep well.

When August came around, the Twins were still in the fight for the pennant, and Killebrew was still making home-run history. In a game against Detroit on August 3rd, he hit a Jim Bunning fast-ball that landed on the leftfield second-deck roof, 340 feet away—bouncing out of the park. This was the first time this feat had been accomplished.

Another dazzling first occurred in the major league no-hitter at the Met, pitched by Jack Kralick against Kansas City on August 26, 1962. Kralick is a wiry pitcher who has a great assortment of slow-breaking stuff, and that day he had the Kansas City batters almost standing on their heads in an effort to hit his tantalizing pitches.

At this time, the Twins were fighting with the New York Yankees for first place with just four games separating the two clubs.

Then overnight, for some unknown reason, the Twins went into a slump. Harmon did his best to keep his hitting streak going, but the pressure of the team's losses got to him, and his hitting fell off. The fans began riding him and every time he failed to get a hit some loud-mouth in the stands would shout, "Harmless Harm! What a killer!"

Killebrew was upset. One night he said to Elaine, "I can't understand what's wrong. I'm swinging the same way as I was when I was hitting."

"Well, you've had slumps before, Harm," she said. "I'm sure you'll pull out of it."

Mele was more specific in his thinking. "Harm, you're turning your head as the pitch comes in and swinging too soon. Keep your eye on the ball as long as you can before committing yourself."

Harmon tried to follow Mele's suggestions, succeeding temporarily, but still he was not consistent in his hitting.

One day, almost like the sun suddenly emerging from behind a cloud, the team broke out of its slump and began winning again. And by late August they pulled within two games of the first-place Yankees.

About this time, when the team was playing in Boston, Mele threw out a challenge to Killebrew. He asked, "Do you know, Harm, that you've hit a homerun in every park in the league except here in Boston?"

"No, I haven't kept track," replied Killebrew.

"How about making it one in every park today?" Mele pressed.

"Maybe. The pitching is good here, Sam," Killebrew said, "but I'll try."

Try he did. And the result? He blasted his thirty-fifth homerun of the season though the Twins lost 7 to 5.

Despite Mele's patient handling, the Twins did not play consistently enough the rest of the season to overtake the Yankees. They would win a few and then lose a few without establishing a winning pattern.

Killebrew seemed to have the same problem with his hitting. Fans began to say, "As Killebrew goes, so go the Twins."

At one low point, Mele benched Killebrew for two days' rest. The brief period of inactivity seemed to be just what the doctor ordered because when Harmon returned to the lineup on September 15th, he started one of the most spectacular hitting streaks in the history of baseball. As incredible as it may seem, each one of the seven hits that he got from September 15th to September 22nd was a homerun. He continued hitting at such a torrid pace that he hit eleven homeruns in the last eleven games and won the league homerun title with 48 homers. He also led the league in runs-batted-in with 126. Meanwhile the Twins wound up the season in second place.

When sportswriters asked Harmon how he felt about his tremendous hitting and winning the two titles, he said, "It's real nice, but I also won another title I'm not proud of. I led the league in strikeouts with 142, and they say its a new major league record. I've got to improve."

the faith to keep going

17

Perhaps it would be well to answer a question that is uppermost in the minds of thousands of fans. "What has kept Harmon Killebrew going despite all of his serious injuries?" He and Elaine are always able to overcome adversity and meet each new day with optimism.

The answer—their deep religious faith. Many people are unaware of this healing and driving force deep within their hearts. They don't wear it on their sleeves.

Some individuals think it is necessary to stand on street corners and shout "Hallelujah" to be recognized as religious. But not the Killebrews. Their religious belief permeates their entire existence, but they don't shout to others about it. Harmon believes his role as a baseball player gives him an opportunity to serve others by the way he plays the game.

Ray Crump, the Twins Equipment Manager, and long-time friend of the Killebrews made this comment about Harmon's faith in action:

"Harm's the type of guy that thinks the Lord put him

here in baseball to do a job for him, and to show kids how to live a straight life and stay on the main road. Why, even the umpires respect him. I remember a time when I was sitting on the bench and Harmon was at bat. The umpire made a bad call. Harm turned and said to the ump, 'You sure made a bad call on that one.' The umpire replied, 'You're right, Harm, I did.' "

"I think so much of Harmon that in 1965, when I was married, I would have liked to ask him to be my best man, but people might have said I was asking for his name and so I didn't.

"To sum Harmon Killebrew up, I want to say that if I had one wish in life, I would want my two sons to grow up and be like Harmon Killebrew—not the ball player—but the person."

Elaine also has implicit trust in God, and she has always been a bulwark of strength to Harmon because of her great faith. When she was telling us about Harmon's struggles to prove his baseball abilities and the many heartaches they both encountered, she made one thing crystal clear, and that was that the most important thing in her life was to have Harmon and her children united with her in a common faith so they could serve God as a family.

In discussing the 1962-63 years she said:

"I think at this point I should interject something about our activity in the church. Before we had moved from Payette, we had attended church quite regularly with our two boys. Even though Harm was not a member of our faith, he attended with me and was receptive to the ways of our church.

"As our boys got older, and we were planning to have more children, I came to the realization that they should attend religious services regularly, to learn just what religion could mean in their lives. As we did this, I began to see for myself the importance of having a closely-knit family who attended church together, learned together and could grow in religion together, so we could meet life's challenges.

Elaine explained that much of the Killebrews' time in 1963 was used remodeling their new house in Ontario. "Because of the remodeling, I lived in Minneapolis only about five weeks during that baseball season. While Harm was away I took charge of the work—and what a mess! Everything was so torn up that we had to live in one part of the house while the other part was being worked on. I usually had to take the children out to eat our main meal because we were completely redesigning the kitchen.

"To make things a bit more difficult, I was pregnant again—expecting our fourth baby about the middle of October. So you can imagine how I felt—morning sickness; no kitchen to cook in; the children irritable; and Harm away. Also, I was getting bigger all the time and was constantly afraid I would lose my balance and trip over one of the loose boards lying around. To put it mildly it was a trying time.

"So it was a blessed relief when we got away to spend five weeks of the summer in Minneapolis with Harm. We rented the Jack Kralick home. He used to be a pitcher for our ball club.

"When Harm met us at the airport, I hugged him and said, 'Oh, honey, it's so good to be away from that remodeling mess. I'm going to relax, lie around and dream, and have some romantic interludes with you.'

"Then wouldn't you know! The first day I was there I had an accident. Harm had carried in our bags, helped us get settled, and then had taken off for practice at the ball park. The boys had gone outside to play, and in a little while, I went out and called to them to come in and bathe. I reached up to pull the garage door down and close it for the night. All of a sudden, the door came slamming down. I had reached up and grabbed it in one of the joints with my fingers, and it came down so quickly that the fingers remained caught in the joint. The pain was excruciating, and I was so afraid that I had lost some of my fingers that I couldn't even look. Since my left hand was caught up high in the door, I had to balance on one foot and lift the door with the other until I could reach it with my free hand and ease it off my pinched fingers.

"Naturally, I let out a scream and the boys came running. I sobbed, 'Hurry to the neighbors for help. I'm afraid I'm going to lose my fingers.'

"Cam and Kenny dashed across the street, and the very neighbor they contacted happened to be an anesthesiologist. Talk about luck! He gave me something to deaden the pain and then called the hospital and made arrangements for me to be taken care of. I phoned Betty Allison (Bob's wife) and she and her sister took me to the hospital while the neighbors stayed with the kids. Fortunately, the doctors were able to sew my fingers and keep them intact, although I was almost sure at the time that I had lost some of them.

"When Harm came home he was so tender and sweet to me that I appreciated being with him more than ever.

"'Honey,' he said, 'There's nothing that hurts me so much as to see you suffer.' Then he took me in his arms, and I knew his very presence would make my fingers heal faster."

Harmon added, "That street where we lived was really something. Down the road was another anesthesiologist; so if you got hurt you could get treatment at both ends—of the street—I mean. Dr. Peterson, we call him Pete, and his wife, Ruth, were very kind to us, and we have been close friends ever since.

"After five happy weeks in Minneapolis, Elaine took the children and returned to Ontario. She couldn't wait to see our newly remodeled kitchen. When she got there, she found that the kitchen wasn't finished. The cabinets weren't in; and the finish man we had engaged to do the work had gone off on another job."

Elaine said, "I felt like crying, but realizing that things had to be done, I got hold of my brother-in-law, Bert Ivie, and the two of us did all of the kitchen painting and the finishing work on our maple cabinets. We spent days painting and varnishing the kitchen and family room and also took many hours putting decorative worm holes on one thing and another. Harm helped when he returned home. We both enjoy decorating, and we spent many pleasant hours together painting the entire house which included texturing the plaster walls."

The 1963 season was a mixture of accomplishment and frustration for Harmon. First, Calvin Griffith showed his appreciation by giving him a $40,000 contract. He paid him such a sum because in addition to batting titles Killebrew had won the previous season, Cal learned that Harmon's homerun frequency was one in 13.1 times at bat, second only to Babe Ruth's record of 11.8. Griffith knew how homerun hitters attracted fans, so he wanted to keep Killebrew happy.

Spring training turned out to be a disaster for the Twins—winning seven out of twenty-seven exhibition games.

Things went even worse for Harmon. One day he slipped on a soggy spot in the infield and suffered what Bill Proffit, team physician, diagnosed as a severe sprain of the right knee. From that time on, Killebrew had to have the knee tightly taped each day before going on the field. The twisted knee threw off his batting rhythm and pained every time he swung at a ball. To make matters worse, he slipped again a few days later and sprained an ankle.

Finally, Mele approached him and said, "Harm, you'd better rest a few days until some of your pain eases up."

"Thanks, Sam," Harmon replied, "but I think I'll work out the soreness faster if I play. If I rest it might tighten up."

Mele turned away and said to himself, "What a guy. I wish all the players had his guts."

As the team approached the opening game of the season, every move that Harmon made sent darts of fire shooting through his knee. Fluid had formed on it and he endured constant pain.

Doc Lentz, the team trainer, tried to talk him out of playing, but he refused to be budged.

"Doc," he said, "I'm being paid to play, not sit on the bench."

Then Elaine attempted to get him to sit out a few games, telling him he didn't need to worry about losing his place in the lineup. "You're the team's star hitter. If you rest up awhile, they'll put you back in just as soon as you feel better."

"Darling," Harmon said looking at her with his calm gaze, "I'm not worrying about my place in the lineup. It's just that I can't let Mr. Griffith and the fans down. He's paying me a lot of money, and they're paying to see me play. I just want to be earning my salary, and I won't if I sit on the bench because of a little pain."

So Harmon played. Dr. Proffit drained the fluid from his knee the morning of the opening game, and Killebrew got some relief.

The Twins lost their opener to Cleveland 5 to 4, and Harmon went hitless as he limped through the game.

In the second game, with the Twins leading 4 to 3, Killebrew added an insurance tally with a homerun in the eighth against Barry Latman. When he met the ball with his powerful swing, the pain from his injured knee seemed to shoot clear up to the top of his head, but he gave no outward expression of it as he rounded the bases to the cheers of the crowd.

Reporters crowded around in the clubhouse after the game, and one said, "Why, you can hit homers standing on one leg!"

"I was just lucky to get hold of one," replied Harmon.

Another reporter moved closer and continued the conversation with, "You're ten days ahead of last year with your first homer. Does that mean you'll break some records this season?"

Killebrew smiled, "It doesn't mean a thing. I hit in streaks; so you can't count on any records being made this early in the season."

A few games later, when the Twins lost to the Kansas City Athletics 5 to 4 and Harmon fanned four times in a row, Mele insisted that he rest, and rookie Jim Hall, a promising long-ball hitter, was put in his place.

Now Killebrew's leg ached day and night. Every step racked his body with pain. He had to get around like he was walking on eggs to avoid twisting the knee more. And at night in bed, if he made the slightest turning movement his leg felt like it was on fire. Yet he never complained or cried out. When he was home, Elaine lay at his side and suffered with him, and used all of her great love and faith to help him get well.

Dr. Proffit tried several therapeutic techniques in treating the ailing knee. He drained the fluid, administered cortisone injections, and prescribed whirlpool treatments.

By May 11th the soreness was gone. Harmon went to Mele and said, "Sam, I'm ready to play again."

"Are you sure?" asked Mele.

"Try me." answered Killebrew.

"Okay, go ahead, but watch it."

Harmon got through five innings as a starter, but then sat out the next game because rain had made the outfield slippery.

Gradually Killebrew fought his way back to his normal hitting form, and from about the middle of May on, the Twins' fortune began to pick up. Everyone hit better, and in a four-game series with Cleveland, Harmon and his teammates hit twelve homeruns.

Some reporters asked Mele if he could account for the Twins' sudden rash of victories.

"Probably the main reason is Killebrew," he said. "When he's playing—and hitting, the whole team becomes more confident and they put pressure on the opposing pitcher. Harm is an inspiration to the other players; and I've noticed that when he is in the game all the fellows play with more spirit."

Earl Battey, catcher for the Twins, expressed the thinking of the team at that time when he said:

"Harmon gives us class. This team, without Killebrew, is like dressing up for a formal affair with white tie and tails and then wearing muddy shoes. Harmon puts us all in bigger shoes and adds a sparkle of polish. We feel like we are among the best with him in the lineup."

From that time on, led by Killebrew, the Twins started to climb in the standings.

There was also another player who deserves special mention for his contribution to the team during the 1963 season—relief pitcher, Bill Dailey. This newcomer who had toiled ten seasons in the minor leagues first attracted attention on May 20th when he did his funny duck-like walk in from the bullpen and threw his fast-ball past the Boston Red Sox for two and one-third innings.

Bill was a colorful character. He was a lanky sidearmer, and when he threw the ball it was with such a violent, lunging motion that it looked like his arm would tear away from his body. I watched him pitch many times and never saw a hurler who put more of himself into his delivery. It seemed sometimes that he would wear himself out pitching to only one batter—he threw so hard.

It got so that whenever the Twins pitcher on the mound was in trouble, everyone would look to the bullpen and hope that Bill Dailey would come to the rescue. He usually did, and while Bill trudged across the field toward the pitcher's mound, Willie Peterson, the stadium organist, would play: "Bill Bailey Won't You Please Come Home." Before the season was over, Dailey pitched in 66 games and compiled a sparkling 1.98 earned run average.

Another Twins Player who went beyond the call of duty that year was Rich Rollins. The fiery little third baseman suffered a broken jaw during the season but kept right on playing. He had the fracture held together with wires, and for a long time the only foods he could eat were liquids such as soup and watery malted milk which he sipped through a straw. But he still "hung in tight" at the plate and got his share of hits. His manner was somewhat reminiscent of a miniature tank that pushed forward come what may.

As the season progressed, Mele got into the habit of

putting Jimmie Hall into the game as a defensive move to rest Killebrew in the late innings. He usually did this when the Twins had a lead. His thinking was, "Killebrew has given us the lead with his bat. Now we'll let Hall defend it with his glove."

In a game against Chicago on May 24th, the maneuver nearly backfired. The Twins seemed to be coasting to victory with a 6-2 lead in the sixth as the result of a grandslam homer by Harmon. So Sam sent in Hall to rest Killebrew. The White Sox hitters took on new life in the ninth and knotted the score at six all.

It so happened that Hall came to bat with two out in the ninth, hitting in Killebrew's slot. Bystanders said it looked like Mele was offering a silent prayer for forgiveness for having taken Killebrew out.

I suppose it will never be known just what Mele's prayer was, but Hall answered it in an unexpected way. He smashed a homerun into the left field stands to win the game.

Later in the clubhouse, Mele shook his head in amazement.

"What a crazy, mixed-up game," he said, "I take out our power hitter Killebrew to shore up our defense with Hall; then Jimmie wallops one out to win for us."

Bob Allison needled Harmon afterward. "Take care, Harm," he said. "That kid, Hall, might grab your job."

"You aren't kidding!" said Killebrew.

The season continued with Killebrew and the Twins fighting to move up in the standings, and by June 12th the club was in fourth place, just two and one-half games behind league-leading Chicago.

Harmon was constantly trying to strengthen his physical condition so he could better resist injuries; and one approach which he felt might be helpful was a method called isometrics. This is a system of static strength development which employs the use of one force against another to strengthen muscles. For example, an individual can push against a wall or pull at an immovable object to build muscular strength.

One day, when the Twins players walked into the clubhouse, they were surprised to see a gymnastic bar set up in the dressing room.

"What's this thing for?" asked Rich Rollins.

"That thing is for exercising," Mele said drily. "Killebrew asked for it, but you're all free to use it."

Allison looked at Killebrew quizzically. "Don't you get enough exercise, Harm?"

"This is to build up my strength," Killebrew replied in a matter-of-fact way.

"Now I've heard everything," said Allison. "The strongest man in baseball exercising to build up his strength."

Harmon grinned, "The system is called isometrics and it's an effective method of using pressure and resistance for exercise without having to move around. Here's a book that explains it."

From that time on, Killebrew worked systematically on the bar. Rich Rollins also become a convert. The rest of the players seemed less interested in the new theory.

The exercises seemed to start paying off for Killebrew, because on June 18th he hit a 432 foot homerun that reached the thirty-ninth row of the Met left field bleachers, one of his longest wallops. And as his hitting picked up once again, the other players followed his lead, and the team won seven straight games.

As was said before, the 1963 season was made up of a mixture of accomplishments and frustrations for Harmon; and just when he seemed set for a string of prodigious clouts, injury struck him again, and he pulled a hamstring muscle in his left leg. It happened in a July Fourth doubleheader with the Tigers when he tried to outrun a double-play ball.

Now Killebrew had miseries in both legs, but he refused to quit playing. He was constantly after Doc Lentz to get them healed fast—and repeatedly telling Sam Mele that he was able to play.

Harmon again was chosen for the All-Star game played on July 9th in Cleveland's Municipal Stadium. He was used sparingly, however, and failed to hit in one time at bat. The National Leaguers won 5 to 3.

Ten days later on July 19th, Killebrew hit his twenty-second homer of the season, which was the two hundredth of his major league career.

When a sportswriter asked him if this special homerun gave him a thrill, Harmon replied, "Each ball you hit over the fence gives you a thrill at the time, but if your team doesn't win the game, homers don't seem very important."

For a short time during the season Killebrew and Allison hit homeruns at an equal pace, and at one time they were tied at twenty-five each. Again, sportswriters started asking questions such as:

"Do you think Allison will take the championship away from you this year?" "Will you feel bad if he edges you out?"

Both Killebrew and Allison were too sensible to be drawn into rivalry, and each in turn tried to explain to the inquiring newsmen that they were interested primarily in helping the team win games, not in who would hit more homeruns.

Harmon kept swinging hard, despite his most recent hamstring injury and his twisted knee; but his ailing knee was affecting his swing, and by August 28th he had hit only twenty-nine homeruns.

At this time, when he must have felt a bit down emotionally, he was asked by Commissioner Ford Frick what he thought of major league baseball. The request was made in a survey of ballplayers in the big leagues and it read, "Tell us in your own words, something of the game's meaning to you."

Harmon's answer, which was contained in a booklet published by the Commissioner's Office, brought so many favorable comments that it was also printed by the Minneapolis Tribune.

It read:

> Signing a big league contract was one of the big thrills of my

> life and one of the smartest things I ever did. It meant heartache, frustration, disappointment, hard work and oftentimes painful injury. But all these things have made staying and playing in the major leagues all the sweeter.
>
> By my connection with the game, I have met some of the most important people of our times—the President, Vice President, and cabinet officers. In fact, it was through the recommendation of my senator from Idaho, the late Herman Welker, that I was first signed.
>
> My earnings have enabled me to provide a better home for my family sooner than I would have been able to otherwise. During the season, I have been able to live and travel first class, eat the best foods and keep in the best physical and mental condition. Through baseball, I was able to get a job as a radio and television feature broadcaster.
>
> The training I have received in this field could prepare me for a career outside baseball after my playing days are over. And, of course, baseball has that wonderful pension program to care for my family and me in later years. Yes, the decision to sign my first baseball contract was a big one.

Again came accomplishment. On August 29th the Twins defeated Washington twice, 14 to 2 and 10 to 1, and in the process hit twelve homeruns. This barrage, added to hits in previous games, set the following new major league records:

The most homeruns in three consecutive games—15.

The most homers in four games—17.

The most homeruns in five-consecutive American League games—18.

Then came frustration. While the team was playing in Washington, Harmon had Dr. George Resta, the Senators team doctor and a friend of long standing, X-ray his ailing knee.

When the doctor looked at the results he was both appalled and amazed.

"Harmon," he said, "your knee is in bad condition, and your pain is due to loose fragments in the area. An operation is the only thing that can set it right. It is amazing to me that you've been able to play on it."

"I knew something must be wrong inside," Harmon said. "I suppose I'll have to have it operated on, but I'll wait until the season is over."

Again, Killebrew went on to accomplishment. Despite

the condition of his knee, he battled with Dick Stuart of the Boston Red Sox for the league homerun title. The duel continued down the final stretch and wasn't decided until the last days of the season.

Dick Stuart could hit the ball a mile, but was awkward on defense. Consequently, he was nick-named "Dr. Strange glove" or "Old hard hands."

He was the type who liked to talk, and once when he was speaking before a group in Boston, he waxed eloquent, pounded on the lectern, and said, "Friends, the most important thing in a ball player's life is to have a good woman backing him up."

Just then, some joker in the back of the hall stood up and shouted. "That's true Dick, and if she's in back of *you*, she'd *better* have a glove on."

When Harmon edged Dick out for the homerun title with 45 homers to Stuart's 42, Dick was really broken up and according to some reports, said it was the saddest day of his life.

The Twins finished the 1963 season in third, 13 games out of first. But Harmon's individual record was a good one. Despite an ailing knee and missing twenty games, he won the league homerun title with 45, had the top slugging percentage of .555, he also led the Twins in total bases, 286—and runs-batted-in, 96!

As he started for home to rejoin Elaine and the children, his happiness in thinking about spending the winter with them was tempered by the fact that he faced a serious knee operation.

"The 1964 Sultan of Swat"

the 1964 sultan of swat

18

"Harm, am I glad to see you," Elaine said when he arrived home. "Our baby was due six days ago. I'm sure it's a girl and she must have been waiting for you to get home before making her grand entrance."

"Well, I don't know," Harmon smiled. "Remember last time how nervous I was when Shawn was born? Perhaps our baby knows that and can't make up her mind whether it's safe to come when I'm around. It could be that you've miscounted the days."

"What a man," said Elaine, her eyes twinkling as she handed Harmon a glass of cold apple juice, "after all our years together you think I can't count. Now, who balances our check book every month and who . . ."

"Hold it! Hold it!" interrupted Harmon laughingly. "You look too big to argue with right now."

Then the two melted into each other's arms and Elaine whispered, "Nervous or not, it's great to have you home."

"Watch out—you'll spill the apple juice," chuckled Harmon.

The new baby girl wasn't in any hurry to be born, and the Killebrews waited three more weeks before she arrived.

Elaine remembers her birth this way:

"Kathy was born early in the morning on October 23, 1963. Harm was with me, and everything went smoothly. Her birth was much easier than that of our first girl, Shawn.

"Neither of us was very nervous this time. We felt like a veteran team of baby-havers.

"Harm was again delighted with our dainty little girl. I remember his saying, 'Now we have two boys and two girls. What'll it be next? Another cheer leader or a third member for our basketball team?'

"'Don't be in such hurry! Time will tell,' I said drowsily and then I fell asleep."

Harmon was home that winter after Kathy was born, taking great delight in helping to care for her. He pitched in, shared the household tasks, helping with the washing, cooking and caring for the children.

He also found time to hunt, going out often in the hills for birds. But being home didn't change the condition of his knee. It still ached with every step. Finally realizing it must be done, he arranged for surgery. He went to Dr. Donald J. Baranco, an Orthopedist in Caldwell, Idaho. Dr. Baranco is a widely-known orthopedic surgeon and many athletes are flown in to him for surgery. He saw Harmon for the first time on November 11, 1963, and on the twelfth of December performed surgery.

Dr. Baranco repaired some ligaments in the injured knee and also removed some calcified cartilage and bone fragments.

Harmon spent some painful days recovering at the hospital and a trying time while convalescing at home.

As mutual admiration developed between Dr. Baranco and Harmon they became good friends. When he learned I was writing a book about the Killebrews, he sent the following account of his association with Harmon:

"I am very pleased to hear that you are writing a book on the life and baseball career of Harmon Killebrew. Without question, I feel that you could not write about a finer young man.

"I saw Harm first on November 7, 1963, probably as a referral from mutual friends of ours, Jerry Kramer and R. C. Owens. Harm gave a history of injuring his knee back in 1952 or 1953 at which time his right knee was operated on. Since then he has had pain and discomfort along with marked instability of the right knee. It's amazing, when I think of his record at that time, that he was doing all of this with a completely unstable right knee; and of course this is the extremity that he pushes off on. In other words he maintains a great deal of his power by pushing off the right knee, and when this knee is unstable it really creates a problem.

"Harm was an extremely easy patient to treat. Everyone in the entire hospital fell in love with him. Even though it was a routine knee, everytime I do surgery on an outstanding athlete there is no question that the pressure builds up when you realize that the patient's entire future depends a lot on what you are doing at that time. I have operated on many athletes, but I don't think that I have ever worked with a more pleasant and cooperative person than Harm. He has a definite quality about him that after you work with him a short time you end up treating a friend and not a routine patient.

"Another interesting quality that Harm has is his ability to meet people and make them feel completely at home. Every visit that he made to the office was quite prolonged because every young high school athlete in the office wanted to be introduced to him. Harm would take his time and visit with the young men asking about their various injuries and plans for the future. He was never too busy to take time out and stop and carry on lengthy conversations with some college football player or some Midget League baseball player.

"Another example of his kindness occurred shortly after my father's death. My mother and father became Killebrew fans right after they knew that he was a patient as well as a friend of mine. I was visiting my mother, and we were discussing Harm, whom she feels is a 'darling.' I asked mother if she would like to speak to Harmon; so with that I put in a long distance call and found out that he was on the road. I was quite anxious to have mother speak to Harm; so I followed it up and put in a call for him at the Yankee Stadium. In short order Harm was on the phone visiting with my mother as he would his own mother.

"I could ramble on for quite some time about his good qualities, but I am quite certain that you are aware of every one of them as well. If there were more Harmon Killebrews in professional athletics today what a wonderful world this would be."

Yours very sincerely,
Donald J. Baranco, M.D.

In talking about the months after Harmon's surgery, Elaine said:

"It was a frustrating winter for both of us. I was busy with Kathy, our new baby, and Harm was crippling around with his disabled knee. He was on crutches much of the time, and after that he spent the rest of his stay at home until spring training, lifting weights and doing exercises to build his knee up. He was under a lot of strain because he didn't know if he would be in shape to run when he reported to Florida."

Harmon says that recovering from knee surgery is just plain agony. "The knee is immobilized so long that adhesions develop. This means, very simply, that inflammation starts new tissues to form, causing parts of the leg to cling together that normally are separate. Consequently, the patient recovering from knee surgery has to stretch his leg to pull these abnormal unions apart so that mobility will come back to his leg. Also he must lift weights with his leg and do other special exercises to strengthen it."

Killebrew had trouble with his hitting and running during spring training and early season play. He found out that his knee had not yet become strong enough to push off when at bat and get full power in his swing. And when he ran he couldn't cut and turn normally. As a result, he was in a hitting slump during the early season, and the other players followed his pattern. Consequently, the Twins were mired in the second division.

Still the team was interesting to watch. One reason was the play of a newcomer to the club named Tony Oliva, a Cuban outfielder with a tooth-paste smile.

Tony-O, as he is nicknamed, moved into the 1964 lineup in right field with much fanfare. He was publicized as having the "sweetest swing this side of heaven," and a "sling shot arm," strong enough to throw a runner out at the plate from deep right field.

Tony-O more than lived up to his advance notices as he combined with Killebrew to form a deadly one-two batting punch in the lineup.

In addition to this, Tony had, and still has, some interesting-to-watch mannerisms. Before he takes his position in the batters' box, he spends several minutes landscaping the bordered oblong of earth. He'll push the soil carefully one way with his left foot, then back with his right—next bounce on the area; and just about the time the opposing pitcher is ready to blow a fuse and the plate umpire is ready to fine him for delaying the game, Tony assumes his stance in the box and begins swinging his bat in a beautiful arc.

Tony has suffered some finger injuries during his career, and as a result cannot always hold onto his bat when he takes a vicious swipe at the ball. So when he is at the plate, his teammate in the on-deck circle, the first and third base coaches, the infield umpires, the fans in the rightfield boxes, the opposing pitcher, and everyone else in the general vicinity, have to be on guard against his bat, which often leaves his hands like a flying missile.

Tony had a great season in 1964. "He became the first

L. to r., Floyd Baker, coach; George Strickland, coach; Sam Mele, manager; Gordon Maltzberger, coach; Ed FitzGerald, coach.

CECIL W. STOUGHTON

Twins players are greeted by President Lyndon B. Johnson and Vice-President Hubert H. Humphrey, 1964

rookie and the first Negro ever to win the American League batting title. He batted .323, leading the league in doubles with 43, in hits with 217, in total bases with 374, and in runs scored with 109."

Harmon was so upset about his slump that he again went to Ossie Bluege for counsel. And Bluege, as usual, reassured him with some sound and simple advice.

He said, "You're a good hitter, Harm. Quit worrying and take your natural cut at the plate. Your timing is off now because your knee prevented you from getting in all of your training. Keep using your natural swing, and the hits will soon start falling in."

Harmon felt relieved, but the slump hung on and he finally went to Sam Mele and said, "Sam, I feel real badly about not doing better this year. I want to apologize."

This was a new experience for Mele to have a star ball player offer an apology in such a humble manner, and he was almost at a loss for words.

"Harm," he managed to say, "you don't have to apologize. We all know you're doing your best. Your luck will change soon.

"Perhaps if we rested your knee a few days it would help. How about it?"

"It's worth a try," replied Killebrew. "I'd like to take some extra batting practice too."

"Fine," agreed Mele.

While Harmon was fighting to get out of his batting slump, Elaine waited until school was out to leave Ontario. Then taking the children, she moved into a house on Logan Avenue and 53rd Street in Minneapolis. She indicated that it was a very special summer for them. "I was happy because when we arrived, Harm was over his slump and hitting homers again. Also, we both acquired a very special and interesting friend.

"Harm had met a fascinating person named Evie Nordley when he was looking for a place to live. She was the Social Director for the Guthrie Theater, and she took care of finding all of the housing for their performers.

"She is a vivacious, outgoing person. She not only helped Harm find a house for us but she introduced us to the Guthrie Theatre. This opened up a whole new world for me in Minneapolis. Since we had become married and settled down to being busy with babies, traveling, and finding houses, I hadn't thought too much about the theater. But I've always liked dramatics and was in some plays in high school; so I was delighted when Evie took me to the Guthrie and showed me around. I found some of the things they did there to be fantastic—almost unbelievable. She took me into the rooms behind the scenes to see how the costumes are made. They make clothing, shoes and everything. And the way they build their settings—talk about creativity. It's out of this world.

"I had a girl named Arlene Rand from Payette living with

us and tending the children that summer. She was a splendid companion and so reliable that I could get away for such activities."

The rest seemed to help Harmon. He returned to the lineup on May 14th in a game against the White Sox.

In the opening inning, he stepped up to the plate with two on and two out. Gary Peters, a sensational rookie, was the opposing pitcher.

As Harmon waited for the ball, disturbing thoughts flashed into his mind. "Will I have my timing back?" "Will my knee hold up if I push hard?" "This game can make or break my season."

Peters got two strikes on Killebrew in a hurry. He threw a fast ball past him, and he fooled him with a breaking curve. The next pitch was another fast ball, and Harmon met it squarely. The ball sailed way up into the left field stands for a three-run homer and his fifth circuit clout of the season. From that game on, Harmon blasted American League pitching, and from May 14th to May 30th, he hit ten homeruns.

Despite Killebrew's hitting siege, the Twins began losing again. There were reasons for this. Battey, who had also undergone knee surgery during the winter, reinjured his knee. And Bill Dailey, the courageous reliever who had helped the team so much the year before, injured his arm.

Finally, in an effort to shake the Twins out of their losing lethargy, the club management began making trades. On June 11th, they sent Vic Power and Lennie Green to the Los Angeles Angels in exchange for infielder Jerry Kindall and infielder-outfielder Frank Kostro. And on June 16th they traded pitcher Lee Stange for Jim (Mudcat) Grant of the Cleveland Indians.

When these moves didn't help, Sam Mele took another approach, got tough and began fining the players for misplays.

There was a break in the slump when Killebrew, Allison and Oliva played in the All-Star game. But after that, the team still continued to skid.

But not Killebrew. He kept up a steady bombardment of the fences. He also sparkled in the field. Although he was not known as a fleet leftfielder, he made several sensational diving catches and it was evident that he was doing his best to light a winning fire under the club. Nevertheless, the team never did get rolling during the 1964 season and finally ended the year in sixth place.

Harmon, despite his early season slump, hit 49 homeruns, and won the homerun title for the third consecutive year. In so doing, he joined the select group of seven major league players who had won three homerun titles in a row. Among them were such notables as Babe Ruth of the Yankees and Ralph Kiner of the Pittsburgh Pirates.

In December of that year Killebrew received another honor. He was invited to the Tops-in-Sports Banquet in Baltimore, Maryland. While there he was named the 1964 Sultan of Swat and was presented with an elegant jeweled crown signifying that he had won the major league homerun championship.

Naturally, he was happy. But he had an even greater reason to be happy. Elaine was expecting another baby.

going into battle without sir lancelot

19

One evening in February, 1965, before Harmon left for spring training, the Killebrew family was seated around the dinner table enjoying some roast duck that Harmon had bagged. Suddenly, Cameron asked a question, "Dad, do you think the Twins will ever win the pennant?"

"Why sure, Cam," Harmon replied, as he turned slightly red. "You know we've come close a couple of times already."

Seven-year-old Kenny chimed in, "Close isn't good enough, dad. My teacher said you don't win coming close. You have to be first."

"You can do it, daddy. You're great!" said three-year-old Shawn.

Two-year-old Kathy just smiled and patted her daddy's arm.

"Goodness," spoke up Elaine. "You children know your daddy can do anything he wants to." Then winking at Harmon, she asked, "Harm, do you think the Twins can win the pennant this year?"

Harmon smiled, "We've got a good chance. We have some new players that have really strengthened the club."

"There now, it's as good as done," said Elaine. "Now all of you finish your dinner. It will soon be bedtime."

Later, when the four small Killebrews were fast asleep, Elaine turned to Harmon, who was reading the paper, and said, "Harm, I'm kind of worried. I'm getting so big. I've never been this large when I was expecting our other babies."

"Does it hurt anywhere?" asked Harmon solicitously.

"Yes and no," answered Elaine. "I feel kind of queer inside. It's a sort of feeling I've never experienced before. Golly! I wish you didn't have to go to spring training."

"I wish I could stay here until you have the baby," said Harmon, as he held his wife's hand. "But always remember I'm as close as the telephone. If you need me, phone, and I'll take the next plane home."

When Harmon arrived in Orlando, he could sense that the players seemed more relaxed than usual, almost like they *could* become a happy family.

During the winter Harmon, Bob Allison, Earl Battey, and Bill Dailey had conducted some baseball clinics and had played baseball on snowshoes in Fairbanks and Anchorage, Alaska. While there, they had discussed the Twins' chances for the coming season, and they were in general agreement that Calvin Griffith had strengthened the team enough so they could make a run for first place money.

One reason for their added confidence was the strong coaching staff Griffith had assembled. He had hired the fiery Billy Martin as the third base coach, saying publicly at the time, "Billy Martin is explosive, and we expect him to build a fire under the Twins."

Jim Lemon, famed slugger and a former Twin, had been brought back as a batting coach.

Johnny Sain, considered by many to be the best pitching coach in the majors, had been added to the club to work with the pitchers.

Harmon Killebrew playing baseball in Alaska, 1964

L. to r., Sam Mele, manager; John Sain, Hal Naragon, Billy Martin, Jim Lemon, coaches.

And Hal Naragon was expected to continue doing an outstanding job in the bullpen.

Griffith had done two other things to set the stage for a successful season. First, he had given the players raises to show his faith in them; Killebrew's salary went up to $50,000. Second, he had resurfaced the entire field at Tinker Field Stadium with Minnesota soil. The original surface had been marred with soft spots and pebbles which had contributed to Killebrew's and Battey's knee injuries, so he wanted to do everything possible to guard against the recurrence of such mishaps.

Calvin announced to the players that the dirt was the same kind that was on the infield at Metropolitan Stadium.

"We should feel right at home then," joked one of the players.

"You'd better," said Calvin, "considering we hauled down three hundred and fifty cubic yards, nearly a million pounds of Minnesota dirt!"

Despite Calvin's encouragment, Mele's efforts, and the knowledge imparted by the new coaches, the team couldn't seem to get going during spring training. Killebrew had been shifted back to first base and was doing well defensively; but the team was lacking in spirit.

Killebrew playing first base 1965

Dissension was rearing its ugly head. And some people claimed that Billy Martin was after Mele's job. Versalles, the fancy-fielding shortstop, and Mele seemed unable to communicate with each other. Gossip mongers were doing their best to blow things sky high. Gradually things were patched up, stories denied, and the club, despite an 11-15 record in exhibition games, left Florida in good spirits for the season's opener in Minnesota.

The Twins got off to a good start, defeating the Yankees 5 to 4 in their first game. In subsequent contests, Killebrew and Oliva began leading the others with a consistent hitting attack, and in early season games Tony was hitting homers and Harmon singles.

Killebrew's first homerun came on May 2nd when he propelled a Hoyt Wilhelm knuckle ball over the center-field fence 425 feet away from home plate. The night before, May 1st, Elaine phoned to tell him that a new baby daughter, whom they named Erin, had been born; so he promptly hit a homerun just as he had done when their other children had arrived. Elaine also told him she needed him with her. The next day being an off day, Harmon flew to see his wife and new daughter.

The birth of Erin had been a complicated one. Sometime in April the doctor suspected possible complications and thought perhaps Elaine was carrying twins. X-rays proved otherwise, but revealed instead that the baby was in an incorrect position for normal presentation.

In talking about the problem, Elaine said that each time she went to the doctor, he would turn the baby to the correct position, but at the next visit to his office it would be turned backwards again. In speaking of her anxiety, she recalled, "At the end of April, I began to hemorrhage and went into labor. I was at the hospital in hard labor for an hour when the contractions and hemorrhaging both stopped. They took me into the delivery room and found on examination that it was placenta previa (a placenta that is implanted very low in the uterus near the opening, often producing serious bleeding during labor). The doctors then decided they would have to deliver the baby by Caesarean section.

"They phoned Harm, but he was playing a ball game; so they left word for him to call. Surgery began at noon. There were some complications. The umbilical cord was cut and blood spurted all over the room. As a result, I needed some blood transfusions. But our little girl was just fine. She weighed ten pounds six and one-half ounces—a beautiful baby. Without a blemish or mark on her, she was rounded and filled out like a two-months old child.

"I was extremely sore and miserable when I woke up. Harm had been trying to get in touch with me, but there was no phone in the room. He called again, after I was awake, so the nurses helped me get on a hospital cart and pushed me down the corridor to the phone.

" 'How are you, sweetheart?' Harm said. 'It's great that we have another girl'—and in the same breath—'I'm so glad you are all right.'

" 'I'm all right,' I repeated. 'But I feel miserable, and oh, I wish you were here!'

"Harm could tell that I felt sorry for myself and how down I was. It gave me a big lift when he said, "Tomorrow is an off day, so I'll fly right out to see you. I'll take the next plane.'

"He arrived the next morning, coming directly to the hospital. He was really tickled with Erin and was so kind and loving to me that everything seemed bright again.

"The press phoned and wanted a picture of us, but I looked so frightful that I wouldn't consent until I put on a wig. Harm stayed with us awhile and then went home to visit with the other children and do some things for them."

Harmon recalled the evening: "I went back to the hospital that night to see Elaine. It so happened that she was in a two-bed room and the other bed was unoccupied. When visiting hours were over, I looked at the other bed and said, 'It would be great if I could stay here with you tonight.'

" 'Why don't you ask the sister in charge?' Elaine suggested.

" 'Well, I don't know. It's probably against the rules,' I said.

"Just then the sister came in and I said, 'I'd sure like to stay here with Elaine tonight. But I suppose. . . .'

" 'Well, I never,' said the sister, her eyes twinkling. Then looking at us both she continued, 'Mr. Killebrew, a baseball star who spends his day off traveling, deserves some consideration. And Mrs. Killebrew, a wife who's just gone through what she has, who wants her man beside her through the night, must love the gentleman very much. I'll tell you what. Mr. Killebrew can just climb into that empty bed, and I'll see that no one bothers either one of you.'

"Well, there we were, happy and contented in the same room where we could talk and enjoy each other's companionship.

"Then bad luck struck again. You'd never guess what happened. It was warm in the room, and the air got so hot that I couldn't sleep, so I got up and opened the window. The result? Elaine caught cold and developed a cough. Everytime she started to cough the pain was dreadful, and she said it felt like her stitches were coming apart. I got so panicky that I signalled the nurses who came running with some cough medicine. I just couldn't stand the thought of Elaine's coughing too hard and having to go back into surgery for repair work.

"I left early the next morning, Tuesday, to rejoin the club, and played a game that night.

Elaine stayed in the hospital for nine days. She said, "I was really quite nervous when I thought of going home and taking care of our five children. Kathy was still in diapers and Shawn was barely three years old. In addition, we had to arrange to leave for Minneapolis in a month.

"There were also some other problems. I wanted so much to nurse Erin, but the Caesarean made it inadvisable. I was also so weak that it was nearly a month before I could even lift her.

"Fortunately, I had two kind and efficient women

help me. Mrs. Larimer our regular baby sitter stayed with the children while I was in the hospital. And after that, Mrs. Huegnot lived with us and accompanied us to Minneapolis.

"Finally, I felt well enough to do some things that didn't require lifting, and I planted a row of flowers along the fence, a job that I perform every spring.

"Everything was going well there; so on the first day of June we all flew to Minneapolis."

When Harmon returned to the team, the Twins began to win consistently. On May 10th they defeated the White Sox and took over first place.

From that time on, and through the month of June, the Twins and the White Sox fought for possession of the top spot.

During this stretch it became obvious to Mele, the players, and the fans, that Killebrew was becoming the acknowledged team leader. It wasn't by being talkative, but rather through his quiet example and unselfishness —his being willing to do what was best for the team.

One example of this took place in mid-June. The Twins were playing in the Detroit Tigers Stadium, a ball field that is known for its short right-field; the players call it a "front porch." At this time Killebrew was playing first base, but the club had an able back-up first baseman named Don Mincher warming the bench. Mincher was a lefthander and a strong pull hitter whose favorite target was rightfield fences. Feeling that Don would strengthen the team's hitting in this situation, Killebrew went to Mele and said, "Sam, if you think Mincher would help the club with his left-handed swing, I'll be glad to switch to third base so he can play first."

Mele looked thoughtful. "Thanks Harm," he said. "I'll think about it."

A few days later, the manager made the shift.

Killebrew's unselfish example influenced the other players, and they all united in a team effort. Pitcher, Jim Grant, who was bothered with arthritis in his knees, volunteered to start and relieve in games. Jim Kaat insisted on taking his regular turn on the mound, even though he had tendonitis in his arm. Zoilo Versalles—handicapped with a pulled groin muscle, two leg bruises, and a sore foot, still covered the area at short stop like a blanket. Pascual pitched despite a pulled back muscle. Battey refused to let repeated injuries keep him from catching. Swollen knees didn't keep Oliva from playing; and several others suffered ailments that sidelined them for short periods of time. Allison fractured a wrist. Jerry Kindall hurt a hip; Jim Hall wrenched a knee; and Dave Boswell developed mononucleosis.

Still, the Twins kept winning with every man contributing his share. At one period of time, injuries were so numerous that Mele was using relief pitchers as starters, and went eight days in a row with a different infield alignment each day.

Despite these troubles, the Twins were leading the league by three and one-half games at the All-Star break.

Minnesota fans were delighted to have the All-Star game played in Metropolitan Stadium for the first time, and the game was sold out weeks in advance. Killebrew played for the seventh time in an All-Star game and hit a homerun, but the National League team won 6 to 5. Other Twins who appeared in the game were Battey, Grant, Hall, Oliva and Versalles.

The Twins' team spirit was again apparent when they defeated the Yankees on July 12th. The New Yorkers were leading 5 to 4 in the last of the ninth. Then with two out, Killebrew came up with Rich Rollins on base. Pete Mikkelson, the Yankee pitcher, got the count to three and two on Harmon and was one pitch away from defeating the Twins. Then he tried to blow a fast ball past the "Killer." You guessed it! Killebrew swung and parked it in left field for a gamewinning homer.

The homerun was Harmon's sixteenth of the season, but it was a memorable one because it strengthened the Twins first-place lead to five games and virtually eliminated the Yankees, always a Twins nemesis, from the pennant race.

The Minnesota players stood up and cheered as Killebrew circled the bases, converging on him with mauling affection when he entered the dugout.

It appeared that the team had it made. They continued winning, and August 1st were still five games ahead of Baltimore and Cleveland, their closest rivals. Harmon's swing was as sweet as ever, and the entire club was confident that this was their year.

Suddenly, on August 2nd, misfortune struck Killebrew again. The Twins were playing Baltimore at Metropolitan Stadium and were leading 2 to 1 in the sixth, when Baltimore centerfield Russ Snyder came to the plate. He swung and hit a slow roller down the third base line. Rich Rollins charged it and fired the ball to Killebrew at first base. The throw went to the home plate side of the base and Killebrew reached out with his left arm to grab it. The ball and Snyder arrived at the same moment, and Russ smashed into Harmon's outstretched arm with all the force of a Florida hurricane. The sound of the collision could be heard on the top row of the stadium, and the fans held their breath in terror as Killebrew writhed in agony on the ground. There, lying disabled on the field, was the man who was one of the key players in the Twins' bid for the pennant. The loyal rooters knew that his injury, added to those of other players, might well end any title hopes for the season.

Things around him appeared as a blurred mass of color as Killebrew was gently lifted onto a stretcher and carried off the field. Searing pain was running through his left arm. Upon examination, Dr. Proffit learned that Harmon had suffered a complete dislocation of the left elbow. The stricken player steeled himself as Proffit pulled the elbow back into place. Later, X-rays showed no fracture, and the doctor patted him on the back. "Don't worry Harm, you'll be back in the lineup in a couple of weeks."

That night was one of torment. Harmon couldn't sleep.

Elaine did everything possible to relieve his pain, but it seemed to get worse, and the next day the elbow was swollen to twice its normal size. Dr. Proffit looked at it again and reassured Killebrew that it would be all right.

But Harmon was worried, and he told the doctor, "My swinging power comes from my left arm, and I just use the right one to guide my bat. I sure hope it will be straight again."

Later, when asked about the injury, Killebrew said:

"It was really bad. It was the most painful thing I'd ever experienced. All the nerves were torn in the elbow, right where the crazy bone is located. I thought I might be through as a player."

But Harmon's courage is not easily shaken. He was not through.

Although he sat out the next 48 games, the elbow mended and Killebrew returned to the lineup in September.

Today, his left arm is as straight as it ever was, and his remarkable recovery can be attributed to three things: Harmon's great faith that he would recover full use of his arm, Elaine's constant encouragement, and the skillful therapy of Doc Lentz.

The good Doc really went to work on the elbow. He made a balloon cast for it "to be sure it would be straight," and then worked with the arm every day to help Harmon regain his strength in it.

Killebrew's injury served to unite the team more than ever. At the time he was injured, he was hitting .280, and was leading the league in RBI's with 70, and in homeruns with 22. Pascual who had an 8 to 3 pitching record was also out with torn back muscles. So the other players had their work cut out for them in order to keep winning.

Mele gave them a pep talk, saying in essence, "We can still win. We'll just have to try harder!"

Bob Fowler, Minneapolis Tribune sportswriter, commented on the talk:

"Mele, telling the team to win without Killebrew was like King Arthur telling his knights to go into battle without Sir Lancelot."

Doc Lentz gives Killebrew therapy for his dislocated elbow, 1965

But the Twins did continue to win. Their motto, pasted on the bulletin board, was: "A hero a day keeps the contenders away."

They lived up to it. In each game a different player did what was needed to win.

Don Mincher took over at first base as though he had never been away. Squad members Sandy Valdespino, Jerry Kindall, Frank Quilici, Joe Nossek and Jerry Zimmerman, who had been relatively unnoticed, made headlines with their play. "Team effort became the theme of the Twins. And they won game after game with final-inning heroics (34 by one run) or in the final time at bat." ("Decade at the Met," p. 14)

Harmon sat on the bench as his teammates battled for the pennant, and although inwardly frustrated, his dugout comments and encouragement helped feed the team's winning spirit.

The Twins clinched the American League pennant on September 19, 1965 in Washington, and it was a thrilling first for Minnesota fans and most of the players.

On September 23rd, Harmon returned to the lineup wondering if he would ever have the strength to hit another homerun. The answer came five days later, on September 28th, when he swung with all his might at a fast ball and almost held his breath as he pulled the bat around with his left arm. For a moment he sensed a fleeting weakness, but his elbow held, and the ball went crashing into the stands. He hit two more homeruns before the season ended and finished with twenty-five. He batted .269 for the year and had batted 75 runners in. Tony Oliva won the league batting championship and Zoilo Versalles was named the Most Valuable Player in the American League.

At last the Twins were the American League Champions—looking forward to meeting the Los Angeles Dodgers in the World Series.

world series fever

20

Have you ever been bitten by the World Series bug? In the fall of 1965, this infectious little creature circulated throughout the state of Minnesota and invaded surrounding states until an epidemic raged throughout the upper mid-west. There was much talk about the ailment, but the only prescription that seemed to cure it was to obtain four tickets to Metropolitan Stadium and use one a day until relief came.

This wasn't easy to do because tickets were as hard to get as an invitation to the White House. Unless you had "inside connections," the procedure was as follows:

Send a certified check or money order weeks in advance to the Twins office, and then pray that fate would favor you with the "luck of the draw."

Such applicants did all sorts of things to catch the eyes of workers opening envelopes received. One of the largest envelopes received was covered with cutouts of baseball players, baseballs, and pictures of Twins officials. Another had the picture of a shapely girl in a revealing outfit pasted on the envelope—undoubtedly calculated to impress a male worker.

Ultimately, only 23,000 persons out of well over a 100,000 applicants received the coveted cardboards.

We applied for several grandstand seats and wound up with two in the rightfield bleachers. The tickets came in sets of four for all home games; so I alternated taking my wife, Elise, and our two teen-age daughters, Julie and Jill with me. Although our seats weren't the best, an unexpected dividend that resulted from their attending the Series was that the girls in the family no longer made resentful noises when I wanted to watch televised games the following baseball season. Sometimes they even sat down and watched with me.

Another result of the Series was a shot in the arm to the economy of the area. More than 25,000 World Series visitors packed the Twin Cities to see the first two games, and hotel owners had to place some of their overflow of guests in neighboring Wisconsin. The money taken in from the visiting fans was estimated at a minimum of $50 a person per day, receipting a staggering total of five million dollars for the four days when games were played at the Met, and these figures did not include money spent for retail shopping or the spending of sports fans who didn't need overnight accommodations.

But back to the Series itself. The Dodgers were expected to win from the start, and the odds-makers posted them as 7-5 favorites. This was because they had two pitchers who were considered unbeatable. One was Sandy Koufax, rated by many as the greatest pitcher in baseball—so good that he had thrown more strikeouts than innings pitched. The other was Don Drysdale—known as one of the toughest competitors in the game as was demonstrated when he refused to miss a pitching turn after being hit in the face by a line drive in Chicago earlier in the year. The Dodgers also had Ron Perranoski, a reliever who "did nothing but get opposing batters out." And there was also Maury Wills, their fleet base runner who could break up any game with a needed run once he got on first base.

Despite the ominous Dodger buildup, the Twins weren't about to roll over and play dead. They had some stars of their own including Harmon Killebrew—home run king, Tony Oliva—American League Batting champion, Zoilo Versalles—phenomenal fielding shortstop, pitcher Jim Kaat, a never-say-die competitor, and Mudcat Grant, billed as "the American League's winningest pitcher," whose jiving rhythm on the pitching mound was as effective as it was entertaining.

The interest in the first game reached fever pitch. Over 1000 fans lined up right after midnight on the morning of the game in order to buy standing room tickets scheduled to be sold at eleven a.m. In order to endure 30-degree temperatures, made more miserable by a few drops of rain, they brought sleeping bags, blankets, salami sandwiches, and hot coffee.

The temperature went up to a sunny 65 degrees by game time, and when Vice-President Hubert Humphrey, the number one Minnesota fan, tossed out the first ball, a sell-out crowd of 47,797 had jammed the stands.

The first game was a honey, not because the Twins won 8 to 2, but due to the way the victory was accomplished. Don Drysdale, the Dodgers pitcher, had started by striking out three Twins hitters and things looked gloomy for the Minnesotans until Don Mincher lit the victory fuse in the second inning with a homerun into the rightfield bleachers. This led to a Twins explosion good for six runs in the third—highlighted by Versalle's homer with two on.

Twin hurler Mudcat Grant pitched a steady game spacing ten hits while walking one and striking out five. And he was backed by sparkling fielding plays all around him.

Harmon, who usually avoids making comments, made some statements after the Twins win which were representative of the team's thinking.

"You get a little tired of hearing how we were going to

Harmon Killebrew chats with Dodger pitching star, Sandy Koufax, at

SCHARFMAN

Metropolitan Stadium during World Series, October, 1965

lose four straight and how we were overmatched in the Series," he said. "I know that one victory doesn't win a World Series, but it was nice to show everybody that we could beat one of the best pitchers in baseball."

In the second game, the Twins bombed Sandy Koufax to win 5 to 1.

Tom Briere, Minneapolis Tribune Staff Writer, started his report of the game as follows:

> The amazing Minnesota Twins made believers of the baseball world—particularly the National League Champion Los Angeles Dodgers—by defeating sainted Sandy Koufax 5-1 in the second game of the World Series Thursday.
>
> At least for one day, Jim Kaat of the Twins turned out to be a better left-handed pitcher than Koufax, according to a vote of 48,700 record-setting spectators at Metropolitan Stadium.

In the win, Jim Kaat pitched a strong game, scattering seven hits. Koufax also pitched well and was living up to his invincible reputation until the 6th inning, when Oliva and Killebrew blasted base hits that gave the Twins a 2 to 0 lead. In the 7th, Koufax was driven to the showers, and the Minnesotans went on to victory.

The Twins again sparkled in the field, but there was one defensive play that stood out above all of the others, a catch by left fielder Bob Allison in the fifth inning which Mele thought "probably saved the game for the Twins."

The score was 0-0 at the time, with singling Ron Fairly at first base. Then Jim Lefebvre, one of the Dodger's power hitters, slashed a vicious liner into the leftfield corner. Allison took off toward the ball like a shot. Seeing that he couldn't reach it by running alone, he left his feet and dived headfirst extending his gloved left hand out as far as he could reach. He managed to backhand the ball inches above the ground, and then his great momentum spun him around; and clutching the pellet he sat upright and slid several feet across the soft turf in a splash of water and mud.

Spectators, including American League President Joe Cronin and Calvin Griffith, called it one of the greatest catches in baseball history.

Harmon Killebrew watching a World Series game, 1965 with Bob Allison and Sam Mele

Harmon Killebrew from his vantage point at third base said, "It was the greatest catch I've ever seen!"

I have no argument with the above statements. I also witnessed the catch and considered it the equivalent to moving a mountain with a faith the size of a grain of mustard seed. Allison had the faith, and through sheer determination he moved the mountain.

The Twins left in good spirits for the third game to be played at Chavez Ravine in Los Angeles. Mele was pleased so far with the pitching and the club's general all-around play. He was also elated because Killebrew who had been sidelined with a dislocated elbow was taking his normal cut at the ball—batting .500 with three hits in six times at the plate.

Killebrew, when interviewed, said, "I'm getting a real good rip at the ball. The elbow isn't giving me any trouble. I don't care whether I hit any out of the park or not, if I can help the team win in other ways."

So the Minnesota Twins departed from Metropolitan Stadium for the journey to Sunset Boulevard. Their two jets carried a jubilant party. The players relaxed while their wives, club officials, and guests sang songs.

Kim Whitney, a Minneapolis rooter, wrote a song that went something like this—with variations:

Pack up all my care and woe,
Here we go, singing low,
Bye, bye Dodgers.

Koufax couldn't make the grade,
Drysdale hit them with a spade,
Bye, bye Dodgers.

Sportswriters never seem to understand us,
Oh, how often all these bums have panned us,

Going to California,
We'll beat them away,
Like we did today,
Dodgers, bye, bye.

The traveling group was welcomed to Los Angeles by

a band, and as the players filed into the Continental Hotel, Bunny Girls from the local Playboy Club made an arch of bats for them to walk under.

The Twins had some anxiety about playing in Chavez Ravine, the Dodgers stadium. They had played there, not too successfully, against the Los Angeles Angels, and had found the infield surface to be extremely hard. They knew the Dodgers were used to it and had learned to make the most of it by deliberately striking down on the pitches so the ball would skid through opposing infielders' gloves—or bounce over their heads. The outfield fences were also farther away than those at the friendly Met.

In the first game, the change of scenery seemed to bother them, and the Twins lost 4 to 0. Their starting pitcher Camilo Pascual pitched fairly well but his sweeping curve ball wasn't working. On the other hand, Claude Osteen of the Dodgers stilled the Twins' bats with a five-hit shut out.

In the second game at Chavez Ravine, the Dodgers employed their bunt-and-run style of baseball to force the Twins into damaging errors. They used their hard-surfaced infield as if it were a pool table, to push and bunt hits in all directions. As a result, the Twins came unglued defensively and failed to cover bases, threw to the wrong base, missed the cutoff man, and seemed to forget baseball fundamentals. Twins hurler Jim Grant was driven to cover in the sixth inning.

Meanwhile, Don Drysdale reversed his losing decision over the Mudcat. With the exception of Killebrew's 400 foot homerun to left in the fifth inning and Oliva's 385 foot wallop to right in the sixth, he had little trouble in breezing to a 7 to 2 victory.

On Monday, October 11, 1965, the Dodgers won their third straight game and took a 3 to 2 lead in the World Series. Sandy Koufax, the ace of their staff, was in magnificent form. He scattered four hits and struck out ten batters in pacing his team to a 7 to 0 win. Meanwhile, the Los Angeles team hit Twins starter Jim Kaat and relievers Dave

Boswell and Jim Perry like they owned them, banging out 14 hits!

In commenting on the games in Los Angeles, Sam Mele said, "The Dodgers are content just to hit the ball in the infield and run like jack rabbits. They handle the bat and maneuver the ball so well that they force us to make mistakes we don't normally make."

The Twins were glad to leave California. In the three games there, they had only collected 14 hits and had a miserable batting average of .157.

Elaine Killebrew had some interesting things to say about her World Series visit in Los Angeles.

"Although our tickets cost twelve dollars apiece, we had trouble even seeing the game. I was even more disgusted when I learned more about the ticket situation. I was standing in front of the ballpark waiting to meet my brother, who was flying down from Modesto, when I saw some scalpers selling tickets. They were practically giving tickets away that were in the same section I had to pay such high prices for. However, I had an experience which more than made up for it, one that I shall always treasure.

"Gordon and Topsy Ritz, Minneapolis friends of ours, were at the Series. After the first game they said they had been invited to visit with Rosalind Russell, the movie star, and asked me to go along. Harm had a TV show after the game, so he couldn't make it. I was thrilled to be entertained in her beautiful home. She was most gracious—a very lovely person. While we were there she served sparkling cold drinks and delicious hors d'oeuvres.

"After our visit, she had her chauffeur drive us back to the hotel.

"During our stay in her house we had mentioned how bad our ballpark seats were, and a short time later, she sent us more desirable seats with this note:

> Dear Mrs. Killebrew,
>
> Enclosed are 2 tickets for the game; I hope they are good seats—at least better than those you have had. See you in Minneapolis.
>
> Rosalind Russell,
> Cheers for your husband.

After the Twins had departed from their Chavez Ravine disaster area and arrived at friendly Metropolitan Stadium, they felt confident they could win the championship. And when the games resumed, Sam Mele called on Jim Grant in an effort to even the Series. Although he was nursing a heavy cold and felt "lousy," he responded in brilliant fashion and pitched the Twins to a 5 to 1 victory with a neat six-hitter. The Twins and Dodgers battled to an 0 to 0 stalemate until the fourth inning when Bob Allison sent Minnesota ahead with a two-run homer off Claude Osteen.

Then Grant turned the Twins fans to hysterics in the sixth. In that inning, Bob Allison drew a walk with one out and then stole second as Don Mincher fanned for out number two. At this point Dodger manager, Walt Alston, ordered an intentional walk to Frank Quilici, feeling it was safer to pitch to Grant who was the next hitter.

The Mudcat spoiled the strategy by whaling reliefer Howie Reed's first pitch 392 feet into the left-center pavilion. Never have I seen a man more ecstatic with joy. Grant jumped up into the air with glee, danced around the diamond and jumped jubilantly on home plate after rounding the bases. At that moment Jim Grant could have run for and been elected to any political office in the state of Minnesota. He had saved the Twins in their "sudden death" game and given the fans new hope for the morrow.

In the final and deciding game of the Series, the Twins again had to face Sandy Koufax, the pitcher who was a paragon of perfection, the control artist who had become the first pitcher in the history of the game to hurl four no-hit, no-run games.

Opposing hitters spoke of Koufax in reverent tones, but the Twins were not shaken by his impressive image. They had already beaten Sandy once in the Series and felt they could do it again. Jim Kaat was going to oppose Koufax on the mound, and the team felt he would battle him with his last breath for the win.

Koufax was shaky in the early innings, and the Twins

threatened to break the game open in the fifth. With one out, Frank Quilici doubled to left, and pinch-hitter Rich Rollins walked. This brought the dangerous swinging Versalles to the plate. With the count one and two, Zoilo pulled Sandy's pitch just inside third base for what appeared to be a sure double—certain to knock in two runs and tie the score. But the Dodgers third baseman, 37-year-old Jim Gilliam backhanded the ball while falling down, and scrambled to his feet in time to force Quilici at third.

Again the Twins threatened when Killebrew singled with one out in the ninth, but Koufax reared back and struck out the next two batters, and the Dodgers won the game 2 to 0, taking the Series four games to three.

The experts say the Twins were beaten by the greatest pitcher in baseball, and after the game Sam Mele remarked, "This Koufax is something. We've never faced anyone better."

So—that's the way the Twins lost the World Series before a record crowd of 50,596 baseball fans. The Minnesota rooters were disappointed but proud of the way their team battled right down to the finish.

Killebrew, according to the paper, got six hits in twenty-one at bats and one homerun during the World Series—a batting average of .286.

One might conjecture as to his showing had he not been recently injured.

Mrs. Sam Mele (Connie) helped her husband bounce back from losing by presenting him with a seven-pound boy, their fifth child, three days after the Series ended. The lad was expected to arrive at the start of the World Series, but obligingly delayed his coming so his dad could concentrate on the Dodgers.

great expectations. but a late start

21

The Killebrews were happy to get back to Ontario and relax after the strain of the World Series. Harmon enjoyed being with Elaine and the children. They spent many happy hours together—being a family.

Elaine is a staunch member of The Church of Jesus Christ of Latter-day Saints and a great granddaughter of Swedish immigrants who were converted in their native land. After joining, they left their possessions behind, crossed the ocean, and undertook the perilous trek across the continent to the West, beginning a new life near the geographical center of their chosen belief. With this heritage, and the additional religious training she received as a child, Elaine has always believed religious activity to be an important part of life.

In order to guide their children with propriety, the Killebrews had followed the recommendation of her Church and used one night a week as a family night during which prayer, songs, and religious discussions took place—followed by games and refreshments.

Although Harmon was not a member of Elaine's Church, he felt these family nights were choice occasions and enjoyed participating in them.

One evening, in February, 1966, he put down the sports-section of the newspaper, turned to Elaine who was busy crocheting and said, "Honey, I've decided to join your Church."

Elaine hastily put aside the sweater she was making and asked, "Oh, Harm! Are you sure you want to?"

"Without any doubt," replied Harmon. "The way of life your Church teaches seems to make sense to me."

"Darling," said Elaine smiling through her tears, "This is the greatest thing you've ever said to me."

"Do you mean that?" asked Harmon teasingly.

"Of course—I mean next to when you asked me to marry you," Elaine put in hurriedly.

"That's better," grinned Harmon.

Arrangements were made, and Harmon was baptized into the Church on February 21, 1966. The mode of baptism is to have the candidate, clothed in white, step down into a baptismal font and after the appropriate prayer, be immersed in the water. He is later confirmed a member by Elders who hold priesthood authority.

Harmon, in looking back upon the event, said, "My life has markedly changed since that time, and I feel that I have greater insight regarding the purpose of our existence here."

Since that day, Harmon has quietly and faithfully lived according to the precepts of his Church. He has never tried to impose his religious thinking upon others, and neither has he ever been ashamed to be identified as a member of the Church.

During the late stages of the 1970 baseball season, the Twins were playing in Boston, and Harmon learned that one of the general authorities of the Church, Elder Paul H. Dunn, was supervising church missionary work there. He immediately got on the phone and said, "Elder Dunn, would it be possible in your schedule to come down

Sunday morning and talk to the Minnesota Twins Ball Club?"

Elder Dunn replied, "I'd be honored, Harmon; what can I do?"

"Just tell them about our religious principles."

Then Elder Dunn asked, "How did you get a religious program arranged?"

"I'm the chairman of our devotional services for that day," Harmon answered.

So Elder Dunn met with the players and their wives and discussed the realities of life and meaningful living in the quiet atmosphere of an upper room in the hotel where the Twins were staying.*

When the Twins began spring training in 1966, their fans had great expectations for the coming season. They reasoned that the club had won the American League pennant despite a rash of injuries the year before; so now with everyone sound, they should repeat as pennant winners and then go on and win the World Series. But the sailing was not to be that smooth.

Grant, Versalles, Oliva, and Pascual wanted raises and couldn't come to terms with Griffith. Calvin said their demands were unrealistic.

Jim Grant had organized a song and dance act called "The Mudcat and His Kittens," so he told Griffith that business was so good maybe he shouldn't rejoin the team.

Calvin shrewdly replied, "Jim, you *are* a pretty fair singer. Maybe you'd do better working in night clubs."

The holdouts all eventually signed but so late that they didn't get all of the conditioning they needed during the exhibition season.

The management's biggest concern was to find a second baseman; they had several candidates trying out for the job. One of them, Bernie Allen, whose knee was sound for

---

*Adapted from "Be Not Ashamed," by Paul H. Dunn, September 29, 1970. Speeches of the Year, Brigham Young University Press, Provo, Utah.

the first time since surgery in 1964, was determined to regain his former pivot position.

The team's general situation was hopeful for several reasons. Top relievers, Johnny Klippstein and Al Worthington were back with the club. Jim Roland, an outstanding rookie pitcher was up from Denver, and catcher Earl Battey was in good shape.

Sam Mele, who had directed the Twins to the pennant in 1965, had not let success go to his head and was still quiet on the field and patient with his men. Despite his additional pennant and World Series earnings of the previous season, he had not introduced caviar into his diet but still ate his usual bowl of hard-boiled eggs after each day's drill.

Harmon, who had signed for $60,000, was in good condition and expected to have an outsanding season.

The perennial question popped up, "Do you predict that you will hit 60 home runs this season?"

And once more came the modest reply, "I honestly don't know. I aim to cut down on strikeouts and try for 40 homeruns."

If Harmon did have any other secret goals he refused to advertise them.

While the battle was being waged for the second base spot with Allen, Rollins, Kindall, Quilici, Tovar, and Renick participating, word came that a rookie second baseman was scheduled to be discharged from the Marines and would join the club in early March. At the time, this news didn't cause much of a stir. But later on, this rookie, Rod Carew, was to become a superstar.

The Twins didn't play much like pennant winners when exhibition games started, and they lost seven straight before they finally defeated the Yankess 5 to 1 on March 18th.

Harmon started hitting homeruns right away, and Bob Allison said, "I've never seen Harm hit so many homeruns so early before."

Still, Killebrew would not predict a record breaking

year for himself, and his modesty won him the title of the "Bashful Basher of Power Alley."

Despite their dismal start, the Twins finally got going and won nine of their last thirteen exhibition games.

The 1966 opening game offered a first for the fans and the players. Before it started, the American League Pennant for 1965, a beautiful banner, was raised on the flagstaff and took its place beside Old Glory.

The Twins won the opener from Kansas City 2 to 1. Mudcat Grant twirled a sharp six-hitter and Cuban Sandy Valdespino, a rotund five-eight dynamo whose distinguishing characteristic was a perpetual chuckle, drove in both runs.

In the second game, the 5 to 3 victory over Kansas City featured an All-Cuban cast as Valdespino and Oliva drove in all five runs with homers and Pascual was the winning pitcher.

The players' early wins further endeared them to the hearts of their fans, and once again they became the talk of the town, with various and assorted experts predicting "a World's Championship this year."

The team members and their activities became a topic for a number of writers. For example, Barbara Flanagan, popular Minneapolis Star columnist, had the following to say after a reportorial tour of the Met:

"I've discovered that the phone number to call from the Twins dugout in 327 if you want to be connected with the bullpen to ask for a relief pitcher. There are all sorts of other conveniences around like an automatic washing machine in the waiting room for the Twins wives.

"Do you think Elaine Killebrew does the family washing there while waiting for Harmon to hit a homerun?"

After all of this adulation, the Twins began to lose. Harmon only hit one homerun in 14 games, and a general batting slump hit the team.

Sam Mele blasted the players for stupid base running. And the papers printed such headlines as, "Foes Slow Twins Go-Go Attack to a Trot."

But the club found a stopper. Mudcat Grant, his knees aching with arthritis, came in time and again to pitch a win and stop a losing streak.

The management began to disagree about the best place to play Killebrew. Griffith wanted to keep him in left field; Mele desired to experiment with him at several positions.

This constant shifting caused one sportswriter to say, "Harmon's a $60,000 homerun slugger, and he's being moved around like a dime-a-dozen utility man."

Killebrew's only comment was, "I'll play where they want me to play."

While Harmon was battling to help the Twins win on the field, Elaine was battling a problem at home. The summer had begun in a beautiful way. She had a lovely girl, Cheril Wilson, accompany her to Minneapolis to help care for the children and provide companionship. Their family had found a beautiful house to rent in suburban Mendota Heights. It was the home of a Dr. Foreman who had been called into the army. It so happened that he is a son of Mr. T. C. Foreman, President of the Foreman and Clark men's clothing chain. His company had been a sponsor for Harmon's television show, and he graciously arranged with his son to have the Killebrews move into the house.

With a lovely home to live in and Cheril to help her while Harmon was traveling with the team, Elaine looked forward to a relaxing and pleasant summer. But things didn't work out that way. It suddenly became necessary for her to undergo surgery.

Elaine told me she would always remember that summer.

"I went to a hospital in St. Paul and had an operation for a deviated septum. The doctors believed this separation between my nostrils was out of line because it had been damaged when I was born.

"After the surgery was performed, I looked an absolute sight for about six weeks. I had bruises all around my eyes and nose, and the whites of my eyes were completely red; everywhere I went, people stared at me; I felt sure everyone thought I had been in a fight.

"But that was not really the horrible part of it. The things that tortured me were the wiring and the cast. I was wired from the center part of my nose down through my upper lip, and the wires were wrapped around my teeth. And the cast! My nose was all packed and also had a cast on it. I had a miserable time trying to eat or breathe. And until those wires were taken out and the cast was removed, I felt like a caged animal that was being deprived of sufficient food and air."

"A bright spot in that summer was the wonderful neighbors we had," Harmon continued. "We had met Bud and Georgianna Cursalle the summer before, and they are still dear friends. During the summer of 1966, we were again fortunate in having Dr. Leonard Michienzi and his family live down the block from us. Dr. Michienzi has since become the Twins club physician. He raises a beautiful garden each summer and very generously shares the vegetables he grows with his friends. As a result he provided us with some delicious foods."

Harmon did everything he could to help Elaine while she was recovering from her operation and he also did everything in his power to help the team win.

During the 1966 season, the club's coaches made a tremendous contribution to help keep the team on the winning path. One of them was pitching coach Johnny Sain. John's coaching approach was to give the pitchers confidence in themselves. He taught them to think positively and to feel that they could control the game when they were out on the mound. He also taught them what he called a hard curve, one that could be thrown with more speed and with a short, sharp break. The Jims of the pitching staff, Jim Kaat, Jim Merritt, and Jim Perry, all seemed to develop more self-confidence and a great bag of pitching tricks under Sain's tutelage.

Sain was very protective of his pitchers. He resented any other staff member saying anything critical about them and insisted that no comments be directed toward them when they were out on the mound.

Billy Martin, the third base coach, also made an immeasurable contribution to the team. He, like Sain, had also been a big factor in the Twins' pennant drive the year before. Billy had been hired by Griffith in 1965, "to light a fire under the team," and that he did. From his third base coaching spot he was constantly encouraging, needling, and doing everything he could to impart his fire to the players on the field.

Martin also spent considerable time working individually with infielders. He established good rapport with the Cuban players and did much to help Versalles, Tovar and Carew develop their latent talents.

Jim Lemon, the lanky batting and first base coach, was also extremely helpful. In his quiet and unassuming manner he drew from his great store of knowledge to give many helpful batting hints to the Twins hitters.

Jim who now has his own business, is one of Harmon's most highly-esteemed friends, and I had the privilege of chatting with him in December, 1970.

Jim said, "The thing that impressed me most about Harmon was his supreme dedication to the game. And he wasn't trying to be successful for monetary reasons—but simply because he wanted to do his best.

"Success didn't come easy to him; he earned it because of his sound mental attitude—always figuring out and planning how to improve. He reminded me of Hank Greenburg who also had this kind of attitude.

"I remember having an interesting experience with him during 1965, the year the Twins won the pennant. I was the batting coach, and we were scheduled to play a game with the Yankees about July 10th that would have a crucial effect on the pennant race. Before the game, I told Harm he didn't seem to be hitting the ball as hard as usual. During the game, he hit a long homerun in the bottom of the eighth to win for us. When he came to the dugout he asked, 'Did I hit that hard enough?'

"I tried to keep a straight face and said, 'Yes, I suppose that will pass.' "

Harmon has lunch with the Twins most renowned fan, Vice-President Hubert H. Humphrey, 1967. Manager Cal Ermer in background.

Harmon visiting patients in the Veterans Hospital, Minneapolis, 1966

Killebrew signing autographs at Metropolitan Stadium, 1966

Hal Naragon kept everyone happy as coach in the bullpen, and the players seemed to be relaxed around him.

So the Twins had sound and understanding management; nevertheless, the team couldn't win consistently.

In May, Killebrew and Oliva both began hitting the longball with regularity, and the team started to win more games.

On May 22, 1965, the "Bashful Basher" slugged the 300th homerun of his career, yet the Twins lost the game to New York on errors.

Harmon showed me that number 300 homerun ball one day when we were visiting the Killebrews. The batboys had retrieved it for him, and Ted Uhlaender, who is a skilled artist, had decorated it attractively.

Something should also be said about Uhlaender's play during the 1966 season. He was called up from Denver during the year and installed as the regular centerfielder on June 20th. Ted scintillated on defense and ranged far and wide to field the ball. He would often leap horizontally and come up with an unlikely catch. At the plate, he was a spray hitter and batted at a .284 clip from August 27th until the season ended.

On May 26th, Harmon hit homerun number 301 to win an overtime victory for the Twins against the Boston Red Sox in Fenway Park. One of his longest circuit clouts of the season was a 476 foot drive on June 21st.

During the season, relief pitcher Al Worthington became known as "The Saver" and was credited with exactly half of the team's total of 22 "saves."

Despite these individual heroics, the team couldn't get going as it had the previous year and consequently, was the target of much criticism.

Through the barrage of negative comments directed toward the team, Killebrew still remained in good standing with the sportswriters.

In mid-June, Charlie Johnson, Sports Editor of the Minneapolis Star, wrote:

"Harmon Killebrew is a mighty valuable man, for my

money. He is willing to play anywhere, at first, third, or in left field. And he gives it the good, old college try wherever he plays."

By August 13, 1966, Harmon had played in all 116 games, done a tremendous job, and was recognized as the team spark plug. It became quite common for Twins fans to say, "As Harmon goes, so go the Twins."

On July 4th, the club finally caught fire and came down the stretch at the fastest clip in the major leagues, winning 54 of 84 games for a percentage of .643.

Killebrew did his share in the winning drive and during a thirty day period, from August 11th to September 12th, hit 11 homeruns and drove in 36.

But the winning streak came too late. Their chief rivals, the Baltimore Orioles, had a major lead in the race for the pennant. So, even though the Twins cut the Orioles' margin by 10 games, they still couldn't overtake them, and when the season ended the Minnesotans had to settle for second money.

Harmon had another good year at bat with a .281 average. He hit 39 homeruns and batted in 110 runs.

There was some speculation as to whether Sam Mele would be rehired for 1967, but Calvin Griffith expressed confidence in him and renewed his contract. So the Twins disbanded for the season, confident that their final stretch winning momentum would carry over into 1967, and bring them another pennant.

Elaine had to return to Ontario before the end of the playing season to put Cameron and Kenny back into school. But at the end of that summer there was a plane strike so she arranged to drive to Ontario.

When the time came for Elaine and the children to leave, nothing but a spacious car would accommodate their group, so they traveled in a station-wagon. Even so, the trip to Ontario was crowded with Elaine and the five Killebrew children, Cheril Wilson, and the family's Shetland sheep dog, Candy.

now and forever

22

The winter of 1967 was a happy one for Harmon and Elaine Killebrew—they got married again.

Before you jump to the conclusion that they quarreled, got a quickie divorce in Mexico, then patched up their differences and remarried, let me explain what really happened.

It had long been Elaine's dream that she might some day be married to Harmon in one of the Temples of The Church of Jesus Christ of Latter-day Saints—for time and eternity.

Now you may think," What does this mean, and how is it accomplished?"

Let's answer these questions in reverse order.

To be eligible for marriage in one of the LDS Temples, both must be members in good standing for a specified period of time. This means that both have faithfully practiced Church principles to the extent that the presiding Church authorities in their area can recommend them as worthy to enter the Temple. The man must have, through dedicated activity, risen to the office of Elder in the priesthood.

At the time the Killebrews went to be married in the Temple, Harmon had been a member for the specified period of time. Both were recommended as being worthy.

A convenient Temple was in Cardston, Canada, so the Killebrews went there and had the ceremony performed. This was on November 18, 1967.

Now to answer the second question, "What does this mean"?

The Temple marriage ceremony is simple, but beautiful. The couple clothed in white for the ceremony, goes into a special room called *The Sealing Room.* Here an Elder in the Church, who holds the special authority to perform the marriage ordinance, talks to them, in the presence of witnesses, explaining the purposes of life and eternal marriage. He then performs the marriage ceremony in which he pronounces them man and wife throughout time and eternity.

Church members believe that this covenant which the husband and wife enter into will be binding after mortality.

In recalling their marriage in the Cardston Temple, Elaine said,

"Even though I had been married to Harm for a number of years at the time, and had always loved him dearly, I felt even more married to him after the Temple ceremony."

Harmon said, "The whole thing was a really wonderful experience for us. A spirit and feeling were there that are hard to describe."

Harmon and Elaine were treated royally by other Church members during their visit to Cardston. They stayed at the home of Mr. and Mrs. Bob Sackley. They were invited to speak before several groups, including young men's and young women's banquets, and gatherings of sports enthusiasts. At one function, Don Fullmer, a former World's Boxing Champion was on the same program. The Killebrews also took part in an old-time parade and rode through town in a stagecoach.

In reliving the experience Harmon said, "The people in Cardston are among the finest I've ever met." They have a wonderful community up there."

One young couple who have been friends of the Killebrews for years accompanied them to the Cardston Temple to act as witnesses to the ceremony. They were the Vernon Laws. Vernon is a former Pittsburg Pirate pitching great.

VaNita Law wrote me a note describing her feelings at the time and graciously gave permission to reproduce it here.

> It was truly a wonderful and spiritual experience for us to be with Harmon and Elaine when they went through the temple at Cardston. We knew it was the culmination of a lifelong dream for Elaine. . . .
>
> For Harmon it was a crowning experience to have his lovely wife sealed to him for time and eternity. Life at this time surely takes on new meaning to all who are involved.
>
> To share this love and spiritual experience was such a blessing to us and we are thankful for the opportunity.
>
> For many years we had agreed Harmon would make a good Latter-day Saint, and knew this was one of Elaine's dreams also. So we were delighted when we learned he had been baptized—then this crowning blessing.
>
> Very sincerely,
> Vernon and VaNita Law

Harmon had been unusually busy since the 1966 season closed. Along with several other sports figures, he had spent about three weeks visiting the servicemen in Viet Nam.

When asked why he made the tour, he explained, "We made the trip to Viet Nam to talk to our servicemen . . . and to let them know that we in baseball had not forgotten them."

He and Elaine also made a combined business and pleasure trip to Hawaii.

In January of 1967, when the fans were again beginning to think of the coming baseball season, Killebrew was voted the "Most Valuable Twins Player" by the Twin Cities' baseball writers at their banquet in the St. Paul Hilton Hotel.

Calvin Griffith left no stone unturned in his efforts to

strengthen the Twins for the 1967 pennant race. During the winter, on consecutive days, he completed two of the biggest and most significant trades of the hot-stove league season.

On December 2nd, he obtained the brilliant righthanded pitcher, Dean Chance (former Cy Young Award Winner) from the California Angels in exchange for outfielder Jimmie Hall, first baseman Don Mincher, and relief pitcher Pete Cimino.

A day later he sent pitcher Camilo Pascual and infielder Bernie Allen to the Washington Senators in exchange for their star relief specialist Ron Kline.

His reasoning was that the Twins pitching staff needed strengthening and that the club had several young players in their farm system who appeared ready for major league status and could, with sufficient opportunity to play, fill the shoes of those who had been traded.

Sam Mele felt that the strengthened pitching staff and a revamped coaching crew would enable the Twins to overtake the Baltimore Club in 1967, bringing the pennant back to Minnesota. Early Wynn, one of the most illustrious pitchers in major league history, had joined the coaching staff and was expected to help the pitchers.

January brought headaches to Calvin Griffith; he had given a number of players nice raises, but combined demands of the team caused him finally to say, "I can't do anymore. Our payroll is already the largest in the American League."

Of course there was rebuttal, as well as all kinds of comment about the statement; and the following story went around town:

"Heard about the kid who tried out at the Twins baseball camp? He was strictly from hayseed country, but his fastball zinged and his curve snaked like a cobra. Griffith was impressed.

" 'I like you; I'm going to give you $750 to sign.'

" 'Mr. Griffith,' the yokel boy said coolly, 'If that's all you can offer, I'd rather wait and sign with a major league team.' "

While possible salaries were being discussed, Calvin was asked if Killebrew would eventually reach the $100,000 level.

"If Harm hits about 60 homeruns a year he'll get there," Griffith replied.

Killebrew signed that year for about $70,000.

As the spring training season neared, Sam Mele was optimistic about the Twins' pennant chances. Sportswriters were saying that the Minnesotans had bought the pennant when they obtained Dean Chance, and they asked Mele if he agreed. Sam wouldn't go that far out on a limb, but he did think that the addition of Chance and relief specialist Ron Kline had made the club's staff one of the strongest in the league.

While discussing the coming season, Mele made several interesting statements. There had been some dissension among the coaches the year before; so to prevent it happening again he set down the policy that coaches Martin, Lemon, and Wynn would make their own ground rules—each being in charge of his domain with no interference from others.

Regarding Killebrew, Mele repeated the thinking that other managers had expressed before and usually didn't hold to. "Killebrew is my first baseman," he said. "That's where he's more at home and I'd like to keep him there permanently."

When spring training began in 1967, everyone was in good condition, and things started out well. Killebrew was a day or two late in arriving, and sportswriter Tom Briere made an interesting observation.

"Spring training is lackluster until Harmon Killebrew arrives. He is to the Twins what Babe Ruth, Joe DiMaggio have been, and Mickey Mantle is now, to the Yankees. When he comes to camp everything picks up."

During his first batting practice, Harmon hit a few fly balls, but nothing of homerun proportions.

"My timing is a little off," confessed Killebrew when asked about his hitting.

The Twins started their exhibition series losing three games in a row by scores of 6 to 8 to the Orioles, 1 to 6 and 0 to 3 to the Tigers.

Their first win, 7 to 2 against the Phillies was led by Killebrew and Rollins.

Rod Carew was sparkling at second base, and when Mele was asked about his chances of staying there, he said, "If Carew sticks he'll have to play leap frog over double-A and triple-A ball because his only experience has been with Wilson in the class A Carolina League."

Carew played well enough to stick and become a 30-day experiment. From there he went on to be chosen second baseman for the All-Star team and Rookie of the Year.

The Grapefruit League ended with the Twins' game record standing at 12 wins and 17 losses.

Killebrew hit 9 homeruns and had one of his best spring seasons.

In the opening game of the season, April 11, 1967, Baltimore jumped on Kaat for 4 runs in the first inning defeating Mele's club 6 to 3.

Carew singled his first time up, which seemed to relax him and, he drove out a second hit. When asked how he prepared for his first start in the major leagues, Carew grinned and said, "I went to bed early last night."

Weather conditions were deplorable for the opening home game at the Met. It rained steadily for an hour before starting time.

Jim Klobuchar, popular Minneapolis Star columnist, described what happened this way:

"Calvin Griffith silently gazed at the Western sky. Then he raised his right arm and signaled to the stadium organist to play a few bars of 'Let a Smile be Your Umbrella'.

"The rain stopped.

"Having tamed the waters at the Met, Calvin next week is going to try the Red Sea."

Anyway, the Twins won. Boswell leading them in defeating the Tigers 5 to 3.

Despite the win, the Twins were off to a poor start;

when the game count was one win and four losses, the management accused the players of mental and physical errors, and poor pitching.

There were also some bright spots in their play.

One was on April 20th when Chance pitched a 3 to 2 win against Baltimore. Killebrew got a two-run homer in the 4th and triggered a ninth inning rally with a single, after which Carew knocked in the deciding run.

As the season went into May the club was sputtering badly.

Again a manager's pre-season statement had to be modified, and Killebrew was shifted to third base. Mele was seeking to bolster the team and the move seemed to be the right one. Harmon didn't object but continued his consistent hitting and dependable fielding.

Several other players did their best to get the team into a winning pattern. Rick Reese, who was stationed at first base, was fielding spectacularly and hitting well. And Cesar Tovar, the mighty mite, was playing when needed, all over the field, filling in well at second base, left field, center field, and right field.

Chance and Grant were pitching well, but weren't backed by solid hitting and consequently lost a number of low-scoring games by one-run margins.

In late May the warm weather seemed to rejuvenate the Twins, and Killebrew and Oliva stepped up their pace in leading the hitters.

During this time, catcher Earl Battey was having some physical problems and reserve catcher Jerry Zimmerman—always ready when called upon—stepped into the lineup and sparked the club to four straight victories.

But the winning pattern didn't last, and the team slumped once more.

By the end of May, the team's critics were choosing up sides regarding Mele. Two of the reasons for the club's losing ways seemed to be pitcher Jim Kaat's ineffectiveness and Tony Oliva's slump in hitting.

Several individual players performed brilliantly in

their efforts to check the team's slump. Jim Merritt pitched two shut-outs in a row leading the Twins to 5 to 0 and 3 to 0 victories over Kansas City and New York. Bob Allison had a hot batting streak, and catcher Russ Nixon came through with timely hits.

Harmon Killebrew, who was also striving to help the team win, made history on June 3, 1970, by driving out the longest homerun ever hit in Metropolitan Stadium. He connected with a pitch thrown by Lew Burdette of the California Angels and sent it 430 feet into Seat 9, Row 5 Section 34 of the upper deck in the left field pavilion at the Met. The seat has since been retired and painted to stand as a constant reminder of Killebrew's power. Players say that no other living man can hit a ball up there.

The ground crew claimed the ball had to travel 530 feet to land where it did.

Amidst all of the tumult and shouting, Harmon was asked to express himself concerning the hit.

His comment: "I think it was a fastball."

On June 5, 1970, Killebrew hit another herculean clout that bounced off the facing of the second deck on the left-field stands. This hit helped the Twins defeat the Angels 8 to 7. The other homerun had led to an 8 to 6 victory.

Harmon, when asked to explain his sudden burst of power, said, "Well, I had been sharing an apartment with Jim Lemon until my family moved here for the summer from Ontario. Jim's a pretty good chef and did a fair job of cooking, but he couldn't seem to open up a carton of eggs without frying the whole dozen.

"Elaine got here from Ontario a couple of days ago and since she's been around to cook, I've been on a homerun diet."

Then he grinned, and said, "Seriously speaking, I think it's the warmer weather."

On the morning of June 9, 1967, Sam Mele's wife Connie and their six children flew to Minneapolis to spend the week-end with Sam. That same afternoon, five hours later, he was fired.

Harmon hits the only homerun ever hit in the upper left field pavilion at Metropolitan Stadium, June 3, 1967 distance 520 feet

Doc Lentz treating Killebrew, 1967

The Twins' record at the time was 25-25, but the fans wanted more, and of course the answer, logical or not, was to change managers. Griffith's statement was, "Sam Mele has lost control of the club."

It was a strange thing, Sam's firing. He's a quiet, reserved gentleman, but like many reserved gentlemen, I suppose he was misunderstood by the players and the fans.

I must confess to being as guilty as the rest in having made a false judgment. I used to become impatient when Sam would walk very slowly out to the mound to change pitchers, and I'd think to myself, "What a showboat! Mele sure likes to spend every minute he can in the limelight."

After Sam Mele was released, I told Harmon my thoughts, and he set me right.

"Sam had a reason for his slow walk," he said, "He did that so the pitchers in the bullpen would have more time to warm up." Harmon's only other comment was, "Mele is a man with a lot of patience."

Sam Mele, who is now with the Boston Red Sox, responded with a letter when I was gathering material for this book. It is reproduced below:

Dear Dr. Anderson,

To be perfectly frank, words cannot express my feelings for this fellow but I'll try. I guess two words will sum it up, "Class Personified." That's on the field, off the field, in the clubhouse, in the dugout, at home, in a group, and wherever he happens to be. He's a ballplayer's ballplayer, a manager's ballplayer, and a fans' ballplayer. He's a quiet but productive leader, and every one of his teammates and opposing players respect him. Naturally the opposing managers, too.

Ordinarily the ballplayers look up to the manager. I as a manager looked up to a ballplayer, a man, Harmon Killebrew.

My best to you and say hello to Harmon for me.

Sincerely yours,
Sam Mele

The man appointed as the Twins' new manager was Cal Ermer. Cal is a patient southerner who had compiled an impressive record in managing the Twins' farm clubs. At the time he was called up, he was managing the Denver team. Cal was known for calm, fair, but firm treatment of players.

Ermer took charge immediately, set down rules, and instituted a rigid curfew.

The club was in sixth place with a 25-25 record when he took over, and from that time on they played at a .589 clip and climbed in the standings.

When All-Star game time came around in July, the team was doing well. Carew, Chance, Oliva and Killebrew were picked to play in the contest.

There were additional reasons besides the change in managers to account for the Twins' turnabout to a winning pattern.

Oliva had recovered from his injuries and was hitting near the .300 mark in the later stages of the season. Killebrew was having one of his best homerun years and was also playing well at first base. Jim Kaat, who had finally recovered from his injuries, regained his pitching rhythm and was winning with consistency. Down the season's stretch he won seven straight games.

Dean Chance was pitching well enough to become a 20-game winner, and Bob Allison had staged a comeback with his hitting.

As a result of this combined effort, the Twins took over first place on August 13th and remained at the top for all but ten days before the Boston Red Sox overtook them on the final day of the season—October 1st.

The final series with Boston was a nightmare. The Twins needed to win only one of two games to capture the pennant and reach the World Series. Instead, they lost them both.

In the first game, they seemed certain to breeze to victory. Jim Kaat was pitching. He had been unbeatable in his last seven appearances, and in this game seemed to have the Red Sox eating out of the palm of his hand. Then in the third inning, misfortune overtook him. He felt a stabbing pain in his left elbow, and his arm went dead. He courageously tried to continue but it was impossible; he couldn't control his pitches. After he retired from the game, the Red Sox went on to win.

The final game on October 1, 1967, was a cliff-hanger. That was the day the Twins lost the pennant or Boston won it—either way you want to put it.

Ermer started Dean Chance on the mound. He was the team's 20-game winner and known as "The Big Boy" on the staff, so the move made sense.

After five and one-half innings the Twins were leading 2 to 0, and Chance was working on a four-hit shut-out.

In the sixth inning, the Red Sox who had been waving feebly at Dean's slants, went into action. First, Jim Lonborg beat out a sacrifice bunt. Then Jerry Adair and Dale Jones both singled to load the bases. With the bases filled, there was no alternative but to pitch to the batter—none other than the feared Carl Yastrzemski. Carl lived up to his reputation and singled to tie the score.

The next batter, Ken Harelson grounded to Versalles. Versalles made a great effort but Jones beat his throw to the plate, and the Red Sox went ahead.

Al Worthington, who had saved many games for the Twins, came in and tried to stem the tide. But there were two on with no one out, and before the inning was completed both runners scored, and Boston heralded a 5 to 3 victory enroute to the World Series.

Dean Chance was so shaken up emotionally that he left the stadium and was on his way to the airport before the game was over. He said later, "If I had stayed in Boston one minute longer, I would have gone out of my mind."

It was a heartbreaking loss for the Twins. Although Harmon was downcast about the defeat, he had completed an outstanding year at bat. He had tied with Carl Yastrzemski for the league homerun title with 44—and had batted in 113 runs—recording a batting average of .269.

It had been a long and tiring season, and he was happy that he could head for Ontario and rejoin Elaine and the children.

"the topsy-turvy twins"

23

The winter of 1968 was a pleasant one for the Killebrews. Harmon had gone through the 1967 season without any serious injury; consequently, he wasn't faced with a rigorous schedule of treatments and could devote more time to the family. The two Killebrew boys, Cameron and Kenny were growing fast and as pre-teen-agers enjoyed roaming the hills with their dad. Shawn, Kathy, and Erin also spent many delightful hours with Harmon and Elaine.

Harmon was again invited to speak at several banquets, and on January, 1968, was honored at the 33rd annual awards dinner of the Touchdown Club. At this time he was presented with the Clark Griffith Memorial Trophy for his outstanding contribution to baseball.

During that winter the two Cals, if I remember correctly, writers were calling them "High-Cal" and "Low-Cal", were optimistic about the team's chances for the 1968 season. They had good reasons to be confident. In late November of 1967, Griffith had negotiated the deal of the year at the major league meetings in Mexico City. With

BABER

Harmon receiving the Clark Griffith Memorial Award from his friend, Jim Lemon, at the Touchdown Club in Washington, D.C. 1968

one trade, he had strengthened the two positions which had given the Twins the most headaches in 1967—catching and relief pitching. He had sent shortstop Zoilo Versalles and pitcher Jim Grant to the Dodgers in exchange for catcher John Roseboro, an outstanding receiver, and pitchers Bob Miller and Ron Perranoski, two of the top relief pitchers in the majors. The club hated to part with Grant and Versalles, but felt that they had sufficient depth to compensate for Mudcat's loss, and a young shortstop named Jackie Hernandez appeared to be ready to fill in the place of Zoilo.

Another reason for their optimism was that the "Cast and Crutch Brigade" was healed. Rich Reese had recovered from knee surgery. Tony Oliva had undergone successful removal of bone chips in his knee. Bob Allison and Ted Uhlaender were physically sound once more. And Rich Rollins had bounced back enthusiastically from a knee operation.

Perhaps those of us who have not had serious knee injuries don't comprehend the feeling of relief that comes to a player after having recovered from successful surgery on the ailing member. Rich Rollins, when interviewed, gave some indication of that relief when he said,

"For the first time in years, I can sleep at night without being stabbed with pain every time I move my leg."

Harmon Killebrew was also optimistic about the coming season and was pleased when he signed with Mr. Griffith for about $85,000.

During the signing sessions, Calvin again expressed concern about club finances. And he immediately got some advice from Jack Benny, perennial motion picture, television, and radio star. Jack said to one of the Twins broadcasting sponsors, "Tell Cal to peddle Killebrew, because all he ever does is drive balls out of the lot at a buck-and-a-half a copy."

The first day of the spring season it rained, but the Twins were in a good mood and went right to work. Ermer said, "We'll keep everybody busy." And he had gathered around him a group of coaches with the same philosophy. Returning were Billy Martin, Early Wynn and Johnny Goryl. Additions were George Case (one of the great base-stealers of all time) and Bob Oldis, a heady bullpen coach.

Cal Ermer was definitely on the spot during the 1968 season. Everyone expected him to bring home the pennant. Sportswriter Paul Foss said,

"Now its up to Ermer to bring home a winner. I don't see how he can possibly miss."

The fact was, Cal Ermer had been handpicked for management by Cal Griffith thirteen years before. He had been brought along in the minors, had been called up to replace Mele, and he responded by doing a magnificent job in 1967; so naturally he was the fair-haired boy from whom everything was expected.

During spring training Killebrew was asked the question that had become as inevitable as the return of the first robin, "Are you going to hit 50 homeruns this year?"

Jerry Zimmerman, Killebrew's friend, and a fellow Oregonian tried to get Harmon off the hook with humor when he said, "We fellas from Oregon will combine for 47 homers this year. Forty-six for me and one for Harm." Zimmerman had hit one homerun for each of the three previous seasons.

But the reporters persisted in interviewing Killebrew, so he gave them his usual answer, "I don't make predictions. My concern is to stay away from injuries. The rest will take care of itself."

Ermer's Twins didn't set the world on fire during the exhibition season. In fact they looked ragged, ending spring training with a record of 11 wins and 16 losses. However, when the regular season started, the team did an about-face and won 6 games in a row.

In the season's opener at Washington, Dean Chance edged Camilo Pascual 2 to 0. Killebrew broke a scoreless tie with a home run in the sixth and Allison made the score 2 to 0 with an eighth inning four-bagger.

Vice-President Hubert H. Humphrey was at the game

and was so enthusiastic over the win that the players gave him the game ball.

In the second game, Killebrew helped Jim Merritt win 5 to 4, with a homer in the fifth inning.

Then Perry blanked the Yankees 6 to 0 for the third straight victory. And Harmon contributed two hits.

The next three games including the home opener were won by scores of 4 to 3, 6 to 3, and 13 to 1.

The Twins showed so much all-around strength in swamping the Yankees 13 to 1 in the season's opener at the Met that the fans started to dream of the pennant, and the players began estimating their World Series cuts. Lieutenant Governor James Goetz tossed out the opening ball, and from that point on the Minnesotans went wild. Killebrew contributed a two-run homer, his third of the year.

Suddenly, Dame Fortune turned her back on the Twins. They began to lose. They lost five games by one run, and on May 4, 1968, suffered the ignominy of losing a no-hit game to Jim Catfish Hunter of the Oakland Athletics.

The erstwhile heroes were now bums in the eyes of the public.

Griffith said, "They are too complacent, need more hustle." The fan-on-the-street commented, "Those guys all need to get a doctor to give them eye examinations. Why, they can't even see the ball."

Cal Ermer became so frustrated that he bought a book on extrasensory perception to see if he could learn how to influence the team to score runs.

And finally, Ermer did what others before him had done when in trouble, he shifted Killebrew, "whose natural position is at first base" back over to the hot-corner at third.

Despite the team's ups and downs, Harmon was doing well, and by May 3rd had hit 6 homeruns, his best start in eight years as a Twin.

One bright spot in the Minnesotans' erratic play was

Three great sluggers meet at Shea Stadium in New York City. L. to r., Harmon Killebrew of the Minnesota Twins, Willie Mays of the San Francisco Giants, and Mickey Mantle of the New York Yankees.

L. to r., Bob Oldis, coach; Billy Martin, coach; Cal Ermer, manager; Early Wynn, coach; George Case, coach.

the effective hurling of relief pitchers, Worthington and Perranoski. It got so that if the Twins were anywhere within winning distance in the late innings, either Al or Ron was expected to come in and guarantee a victory, and most of the time one of them did.

On May 28, Billy Martin agreed to leave his coaching position with the team and manage the Denver Bears, the Twins' top farm club. He did a tremendous job while there and turned the club into a winning aggregation.

It is difficult to say whether Martin's departure took away some of the team's zip. No matter what the reason, the Twins continued to play erratic ball, and it became quite commonplace for fans to call them the "Topsy-Turvy Twins." When the pitchers were going strong, the batters seemed to slump, and when the hitters found their batting eyes, the hurlers lost their stuff.

Cal Ermer, who had been considered a managerial genius, was getting criticism, and in June, when Jim Merritt stopped the Angels with a well-pitched game, the papers flatly stated, "Merritt's win may have saved Ermer's job."

Whether the Twins won or lost, Killebrew was always under pressure because statisticians were continuously computing his homerun ratio as related to times at bat. In June they announced that "The Killer's" ratio had fallen off, and he was only hitting 1 homerun in 15.58 times at bat as compared with his overall average of 1 in 13. Harmon was in a slump with a batting average under .220; so the statistical fanatics would have been more helpful if they had kept quiet.

One of the Twins players who gave the fans something to cheer about in June was Frank Quilici. The colorful Italian came off the bench and sparked the team to six straight wins. Frank was really pounding the ball, and his play in the field was spectacular. I went to see a game during the winning streak and was surprised to see the spectators applaud Frank's every move, even when he made a routine put out.

But Quilici is not a superman, and eventually, despite

his courageous efforts, the topsy-turvy pattern of play came back. Someone said, "When the pitchers top, the batters flop."

On June 21, 1968, Harmon Killebrew was honored at the annual 4H Club recognition banquet sponsored by the Greater Minneapolis Chamber of Commerce. He was given an award "for the inspiration he provides for the youth of Minnesota and the nation."

In late June, Harmon was voted in as starting first baseman for the All-Star game on July 9th at Houston. He happily acknowledged the honor but said, "I was never more surprised in my life. Maybe there will be a recount."

Surely Killebrew was deserving of the honor, but the way things turned out he would have been better off if he had not been elected.

By July 8th, the Twins seemed to have collapsed, and the reason was a mystery that neither Calvin Griffith nor Calvin Ermer seemed to be able to solve.

On July 9, in the All-Star game at the Astrodome in Houston, the final crusher was put on the Twins' fading pennant hopes. Killebrew, who was playing first base, reached out to catch a low, wide throw from shortstop Jim Fregosi. Curt Flood was streaking toward first. As Harmon stretched to the limit, the powdery, artificial soil in the the Astrodome gave way, and he did a complete split. His huge left hamstring muscle tore with a loud pop that could be heard all over the field. Virtually helpless, he was carried away on a stretcher, and with his injury went the last of the Twins' pennant hopes. It was thought at the time that he might never play again.

He did recover enough to come back in the closing weeks of the season, but it was too late at the time to help lift the Twins in the standings.

With the "Killer" out, the rest of the Twins faced a steady diet of left-handed pitching. It upset them so much that they became anemic with low hitting pressure.

Adding to their woes, Tony Oliva suffered a dislocated left shoulder. It happened when he attempted to catch a difficult fly-ball on September 1st, in a losing 5 to 4 effort against Chicago.

The collapse of the Twins caused Griffith to comment, "This season is the most frustrating of my lifetime in baseball."

While the Twins were struggling on the field, Harmon was fighting to regain the use of his left leg. Doc Lentz said the injury was so bad that Harmon couldn't bend his leg to sit down. He had to eat standing up for a month! Still Killebrew fought gamely to get back and help the team.

During this period when Harmon was injured, he and Elaine were attending a Sunday School class that I teach. The Sunday before the All-Star game, I had asked him if he would give a talk to the class on self-discipline.

He replied, "I would be happy to."

Then he was injured several days later. As soon as he was able to talk on the telephone at home, I dialed him, expressed my concern, and said, "I suppose we'll have to forget your talk to our Sunday School class."

I shall never forget his answer, "I'll be glad to come, if you don't mind my standing up during the entire meeting. You see I can stand up or lie down, but I can't bend my leg enough to sit yet."

"But Harmon," I remonstrated, "won't that be too hard on you?"

"Not at all," he replied. "Glad you still want me to do it."

So Harmon came to class and gave an excellent talk on self-discipline before about one-hundred people.

After his presentation, there were questions of all kinds. But he stood there patiently (I know he was in pain) and cheerfully answered them all.

With Doc Lentz's skilled treatment, Elaine's love and inspiration, and hours of exercise, Killebrew recovered the use of his leg sufficiently to rejoin the Twins on September 1, 1968.

On Monday, September 2nd, the Minnesotans were

trailing Chicago 5 to 3 in the last of the ninth inning. With two outs, Killebrew was called on to pinch-hit, and the fans gave him a standing ovation as he emerged from the dugout.

As the "Killer" took his position at the plate there was respectful silence in the stands.

Would the Twins' slugger ever be able to hit one out again, or were those days in the past?

Harmon himself didn't know the answer.

Wilbur Woods, the Chicago pitcher, threw one on the outside.

The fans booed loudly.

Harmon knew the next one would be in there. As he faced the Chicago pitcher, he took a deep breath and thought, "We have no chance of winning this game unless I can hit one out. But almost simultaneously the idea flashed into his mind, "If I swing too hard, I may tear the muscle in my leg again and end my playing days for good."

As he hesitated, for a split-second, in making his decision, Elaine's face flashed before his eyes and he heard her say, as if she were right beside him, "You can do it, Harm. You can do anything you want to do."

Relaxed, his mind made up, he swung at the oncoming pitch with all his might. There was a resounding crack as his bat connected and the ball shot 402 feet into the left-centerfield stands for a homerun!

His leg had held! Killebrew's heart was filled with gratitude and joy as he paused momentarily to watch the ball in its flight, and then circled the bases.

An audible sigh of relief came from the other players and the spectators as the "Big Guy" touched home plate. They had learned that Harmon Killebrew, the team's leading power hitter, was physically sound once more.

He had hit his first homerun since June 26th and his 14th of the year.

Although the Twins lost the game, Cal Ermer said, "I don't like losing, but Harm's homer in the 9th sure took a lot of sting out of the loss for me.

"It's just too bad there wasn't at least one man aboard. Here's a guy who goes up there after being out for nearly two months and rips one into the seats.

"To me, he's one of the greatest pros who ever played the game. It's a shame we don't have more like him."

In the clubhouse afterward, Killebrew said, "It was a great feeling to get that much wood on the ball after being out so long."

Months later, when he was asked by a sportswriter to list his most memorable homeruns he said, "I suppose the first one I hit after recovering from the rupture of my hamstring muscle meant the most to me, because I knew that I could still hit the ball out."

The 1968 season ground to a close on a dismal note. Cal Ermer was fired on September 30th.

A sportswriter in commenting on the dismissal said, "Cal Ermer is a stalwart character with abundant courage and a pleasant personality. He also has a thorough knowledge of baseball, but because the Twins flouted his authority, he is out of a job."

Cal Ermer remained a true southern gentleman right to the last. His single comment was,

"I only wish it could have turned out differently. I enjoy the area. And the fans here are the greatest anywhere. I don't regret at all being associated with the Twins."

Killebrew as a banquet speaker, 1969, with Twins director of public relations, Tom Mee on his left

player of the year

24

When the 1968 season ended, the Killebrews returned to their Ontario home. The move was a bit more difficult this time, not for geographical but for sentimental reasons. The family had purchased an attractive rambling home in Edina, Minnesota, a beautiful community southwest of the Twin Cities. They were now torn between living there or in their home in Ontario. They had also extended their circle of friends in Minnesota until they felt almost as much at home there as they did in Ontario.

There were two things uppermost in their minds after they got settled in their comfortable Ontario home. One was professional—the other was spiritual.

In order to resume his career as a baseball player, Harmon knew he must regain full strength in his injured leg; so he spent long hours of exercise and walking during the winter months to build it up. He also climbed the hills around Ontario hunting pheasants for exercise. By the time the spring training season came around, he felt he was ready to thoroughly test the healed muscle.

The spiritual goal in the Killebrews' minds was to go to the temple at Salt Lake City and have their children sealed to them. It is the doctrine of the Church that a couple—married in the temple before their children are born—will have their children with them as a family unit in the life after death; however, if the couple does not participate in this temple ordinance before the birth of their children, they may then have their children sealed to them later.

Harmon and Elaine love their children dearly, consequently they went to the temple, and the sealing was done on December 27, 1968.

After the Twins had finished three seasons in a row as "also-rans," Calvin Griffith was determined to change things in 1969. The '68 season had been deeply disappointing, and in reviewing it, Griffith became convinced that the club's troubles had stemmed from the lack of firm control over the players. Therefore, his first step was to turn the reins of his team over to the fiery Billy Martin. Billy was known as a "take charge" guy and Calvin felt that he could get the Twins on the pennant-winning path once more.

Griffith also realized that the team had a defensive weakness at shortstop in 1968, and he said, "We lost thirty games last year because of the hole there." To plug this gap in the infield, Calvin took advantage of the opportunity to obtain the veteran shortstop, Leo Cardenas, a four-time National League All-Star, from the Cincinnati Reds. He paid a high price for Cardenas—giving up standout left-handed hurler Jim Merritt in exchange.

At Martin's request, the coaching staff was also changed. Art Fowler, Martin's pitching coach at Denver the year before, was brought up to assist Wynn in coaching the hurlers. Vern Morgan, veteran manager in the Twins minor league system, was named third base coach. Charlie Silvera became the Bullpen coach; and John Goryl was retained for first base duties.

The club management felt the adjustments had finally

L. to r., John Goryl, Charlie Silvera, Art Fowler, Vern Morgan, Early Wynn, coaches; Billy Martin, manager.

set the Twins for a run at the pennant. Their optimism was also heightened by the conditioning of pitchers Jim Kaat, Dean Chance, and Jim Perry—all expected to have a winning year.

Something should be said here about Martin's leadership. Art Fowler, who coached under Billy at Denver in 1968, had these comments:

"Martin is a great manager for several reasons:

1. He has a thorough knowledge of baseball.
2. He possesses the ability to handle men.
3. He has the knack of getting along with players and gaining their respect.
4. He can get mad and kick up a storm very often but also forgives and forgets."

The fourth point as stated by Fowler was the one that bothered Griffith, and he told the press, "I feel like I'm sitting on a keg of dynamite because Billy is so unpredictable. But I'm hoping for the best."

Martin let the team know who was boss as soon as

spring training started. And when asked how he was going to handle the players, he answered, "If they act like men, I'll treat them like men; but if they act like little boys, they may get spanked."

In the spring of 1969 the pre-season training of the major league clubs was slowed down by a threatened players' strike over the amounts of their pension funds. Inasmuch as an agreement was not reached until February 26, 1969, the veterans on the teams reported late.

Killebrew signed a contract for $70,000 that year, feeling that he was physically in condition for a good season.

On the first day of spring training, 16 out of the squad of 32 were present at Tinker Field, and several days passed before the full team appeared.

Martin posted his training rules on the blackboard in the clubhouse so no one would misunderstand what was expected.

They read:

Curfew at 12:00, midnight.

Learn the signs.

No swimming.

Be on time for photographers.

There were some newcomers in camp who immediately attracted attention. Among them were Joe Grzenda—veteran reliever from Denver, rookie Charlie Manual—a long-ball hitter, and young pitchers Tom Hall, Bill Zepp, and Dick Woodson.

Pitcher Dave Boswell looked like he was headed for a great year, and Arno Goethel wrote for the St. Paul Pioneer Press on January 26, 1969:

"The New Boswell is Serious—Tolerant—Careful—Dedicated—Philosophical—A Home-man—Mature—Sensible."

Then paradoxically, a short time later, Dave sidelined himself while cleaning a fish. The knife slipped and severed two tendons in his hand.

Harmon Killebrew had suffered his severe hamstring injury the year before; so Martin told him to be careful and get ready in his own way.

The Twins' play in the Grapefruit League was a bit erratic. They lost their first three games and then later won seven straight. But they had a good training season and approached the beginning of league competition with confidence.

However, by the time the opening game rolled around, a rash of injuries had hit the club. Boswell's hand was not completely healed. Allision had a stiff neck—Kaat a pulled groin muscle, and Roseboro had a sore thumb. Carew incurred a thigh injury. And Chance's condition was questionable.

The Twins lost the season's opener to Kansas City in twelve innings 4 to 3, and Harmon hit one single in five times at bat. The team continued to lose to the tune of four straight.

Despite the worst beginning-of-the-year losing streak in ten seasons at Minnesota, Martin was supremely confident. When interviewed he said, "I think I'll buy some season tickets right now, so I'll have priority for good World Series seats for my friends."

The turning point in the Twins' fortune came on April 13, 1969 in a game at the Met against the California Angels. And it occurred when Killebrew passed one of the most crucial tests of his entire career, namely, that of finding out if he had retained his ability to swing with power after recovering from his serious hamstring injury. Although he had hit 4 homeruns after his injury had healed, and he had returned to the lineup for the closing weeks of the 1968 season, he was still uncertain about his future. The question was, would the leg hold up during an entire season of rigorous play?

He had spent long months of walking and exercising during the winter to strengthen his leg. But the hamstring tear had been so severe that he didn't know even then if it would continue to hold up under the pressure of his powerful swing. When he arrived in Orlando he began conditioning himself carefully, and when batting, took slow, easy swings in an effort to regain his timing. In his times at bat during the exhibition season, he avoided putting everything into his swing.

When the season started, he hit well, but the long-ball was missing. Finally, after punching out eleven straight singles, he felt he must undergo the ultimate. Would his leg still hold up when he went all out to hit a homerun in regular league play?

The effort took place on April 13 in the aforementioned game at the Met. Harmon stepped to the plate in the eighth inning with the Twins trailing 3 to 0.

As he faced the Angels pitcher, he took a deep breath "We may never win this game unless I can hit one out. The leg held last fall. Why shouldn't it still hold up now?"

So, he steeled himself and swung with all his might at a fastball that came right down the middle. He met the ball squarely, and it soared 398 feet over the left centerfield fence for a homerun. The blast led to a 4 to 3 victory, the Twins' first of the season.

Harmon's leg was sound, in fact so completely healed that he went on to play in every game of the 1969 season.

Billy Martin holding back his emotions said, "Now we can relax and win some games."

And they did. Cardenas glued the infield together. Mitterwald helped with the catching. Oliva began hitting. Kaat rounded into form, and Perranoski began saving games with his superb relief hurling. By April 16th, the Twins had hit 10 homers in the last four games and approached the home opener on April 18, in high spirits. Twenty-five thousand fans cheered that day as Minnesota's Governor Harold LeVander threw out the first ball, and the Twins went on to defeat the California Angels 6 to 0 on Tom Hall's two-hitter.

Killebrew was swinging smoothly and started rallies with two infield singles.

By April 22nd, the Twins were in first place, and on April 28th, Harmon reached another milestone in his career, hitting his 400th homerun.

When Elaine Killebrew was asked how she felt about

it, her blue eyes twinkled as she replied, "Four hundred homeruns are great, but I won't let Harm quit until he hits six hundred."

The Twins of 1969 were an exciting team to watch because of their daring base running. Martin had said, "This year we're going to bunt and run, and we're going after all the marbles."

Bunt and run they did. Led by the Cuban comets, Oliva, Tovar and Carew, the Minnesotans made life miserable for opposing pitchers.

Oliva with his graceful stride would stretch a single to a triple if the opposing outfielders weren't on their toes.

As soon as Tovar got on first base, he drove the rival pitcher crazy with his antics. He would take a daring lead toward second and then dive back head first to the initial sack, all the time grinning like a mischievous kid at the hurler's futile efforts to pick him off.

And Carew, he was something else! He stole home five times in five attempts. It was worth the price of admission to see him approach the plate in a blur of speed and gracefully hook the corner of the base with a slide, making it impossible for the rival catcher to tag him.

A look at the statistics in May, 1969, gave tangible evidence that Killebrew was the team's bread-and-butter player. In seventeen victories he had hit for a .440 batting average and in 8 losses at a low .121 clip.

Martin played every hunch he could to drive the team to the pennant. He made Jim Perry a regular starting pitcher —it paid off.

He pitched Bob Miller frequently—it paid off.

He even ordered the ground crew to cut the infield grass long to help the Twins' bunting—it paid off.

And his fiery spirit so permeated the team that on June 8th, Don Riley wrote in the St. Paul Pioneer Press, "Martin's put more fire under the Twins than a tungsten burner in a pile of dry leaves."

During the team's drive to the pennant, Ron Perranoski, who was affectionately dubbed the "Polish Ambassador," appeared so many times in relief that by June 5th, he had worked in 25 games, saved 11, posted a 3-2 record and figured in more than half of the Twins' victories.

Ron was known as a vocalist with a "perfect pitch," and the Twins starting pitcher, feeling that his throwing muscles were equally as good as his singing cords, urged the management to take out an expensive insurance policy on his pitching arm.

When asked the secret of his success Ron modestly said, "I just try to get them to hit the ball on the ground."

Yes, Martin had lit a fire under the players, and he got them to win by cajoling, needling, encouraging, and sometimes spanking.

Billy had been required to fight his way up to major league status. As a result, he sometimes exploded and said and did things before he thought them over.

On one such occasion he decked Dave Boswell with a right cross in a confrontation outside a bar in Detroit. Afterward he treated Boswell like a loving father and did everything he could to patch up their differences.

Killebrew suffered a bruised elbow late in the season, and Rick Renick took over temporarily at third base and saved one game with a brilliant defensive play.

On July 10th Harmon again played in the All-Star game, and small wonder. He, Oliva, and Reese had all been hitting at a torrid pace and by July 17th, one week later, Killebrew had hit 23 homeruns in 80 games, with five coming in the last five games. This was his best homerun pace since 1964.

On July 29th the Twins reached the summit of their success when they defeated the Detroit Tigers pitching aces in a double header. Jim Perry outpitched Mickey Lolich 5 to 2; and Bob Miller out-hurled Denny McLain 11 to 5.

From that time on the Minnesotans' winning momentum could not be checked. They went on to win the pennant by a wide margin.

The club's chief rival for the Division Championship in

1969 was Oakland, and one reason the Twins captured the crown was because they played so well against the Athletics, winning one crucial series after another. Killebrew rained their pitchers' offerings all over the field and rattled the fences so often that Oakland's pitchers could hardly get him out.

The Twins ended the Oakland Athletics' pennant hopes on Tuesday, September 16, when Jim Perry won against them 11 to 3, his nineteenth victory of the season. Harmon Killebrew, in a typical display of his power, gave the Minnesotans a 3 to 0 lead in the first inning with a homerun off loser, Jim Nash. The blast was his eleventh of the season against Oakland and his 44th of the year.

A look at the statistics shows how well the Twins played against Oakland that year. They won the season's series 13 to 5, winning seven of nine at home and six of nine in Oakland.

When Oakland manager Hank Bauer was asked, at the end of the season, to explain why his team lost out in the race for first place, his answer was brief and to the point. He said, "Our losing the pennant can be explained very simply; the 'Killer' killed us."

Harmon had a great year against all of the American League teams in 1969. And he achieved it despite being plagued with an assortment of injuries.

Doc Lentz, the Twins trainer, said Killebrew had so many injuries that he couldn't remember them all. Some of them were bruised ribs, a pulled muscle, a banged-up knee, a swollen arm and a battered elbow.

Refusing to be sidelined by these painful hurts, Killebrew kept going and didn't miss a game. Doc Lentz's comment on this was, "He never complains, and he plays every game. That's your money player."

Billy Martin felt the same way about Killebrew. He said, "Harmon Killebrew is a great player and a great person. Very few guys could keep playing with the injuries he has had."

Even though Harmon had a banner year, he suffered

one bitter disappointment in the final game of the season. At that time he had hit 49 homeruns during 1969 and needed one more to set a personal record of 50. In previous seasons he had hit 49 and 48, but never 50.

Everyone at the Met felt sure that this would be Harmon's day to crash that fiftieth barrier. But things didn't work out that way. Fate seemed to be against him. Twice he hit long fly balls that came down inches inside of the fence, and when the game was over, although the Twins defeated the White Sox 6 to 5, everyone was disappointed.

In post-game interviews, Harmon made no alibis and avoided giving expression to his disappointment. He simply said, "I never saw so many good pitches as I had today. I suppose the problem was that I was getting too far under the ball on my swing."

A perennial Twins fan who is a great Killebrew booster, and who did much to enliven the season of 1969, is former Vice-President Hubert Humphrey. Once or twice, when he was watching a game at the Met, he visited the sports announcers in their booth. The conversations that followed were a delight to hear. Mr. Humphrey was so enthusiastically interested in the game and so knowledgeable about the various ball players that he nearly took over the play-by-play broadcasting.

The Twins entered the play-off series with Baltimore, the Eastern Division winners, confident that they could win. They had two twenty-game winners in Jim Perry and Dave Boswell and a lineup of strong hitters led by Killebrew, Oliva, Carew and Reese. Killebrew had won the homerun title with 49, and Carew was the American League batting champion with an average of .332. In addition, he had tied a major league record with seven thefts of home.

Oliva and Reese had also hit well above the .300 mark.

Martin pitched his twenty-game winner—Jim Perry—in the opening game against the Orioles' Mike Cuellar in Baltimore. The hard-fought contest went 12 innings before the Orioles finally won 4 to 3 on Paul Blair's perfectly placed two-out bunt.

In the second game, Dave Boswell was determined to show the fans in his home town of Baltimore his best pitching stuff. He did, battling Baltimore's Dave McNally in a nearly scoreless pitching duel that ended 1 to 0 in Baltimore's favor. The hit came in the 11th inning when Curt Motton hit a pinch single off the Twins' reliever, Ron Perranoski.

The third and final game of the series was played at Metropolitan Stadium. Calvin Griffith indicated that he would prefer to have Jim Kaat as the starting pitcher. Jim was known as a tough competitor and had beaten Baltimore twice during the regular season.

Martin favored Bob Miller who had been a work horse during the year and consequently went along with him.

Miller didn't have his stuff that day, and the Baltimore sluggers pounced on him early. Billy then called on Woodson, Hall, Worthington, and Chance in an effort to stop the Orioles, but to no avail. The Twins lost 11 to 2.

So the Minnesota team disbanded for the season and traveled to their various homes, downcast that they had lost their chance to compete in the World Series.

They felt even a bit more down when the Orioles, who had vanquished them, lost four straight to the amazing New York Mets in the World Series.

Harmon's record for 1969 was outstanding. He won the homerun crown, with 49 circuit clouts, led the league in runs batted in with 140, and also drew the most bases on balls, 145. In addition, in the eighty games he played at first base, he led the league's first basemen with a fielding average of .997. And amazingly, he stole eight bases out of ten tries, bad leg and all.

He had often been mentioned as a candidate for the most valuable player in the American League, and when he was resting and enjoying his family in their Ontario home, the formal recognition came to him from two different groups.

In the month of October, 1969, he received the awards. First, he was recognized as "The Sporting News' Player of the Year" in the American League. Receiving this recognition is a great honor because the winner is selected in balloting by American League Players. It was the first time Killebrew had received the award, and he commented on it with typical modesty saying, "To have the players vote me this honor means an awful lot."

Then he was named the "Most Valuable Player in the American League for 1969" by the Baseball Writers' Association. He was accorded "Most Valuable" honors by the large margin of 249 votes to 227 for runner-up Boog Powell of Baltimore.

Thus, Harmon Killebrew reached the pinnacle of one of baseball's greatest careers in 1969.

The awards were doubly meaningful, because for Killebrew the baseball year of 1969 was the year that almost wasn't.

When he had slipped and ruptured his left medial hamstring muscle in the All-Star Game in Houston on July 9, 1968, attending physicians, including Dr. Harvey O'Phelan, thought it would be the end of his career.

But they didn't realize how strong Harmon's faith was that he would play again. Nor could they measure the deep well of inspiration that his wife, Elaine, would provide.

And then there was Doc Lentz. . . . No one could foresee the many hours of treatment that the genial Twins trainer would administer to "his boy" to help him recover.

So Harmon Killebrew came back.

a dream come true

25

After the season ended in 1969, Harmon did something he had wanted to do for several years—he went to Japan. He had been asked to go once before to take Rocky Colavito's place on a Detroit Tigers exhibition tour, but League officials had denied permission.

Harmon said, in recalling his 1969 trip, "I was extremely interested in seeing Japan because I had heard a lot about organized baseball there and the great enthusiasm the fans have for the sport. Our group spent about a week there and it was one of the most pleasant experiences Elaine and I have ever had."

During the following winter, the Twins slugger was speaking at so many banquets because of his "Most valuable" and "Player of the Year" awards that he was away from the Killebrew home a great part of the time. He accepted every request to speak that he possibly could, as he felt a dual obligation to represent the game of baseball and to serve the fans who supported it.

Elaine went with him when she could get away. Other

times she drove him from Ontario to the Boise airport, gave him an affectionate kiss and watched him board the plane.

Traveling the "Knife and Fork" circuit can become a strain, and by the time spring training season came around, Harmon was tired, and his knee was bothering him. Due to his crowded speaking schedule, he had not had the opportunity to exercise and walk in the hills as much as was his custom; so he knew that during the first days of spring training he would have to work particularly hard to get into condition.

When he arrived in Orlando he was greeted by a new manager. Billy Martin had been replaced by Bill Rigney.

Rigney was on the spot as the club's new pilot because Martin's firing, after the last baseball season, had caused an upheaval among the baseball fans in Minnesota. The fans seemed stunned that their popular, pennant-winning manager had been discharged. And in their anger they flooded Calvin Griffith's office with uncomplimentary letters; however, a large number of the Twins followers took Calvin's side.

Excerpts from a few letters reveal the tenor of the fans' remarks:

"Calvin Griffith, in my judgment, history will record your decision on Billy Martin along with decisions that were made by Henry Ford, Adolf Hitler, and Napoleon when they took it upon themselves, in defense of their own egos, to determine what was good for all the people. . . . You have made a monstrous mistake. Are you man enough to admit it?"

"The public outcry on the part of the fans and sportswriters against the firing of Billy Martin is laughable to say the least. . . . I agree with Griffith 100 per cent. No owner who has any sense of responsibility to his own organization could possibly tolerate the actions of Martin during the past year."

"Who put the spark and life into a team that was in its

death throes? Who drove his players onto their best season in the majors? . . . Who was the most spirited, aggressive, gutsy, best-loved manager ever in Twins-land? And who was just fired by his Royal Majesty, Calvin Griffith? The unbelievable answer is, yes friends, Billy Martin."

"I am surprised at the criticism of Calvin Griffith for his removal of Billy Martin . . . I live in an average small town. And the majority of fans out this way were not supporters of Martin. . . . I heard many condemnations of Martin's decisions. For example, it seemed that Billy could never make up his mind about taking a pitcher out until it was too late. Then 'boom' the game was lost."

One might conjecture as to the reason for Martin's abrupt termination which in all probability was due to personality differences.

When Calvin announced to the press that he was not rehiring Martin, he said Billy was ignoring the club's administrative policies. ". . . I thought there was a distinct lack of communication between us."

In the final analysis, one must conclude that both Griffith and Martin are dedicated and talented baseball men. However, in Martin's firing, the same thing happened that always happens if there is an irreconcilable personality conflict between the boss and his employee. The head man exercises his prerogative to discharge the dissenter.

Although Bill Rigney's managerial talents were under scrutiny during the 1970 season, he had the background and skills to demonstrate that he, like Martin, is a winner. The white-haired, 52-year-old Rigney projects somewhat a father-image to his players. He doesn't condone mistakes on the ball field, but unlike Martin is less demonstrative in pointing them out. Fans who thought all of the managerial fire left with the departure of Billy have learned

---

(Excerpts of letters which appeared in the Minneapolis Star, October 17, 18, 1969.)

that Rigney has fire of his own but shows it in a different way. He paces the dugout constantly, is completely involved in every play and is willing to take chances to get a run.

The Twins had a rough time getting started during spring training in 1970 and lost 15 out of their first 16 games! When Rigney was asked the reason he said, "We miss the 'Big Guy's' hitting. When Harmon doesn't play we seem to lose our spark, and when he does, his ailing knee slows him down. I also think there could be another contributing factor. The players know I'm on the spot as their new manager, and they might be pressing a little too hard in order to win."

Harmon had to take treatments every day for his right knee. He explained that the fluid on it is a recurring condition—a result of a 1963 spring training injury and an operation in December of that year. The operation was to tighten up a ligament that had ruptured, and the tightening has caused subsequent trouble.

Killebrew said, with an optimistic smile, "Doc Lentz has fixed me up with an elastic brace that gives me a lot more support."

It was a slow, painful process but he gradually worked himself into condition.

The Twins management made a trade during March that brought more batting punch to their outfield. They sent pitchers Joe Grzenda and Charlie Walters to the Washington Senators in exchange for Brant Alyea, a six-foot-three, 215 pound long-ball hitter.

The club had also made another trade during the off-season in an effort to bolster their pitching staff. They made a deal with Cleveland in which they exchanged Dean Chance, Ted Uhlaender, Bob Miller, and Graig Nettles for pitchers Stan Williams and Luis Tiant. Both of the new hurlers were working hard in camp and gave promise of making a good contribution.

The overwhelming number of losses was hard on Rigney and on the players, so as a humorous gesture, Bill had a slip of paper with a big black dot in the center posted on the bulletin board outside his office. Below it were the words: "The Panic Button." No one ever got around to pushing it.

The Twins wound up their spring training season with 7 wins and 19 losses—a dismal record. Nevertheless, two rays of hope penetrated the gloom. Tony Oliva had his sweet swing going and had hit seven homeruns during the period and Harmon had rapped out 10 hits in his last 28 times at bat, hitting in eight games in a row.

In the opening game of the season against the White Sox on April 7th, the Twins unleashed their pent-up frustrations in a barrage of hits defeating the Chicago team 12 to 0. The star of the show was Brant Alyea who drove in seven runs on two three-run homers and two singles.

After the game, Alyea was surrounded by reporters in the Twins dressing room. While he was patiently answering questions, the news-hawks milled around so much that smaller teammates like Leo Cardenas couldn't get close enough to their lockers to put their clothes on.

The crowd roared when Oliva shouted, "Hey, who die over there?"

Alyea's performance pleased Rigney and Griffith. They both felt he could balance the team's hitting attack. The Twins had started the season the way Rigney desired, "off and running."

Jim Perry had come through with a sparkling shut-out, and the hitters seemed to have found their batting eyes.

The Twins won another game from the White Sox 6 to 4 and then continued to win with consistency. Jim Kaat helped by pitching them to an 8 to 2 victory over the Oakland Athletics at the home opener on April 11, 1970.

Alyea went on with his torrid hitting during early season play and attracted so much attention that sportswriters and fans made a special effort to pronounce his name correctly. That is—his abbreviated name. He is of French descent, and the record shows that his full name is Garabrant Ryerson Alyea.

As the season progressed, Harmon, through patient persistence, got his timing back, seemed to be swinging with a good pivot again, and resumed his role of getting key hits. Typical of such play was his three-run homer in the sixth against Chicago on April 22nd. The blast enabled the Twins' Kaat to earn a 4 to 3 win.

Rigney's comment was, "The 'Big Guy' (Killebrew) has done it enough against me. It's nice to have him on my side."

Bill Rigney proved to the Twins fans in 1970 that he is a colorful manager. Spectators sense his complete dedication to winning as he paces the dugout. When he changes a pitcher, he runs out to the mound, giving the impression that every moment the team is not in action is wasted. Rig is also a likable guy, and the players soon learned that he treats veterans and rookies alike. His temper occasionally flares, but when it does, he ventilates his anger by slamming his cap on the ground and drop-kicking it expertly, his white hair fluttering in the breeze.

The Harmon Killebrew of 1970 was also a colorful personality to watch. His sixteen years in baseball had given him unmistakable polish. Today, he stands out from other players, and even before the game starts and the teams line up while "The Star Spangled Banner" is played, you are conscious of his maturity. You notice that his hair is thinning and realize that he is no longer the curly-haired, rosy-cheeked kid of seventeen who startled the baseball world with his powerful hitting. You feel a personal pride that he is on your team—part of your community.

As play gets underway, you sense his dependability when on defense and you think, "The Twins will never lose their poise as long as Killebrew is in there."

If the pitcher falters a bit, a glance or a word from Harmon seems to calm him down.

And at bat? The air is charged with electricity every time the "Killer" steps to the plate. His swing is power personified, and whether he hits the ball or strikes out, you realize that you are seeing one of the great right-handed sluggers of all time in action.

Killebrew's influence spreads far beyond the playing field. He receives thousands of fan letters that he always tries to answer, and before most games he can be found standing beside a large mail box in front of his locker going through them.

After the games he is besieged for autographs. You hear a youngster say to his buddy, "Here comes the 'Big Guy.' You try to get him on this side, and if he gets by, I'll be waiting on the other."

I remember one time when I was waiting for Harmon at the entrance to the players' tunnel. As different team members came out there was a mild stir and a few autograph seekers approached them. But when Killebrew finally appeared, I was amazed at the crowd reaction. Everyone pushed around and followed him en masse to his car. And there he stood, pleasantly and patiently signing his name until the last outstretched hand clutched his signature.

Members of the club's organization who work behind the scenes are also Killebrew boosters, and they have been friendly and cooperative in my contacts with them.

In Orlando, Florida, I met the friendliest box-office man I have ever encountered—a man with a big smile—Earl Godfrey; I think I would buy a ticket from him just to enjoy the sunshine of his presence.

I mentioned to Art Johlfs, sports forecaster and Minneapolis realtor, that I was writing about Killebrew. And Art's admiration for Harmon was almost incredible. He talked about him as if Killebrew were a son.

Those in the Twins Public Relations Department have been helpful. Marlene Peters, the secretary, has cheerfully assisted with research.

Jim Rantz, assistant Director of Public Relations and a former student of mine, has given me continued encouragement, and Tom Mee, Director of Public Relations has patiently fulfilled my requests for assistance.

Tom told me something about Harmon that bears repeating.

"A Dream Come True" Minnesota Twins Baseball Club 1970

"I remember an incident that has always stood out in my mind where Harmon Killebrew is concerned. On June 3, 1967, Harmon hit a homerun into our second deck in Metropolitan Stadium, the only ball ever hit into that section. After the game we had the particular seat appropriately marked for all to see from that point forward. In the first inning of the next day's game, I instructed our public address announcer Bob Casey to read a piece of copy I had prepared concerning the marked seat and Killebrew's homerun. I instructed Casey to read this copy just as he introduced Killebrew on his first time at bat in the Sunday game. Casey introduced Killebrew and read the copy. Just as he finished reading the last word of the brief text, California's pitcher Jack Sanford delivered his first pitch to Killebrew. Harmon swung and hit a drive toward left-center field that actually carried even farther than the ball he had hit the day before, but because it was hit toward left-

Two of the Cuban Comets, Oliva and Cardenas, greet Harmon after a homerun, 1970

center field and not to dead leftfield, it didn't go all the way into the second deck. Instead it hit the facing along the front of the second deck.

"In all my career in sports, I have never seen a player respond to such a dramatic situation in so unbelievable a manner. More than anything else, this particular situation portrayed to me the incredible ability of this player to respond to the pressure situations."

Killebrew's popularity with his teammates has already been discussed, but one pleasing facet of his personality has not been mentioned. He treats everyone he meets with respect and does it in a natural and friendly manner. In other words, he puts no emphasis on economic or social status and is not clannish. He accepts people for what they are, not for what they have. In the clubhouse, he mingles as naturally with the rookies as with the established stars. One of his closest friendships has been with Jerry Zimmerman, former Twins utility catcher, who is now with the Montreal Expos.

Zimmerman is a nice, quiet person who resides in Milwaukee, Oregon during the off-season. And the Killebrew and Zimmerman families have been on trips together. In talking about Harmon, he told me:

"Harmon is one of the most unselfish men I have ever met in or out of baseball. I have never once heard him complain. He is a respected team man and a quiet leader. Harmon's image as a gentleman is genuine. He would never disappoint his family, team, or fans. Being a teammate and friend of Harmon Killebrew has been one of the high points of my life."

As the Twins continued the season, several newcomers contributed to their wins. One of them was Rick Renick, who started to fill in at third base when Harmon was shifted to first. Rick hit a grandslam homerun in April against Oakland that not only won the game, but also showed his power as a hitter. Rick is a product of Ohio State University and spends the off-season as a cattleman in his native Ohio. He broke into the major leagues with a homerun in his first time at bat on July 11, 1968.

Elaine Killebrew and I were sitting beside his attractive wife, Libby, during one game when Renick was called on to pinch-hit. Never have I seen a wife more involved in her mate's efforts. All the time Rick was at the plate, Libby was nervously clenching her hands and fumbling with a ring in her efforts to control her tension.

"Strike one," called the umpire.

Libby groaned.

"Ball one."

She relaxed.

"Ball two."

She even smiled.

"Strike two."

Another groan.

"Ball three."

Libby held her breath and almost slid under the seat.

"Ball four."

Libby Renick straightened up and gave a gasping sigh of relief as she resumed breathing.

Elaine, who is always understanding, leaned over and said, "Libby, your husband has what it takes; he'll be a star some day."

Rick and Libby Renick are typical of the fine young couples who are part of the Twins organization. I asked her if it is hard to be separated from Rick when he is traveling. Wouldn't it have been easier to have a husband who has an 8 to 5 come-home-every-night job so she could know what he was doing?

Libby's brown eyes sparkled as she said, "Rick and I got married because we love each other, which to us also means to trust. We went together six years and agreed on our mutual goals before we married. So we knew ahead of time that there would be moving around and times of separation. I'm completely happy the way things are."

Libby also told me that she had attended a dental college for several years and had emerged as a trained dental assistant so she could help with family finances if necessary. It was gratifying to hear such sound thinking.

As the season progressed, the Twins established a winning pattern and by mid-May were leading the league.

Harmon was making consistent contributions to the club's victories. On May 4th, he helped the team win against Baltimore in an unusual way. In the ninth inning, with the Minnesotans trailing 3 to 2 and Tony Oliva on base, Killebrew tried to hit to right field in order to move Oliva to third. He connected for his intended place single, and the ball sailed for a homerun giving the Twins a 4 to 3 victory.

"That Killebrew doesn't know how strong he really is," commented an Oriole player afterwards. "He just needs to get a piece of the ball, and out it goes."

Statistics showed that Harmon was having his best early season since 1961. In 25 games he had 9 homeruns, 23 runs-batted-in, and was hitting over .330.

At this time, a newcomer who was aiding the cause was pitcher, Luis Tiant. He had won 5 straight on the mound and was keeping the players relaxed in the dugout. He was always joking—calling everyone, "Buddy Boy," and his special name for Killebrew was "Killy Baby."

The other new pitcher who was making a tremendous contribution to the Twins victories was right-hander Stan Williams. He was so dependable in relief that Rigney invariably signaled for him when the opposing team's right-handed hitters were coming up.

On May 31, 1970, in a game with the New York Yankees at the Met, Harmon thrilled a large camera day crowd with his second homer of the game to give the Minnesota Twins a 7 to 6 victory.

In reporting the game, Jon Roe, Minneapolis Tribune writer, said, "There is an excitement which runs through the crowd as he leaves the dugout and heads for home plate. And when his name is announced—'now batting for the Twins number three, Harmon Killebrew'—the murmur of excitement turns to applause and cheers.

"It occurred again yesterday at 4:30 p.m., and Killebrew rewarded the ticket holders with their money's worth. He hit a homerun—a drive 421 feet into the leftfield bleachers—to bring the Minnesota Twins a 7 to 6 ten inning victory over New York."

Harmon's winning hit marked the fifth time in the year he had driven in the deciding run, three on late-inning homers.

Killebrew continued pounding his game-winning hits, and on Tuesday, June 16th, he brought the Twins from a 3 to 2 deficit with a three-run homer in the seventh. The 5-3 victory over Washington caused their pitcher Joe Coleman to say, "I didn't think it would carry out against the wind, but Harmon hit that ball with that overspin on it and it just kept climbing until it cleared the fence."

As the team neared the break for the All-Star game, Bill Rigney felt that Killebrew, Carew, Perry, and Perranoski were certain to make the American League All-Star squad. But before the All-Star game break, a dramatic event took place in Met Stadium on the next to the last day of June.

The night of June 29, 1970 at Metropolitan Stadium was a night that thousands of Minnesota baseball fans will always remember. It was a hot, humid evening that made you feel like you were sitting in a steam bath. The sticky heat was so debilitating that pitcher Jim Perry, losing eight pounds during the game, was so weary near the end, that Bill Rigney called on Perranoski to get the final man out during the ninth and preserve a 5 to 4 Twins victory over Kansas City.

But something happened before the game that outweighed the discomforts of the evening. It was Harmon Killebrew's 34th birthday. And in a pre-game ceremony, American League president, Joe Cronin, presented him with a magnificent silver plaque, the award for his selection as the American League's Most Valuable Player in 1969.

As Harmon stood with cap off and head bowed to acknowledge the honor, the 20,000 fans in the stadium rose to their feet and sang "Happy Birthday" to him.

As the strains of "Happy birthday, dear Harmon," floated through the hot, night air, Elaine Killebrew, who was seated in the grandstand behind home plate, was softly humming a different melody, "To dream the impossible dream, to fight the unbeatable foe. . . .

"This is our quest . . . to reach, the unreachable stars."

She thought, "It has taken seventeen years. In that time, Harmon has doubled in age. There have been heartaches and joys, but never defeat. Through all of those years, Harm and I have followed our star together. Tonight, the beautiful plaque he received makes our dream come true. Harm is recognized as one of the greats in major league baseball."

I asked Harmon how he felt out there when he received the plaque and 20,000 fans stood and sang "Happy Birthday" to him.

He looked thoughtful and replied, "It was almost overwhelming. It makes you wonder what you're doing out there."

MOUNTAIN
BASEBALL

most valuable

Part II

If there is some special secret to athletic victory, I don't know it. From what I've seen of champions, their success is an open book, easy to read, hard to apply: good health habits, moderation, discipline, and so forth. Most important, an athlete needs both faith in himself and faith in a higher power.

—Bob Mathias, Congressman, Olympic Star

American League president, Joe Cronin, presents Harmon with a silver plaque—the award for his selection as the American League's Most Valuable Player in 1969 Metropolitan Stadium June 29, 1960 (Harmon's 34th birthday)

THE WHITE HOUSE

WASHINGTON

November 20, 1969

Dear Harmon:

Baseball fans across the nation share your pride in seeing your name on top as the American League's "Most Valuable Player" for 1969. The Nixon family joins in adding our congratulations to the many that are coming your way on this significant occasion. We wish you many more successes in the days to come!

Sincerely,

Richard Nixon

Mr. Harmon Killebrew
Minnesota Twins
8001 Cedar Avenue
Minneapolis, Minnesota

most valuable

26

It was Tuesday and a beautiful autumn day in Ontario, Oregon. Elaine Killebrew was doing the family ironing. Gazing through the back window she could see brilliant patches of color made by the apple and birch trees whose leaves had turned to vivid shades of autumn hues. She hummed contentedly as her eyes feasted on the beauties of nature, and she thought about the pleasant days ahead.

Harmon was home again after having completed an outstanding 1969 season with the Minnesota Twins. It had been a trying year for both of them. Her husband had played in every single game on the baseball schedule (162), and had given every ounce of energy he possessed to help the Twins win the Western Division title in the American League. Then had come the playoff series with the Baltimore Orioles for the American League Pennant. She had flown to be with Harmon, optimistic that the Twins would go all the way and win the World Series. But they didn't. Baltimore won the playoff from the Twins and went on to lose to the New York Mets in the World Series.

Elaine was disappointed, but not discouraged. She has often said she does not get discouraged because she is "a stubborn Swede—with the Viking blood of adventure flowing in her veins." So with fierce pride she had consoled her husband with her oft repeated phrase that keeps the flame of ambition burning in Harmon's breast. "You can still do it, Harm," she said. "Next year, you'll go *all* the way."

But now the hectic baseball season was in the past. They would have time to spend delightful hours together on horseback. They could check work that needed to be done around their ranch-style home, or on their nineteen acre tract overlooking the Snake River Valley. Perhaps they would even find a few moments to do some skeet shooting, (a sport in which they both excel according to Dave Yaeger, a former national champion who tutored them).

Elaine smiled as she thought about how much their five children would enjoy having their daddy home again. They had missed him sorely during the long months he had been away and were bubbling over with enthusiasm at the prospect of chatting, playing games, and having a romping good time with their doting dad.

All these thoughts were in Elaine Killebrew's mind on that October day when a phone call came from New York City. Harmon answered it and was told that he had been voted the "Most Valuable Player in the American League."

Elaine said, "Things weren't quite the same after that call came. For two days the phone never stopped ringing, and it finally got to the point that we locked the house and drove seven miles to Payette, Idaho where we stayed a day with Harm's mother. Even there, one newsman tracked us down."

In the days and months that followed, Harmon traveled by plane to a continual round of award dinners. Writers in cities across the nation arranged banquets in his honor, and being too considerate to decline an invitation without a good reason, Harmon would accept if it were at all possible to attend.

Harmon's longest trip lasted three weeks, and Elaine accompanied him part of the way, stopping in Washington, D. C. and Minneapolis, before returning alone to Ontario. While Elaine was in Minneapolis we were privileged to have her as a house guest. In quiet evénings of conversation my wife and I grew to appreciate her remarkable personality and to sense her great love for Harmon and their children. She said, "Of course I get lonesome and start feeling sorry for myself when Harm's away so much of the time, but then I remember that I'm so fortunate with five beautiful children and a wonderful husband who loves me and provides for me. And not only that, it's great to belong to a man whom I love with all my heart."

Despite these periods of separation, Elaine does not sit passively by and await Harmon's return. Although she misses him deeply, she is as busy in her own way as he is in his. She leads a life of service to others.

Just what made Harmon Killebrew the "American League's Most Valuable Player for 1969?" It would be easy to quote statistics and write the answer off with the following records:

He led the league in:

Homeruns 49

Runs-batted-in 140

Walks 145 (an indication of opposing pitchers' respect for him)

Best fielding first baseman—80 games

A further break-down of the statistics would show other achievements which made him most valuable. However, when a player is chosen most valuable by such a wide voting margin as Killebrew was, there are intangibles to be considered which do not appear on the records. He won first place votes from 16 of 24 baseball writers, two from each league city, and his 294 point total was 67 more than John "Boog" Powell's, who finished second with 227 points and six first place votes.

The intangibles which helped propel Harmon to the top

award were complete dedication to his profession, the will to win, a cooperative team attitude, and the respect of his associates.

A brief look at the comments of other ballplayers, teammates, personal friends, fans, and sportswriters, affirms the thinking that Harmon Killebrew displayed all of these qualities and more during the 1969 baseball season.

Johnny Klippstein, Harmon's former teammate, and at present a scout for the Detroit Tigers, sent the following comment to the writer.

Dear Dr. Anderson:

I would consider it a pleasure to give a few comments on Harmon.

In my twenty-three years as a player, I have never seen any player more dedicated to his profession than Harmon. When things were maybe not going too well for him at times or he was hobbled with an injury, not once did I ever hear him complain.

He was not only respected by his fellow players but also by the umpires and the players on the opposing teams.

Although Harmon is quiet and reserved, he accepted the rookie players well, and probably more by deeds than words he showed them that hard work and desire is the name of the game.

I can still remember Harmon the first time I saw him in a Washington uniform. The larger waistline and excess pounds are now gone. Chasing the curve ball in the dirt and going after the high fastball are not bad habits any longer, but the two things that did not change are his patience and desire, which have made him one of the top hitters in professional baseball.

It was a real pleasure to play with Harm—an association I shall always remember.

Kind Regards,
Johnny Klippstein

Do Harmon's present teammates feel that he helped them during the year? Was he the most valuable to them? Typical of congratulatory messages sent to him were the following two from Twins Coach Vern Morgan and pitcher Jim Kaat:

Congratulations on MVP Award. You're the greatest. It's an honor to me to be on the same team.

Vern V. Morgan

Dear Harmon. Congrats on an honor you deserved long before this year. You have been "Most valuable" in many ways for a long time. Enjoy the winter. Your friends

The Kaats

The writer's conversations with other players brought the following comments:

Jim Perry, the Twins pitching ace and twenty-game winner, said:

Harmon never gets angry and is one of the finest gentlemen in baseball. In the team meetings he doesn't say much. But when he does say something we take notice . . . because he is really right when he says it.

He'll say something to cheer a guy on, but he doesn't like to interfere unless a guy asks for a suggestion, then he helps. All the guys respect Harmon and they don't have any wrong thinking about him. He'll speak his piece and say, "This is the way I believe,"but he doesn't try to push things on other people. We live near each other, and I like to have him as a neighbor. My kids play with his. When I'm pitching I'll say, "All right do something good for your neighbor." When he comes to the plate he puts a lot of fear in the opposition. They think twice before they throw him something. I'll sure be trying hard to win 20 games again, and I know he'll help me a lot.

Another thing, he's highly thought of all over the league.

Frank Quilici, the likable utility infielder who is inserted into the line-up at intervals to play defense, or spark the team with his unflagging enthusiasm, had this to say about Harmon:

You're writing about a regular "All-American." Harm's very shy in outward appearance and when he gets teed off he never shows anger. This was true even before he was a super-star. Instead, he tries to reason things out as an intellectual. Even so he's our silent leader. He's fantastic when he does say something. He gets results and he can influence people with a look.

The last two years we've judged how bad the umpiring is by the number of times Harm turns around and looks at them when he is at the plate. I don't want to give away any secrets, but when he swings at the ball and his lips get tense and move like he's talking from the side of his mouth, he always hits a homerun.

Harm's so solid that I always give him a bad time by kidding him. Sometimes I tell him he's sickening because he's not opinionated. I was like his caddie this past year, so I told him we should negotiate our contract next year like Koufax and Drysdale did for $125,000.00. He could take the $100,000.00 and I what was left.

> He passes out congratulations to any player getting a key hit. That's his way of making the players feel good. He shares in the excitement, but he doesn't show it outwardly, still the emotion is there.

Bob Allison, the handsome, towering specimen of manhood who patrols left field for the Twins, and has been labelled the "All American Boy," had an almost protective tone in his voice as if he wanted to shield Harmon from any possible criticism as he reminisced about their playing days together. Bob first met Harmon in 1955 at spring training before playing at Charlotte, North Carolina, and they have been teammates since they both started playing with the Washington Senators in 1959. Bob said:

> Harm hasn't changed over the years. Although he's more mature, he's basically the same. He's still quiet and unassuming and all of the younger players like him. He doesn't drink or play cards, but he still doesn't make people think he's self-righteous. We've roomed together on the road for years and he spends his spare time reading or watching television. He knows the TV Guide better than the guys who wrote it. Sometimes we go to the theater together. I suppose Harm's had more than his share of injuries, but he's always felt he'd recover and continue playing.

Billy Martin, fiery manager of the Twins who led them to their divisional title during 1969, often referred to Killebrew as the team's "bread and butter" player. When Killebrew was chosen Most Valuable for 1969 and statisticians presented his amazing batting record, Martin commented that the figures still did not reveal all the ways Harmon had helped the Twins. He said:

> Everybody told me not to play Harmon at third base. Well, he has done a helluva job there. I know what Killebrew means to me as a manager. He does everything he is asked to do. His temperament and willingness are ideal. He's a tremendous team man, and he never has a complaint or an alibi. Once when he was hit with a pitch his arm swelled up so much I thought it was going to bloom. He had an awful lot of blood in there and very few guys could have played the next day. But Harm did, and he also hit a homerun. He's a real pro. He played first and third base for us and his performance on the field provided leadership for the club. I couldn't be happier for him now that he's won this award.

George (Doc) Lentz, the Twins trainer who perhaps

knows Killebrew's personality as well as any man, because he has ministered to Harm's many injuries, had this to say about the slugger:

> He's had just about everything in the way of injuries. He reports them at once, but he never complains about them. Among other things he's had pulled muscles, bruised ribs, a swollen arm and a twisted knee. But he still gets out there and plays every game.

Calvin Griffith, owner of the Twins, also holds Killebrew in high esteem. He has frequently said,

> Harmon is the most unselfish star player I have ever known.

When Harmon won the award Calvin's comment was:

> This is the greatest honor a ballplayer can achieve in his lifetime. Harmon has certainly been close to the award before. He is just an All-American fellow. . . . It's virtually certain that Killebrew will become the first $100,000 Twins player.

Harmon Killebrew makes friends wherever he goes. Consequently, when he won the Most Valuable Player award, congratulations poured in from coast to coast. To show the esteem in which Harmon is held a few typical messages from personal friends are reproduced here.

> Congratulations on being named "American League's Most Valuable Player." You are very deserving of this award and you will always be, in our book. Say Hi to Elaine and kids and we'll see you soon.
> Bob and Betty, Minneapolis, Minnesota

> Louise and Sharon join me in sending congratulations to you for your MVP Award. Looking forward to spring training.
> Foley Hooper, Apopka, Florida

> Congratulations on your being voted the American League's Most Valuable Player. It's a great honor and it went to a great player.
> Joe Reichler, New York City, N.Y.

> We know what a huge thrill this must be for you and Elaine. Was quite a thrill for us too. Best wishes to you two and the children.
> Bill and Pat Carrothers, Excelsior, Minnesota

> Congratulations on being named "American Leagues' Most Valuable Player" Looking forward to seeing you in 1970 and your continued success.
> Harold and Jan Baer, Lakewood, California

Congratulations Harmon,
Wayne Crosby, Emmett Idaho

A great award for an even greater guy.
"Pete" Wiesner Family, St. Paul, Minnesota

Congratulations to a most valuable man.
Tom Williams, Coshocton, Ohio

Congratulations on winning MVP award.
Bud, Chattanooga, Tennessee

A few of the telegrams from professional and business friends are printed below.

Congratulations on winning the 1969 American League Most Valuable Player Award. You are tremendously deserving and perfectly represent the ultimate purpose of this great award. We are all extremely proud for you and your family.

Calvin Griffith, Ossie Bluege, Howard Fox, Billy Robertson, Jimmy Robertson, Sherry Robertson, Clark Griffith, Tom Cronin, George Brophy, Tom Mee, Don Cassidy, Jim Rantz, Charlie Lavender, Gil Lansdale, Minneapolis, Minn.

Heartiest Congratulation on your selection as the Most Valuable Player in the American League for the 1969 Season. Sincerely hope you enjoy many more happy successful years. You have been a credit to our game. Personal regards.

Joe Cronin, Pres. American League, Boston, Mass.

Congratulations. It couldn't happen to a more deserving or better fellow. May you have many more years like the past one.

George Brophy, St. Petersburg, Florida

Congratulations on a well deserved honor. May your great career continue long. With best wishes to you and your family for pleasant holidays. Regards.

H. Gabriel Murphy, Washington, D.C.

Congratulations on a job well done and well qualified in becoming the American League's Most Valuable Player. Your Old general manager. . .

Phil Howser, Charlotte, North Carolina

Congratulations on being selected as most valuable player in the American League from all your friends at the Richfield Bank and Trust Co.

Monroe Stenerson, Vice President,
Public Relations Department, Richfield, Minnesota

Congratulations on being named American League's Most Valuable Player. It is an honor that is richly deserved. Couldn't happen to a better ball player or a finer guy.

Gary Capps, KGRL Radio, Bend, Oregon

Congratulations that Harmon Killebrew was chosen the American League's most Valuable Player.

Glenn Miller of Letterman Magazine, Whittier, California

We at Neo-Life were thrilled to hear Harmon had been voted most Valuable Player of American League. Our heartiest congratulations. We look forward to seeing the homerun record added to your laurels next year.

Don Pickett, President, San Lorenzo, California

I would like to take this time to send along my congratulations on your being named M.V.P. for the American League for 1969. It is a great tribute to one of the finest players, and gentlemen, this game has ever known.

I know that your great year in 1969 will be hard to top. I hope you have as good as, or better year. It is a real thrill to watch a performer like you. Also thank you for all the fine courtesies shown me over the years. My life has certainly been much richer knowing such a fine person.

Kansas City Royals—Dick Hager, Kansas City, Missouri

Congratulations on your award as the American League's Most Valuable Player. You are a credit to your state of Idaho in every sense of the word. My best wishes for an even greater season next year.

Len B. Jordan, U. S. Senator, Idaho, Washington, D.C.

Delighted to learn that baseball writers association has admitted what Idahoans have known all along, that you are Most Valuable Player in the American League. My entire family and staff join me in sending warmest regards and congratulations. We are proud of you and the fact that you continue to represent the best in American sports and manhood. You are a great credit to the State of Idaho.

Sincerely
Orval Hansen
Member of Congress Idaho Second District,
Washington, D.C.

I am so very happy you were named the American League's Most Valuable Player for 1969. You are most deserving of this recognition. Congratulations and best wishes for many more good years with the Twins.

Eugene J. McCarthy USS, Washington, D.C.

JAMES A. McCLURE
1st District, Idaho

1034 Longworth Building
(Code 202) 225-6611

District Office:
805 Idaho Street, Room 319
Boise, Idaho 83702
(Code 208) 343-1421

James A. Goller
District Assistant

Congress of the United States
House of Representatives
Washington, D.C. 20515

Committees—Subcommittees
INTERIOR AND INSULAR AFFAIRS
IRRIGATION AND RECLAMATION
PARKS AND RECREATION
MINES AND MINING

POST OFFICE AND CIVIL SERVICE
POSITION CLASSIFICATION
POSTAL OPERATIONS

RICHARD K. THOMPSON
ADMINISTRATIVE ASSISTANT

November ~~10~~ 13th, 1969

Mr. Harmon Killebrew
Ontario
Oregon

Dear Harmon:

Louise and I were sorry that we couldn't be in Ontario last month to join the Payette and Ontario Chambers of Commerce in paying tribute to you. From the reports I've had, it was a great success!

I hope that during the next season when the Twins are in Washington, you will try to find time to drop by the office. It would be good to see you again. Perhaps we can have lunch.

Best wishes.

Sincerely yours,

Jim

James A. McClure
Member of Congress

McC:s

——— and the Most Valuable Player award could not possibly have been voted to anyone else this year. Congratulations!

HUBERT H. HUMPHREY

November 14, 1969

Dear Harmon:

As one of your most devoted fans, I was pleased and delighted beyond words with the announcement of your selection as the most valuable player in the American League for 1969. You richly deserve this high honor, and if I had been the judge you would have been the most valuable player in both leagues. You are not only a great ball player but you are a great and good man. It is for this above all else that I respect you.

With sincere admiration and friendship.

Sincerely,

Hubert H. Humphrey

Mr. Harmon Killebrew
Minnesota Twins Baseball Club
Executive Offices
Metropolitan Stadium
Bloomington, Minnesota 55420

1510 H STREET, NORTHWEST • WASHINGTON, D.C. 20005 • 202 638-4508

Remarks made in the Congressional Record by Len B. Jordan, United States Senator on the floor of the U.S. Senate on November 13, 1969.

HARMON KILLEBREW, MOST VALUABLE PLAYER

Mr. JORDAN of Idaho. Mr. President, yesterday a native Idahoan, Harmon Killebrew, was named the recipient of baseball's most prestigious award—that of most valuable player. Selected by the baseball writers of America, the American League's MVP winners include the game's greatest stars—Ted Williams, Joe DiMaggio, Jimmie Foxx, Joe Gordon, Lefty Grove—just to mention a few. The addition of Harmon Killebrew to this distinguished roster is a fitting capstone to the truly outstanding season which Harmon enjoyed this year.

The records which Harmon has set, and will continue to set in the years to come are sufficient testimony to his skills as a major leaguer. What the record books do not indicate, however, is that Harmon is every bit the major leaguer off the field as well as on. The respect that Harmon enjoys by those who know him personally cannot be generated by athletic prowess alone and will continue long after his playing days are over. My congratulations to a man who is a credit to his home State in every sense of the word.

Sportswriters Comments:

Sportswriters who try to be objective in their evaluation of a player's performance but sometimes are more inclined to throw brickbats than bouquets at popular athletes were nearly unanimous in approving Harmon Killebrew's selection as Most Valuable Player. The table shows the results of their voting:

Their subsequent comments after the selection were also favorable.

In addition to being chosen Most Valuable, Harmon was also named winner of the Babe Ruth crown for 1969 by the Maryland Professional Baseball Players Association; The Sporting News player of the year in the American League in balloting by American League players; was selected for the Associated Press major league all star team at both first and third base and also was voted the most valuable Twins player by his teammates. Other awards were given to him by different communities. Typical of such were

It's Harmon . . . By Country Mile

Player	1	2	3	4	5	6	7	8	9	10	Tot. Pts.
Harmon Killebrew	16	7		1							294
Boog Powell	6	7	7	3				1			227
Frank Robinson	3	4	6	3	3	2				1	162
Frank Howard		1	3	3	5	3	3		1	2	115
Reggie Jackson			1	6	3	5	1	3	2		110
Dennis McLain		1	1		4	2	7	2			85
Rico Petrocelli		2		2	1	2	3	3	1		71
Mike Cuellar		1		2	2	2		2	2		55
Jim Perry			1	2	1		3				40
Rod Carew		1	1				1	2		3	30
Paul Blair				1		1	2		3	2	28
Leo Cardenas			1	1	1		1			2	27
Ron Perranoski			2					2	1	1	25
Dave McNally			1		1	1	1		1		23
Tony Oliva						2		2	1	3	21
Sal Bando						1	1	2	1	1	18
Cesar Tovar					1			1			9
Mel Stottlemyre					1				1		8
Carl Yastrzemski						1			1	1	8
Ed Brinkman					1					1	7
Jim Fregosi						1			1		7
Reggie Smith								1	1	1	6
Del Unser						1					5
Brooks Robinson									2	1	5
Mike Epstein							1				4
Mike Andrews								1			3
Dave Rosman								1			3
Bill Freehan								1			3
Tommy Harper										1	2
Andy Messersmith									1		2
Rich Reese									1		2
Ken Tatum									1		2
Roy White									1		2
Mark Belanger										2	2
Dick Green										1	1
Jim Northrup										1	1
Lou Piniella										1	1

Fourteen points for first place, 9 for second, 8 for third, etc.

those given by fans in Orlando, Florida, Payette, Idaho, and the Exemplary Manhood award conferred by Brigham Young University.

Representative comments by sportswriters included the following:

Jack Lang in a press release from New York City wrote:

"Killebrew richly deserves the honor. . . . He slugged 49 homers, drove in 140 runs and 20 times during the season drove in his team's winning runs . . . that he was even playing this year was a miracle after the near crippling injury he suffered in the 1968 All-Star Game. . . . Harmon so severely ruptured his left hamstring muscle that doctors thought he might never play again. But Killebrew persevered and, through long winter months, exercised his leg to the point where it was strengthened enough for a 162 game comeback. He did not miss a single game the Twins played."

Ontario Argus Observer November 13, 1969.

". . . The year 1969 produced an amazing comeback for Killebrew, who was seriously injured the season before in an All-Star game. Medical opinion about his future in baseball at that time was not good. But Killebrew didn't give up. After long months of exercise and walking. . . . the Twins slugger staged a comeback and what a comeback it was!"

The Daily Hampshire Gazette:

"1968 Injury Fails to Stop Killebrew . . . today Killebrew is the American League's Most Valuable Player for 1969."

The Springfield Union, Massachusetts, Nov. 13, 1969.

"Harmon Killebrew, a quiet baldish man who led the major leagues with 49 homeruns and 140 runs-batted-in for the Minnesota Twins, was named Most Valuable Player in the American League for 1969. The muscular Killebrew bounced back strong from an injury in 1968 that threatened to end his career and was a decisive winner over John "Boog" Powell of the pennant winning Baltimore Orioles. . . ."

Hal Wood in the Honolulu Advertiser said, "That Harmon Killebrew is my kind of people, he's as bald as the bat he wields and twice as nice."

Ferd Borsch of the Honolulu Advertiser wrote: "A year ago Harmon Killebrew was walking the hills of eastern Oregon and Western Idaho, hunting for chukkar and pheasant—and wondering about his future in baseball. Today he is basking in the warm Waikiki sun as a very modest recipient of the American League's Most Valuable Player award following one of the finest comebacks in recent baseball history . . . Harmon is most unselfish in explaining his tremendous comeback.

"We had a lot of fellows on the club who were hitting, so there were a lot of runners on base and I had a lot of chances to drive them in,' he said.

"Which earns him the VMP (Very Modest Player) award as well a the MVP."

John P. Carmichael of the Chicago Daily News wrote:

It is right and just, fitting and proper, that Harmon Clayton Killebrew of the Minnesota Twins represents all the American League's valuable players as most valuable. When you lead the major leagues in homers and runs-batted-in, you've done it all, besides playing third base between times at bat.

Fifteen years ago the late Clark Griffith, who owned the Washington Senators, was breaking bread with Herman Welker, then U.S. senator from Idaho. The solon was bragging how he had discovered pitcher Vernon Law for the Pirates and "my good friend Bing Crosby."

"You're not back in Idaho now," said Griffith. "You're living here. So if you get another one, give him to me."

Welker promised and that's how Killebrew, from Payette, Idaho, came to the big leagues and played his first game in old Comiskey Park in 1954. "You knew he was going to be a hitter," said Paul Richards, then White Sox manager. "He was just a kid, but he was built to power the ball."

Has never hit .300 in majors

The "Killer" has been doing that ever since, although he has never hit .300 for a full season in the majors. But six times he led the AL in homeruns for a lifetime total of 446 and he has driven in 1,148 runs for both the old Nats and the present-day Twins. For a guy who has been shuttled from first to third to the outfield "to find a place for him" this has to be a remarkable exhibition of concentration on his specialty.

CAL ERMER, WHO ONCE MANAGED the Twins and had Killebrew in the minors, said of him: "He did everything to make himself a ballplayer. He worked hard, which is the trademark of success. He never shirked, never complained, never let himself down. He takes care of himself and responds to pressure and rarely does he fail to hit a ball good in every game, even if it doesn't go safe."

Those are some pretty good traits for any athlete and, at 33, the Killer finally won the MVP award over such runners-up as "Boog" Powell of the Orioles and Frank Robinson of the same team, the only other men to receive first-place votes. What's more, he sparked the entire team to a division championship and carried along five more Twins who finished in the first 16 for the MVP honor. . . .

FOR SOME OF THE BIG BONUSES of the '60's, Killebrew was born too soon. He did get $12,000 after Sen. Welker urged Griff to send a scout out there. The Red Sox, Giants, Dodgers and Reds had observed Harmon, but didn't make him an offer. So he took the 12 g's with alacrity and also got a three-year pact for $6,000 a season. Then he buckled down to improve his faulty fielding and his stiff-arm throwing, like that of a football player.

But eventually this diamond-in-the-rough began to glow, to recoin an old phrase, and in 1961 he hit 46 homers for the Twins. But that was the year Roger Maris belted 61 and Mickey Mantle notched 54, so Killebrew's achievement went all but unnoticed except, of course, in Minnesota. His wages were raised to $36,000 in 1962 and from that time on the Killer has climbed steadily in production and the financial award of $75,000 per year.

Just tries to meet ball

Like most sluggers who want to get the last possible look at a pitch, Harmon stands deep in the batter's box and crowds the knob of the bat with both fists. "I really don't concentrate on homeruns," he said. "I'm here to help the team and whenever I get on base, I'm doing that.

"IF THE BALL GOES OUT OF THE PARK, fine, and there are times when you do hope it does because it could mean the game in a late inning. But if I just get good wood on the ball, it'll take care of itself."

In contrast to the majority of his contemporaries, Killebrew doesn't smoke or drink and he derives the same satisfaction out of the Mormon religion as does Billy Casper, the golfer. As an offshoot of this, Harmon can't be drawn into discussions of other players, especially if the topic is derogatory.

"I don't believe in that sort of thing," he said. For a guy who is so muscular and wide-shouldered, with thick forearms and wrists, he belies any belligerency of makeup with a soft voice and almost shy demeanor.

Harmon Clayton Killebrew is the ideal MVP, on and off the field!

By Jim Murray, Sports columnist, Los Angeles Times and the Times Syndicate

ALL RIGHT, class, the subject today is baseball. Remember neatness counts. Give one answer and one answer only. If you don't know, leave the space blank. Don't be a guess hitter. Ready? No erasures, please.

QUESTION—Give the infield-fly rule in Latin—no wait a minute, that's the umpires test. Here's the fans test:

QUESTION—In the history of baseball, only two men have hit more than 40 homeruns in seven or more seasons. I'll give you a hint: One of them was Babe Ruth. For an autographed photograph of Randy Moore, and a pair of the original Black Sox of 1919, who was the other?

ANSWER—Harmon Killebrew, of course. Ruth hit over 40 homers in 11 seasons. Killebrew in seven.

Q—Babe Ruth hit homeruns oftener (per times at bat) than any player who ever lived. For a free picture of Sick Stadium in Seattle, was Willie Mays, Ted Williams, Jimmie Foxx or Mickey Mantle second?

A—None of them. Harmon Killebrew was second. Ruth hit 8.5 homers every 100 times at bat or one every 11.7 plate appearances. Harmon's percentages were 7.6, or one homer every 13 times at bat.

Q—If we accept the dictum, "A walk is as good as a hit," Willie Mays is the only active player in the top 25 all-time in this important category. But who will break into it this year?

Walked 124 Times This Year

A—Harmon Killebrew has walked 124 times already this year, which puts him over 1,000 career walks, and boosts him past Kiner, Slaughter, Gilliam, Hornsby, Max Carey, Eddie Joost and Joe Cronin; and he needs only 30 more to boost him to 23rd all-time position.

Q—A general manager considers the runs-batted-in category the best salary measure. Henry Aaron has won the league title four times, Ernie Banks twice, Orlando Cepeda twice. But, barring accident, who will be the only active American Leaguer to win it twice by the time this season is over?

A—With a 10-run bulge, Harmon Killebrew will. No other active former winner is in the hunt unless Carl Yastrzemski (28 behind) bats .908 the rest of the year or breaks the all-time record for bases-loaded homeruns.

Q—In what department is Harmon Killebrew pressing Baby Ruth closest?

A—Strikeouts. Harmon has 1,200 lifetime, only 17 behind Duke Snyder. Oddly, this list reads like an all-time who's who. Mickey Mantle leads, followed by Eddie Mathews, Ruth, Foxx. Mays is hot on the heels of Killebrew and may overtake him because Harmon this year has cut his strikeouts from a league-leading high of 142 in 1961 down to his own all-time low of 66 this year.

Q—Only five active players are among the top 25 all-time homerun hitters. Who moved up the ladder this year?

Aaron From 8th to 3rd

A—Aaron went from eighth to third. Banks went from 11th to 8th. Killebrew went from 14th to 11th (assuming Frank Robinson does not break the month of September homerun record).

Q—If the Minnesota Twins win the pennant, Cesar Tovar will command attention as most valuable player for his .348 batting average; so will Rich Reese for his .326. Neither would be an unworthy winner, but what would the voters be overlooking?

A—Killebrew has only two less hits than Cesar, 10 more than Rich. Totaling his hits and walks, he has been on base 254 times vs. Tovar's 163 and Reese's 141. Total bases and runs scored is no contest, Killebrew is even third on the club in stolen bases.

Q—List reasons in the order of importance, why Killebrew is MVP every year.

A—He is kind to animals—and people. He is a country boy who never raises his voice. He is a man of monumental strength who uses it only to hit baseballs. He's so humble you'd think they platooned him. He blushes. He never argues with the umpire or fights the manager. He shows up for 8 p.m. games at 3 in the afternoon. He hangs in there on pitches that rip buttons off his shirt. He's as popular as Santa Claus, as taken-for-granted as electricity, as cheerful as a Kansas picnic, as temperamental as a penitential monk. His language could be used in the Vatican. If they had a category for 25 all-time "nicest," he would be so far out in front that whoever was second would be in a monastery.

Twin Cities sportswriters went all out praising the selection of Killebrew as Most Valuable Player. Dick Cullum, veteran sports columnist for the Minneapolis Tribune, had the following to say:

HARMON KILLEBREW NEEDED only a season free of injuries to qualify as the Most Valuable Player in the American League.

It couldn't have happened to a nicer guy—or a more valuable player.

Killebrew's value goes beyond his batting average, the number of runs he scores, the number he drives in or the number of bases he is given, although 145 bases on balls are useful.

His presence in the batting order compels opponents to modify their tactics in any inning in which he is likely to come to bat.

No batter in the league sees fewer good pitches to hit, but this means that men who precede him in the batting order are seeing the good pitches. Pitchers don't want to get behind those batters in the ball and strike count.

At least four times in a game Killebrew is an embarrassment to the opponent. In manager Bill Rigney's opinion he is the most embarrassing player in the league.

It is something extra, but should count in the award, that he is the best influence on a team that can be found in the league because of character, personality and unselfish dedication to the job.

Mike Lamey, Minneapolis Star staff writer

Homerun and runs-batted-in totals tell only part of the story of Harmon Killebrew's value to the Twins in the best all-around baseball season of his 11-year major league career.

He was going for a career-high of 50 homers in today's season finale after hitting No. 49 in Wednesday's 4-3 loss to the Chicago White Sox at Metropolitan Stadium. He also had 140 RBI's before today's Chicago game. But that's just scratching the surface.

Killebrew's bat has delivered hits for winning runs in 20 of Minnesota's 96 victories before today. That's more than one-fifth. And that also is almost twice as many as any other Twin has produced.

Harmon has 28 hits for go-ahead runs—runs that gave the Twins leads, eight hits that have produced game-tying runs and three that have pulled the Twins from behind to within one run of the opposition.

Six times Killebrew has won games in the seventh inning or later.

His batting average was .278 after yesterday. His best averages in other years were .288 in 1961, .281 in 1966 and .276 in 1960. Also Harmon has set a club record of 144 walks and has held his strikeouts to 83. . . .

Of his walks 20 were intentional. That's also a club record. The major league record for walks was set at 170 by Babe Ruth.

Harmon's Response

How did Harmon acknowledge all his honors? His statements to the press give considerable insight into his personality. He said:

"I thought that Boog or Robby might get the award since they were on the league pennant winner. . . . We had a lot of fellows on the club who were hitting, so there were a lot of runners on base and I had chances to drive them in. . . .

"I've always felt this was the No. 1 award, so I feel real good. Last year I was injured so I was just really hoping

I'd get to play a lot this year. I've always felt it is difficult to pick one guy for the MVP. It takes a lot of guys to win. It's great to receive the award."

A look at the official statistics for 1969 give final evidence of Killebrew's value to his team. Although a number of other players made impressive records, Harmon's statistics stand out from the rest like the National Debt.

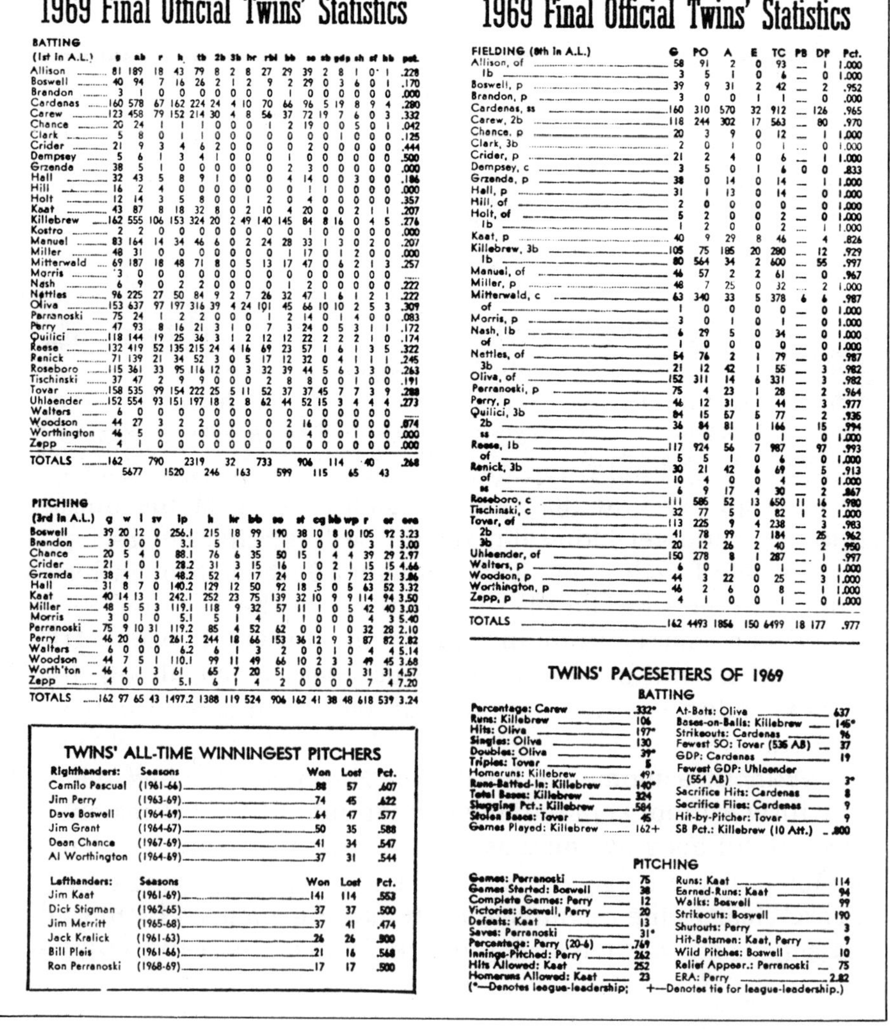

1969 Final Official Twins' Statistics

BATTING

(1st in A.L.)	g	ab	r	h	tb	2b	3b	hr	rbi	bb	so	sb	gdp	sh	sf	hb	pct.
Allison	81	189	18	43	79	8	2	8	27	29	39	2	8	1	0	1	.228
Boswell	40	94	7	16	26	2	1	2	9	2	29	0	3	6	0	1	.170
Brandon	3	1	0	0	0	0	0	0	0	1	0	0	0	0	0	0	.000
Cardenas	160	578	67	162	224	24	4	10	70	66	96	5	19	8	9	4	.280
Carew	123	458	79	152	214	30	4	8	56	37	72	19	7	6	0	3	.332
Chance	20	24	1	1	1	0	0	0	1	2	19	0	0	5	0	1	.042
Clark	5	8	0	1	1	0	0	0	0	0	0	0	1	0	0	0	.125
Crider	21	9	3	4	6	2	0	0	0	0	2	0	0	0	0	0	.444
Dempsey	5	6	1	3	4	1	0	0	0	1	0	0	0	0	0	0	.500
Grzenda	38	5	1	0	0	0	0	0	0	2	3	0	0	0	0	0	.000
Hall	32	43	5	8	9	1	0	0	0	4	14	0	0	3	0	0	.186
Hill	16	2	4	0	0	0	0	0	0	0	1	1	0	0	0	0	.000
Holt	12	14	3	5	8	0	1	2	0	4	0	0	0	0	0	0	.357
Kaat	43	87	8	18	32	8	0	2	10	4	20	0	0	2	1	1	.207
Killebrew	162	555	106	153	324	20	2	49	140	145	84	8	16	0	4	5	.276
Kostro	2	2	0	0	0	0	0	0	0	0	1	0	0	0	0	0	.000
Manuel	83	164	14	34	46	6	0	2	24	28	33	1	3	0	2	0	.207
Miller	48	31	0	0	0	0	0	0	0	1	17	0	1	2	0	0	.000
Mitterwald	69	187	18	48	71	8	0	5	13	17	47	0	6	2	1	3	.257
Morris	3	0	0	0	0	0	0	0	0	0	0	0	0	0	0	0	....
Nash	6	9	0	2	2	0	0	0	0	1	2	0	0	0	0	0	.222
Nettles	96	225	27	50	84	9	2	7	26	32	47	1	6	1	2	1	.222
Oliva	153	637	97	197	316	39	4	24	101	45	66	10	10	2	5	3	.309
Perranoski	75	24	1	2	2	0	0	0	1	2	14	0	1	4	0	0	.083
Perry	47	93	8	16	21	3	1	0	7	3	24	0	5	3	1	1	.172
Quilici	118	144	19	25	36	3	1	2	12	12	22	2	2	2	1	0	.174
Reese	132	419	52	135	215	24	4	16	69	23	57	1	6	1	3	5	.322
Renick	71	139	21	34	52	3	0	5	17	12	32	0	4	1	1	1	.245
Roseboro	115	361	33	95	116	12	0	3	32	39	44	5	6	3	3	0	.263
Tischinski	37	47	2	9	9	0	0	0	2	8	8	0	0	1	0	0	.191
Tovar	158	535	99	154	222	25	5	11	52	37	37	45	7	7	3	9	.288
Uhlaender	152	554	93	151	197	18	2	8	62	44	52	15	3	4	4	4	.273
Walters	6	0	0	0	0	0	0	0	0	0	0	0	0	0	0	0	
Woodson	44	27	3	2	2	0	0	0	0	2	16	0	0	0	0	0	.074
Worthington	46	5	0	0	0	0	0	0	0	0	4	0	1	0	0	0	.000
Zepp	4	1	0	0	0	0	0	0	0	0	0	0	0	0	0	0	.000
TOTALS	162	5677	790	1520	2319	246	32	163	733	599	906	115	114	65	40	43	.268

PITCHING

(3rd in A.L.)	g	w	l	sv	ip	h	hr	bb	so	st	cg	hb	wp	r	er	era
Boswell	39	20	12	0	256.1	215	18	99	190	38	10	8	10	105	92	3.23
Brandon	3	0	0	0	3.1	5	1	3	1	0	0	0	0	3	1	3.00
Chance	20	5	4	0	88.1	76	6	35	50	15	1	4	4	39	29	2.97
Crider	21	1	0	1	28.2	31	3	15	16	1	0	2	1	15	15	4.66
Grzenda	38	4	1	3	48.2	52	4	17	24	0	0	1	7	23	21	3.86
Hall	31	8	7	0	140.2	129	12	50	92	18	5	0	5	63	52	3.32
Kaat	40	14	13	1	242.1	252	23	75	139	32	10	9	9	114	94	3.50
Miller	48	5	5	3	119.1	118	9	32	57	11	1	0	5	42	40	3.03
Morris	3	0	1	0	5.1	5	1	4	1	1	0	0	0	4	3	5.40
Perranoski	75	9	10	31	119.2	85	4	52	62	0	0	1	0	32	28	2.10
Perry	46	20	6	0	261.2	244	18	66	153	36	12	9	3	87	82	2.82
Walters	6	0	0	0	6.2	6	1	3	2	0	0	1	0	4	4	5.14
Woodson	44	7	5	1	110.1	99	11	49	66	10	2	3	3	49	45	3.68
Worth'ton	46	4	1	3	61	65	7	20	51	0	0	0	1	31	31	4.57
Zepp	4	0	0	0	5.1	6	1	4	2	0	0	0	0	7	4	7.20
TOTALS	162	97	65	43	1497.2	1388	119	524	906	162	41	38	48	618	539	3.24

TWINS' ALL-TIME WINNINGEST PITCHERS

Righthanders:	Seasons	Won	Lost	Pct.
Camilo Pascual	(1961-66)	88	57	.607
Jim Perry	(1963-69)	74	45	.622
Dave Boswell	(1964-69)	64	47	.577
Jim Grant	(1964-67)	50	35	.588
Dean Chance	(1967-69)	41	34	.547
Al Worthington	(1964-69)	37	31	.544

Lefthanders:	Seasons	Won	Lost	Pct.
Jim Kaat	(1961-69)	141	114	.553
Dick Stigman	(1962-65)	37	37	.500
Jim Merritt	(1965-68)	37	41	.474
Jack Kralick	(1961-63)	26	26	.500
Bill Pleis	(1961-66)	21	16	.568
Ron Perranoski	(1968-69)	17	17	.500

1969 Final Official Twins' Statistics

FIELDING (8th in A.L.)	G	PO	A	E	TC	PB	DP	Pct.
Allison, of	58	91	2	0	93	—	1	1.000
1b	3	5	1	0	6	—	0	1.000
Boswell, p	39	9	31	2	42	—	2	.952
Brandon, p	3	0	0	1	1	—	0	.000
Cardenas, ss	160	310	570	32	912	—	126	.965
Carew, 2b	118	244	302	17	563	—	80	.970
Chance, p	20	3	9	0	12	—	1	1.000
Clark, 3b	2	0	1	0	1	...	0	1.000
Crider, p	21	2	4	0	6	—	1	1.000
Dempsey, c	3	5	0	1	6	0	0	.833
Grzenda, p	38	0	14	0	14	—	1	1.000
Hall, p	31	1	13	0	14	—	0	1.000
Hill, of	2	0	0	0	0	—	0	1.000
Holt, of	5	2	0	0	2	—	0	1.000
1b	1	2	0	0	2	...	1	1.000
Kaat, p	40	9	29	8	46	...	4	.826
Killebrew, 3b	105	75	185	20	280	...	12	.929
1b	80	564	34	2	600	...	55	.997
Manuel, of	46	57	2	2	61	—	0	.967
Miller, p	48	7	25	0	32	...	2	1.000
Mitterwald, c	63	340	33	5	378	6	6	.987
of	1	0	0	0	0	—	0	1.000
Morris, p	3	0	1	0	1	—	0	1.000
Nash, 1b	6	29	5	0	34	—	0	1.000
of	1	0	0	0	0	—	0	1.000
Nettles, of	54	76	2	1	79	—	0	.987
3b	21	12	42	1	55	—	3	.982
Oliva, of	152	311	14	6	331	—	3	.982
Perranoski, p	75	4	23	1	28	—	2	.964
Perry, p	46	12	31	1	44	—	3	.977
Quilici, 3b	84	15	57	5	77	—	2	.936
2b	36	84	81	1	166	—	15	.994
ss	1	0	1	0	1	—	0	1.000
Reese, 1b	117	924	56	7	987	—	97	.993
of	5	5	1	0	6	—	0	1.000
Renick, 3b	30	21	42	6	69	—	5	.913
of	10	4	0	0	4	—	0	1.000
ss	6	9	17	4	30	—	2	.867
Roseboro, c	111	585	52	13	650	11	16	.980
Tischinski, c	32	77	5	0	82	1	2	1.000
Tovar, of	113	225	9	4	238	—	3	.983
2b	41	78	99	7	184	—	25	.962
3b	20	12	26	2	40	—	2	.950
Uhlaender, of	150	278	8	1	287	—	1	.997
Walters, p	6	0	1	0	1	—	0	1.000
Woodson, p	44	3	22	0	25	—	3	1.000
Worthington, p	46	2	6	0	8	—	1	1.000
Zepp, p	4	1	0	0	1	—	0	1.000
TOTALS	162	4493	1856	150	6499	18	177	.977

TWINS' PACESETTERS OF 1969

BATTING

Percentage: Carew	.332*	At-Bats: Oliva	637
Runs: Killebrew	106	Bases-on-Balls: Killebrew	145*
Hits: Oliva	197*	Strikeouts: Cardenas	96
Singles: Oliva	130	Fewest SO: Tovar (535 AB)	37
Doubles: Oliva	39*	GDP: Cardenas	19
Triples: Tovar	5	Fewest GDP: Uhlaender (554 AB)	3*
Homeruns: Killebrew	49*	Sacrifice Hits: Cardenas	8
Runs-Batted-In: Killebrew	140*	Sacrifice Flies: Cardenas	9
Total Bases: Killebrew	324	Hit-by-Pitcher: Tovar	9
Slugging Pct.: Killebrew	.584	SB Pct.: Killebrew (10 Att.)	.800
Stolen Bases: Tovar	45		
Games Played: Killebrew	162+		

PITCHING

Games: Perranoski	75	Runs: Kaat	114
Games Started: Boswell	38	Earned-Runs: Kaat	94
Complete Games: Perry	12	Walks: Boswell	99
Victories: Boswell, Perry	20	Strikeouts: Boswell	190
Defeats: Kaat	13	Shutouts: Perry	3
Saves: Perranoski	31*	Hit-Batsmen: Kaat, Perry	9
Percentage: Perry (20-6)	.769	Wild Pitches: Boswell	10
Innings-Pitched: Perry	262	Relief Appear.: Perranoski	75
Hits Allowed: Kaat	252	ERA: Perry	2.82
Homeruns Allowed: Kaat	23		

(*—Denotes league-leadership; +—Denotes tie for league-leadership.)

for the team

27

Curt Flood hit the ball sharply and with the crack of his bat was off like a shot toward first base. Shortstop Jim Fregosi fielded the ball cleanly in deep short, but his throw to Killebrew at first was low and wide. As Harmon saw the fleet Flood approaching first base he was faced with a split-second decision. He could see that the only way he could get Flood out would be to stretch out as far as possible for the ball. Two thoughts flashed through his mind, "Should he play it safe, remain on the bag, and let Fregosi be charged with an error on his throw, or reach out for the ball and gamble that the powdery artificial soil in the Astrodome would support his weight and try for the put out?"

Without a moment's hesitation Harmon stretched out. His forward foot kept moving farther out until at the instant the ball hit his glove he was in an almost total split. At that moment, his left leg gave way with a loud pop that could be heard clear to the dugouts and up into the stands. His huge hamstring muscle had torn, rendering him helpless. When he caught the ball he half-rolled onto his back and lay virtually motionless. As he remained prostrate and helpless on the ground a hushed silence swept over the spectators who had jammed the Houston Astrodome to witness the All-Star game on July 9, 1968. Medical attendants came swiftly to Killebrew's aid, and when he was lifted on a stretcher the thousands of fans at the game and the millions watching on television could perceive that his strong body was racked with pain. The stretcher bearers carried him slowly and carefully to the clubhouse, and the game resumed with "Boog" Powell of the Baltimore Orioles taking his place at first base.

Although the game continued on to an exciting finish in the brightly-colored Astrodome, there was darkest gloom in the clubhouse. Joe Cronin, the American League President came in and spoke consoling words to Harmon as the 210 pound athlete writhed in agony on the training table. Cronin seemed so concerned with Killebrew's injury that he appeared oblivious to the fact that his American League had lost its sixth straight All-Star game.

Calvin Griffith, Twins owner, who thinks the world of Killebrew, stood nearby, looking as if he had lost his best friend.

Cal Ermer, Twins Manager, who was coaching at third base for the American Leaguers, said in a heart-broken voice, "The dirt was dry and powdery. It wasn't quite what Harmon is used to outside."

"Boog" Powell, the blond giant from Baltimore, whom Killebrew had beaten out of the American League's starting first base job, and California's spectacular shortstop Jim Fregosi, whose throw had preceded the injury, stood by silently, powerless to help.

As soon as Harmon was able to speak, he was asked to tell what happened. His reply was typical—brief and to the point. "I stretched as far as I could and then the ground gave way," he said.

Weeks later when he was fighting his way back to playing condition, I asked him the same question. He had taken me out on the back lawn of his Edina, Minnesota home to show me how he was gradually regaining his mobility. I put the question to him point blank and said, "Tell me what really happened when you pulled that hamstring muscle, Harmon. Surely you had worked out on the Astrodome infield and were aware that its mealy soil might not hold your spikes. Why did you stretch out and risk injury?"

He looked at me calmly and said, "I always stretch out as far as I can, if it is necessary to catch the ball. In the Astrodome, the powdery dirt didn't hold; it gave way under my spikes." There were no regrets expressed by Harmon in the form of "I wish I hadn't reached out," no criticisms of the playing field's surface, no evidences of self-pity; nor were there any details given of the agonizing hours he had spent recovering from his injury. He simply made it clear to me that when he plays baseball, no matter what the circumstances, he gives his all for the team.

Numerous post-game comments regarding Harmon's injury and his role in the game were aired by both the players and the press.

Don Drysdale, the winning pitcher for the National League All-Stars, who won the game by a score of one to nothing, said, "Killebrew's injury was so severe that from the dugout you could hear his leg pop."

John Roseboro, the Twins All-Star catcher commented, "I've seen many first basemen go down doing the splits like Harmon did and I've seen a lot of them get hurt, but this is the first time I've seen one like that. I knew he had trouble with his legs before, and it wasn't hard to figure out what had happened."

Bob Allison, who has been rooming for years with Killebrew when the Twins are on the road, and thinks of Harmon almost as a brother, did not see the game, but he was one of the first to reach Harmon by telephone after the injury. He said, "I called Harmon last night. He didn't say too much except that it made a loud popping noise when he pulled the hamstring muscle. He's had a lot of bad leg and knee injuries over the years, and I imagine he won't be able to play for quite awhile."

The following were representative of comments by the press: Dick Gordon of the Minneapolis Star wrote: (July 10, 1968) "Killebrew's loss is a stunning blow to Twin hopes . . . two innings after hard luck Harmon's error set up the only run in the National League's one to nothing victory, he was prostrate near the first base bag. Umpire Larry Napp was signalling Curt Flood out, and Killebrew still held on to the ball. But what price glory? He had reached his tired muscles to the limit for Fregosi's low throw on Curt Flood's grounder to deep short."

George Edmond of the St. Paul Dispatch (July 10, 1968) said: "It would be difficult to say which is worse in the case of things that happened to Harmon Killebrew in the All-Star game Tuesday.

"Most fans would probably look at it this way: 'It's bad enough to suffer an injury that means a stretch on the bench, but to get a more than average share of the blame for the American League's defeat is adding insult to injury —quite literally.'

"The Twins first baseman, who started in that position against the National League in the annual game at Houston, was charged with a first inning error on which Willie Mays reached second base, from where he scored the game's only run.

"Now, however, it develops that there is considerable question on whether Harmon deserved the error. There was opinion in the press box that it should have been given instead to Luis Tiant, Cleveland Pitcher. Tiant tried (for the second time) to pick Mays off first base and the ball got away from Harmon.

"There are those who witnessed the play who now say the throw was at fault, not Harmon. Mays says he believes the ball hit him in the back, but he's not sure.

"Tiant, himself, contributes toward absolving the Twins slugger. He admits he may have thrown a curve ball which, one may offer, is not a throw designed for picking off base runners.

"Even if Harmon deserved the error, it hardly would be fair to charge him with the defeat.

"An equal share of blame should go to all others in the lineup who couldn't produce even one run. If you can't score you can't win, whatever the opposition may do."

A nationally syndicated sportswriter had some caustic remarks to make concerning the game and Killebrew's role. He wrote:

(Houston) "An All-Star game is not really a contest unless you consider 'LaBoheme' a contest. . . . (This critic thought it would do better as a musical. On the purely personal level, the review might read like this): Harmon Killebrew appeared to have great unfamiliarity with his role. The program listed him as 'first baseman' but it was beyond the scope of his capabilities, and the poor fellow overtaxed himself catching a thrown ball in the third inning, thus robbing the performance of much, but not all of its comic relief. His replacement Boog Powell, managed to remain in the game largely by not straining himself reaching too far for any hit or thrown balls. You might say Powell handled the role with great restraint. . . ."

One wonders if such comments by a sportswriter are evidence of not pulling off enough flies wings during boyhood—or, if they indicate a sour grapes rationalization suggesting that the writer aspired to play professional baseball, failed to make the grade, and subsequently took out his bitterness on those who did.

Some insightful comments on Harmon's injury were made by Dick Cullum of the Minneapolis Tribune (July 11, 1968). He wrote under the heading, "Incidentally a Great Play," the following observations. "When the telecasters were discussing Harmon's injury in the All-Star game, they talked about this and that including the comment that, 'after all Killebrew's no gazelle.' They might have thrown in the additional comment that for a man who is no gazelle, Killebrew made an amazing play on Jim Fregosi's low, wide throw. Another comment, more to the point, might have been that Killebrew was the victim of the Astrodome. Everything is artificial there, including the unweathered base paths. When Harmon made his stretch for the bad throw, he expected the same kind of footing he would have on an outdoor field. It wasn't there. The mealy soil did not hold his spikes. The result was a split and a torn hamstring. This is an injury, in Harmon's huge leg muscle, about which he and the Twins must have deep concern."

Just how serious was Harmon's injury? Dr. Harvey O'Phelan, the Twins' physician who is one of the top orthopedic surgeons in the nation, said, "Harmon has a partial rupture of the left hamstring muscle. His injury is as bad as has been feared. His disability is relatively severe, and he will be unable to play for six to eight weeks. He's had something on both sides now. (Harmon told reporters at the airport that he had suffered two previous pulled hamstrings and two groin injuries, "but this may be the worst of them.") The treatment involves rest and physical therapy. He's on crutches now and I hope he'll be walking in five to seven days. He led me to believe that this was his worst injury, and I agree. But that man has marvelous recuperative abilities."

I had the opportunity to talk to Doc Lentz, the Twins trainer at the 1970 spring training camp, about the injury. Doc is the kind, fatherly type who watches over the Twins players as tenderly as a mother hen does her baby chicks. He had the following to say: "That torn hamstring was the worst injury I've ever treated. When I first saw it, I didn't think Harm would ever play again. His left leg was a mass of blue where the blood vessels had ruptured from his hip clear down to the ankle. He had to stand up to eat for nearly a month."

Harmon said after he was injured and went to the hotel in Houston he was unable to change to his civilian clothes and that "Ted Uhlaender stayed right with me and helped me dress. The plane flight from Houston to Chicago was torture. Every seat was filled; consequently they could not move anything out of the way so I could stretch out. The flight from Chicago to Minneapolis was better because they could make room for me.

"I remember that Jimmy Robertson was one of the first to call at the hotel after I was injured."

When Harmon flew back to Minneapolis after the injury, his wife Elaine was at the airport to greet him with a wheelchair. He tried to sit in it, but when he attempted to pull his leg in a sitting position the pain was unbearable; so he continued on his crutches to Dr. O'Phelan's office.

Although Elaine was terrifically upset by the injury, she controlled her emotions by saying, "Every time Harm gets hurt it tears me apart inside, but then I think at least we'll see more of him at home. But it doesn't work out that way. It seems that he has to spend even more time at the ball park to get back into shape."

What Elaine did not say for public consumption was that she would be watching over her injured husband and giving him all of her love in nursing him back to health, and during his darkest moments when he wondered if he could come back she would embrace him and say, "You can do it, Harm, You'll come back."

Harmon has always followed a pattern of giving his all for the good of the team.

When he was seventeen and unmarried and was offered a bonus to sign with the Washington Senators, he had to choose between accepting the appointment or a scholarship offer at the University of Oregon. The circumstances surrounding this decision have been discussed earlier. Although Harmon doesn't say this, the writer is certain that the scales were tipped in favor of signing with the Senators because it would help ease the financial situation of his family.

On opening day in 1959, he started the season for the first time in the field instead of on the bench. Over 25,000 fans, including such notables as then Vice-President Richard Nixon, were there to cheer the Senators on. Harmon, with all of the enthusiasm of a 22 year-old, took his position at third base and waited for his big moment. It came on the first play of the game. Pedro Ramos, who was pitching against the Baltimore Orioles and had a count of one and one on Tasby, their first hitter, attempted to put over a strike on the inside of the plate. Tasby swung and shot a grounder toward third. Harmon moved to his right to pick it up. But the ball, instead of taking the hop he anticipated, scooted along the ground. As a result, it hit the heel of his glove and bounced away. Of course Tasby was safe on first. Harmon could hear a low groan in the stands. And when the inning ended, even though his error had not damaged his team's cause, he felt like digging a hole in the ground and crawling into it. He thought to himself, "I've got to prove I can help this team." He did just that in his second time at bat, facing Baltimore's Hoyt Wilhelm.

Wilhelm—renowned knuckle ball pitcher—possessed a knuckler that made so many weird gyrations on its way to the plate that strong batters would almost break their backs trying to hit it while weaker hitters would wave at it with despair as it fluttered past them. But Harmon maintained his composure.

On Wilhelm's third pitch he timed his swing just right and the ball sailed into the stands for a homerun.

Washington went on to win the game 9 to 2. But the most important thing that happened that opening day was the realization by his teammates and the crowd that Harmon Killebrew was a team man. He wouldn't fold under pressure, and if he made a mistake he would fight back with dogged determination to make up for it and help the team.

Another evidence of Harmon's desire to help the team is his willingness to play at any position where "I can help the team the most." This has been the story of his career—changing positions and adjusting his playing according to team needs.

In 1961, the first year the Twins moved to Minnesota, Harmon was instructed by Manager Cookie Lavagetto to "Bring a first baseman's mitt and a third baseman's glove to spring training." And he added, "You ought to wind up at one of those places." Harmon wound up at both places,

Harmon with his long-time friend Bob Allison, 1968

and during the season he was shuttled back and forth between first and third base so much that he began to think of himself as "just a utility infielder."

During the latter part of the 1961 season, when manager Sam Mele had taken over the club's reins, Harmon was supposedly installed permanently at first base. Mele said, "I've decided first base is Harmon's best position." Killebrew's brief comment was "I'd rather play there."

Despite this commitment by Mele, when Harmon reported to Tinker Field for spring training in 1962—the top-salaried man on the team—he was again a player without a position. Rich Rollins, a second-year-man, was showing outstanding promise at third base; so Harmon assumed first base was his spot. But before the season began, Calvin Griffith obtained fancy-fielding first baseman Vic Power from Cleveland in a trade and Harmon found himself installed in left field. Harmon did not complain but set about to learn the intricacies of playing left field. Those who watched him play there said that he always seemed to get to the necessary place to field the ball.

After Vic Power left the team, Harmon was reinstalled at first base. Subsequently, the Twins acquired Don Mincher, a powerful hitting left-handed first baseman, to improve the strength on their bench.

In 1965 the Twins were involved in a battle down to the wire for the American League pennant. Harmon, feeling that the club would be a stronger team with Mincher in the line-up, went to Mele and said, "Sam, if you think Mincher will help us when we're facing right-handed pitchers, I'll be happy to switch to third base." Mele followed the suggestion, and again Harmon was a man with no set position.

At this writing, Harmon is still following his pattern of doing what is best for the team, playing where he is needed. An incident happened as this was being written that illustrates this team spirit. The Twins lost a 3-1 game to Cleveland because no one caught a foul pop fly that led to two unearned runs in the ninth inning. The post-game discussion of the misplay brought a variety of comments. Whose fault? The official scorer simply gave Killebrew an error because he had attempted to catch the ball and did not hang onto it. But team members gave different versions of the "goof".

Manager Rigney said, "Jim Perry, who was pitching, should have called for Mitterwald to take it." (The ball came down five feet behind the plate.)

Twins first baseman Rich Reese observed, "It was not my ball. I couldn't get to it."

George Mitterwald, the catcher said, "I didn't hear anyone call, or I could have caught it."

Pitcher Jim Perry said, "When a ball is up that high, it's up to the individual, although I did call for Reese to take it."

Rigney added, "Harmon had to come 120 feet to reach the ball. When I played third base, I hated plays like that because third was the toughest spot from which to make them."

What did Harmon who was charged with the error say? His comment was, "We just missed the ball. I blew it."

A few mornings later, and the day after Killebrew had won a game with a homerun, Paul Giel, WCCO sports editor, who was an All-American halfback at Minnesota and a major league pitcher, had the following to say in his early-morning broadcast:

"I lockered next to Willie Mays when I played for the Giants, but no one gives me the same thrill as Harmon Killebrew does. When he comes to the plate he is power personified. I don't want to miss that number 3 when it comes up. When I played for the Twins, I never heard him make an excuse either on or off the field. He's played first base, third base, and left field."

Howard Vikan, popular WCCO radio personality who was participating in the broadcast added, "I don't always agree with you Paul, but this time I do. Harm should get a raise on his raise. He's great!"

Paul continued, "Yes, Harmon is great and what's more he's a good family man.

"Remember that pop fly that everyone was making excuses for not catching, Harmon who was charged with the error did not alibi. He simply said, 'I blew it.'

"He's our man for today and everyday."

I talked to Harmon the day after the pop foul incident. Before asking for his off-the-record opinion, I said, "The spectators who were near the play said that Mitterwald called for you to make the catch so late that you had to make a desperate lunge to attempt an almost impossible catch. I don't think you should have been charged with an error."

Harmon looked at me in his calm, pleasant way and replied, "There just isn't any point in discussing an incident like that and trying to fix the blame on anyone. It's not good for the team."

I could see that he did not want to spend any more time discussing the matter, so I started to talk about other things. But then Harmon said something that gave me deeper insight into his remarkable ability to keep his emotions in check and avoid making critical comments about others.

"You know," he said, "Elaine phoned me long distance from Ontario last night. [She and their children live in the family home in Ontario until June; so Harmon lives alone while in Minneapolis for home games during early season play.] She said she had heard the report about my dropping the pop foul and thought I would feel down, so she called to cheer me up. She is down with the flu herself and to add to her worries two of our girls have the measles. She's quite a girl."

Harmon did not tell me what Elaine said, but there was no need to. I sensed once more that his wife is a wellspring of encouragement who helps Harm keep his composure when difficult situations arise. Yes, he is a team man, and his wife is also a team woman.

People often ask, "When a guy is as modest and unassuming as Killebrew, won't his associates tend to step on him and look on him as sort of a milquetoast?" The complete reverse is true. Numerous incidents bear this out.

During the 1961 season, one sportswriter described Killebrew in the following way: "Everything about him suggests the characteristics of the humble apple of the earth, the state fruit of Idaho—modest, unassuming, self-effacing, mild-mannered, folksy—all of those."

Yet, during this same season, when Harmon was only 25, manager Cookie Lavagetto made him team captain. Lavagetto realized that although Killebrew was a bit quiet, he nevertheless possessed leadership qualities that would inspire his teammates.

Harmon responded to the honor with sincere appreciation. He said, "I'm not much of a talker, but I'll do my best to set the right kind of example on the field."

This he has done. He has constantly encouraged his teammates, rookies, and veterans alike, but never in an annoying way. He is their silent leader, the stabilizer on the team, the one who instills into them the confidence that they can win. They appreciate and respect him for it. As a result, sportswriters have called him, "one of the quietest team leaders of all time."

I was talking about this seemingly strange phenomenon with Doc Lentz. I said, "It's difficult to understand how Harmon can command such great respect without losing his temper. Haven't you ever seen him get angry?"

Doc Lentz grinned. "Of course I have. Harmon's human. I've seen him get so angry that his face has turned as white as that pillow. But he never says a word. He controls it."

That's Harmon's secret, control of his emotions. In a lecture on mental health in one of my university classes, I used him as an example of a person with superb emotional control.

One of the students commented, "Maybe that's why he hits so many homeruns, he takes his hostilities out on the ball." It could be.

Whatever the reason, Harmon is an individual who commands respect.

When you shake his hand, you sense the latent strength behind the gentle and friendly grip, and when you walk behind him and observe his broad and powerful shoulders you think to yourself, "Here is a man who could tear his enemies into little pieces." But Harmon doesn't. He directs his great power into constructive channels. That is why he is a team man and a team leader.

Elaine Killebrew and children on the shores of Lake Eola, Orlando, Florida, March, 1970

harmon killebrew day in orlando

28

"What do I think of Harmon Killebrew?" Our cabman twisted around in his seat, flashed a smile, and said, "I love the guy."

Then turning his attention back to driving he added, "For my money, Harmon Killebrew and Mickey Mantle are the two greatest players in the game. You know, it's a funny thing about Killebrew, my ten-year-old kid wants to be a catcher, but he still picked Harmon as his idol."

Everywhere we went in Orlando we heard the same sentiments.

"You can't say anything bad about Killebrew."

"He's just a nice guy."

"We think the world of Harmon."

"The whole town loves him."

In fact, the comments sounded so much like a broken record that we began to wonder if the townspeople were putting us on.

Harmon Killebrew Day on March 22, 1970, proved otherwise. They do "love the guy."

Harmon thanks his wife, Elaine, for her inspirational help on Harmon Killebrew Day at Tinker Field, Orlando, Florida, March 22, 1970 ROY MILL

Although it was a gray day with menacing clouds shutting out the Florida sun, over 3000 fans jammed the Tinker Field ballpark in Orlando to pay tribute to the Minnesota Twins' great slugger.

The ceremonies at home plate before the game presented a scene that will be long remembered. As an opening prayer was spoken, Harmon stood with cap off, flanked on one side by Twins owner Calvin Griffith and Twins manager Bill Rigney and on the other by Henri Guertin, the master of ceremonies. Behind Harmon forming a semi-circle were his wife, Elaine and four of their five children. As the entire group stood with heads bowed, an attitude of deep reverence extended all the way down to four-year-old Erin Killebrew who stood with eyes tightly-closed and arms folded, appearing as if she were offering her own special prayer for her daddy.

Harmon with his family behind him on Harmon Killebrew Day at Tinker Field, Orlando, Florida, March 22, 1970 ROY MILLER

As the ceremonies continued, Harmon's wife was presented with a bouquet of red roses and each of their children received a camera.

Henri Guertin, Calvin Griffith, and Bill Rigney paid tributes to Harmon. Then he was presented with a $2000 check as a joint tribute from his admirers in the cities of Orlando and Winter Park. When Harmon walked to the mike to respond to the fans' generosity, everyone in the stands stood up, and a thunder of applause filled the air.

As he spoke, my eyes strayed to his family—still standing in a semicircle behind him. His two pre-teen sons, Cameron and Kenny, stood tall and attentive, masking their pride in their dad with typical Killebrew modesty. One sensed that they possessed the ability to excel in the Killebrew tradition.

Six-year-old Kathryn and four-year-old Erin—dressed

in dark blue coats—looked like two tiny sentries who were posted and prepared to protect their father from any impending danger.

Elaine stood erect, her golden hair framing her oval face and her clear blue eyes filled with pride. The red roses which she held clasped to her bosom seemed to form a bodice over her attractive red coat, and her appearance was that of a queen whose husband had just ascended to the throne. Before I turned my attention back to Harmon, I could see that she was fighting to hold back the tears.

Harmon's response was sincere and to the point. As he stood with his ailing right knee locked tightly in a brand new brace, he said:

"I'd like to thank Mr. Guertin and everyone involved in this occasion, including the Chambers of Commerce of Orlando and Winter Park. I'd also like to particularly thank Champ Williams." (Williams suggested 'Harmon Killebrew Day'.)

"It's a wonderful honor to receive this award, particularly in a place like Orlando. I want you to know that I've learned to love Orlando and all of you people in it.

"I'd also like to thank the Griffith organization, and especially Mr. Griffith, for the faith they've had in me through the years, and my wife Elaine who has always been an inspiration to me.

"I also want to thank all the managers, coaches and players I have played with.

"Thank you all from the bottom of my heart."

Bill Rigney had not wanted to play Harmon on "Killebrew Day" because of the condition of Harmon's right knee which was painfully swollen. Consequently, in Rigney's original lineup, sent to the pressbox Sunday, he left Killebrew out. However, when Bill saw the stands filling he had a change of heart; and when the game began, Harmon took his position at first base. After the first Red Sox batter went out, the second one walked, and Killebrew moved to the bag to hold him close.

Then the next hitter, Reggie Smith, smashed a scorching

grounder about 10 feet inside the first base line. What followed made it apparent why Rigney was so concerned about having Killebrew play. Harmon made a game effort to field the ball. Pushing his muscular body to the near-breaking point, he reached the sizzler, but could not get low enough to scoop it up. Boston was on the way to its first run.

In the Twins' half of the first inning, Oliva homered with two out to knot the score at 1 to 1. Then Killebrew came to bat. One can only guess at what thoughts flashed through his mind. The odds were 100 to 1 that he wanted to get a base hit, perhaps as much as he ever wanted any during his career.

Vicente Romo, the Boston hurler, threw his first pitch right down the pike. Harmon swung and fouled it. Then after throwing one more strike, Romo tried to get Killebrew to bite at four balls around the edges of the plate. Even though Harmon desperately wanted a hit, he maintained his composure, refused to swing, and took his walk to first base. Rich Reese was sent in to run for him, and the ailing slugger walked slowly to the dressing room. It was evident as he left the field that he was making a great effort to hide the pain as he tried to move his right leg without revealing a perceptible limp.

It seemed almost anticlimactic that the Twins went on to lose the game, their 14th loss in 15 starts.

After the game, Bill Rigney was in a rage. He paced around the dugout like a caged tiger and gave vent to his feelings with:

"I'm not supposed to get mad on Sunday, but this is ridiculous. After a month's work, this takes place. It's a disgrace. Fifteen walks in one game! Gentlemen, this has got to halt. I asked my hitters to go out and get seven runs. Well there they are on the scoreboard. But our pitchers gave Boston ten. Seven runs and we still lose. It's simply ridiculous."

Rigney paused a moment, then pointed at the dark clouds and said: "You know there was only one real ray of sunshine today as far as I was concerned. That was Killebrew. On that one swing, men, he looked like the Killebrew of old, and he told me later he felt the same way —said the knee actually felt better than it had all spring. Doc Lentz fixed him up with a brace instead of the bandaging today and he pushed off real hard with that back leg.

"I'm going to have Harmon sit out of exhibitions for awhile and give him some rest. He's a pro, and if there's any way, he'll be ready when the bell rings April 7th."

We could sense on "Harmon Killebrew Day" the high esteem that Floridians have for Killebrew. The feeling that he is their idol was reinforced when we read comments about him in the Orlando Sentinel. On the Sunday morning of the game, the following article appeared on the editorial page.

Harmon Killebrew Day

HARMON KILLEBREW will have his day at Tinker Field today as local baseball aficionados join with Twins loyals from the rest of the nation—impatient for spring's wedding of ash and horsehide—to pay tribute to the Minnesota third baseman as he launches into his 17th professional year.

Coming off the 1969 success in which he was named Most Valuable Player in the American League by a whopping margin, the Payette, Idaho native now ranks 13th among all-time home run hitters and bids fair to move up at least three notches before the 1970 schedule goes into the record books.

What is more, he ranks fifth among currently active artists of the big blow and has led his league six times in the 11 years since he made the major leagues on a permanent basis.

Honors are not new for Killebrew. In addition to his MVP award and numerous batting crowns, he has been on 11 All Star teams, including the last seven in a row. And his name is in the record books for more than home runs and runs batted in.

But Sunday his fans honor Harmon Killebrew for something that isn't categorized in the statistics—his spirit of fair competition, his modesty despite success, his devotion to, and respect for, his teammates and followers and that inspiration that comes only from the truly great.

Have a good day, Harmon Killebrew—and a good season.

Bill Clark, sportswriter for the Orlando Sentinel, also wrote a glowing account of Killebrew's personality which appeared in the same issue as follows:

Today's Tinker Toast: The Untypical Slugger

By BILL CLARK Sentinel Staff

They call him "Harm" and they call him "The Killer." Just from the sounds, Harmon Killebrew comes across as a guy who should be lockered next to Joe Bananas and Machine Gun Kelly rather than by solid citizens named Jim Perry, Tony Oliva and Bob Allison.

Then again, it depends largely on your viewpoint. To big league pitchers of baseballs, Harmon Killebrew has to be public enemy No. 1 after leading both circuits in homers and runs batted in a year ago.

Kelly and his persuader and Bananas with a burp gun could hardly be more destructive from 60 feet.

And yet, the nicknames still seem peculiarly out of place because Harm, the Killer, may be baseball's all-time nice guy. There is no way of knowing, of course, because they do not keep statistics on this as they do, for example, on homerun frequency, a department in which Harm ranks just behind Babe Ruth. (Ruth took a roundtrip every 11.76 trips to the plate, Killebrew every 12.99 . . . and Williams, Mays, Foxx, Kiner, Aaron, Mantle, Maris, Ott and fellows like that are all spread out to the rear).

BUT BACK TO the nice guy business; the Killer is virtually unique. From the Griffith family which has owned his contract all through the years on down through the six or seven managers he has had, his teammates, trainers, the locker room personnel and finally on to the public, it would be hard to find one single Killebrew detractor.

And you can add umpires to this list because Harmon does not quibble over balls and strikes.

In a very real sense, he thus defies baseball's Law of Labelling. Many if not most of the bona fide sluggers the game has produced were men with idiosyncrasies. Everyone knows that. With some, it was called temperament, with others temper.

Call it what you will, these men often were candidates for Most Popular Member of the Class only to the outsider.

Killebrew's candidacy is just as strong in the inner circles.

Bob Allison is 35 years old, two years Harmon's senior, and for all practical purposes, they came to the majors at the same time. Allison, a onetime Kansas University football player, has had homerun years of 30, 15, 29, 29, 35, 32, 23, 24, 22. On most ballclubs, that would be good enough to rank him as The Big Guy. With the Twins, however, Allison has led in HR's only once because Killebrew was posting fancier figures like 42, 31, 46, 48, 45, 49, 25, 39, 44, 49.

BECAUSE HARMON is the kind of guy he is—and also because Allison is the type he is—the latter is one of the former's top admirers. They have, in fact, roomed harmoniously on road trips for the better part of their careers.

"He doesn't talk your ear off exactly," the Twins' all-time No. 2 homer hitter explains when asked about the guy up ahead, "and of course he doesn't smoke or drink. Lives as clean a life as any athlete I

DON WINGFIELD

Harmon in his first spring training season at Orlando, Florida, 1955

know. On the road, you can count on finding him in front of a TV set. I don't even buy TV Guide anymore. Harmon knows what time all the programs come on and the name of just about every actor and actress. In New York, he may go to a Broadway show. Other than that or an occasional movie, he stays close to the hotel."

Allison says he can not ever remember seeing Killebrew blood-in-the-eye mad. That does not mean, however, that if an opposing pitcher throws one at somebody's head and a fight ensues that Killebrew stands clear.

"Oh no," says Allison. "He'll be out there, but not like a wild man. He'll be out there mainly trying to get things settled."

BOB STORM HAS not known the Killer as long as Allison has. He met him, in fact, just last month here in Orlando.

Storm is a rookie outfield hopeful with the Twins, 21 years old and fresh up from leading the New York-Pennsylvania League in RBI last year. A lanky righthand hitter, Storm believes in himself which is good.

"When I first met him this spring," grins the Rook, "he was in street clothes in the hotel lobby here. To be honest, I was almost disappointed after reading so much about him for so long. I'm a fairly tall guy, you know, about 6-3, and Harmon's not too tall. Well anyway, I met him over there and I gotta say I felt pretty good about my chances all of a sudden. Then the next day, we get in uniform and I see him swing. Good gosh," says Bob Storm, "I never saw a guy look so big."

Twins' equipment manager Ray Crump was the Washington Senator batboy when Harmon first arrived in June of 1954, a bonus boy fresh out of a smalltown high school in Payette, Idaho. Crump recalls that first day vividly.

"HE WAS THE quietest guy I ever saw. Don't think he said a word to anybody. But that doesn't mean nobody paid any attention to him. He'd gotten what I believe was the biggest bonus the club had ever paid up to that time and there was no doubt about it right from the start . . . the guy could hit."

Even so, the early climbing was slow, Harmon banged around from Charlotte to Chattanooga to Indianapolis and back to Chattanooga before finally making the big club to stay in 1959. Immediately, he busted loose with 42 homers and 105 RBI.

With really only one lapse—that in 1968 when he was injured—the 5-11, 214-pounder has been hammering at that same rousing clip for over a decade. And Minnesota, interestingly, has been no lower than second in the American League since 1964 with that single exception of 1968.

LIKE GOLFER Billy Casper, the balding Killer is of the Mormon faith. He was introduced to the religion years ago by his wife Elaine, mother of the five Killebrew youngsters. Harmon joined the church in 1966.

Perhaps it is sheer coincidence, but he and Casper are amazingly similar in the tranquility of their natures regardless of the bedlam surrounding them.

"If I had to size him up," says 20-game winner Dave Boswell, "I'd call him The Quiet Killer. Or, if you want to use today's language, just call him one beautiful guy."

After the game, my wife, Elise and I went to the Killebrew's hotel suite to visit Elaine and the children and to see their eight-year-old daughter, Shawn, who was confined to her room with an acute case of chicken pox. Harmon had remained at Tinker Field to receive treatment for his leg.

Shawn, a brown-haired little tyke with a pixie-like face, was in misery. Ugly pox had erupted all over her tiny body, and her condition had been made worse due to the fact that she had incurred a severe sunburn while sitting beside the hotel pool. This had happened at a time when no one was aware she was coming down with chicken pox. As Shawn sobbed and trembled in torment, Elaine, showing the patience born of deep love, attempted to ease her daughter's pain in every conceivable manner. She held Shawn on her lap and consoled her, patted soothing ointments on her sores, and put her in the bathtub to help her relax in warm water. Nothing seemed to help.

In the meantime, Elise and I were trying to keep the other children occupied so the general atmosphere would not become tense. As time went by, it seemed that there was nothing any of us could do to relieve Shawn's pain. At this moment of frustration, Harmon arrived. Elise and I had the privilege of seeing the Killebrew partnership of Harmon and Elaine in action.

Harmon took Shawn into his arms with the same love and compassion that Elaine had exhibited. He held her close and began to console her with all the affection a father could give. Nevertheless, little Shawn still trembled with pain, becoming almost hysterical; and it seemed that she might go into convulsions. At this time the deep spiritual faith of the Killebrews became evident. Harmon turned to me and said, "You know, more than anything else I would like Shawn to be administered to and given a blessing."

Harmon is an Elder in The Church of Jesus Christ of Latter-day Saints (Mormon), and in this capacity has the

Wayne Anderson and Harmon Killebrew at Tinker Field, Orlando, Florida, March 1970

Harmon and Elaine Killebrew with Elise Anderson in Park Plaza Hotel, Orlando, Florida, March 1970

authority to exercise this priesthood in administering to individuals who are ill.

Inasmuch as I also hold the office of Elder, Harmon asked me if I would participate with him in blessing little Shawn. Of course I considered it a special privilege to be asked. So we placed our hands on Shawn's head and united in anointing and blessing his tormented daughter.

As we finished, Shawn calmed down, and we all felt that she had made the turn on the road to recovery. I remember Harmon saying, "Isn't it wonderful. Shawn seems to feel better already."

After this took place, Shawn quieted down enough to lie on her bed, and Harmon discovered that if he bent over and blew lightly on her back it seemed to ease her suffering. As he knelt over her, his broad shoulders arched over the bed and his ailing right leg stretched out at an angle that enabled him to endure his own pain; I thought to myself, "There is a scene I shall always remember—a man who has just come from the plaudits of thousands, losing himself in helping his wife nurse their daughter back to health."

When we left the Killebrews, much later, Harmon was still bending over Shawn and blowing lightly on her back to relieve her pain.

Back to Harmon and the citizens of Orlando. I can easily understand why he loves the residents of Orlando and their beautiful city. The people are friendly. They chat with strangers and make them feel welcome. They seem so calm. The clerks in the shops, the cabbies, the bus drivers, the hotel attendants. And the people on the street all make one feel that he is indeed among friends.

One suspects that Harmon and the good people of that area felt a mutual attraction when he first came there for spring training as a rookie of seventeen, and that the admiration has grown in depth over the years.

The town of Orlando is a delightful place. It is located at the juncture of the temperate and sub-tropical zones and consequently enjoys a climate that draws from the best features of both. Colorful orange groves line its outskirts, and the landscape is dotted with lakes that provide a variety of sports—including water-skiing, scuba diving, snorkeling, fishing, and relaxing swimming. Additional beauty and shade are provided by stately palms and magnolias, with their fragrant pink or purple flowers, and the oaks and pines that are native to the Smokies.

The area is experiencing tremendous growth, and a chain of other attractive cities including Winter Park and Maitland touch borders with Orlando.

The fabulous Cypress Gardens, the famed Kennedy Space Center, and the white sands of Daytona Beach are but short drives away. An additional attraction will be the huge Walt Disney World which is being constructed just 15 miles away.

Orlando's metropolitan area numbers about 200,000 residents who are provided with an abundance of educational, cultural, and recreational opportunities.

The streets are clean and quiet, the stores filled with tantalizing merchandise. It is easy to understand why Harmon Killebrew said, "I want you all to know that I've learned to love Orlando and all of you people in it."

When he was asked if he and his family may someday move there, his reply was, "You can never tell. We do like it down here, and I really mean that. But we're like everybody else, I suppose. We like it where we were born and raised—can't help being a little partial to that part of the country."

The people of Orlando will continue to root for Harmon, whether he moves there or not.

the big guy

It was the spring training season of 1970. The Twins, playing out of their home base at Orlando, Florida, had put together a string of 14 losses against one win. Sportswriters were ridiculing the team's efforts and were writing such things as: "The Twins will try to make it 15 out of 16 today."

Bill Rigney, the Twins' new manager, was also baffled by the team's dismal showing.

And the fans? The air was filled with their criticisms which took the following tone:

"It's . . . Calvin's fault."

"Bring back Billy Martin."

"The Twins hired a loser."

Instead of joining in the criticism, Dick Cullum, popular Minneapolis Tribune sports columnist, took the sensible approach; he tried to find out what was really causing the Twins' frequent losses. He put the question to manager Bill Rigney of the Minnesota Twins and reported the conversation in his daily column:

Bill, is there any one thing chiefly responsible for your frequent defeats?

His immediate reply, "The Big Guy. He isn't playing much and when he does play he is hurting on his bad knee."

Can Harmon Killebrew's ailments account more than all other factors for what is going on down there?

"Well, it's a big thing. With him hitting, we'd have turned some of those one-run defeats around, and winning a few might have helped us win a few more. . . .

"Probably a team can start winning streaks just as it can start losing streaks. Killebrew's presence and leadership, as well as his bat, have been important in many of the Twins' winning streaks."

Rigney said, "Harmon's trouble is that he can't push off on his right leg. While trying he is likely to develop some bad habits in his swing. He's got the prettiest swing in baseball. I'd hate to have him throw it off while favoring his knee."

If that happens it may take the big guy additional time to get smoothed out again after his injury mends.

"We're really concerned," Rigney said.

Is there any other factor causing defeats?

"We have had to pay for every mistake. It seems that each mistake lets in a run. And another thing," Rigney continued. "These players all know I'm on a spot as the new manager. Sometimes I think they are trying too hard to help me. They may be pressing, and that may account for some of the costly misplays."

Rigney appears to be concerned lest his players forget that, despite their losses, they are a first-rate baseball team.

"We have the players," he said, "and I don't think they'll forget they are a good team."

But Rig will feel better when the Big Guy starts using that beautiful swing in his old, healthy rhythm.

When we read that Rigney felt Harmon's absence from the lineup, and his ailments which were cramping his style, constituted the chief reason for the Twins' frequent defeats, we decided to make our own investigation of the situation. Consequently, we went down to Orlando to learn if the Big Guy's presence and "beautiful, healthy swing" did contribute that much to the Twins victories.

A spring training camp constitutes a city of its own. First, the players must have a place to live, and the Twins management selected an ideal spot. The entire organization is housed in the Park Plaza Hotel which is on the shores of Lake Eola. Its lakeside windows offer a panoramic view of blue water surrounded by beautifully kept lawns, color-

L. to r., Frank Crosetti, coach; Bob Rodgers, coach; Bill Rigney, manager, Marv Grissom, coach, Vern Morgan, coach.

ful flower beds, and trees in great variety. In the center of the lake is the Centennial Fountain, whose dancing sprays light the sky with a kaleidoscopic pattern of colors. Adjoining the hotel is a large swimming pool which is set in a tropical garden of flowers and shrubs.

There is an air of conviviality within the hotel which gives one a comfortable and homey feeling. For those who like exquisite dining, the Columbia, a famous Spanish restaurant, features a delightful selection of special foods. And for those who like to lounge in the lobby and talk sports there are always several friendly persons about with whom one can make conversation.

One person who seemed to be in perpetual motion in the lobby was the Twins' club physician, Harvey O'Phelan. Every time I met him he was either "coming from or going to." I did succeed in getting him to stop long enough to tell me why, and he replied, "I'm the visiting fireman here. It's my job to offer medical assistance whenever or wherever it is needed."

I found out later how completely Dr. O'Phelan fills his role when I encountered him in the Killebrew suite giving of his time and skill to help little Shawn recover from chicken pox.

It's no problem to get to the ballpark from the hotel. One can take a short cab ride or catch a bus that stops at the corner of Tinker Field.

Tinker Field is an attractive facility. Well-kept lawns and palm trees make the entrance inviting. Cream-colored ticket booths and a small office building also add to the pleasing appearance. There is a grandstand that seats about 3000 spectators. And there are dugouts for the competing teams. Palms and a variety of other trees form a background for the billboard covered walls, and the rightfield fence borders along the back of the bleachers of the Tangerine Bowl, a football stadium where college champions play. The field has good dimensions with right and left field foul lines extending 332 feet and the center field batting eye situated 412 feet away from home plate.

Tom Mee, personable Twins Director of Public Relations, made arrangements for me to meet the players and did everything possible to make my visit a profitable one.

A spring training camp is a beehive of activity. The crack of ball and bat fill the air, and everywhere you look men are in motion. Infielders are scooping up grounders, outfielders flagging down flies, pitchers limbering up arms, and other players not so engaged are sprinting back and forth to strengthen their legs and build up their wind. A rigid schedule is observed which starts early in the morning and ends in late afternoon. During this time, players engage in alternate periods of batting and fielding practice and conditioning exercises.

Tom Mee took me out on the field, introduced me to Bill Rigney, and requested that I have permission to talk to team members when they weren't actively engaged in practice. Never have I met a man who was more engrossed in his work. There must have been at least two dozen players working out, and Rigney had his eyes glued on each one of them. I could feel the tension emanate from Bill's wiry frame, and his features were set in such a way that it looked like he was trying to send out winning thought waves to each performer. I attempted a bit of conversation such as: "How's Killebrew doing? Where do you plan on playing him this year?"

Rigney's answer was short and to the point, "Harm's knee has been slow coming around. I'm counting on him at third." So saying, Bill turned away and directed a rookie to move to a different playing position.

Bill Rigney's brevity was understandable. After all, it was not the proper time for a press conference, and in addition, he was on the spot. Here was a man who had become almost an institution as manager of the California Angels. During nine years there he had turned down numerous attractive offers to manage elsewhere. Then with a change in general managers, Rigney's supposed lifetime security with the Angels had abruptly ended with his release. Now, Calvin Griffith had lured Bill out of retirement to manage the Twins. The assignment was extremely difficult because Rigney was replacing the popular Billy Martin who had piloted Minnesota to the Western Division championship of the American League, the year before. To make matters worse, the Twins had already lost 14 out of 15 spring training games under Rigney's leadership. Yes, Bill had a right to feel tense. But he's also the type of man who can bounce back from problems. The Twins won their game that afternoon, after I had talked to him; and the next day he called out a cheery "Nice day," when he saw me. Close observation of Rigney during my subsequent visits to Tinker Field convinced me that the Twins were in good managerial hands. Bill came across as a stable, knowledgeable, likable, and driving leader.

After leaving Bill, I spied Rod Carew standing near the batting cage, so I sauntered over and casually asked, "Can you spare a couple of minutes to talk, Rod?"

The lithe athlete—the American League Batting Champion for 1969—revealed his sense of humor immediately. He grinned and said, "I've got one second, maybe just half a second; my time is awful valuable."

"Okay then," I said, "Just one question. Do you have a hard time getting along with Killebrew?"

Rod's voice rose."Anyone who doesn't like Killebrew deserves a punch in the mouth." Then he calmed down and continued. "I sure admire him. People expect so much, like a homerun every time he comes up, but he shakes it off and keeps going."

Carew also knows something about shaking things off. Despite being out of action much of the 1969 season, due to military service, he still led the league in hitting. The fact that the slender athlete stole home the first seven times he tried, and equalled the major league record of steals of home for the season, is evidence of his great speed and determination to excel.

Just then Cesar Tovar, the Twin who can play any position on the field, came over. It is amazing how small he looks close up, and he acts almost like your 10-year-old son or your little brother would—throwing his baseball against the house or taking practice swings with his bat. Tovar has been accused of being a showboat, which he vigorously denies with, "I no showboat. I just having fun. Nothing bother me."

I had been watching Cesar before, and it was apparent that baseball is fun to him. He teased the other players to let him in ahead of them in the batting cage, and he would move to any infield position that was vacated for a moment, to show how far he could stretch his 5-foot-9 inches to take a throw. He was so much in motion that it was difficult to get him to stand still long enough to talk, but in a momentary lull he did say, "Killebrew? He's a good guy."

Frank Quilici is another player who lends color to the Twins baseball scene—not with the nervous energy and antics of a Tovar, but with a string of good-natured comments that keep his teammates relaxed and on their toes. Frank had already chatted with me over the phone, but in his friendly way he still took time to give some additional comments about Killebrew.

He said, "You know, Harm wanted it to rain yesterday, so they would have to call off Harmon Killebrew Day. But I told him, 'You know Harm, that Mormon church you belong to may be strong, but I don't think they can bring rain to you.' "

Quilici is a definite asset to the Twins. Bill Rigney didn't use him much during spring training, and Frank wondered if he would be cut from the squad. But Rigney dispelled all ideas of his cutting Quilici when he said, "I knew Quilici was around, because I could always hear him yelling. I never gave a thought to cutting Frank. He's a major leaguer and a winner."

Quilici is the ideal utility man. He can fill in at second, third, or short with equal effectiveness. His defensive ability shows in the statistics column. He has only made one error in 103 games and 406 fielding chances since 1965. He often comes up with a game saving spectacular play in the field. And his bat has helped the Twins many times when they needed some punch in their attack.

Although Frank spends much of his time on the bench, he doesn't brood about it. Instead, he keeps up the same snappy chatter that helps keep his teammates hustling.

I was surprised when I met Rich Reese. Press releases about him had led me to believe that he was a flamboyant swinger—a man-about-town. Instead, I found him to be a quiet, articulate gentleman. Although Reese dresses in mod fashion and wears long sideburns, his personality seems at variance with his appearance. He is an intense competitor and sets high standards for himself. Rather than talk about his problems he keeps them to himself, and being a bachelor he has no pretty young wife waiting at home to snap him out of his moods. For three years he played in Killebrew's shadow hoping that eventually his superb fielding would win him a permanent place at first base, which happened in 1969. Sensing that this might be a sensitive area for discussion, I brought it up.

Rich's reply was forthright and rang sincere. "I sat on the bench for three years behind Killebrew, but I didn't mind it because of the kind of man he is. In fact, it was a privilege to play behind him. Last year I hit behind him in the lineup, and I saw him come home after each of his 49 homeruns. Never once did his expression change. It was always the same—calm and pleasant. He's a great guy."

I encountered the Twins shortstop, Leo Cardenas, on his way to the locker room. He is a lot like Tovar, boyish in appearance and filled with restless energy. The Twins obtained him from Cincinnati for left-handed pitcher, Jim Merritt, in November, 1968. Both clubs agree that it was a "perfect" baseball trade. At this writing, Merritt is leading major league pitchers with an 8-1 record, and Cardenas has welded the Twins' infield into a strong defensive unit. Leo has wide range and often picks off grounders behind second base or deep in the hole, and in the process makes the play and the resulting put-out look easy.

I had a special question for Cardenas. Having read so much about Killebrew's slowness afoot and his alleged defensive weaknesses, I approached Cardenas on the subject, thinking that I would finally get a comment about Harmon that would be on the negative side. Trying to be subtle and trap Leo into a spontaneous critical expression, I led with, "I suppose with Killebrew playing third base it makes your job at shortstop a little harder because you have to cover more ground?"

"Harm does a great job at third," Leo replied, flashing a gleaming, white smile. "We always talk about what we're going to do before a game and how we will play things. There's no guy I have more confidence in."

I had struck out again in my quest to elicit a derogatory comment about Killebrew. He was still the "Big Guy."

Just then I spied Tony Oliva coming in from the outfield. I felt that I must talk to him. Halsey Hall, the Twins' popular sportscaster, calls Tovar, Carew, and Oliva the Caribbean Comets; and Oliva, like the others, fits the description perfectly. Since entering the majors, his hitting exploits have continually lighted up the baseball skies, and he has often been called the most natural hitter in the game. Tony has a major league career batting average of .308. In his six years in the majors, he has led the league in base hits four times and has been named to the All-Star team six consecutive seasons.

Oliva loves to play baseball and is smiling most of the time because he enjoys the game so much.

In a game against the Red Sox at Tinker Field, Tony swung his bat around so fast that the deflected baseball nipped him on the ankle. While Doc Lentz was treating the resulting swelling, Tovar and Carew dropped into the training room. Carew needled Tony with, "If that happened to me, I'd shake it off and go right back in."

Tony did just that. Later I saw him limping slightly and overheard Bill Rigney, who has taken a great liking to Oliva, say, "You can play or not. It's up to you."

When Tony started to talk about Harm Killebrew, his face lit up with his winning smile. "Harmon's a good man, a nice guy," he said. "If we had 25 guys with his temperament on the team, we'd have no problems. I've played six years with Harmon and enjoyed them all. I hope I can play many more with him."

During our stay in Orlando and our daily visits to Tinker Field, a few of the Twins began to stand out from the group because of distinguishing personality characteristics. One of these was pitcher Dave Boswell. Although Dave is a serious student of the game, and was a 20 game winner during the 1969 season, he is also a mischievous, fun-loving guy. He gave me the impression of being the clown prince of the team. As he was moving around the field, he was tossing off witty one-liners, and he exuded an almost cocky air of confidence. He seems to be a combination of skill, humor, and a rather devil-may-care attitude. In a moment of disgust at his lack of control, he threw the ball over the grandstand.

One day I saw Dave sitting apart from the others in the dugout; so I sat beside him. Eventually, the conversation got around to Killebrew. "Tell me something bad about the guy," I said.

Dave grinned, "You know it's kind of corny," he replied, "but you can't say anything wrong about him. He's an enviable guy—a perfect guy. You people in Minneapolis should name a street after him. You know, Harmon Avenue or Killebrew Street. They have a Babe Ruth Square in Baltimore, so you should do it for Harm in Minneapolis."

While Boswell was talking, I noticed that the little finger on his left hand stood straight out. Remembering that he had cut a tendon in it while cleaning fish during spring training of 1968, I said, "I notice that your little finger is still stiff. Doesn't it bother you?"

"Not a bit," said Bos. "I've got so I don't even notice it. I just stick it in my pitcher's glove and forget it." Then he reflected a moment and grinned. "Of course it does bother me when I have cocktails. It sometimes bumps into the glass and tips it over."

I didn't ask Dave at the time, but I wondered why he had not had his stiff finger surgically repaired so he could bend it. I heard the story later. I was told that Boswell went to a surgeon to have the finger examined and repaired. During the examination the doctor squinted at the injured area. Then he took a ballpoint pen and drew an outline in ink down Dave's finger, across his palm and up his arm to show just how he would lay open the flesh and make the necessary repairs. While the doctor was drawing this surgical diagram, he inadvertently dropped his pen, and then in attempting to retrieve the ballpoint, stepped on it, crushing it. This was too much for Bos. He left the doctor's office vowing never to return. He told his teammates later that any doc who was so shaky he couldn't hold a pen, and so near-sighted that he couldn't pick it up, was not going to operate on him.

After interviewing Boswell, it occurred to me that all of my discussions had been with established stars and that perhaps I could get a more objective appraisal of Harmon from newcomers to the squad. The first one I approached was catcher, George Mitterwald. George is a tall, well-built young man who had an outstanding rookie season in 1969. He is a long-ball hitter and has a tremendous throwing arm, with which he threw out 16 of 34 players who tried to steal on him in 1969.

Mitterwald was shy but friendly. He said, "The first day—when I came from St. Cloud to join the Twins—Harmon Killebrew made me welcome. One day he noticed I was swinging my bat wrong and locking my hip. He helped me smooth it out. It's a great thing to know him."

Pitching rookie Gerry Christman gave me his reaction to Killebrew. Gerry is a promising young left-handed pitcher, 21 years of age, who formerly pitched for the University of Michigan, and is at present a second semester senior there with a major in mechanical engineering. He was the strikeout leader of the Northern League in 1969.

"Harmon Killebrew went out of his way to make me feel at home," he said, "but you know, the first time I pitched to him in an intra-squad game he scared me to death. I had never seen a batter look so powerful. Incidentally, I walked him. The second time around he hit into a double play. I still don't know how it happened."

I had an interesting chat with 21-year-old rookie outfielder Bob Storm—the runs-batted-in leader of the New York-Pennsylvania League in 1969. Bob is a rangy six feet, three inches and played baseball at the University of Indiana.

"Killebrew's a great guy and a good ball player," Bob said. "If you saw him on the street you wouldn't pay any attention to him. When I first met him a couple of weeks ago, he was in street clothes over in the hotel lobby. He's not too tall, and I was almost disappointed after all I'd read about him.

"Then the next day we got into uniform, and I saw him swing at the ball. Gosh, I never saw a guy look so big. He looked like this." Bob used his hands and arms to form a huge inverted pyramid.

Then he went on, "Harmon goes out of his way to be friendly. It's more than he's a superstar; he's a nice person. In my mind you have to give yourself wholly to anything you do if you're going to succeed. He is completely dedicated to playing the game."

As I was crossing the field after talking to Bob Storm, I encountered Frank Crossetti, the Twins' new third base coach. Frank is nearing 60, but he is still as spry as a rookie. His fame has spread far and wide, and he has played in more World Series than any other individual in history. Despite his record of achievements, he is very friendly.

"This is my first year with the Twins," he said. "But I can tell already that Harmon's one helluva guy, and I know he's respected all over the league."

Crossetti asked about the University of Minnesota baseball team and said that their coach, Dick Siebert, was known as one of the best in the game.

Our stay in Orlando did not allow time to meet all of the Twins squad, but a few things I observed gave me the impression that the other players and coaches were all of the same high calibre.

Marv Grissom, their pitching coach, came across as a knowledgeable veteran who could sit comfortably beside the pitchers and give them the benefit of his many years experience in a friendly and helpful way.

Vern Morgan, first base coach, appeared to be a solid individual who was dedicated to helping in any way possible.

I noticed that Bob Allison, veteran 36-year-old right fielder, was still playing with enthusiasm equal to that of the freshest rookie.

Two rookies who were scintillating on defense were Danny Thompson who was ranging far and wide at shortstop and Paul Powell, outfielder, who was so fleet of foot that he could cover an area from a few feet back of second base all the way to the center field fence. Rookie pitcher, Bert Blyleven, also looked great.

I was convinced after my discussion and observation that Harmon Killebrew was also "The Big Guy" in the eyes of other team members. The games I watched also bore this out. When he was out of the lineup, the team did not seem quite complete.

Then some other thoughts entered my mind. Sure, the players have climbed on the Killebrew bandwagon because he helps them win, but what about the club's administrators? Do they also consider him a vital cog in their club machine? They pay him a huge salary. Do they consider him as simply a valuable professional property? In order to find the answers, I made appointments with Howard T. Fox, Jr. and Calvin R. Griffith.

Howie Fox, smartly dressed in slacks and a turtleneck knit shirt, looked like a clean-cut college student. Wiry and dynamic, Fox is vice-president of the Twins—in charge of all team travel arrangements. He is not afraid to fight for his convictions. I was interested in his feelings toward Harmon Killebrew, so I asked if he would reminisce a bit and give me his impressions of Harmon beginning with their first meeting. Howie seemed to enjoy recalling the past.

He said, "I first met Harm when he reported to us in Chicago in 1954. He was a quiet, humble kid and I suppose almost scared-to-death. I don't think he had ever been out of Idaho before. It was our last stop of a two week road trip. Ossie Bluege was the only one who had seen Harm before, and we didn't quite know how he would react to public attention. Nevertheless, Clark Griffith put both himself and Harm on the spot by holding a press conference just as soon as Otto Bluege, Ossie's brother, had brought Harm from the airport to our hotel. There to welcome Harm were Clark Griffith, president of our Washington Club, Senator Herman Welker of Idaho, and our club manager Bucky Harris. Harm was given a warm reception, and it helped him feel at home. Very soon, though, reporters and photographers gathered around him. I'm sure Harm couldn't understand why he was considered such important news, but he got through the interview in his natural, unassuming way."

For a moment our conversation was interrupted by a telephone call to Howie. After returning the phone to its cradle, he said, "That was from Mr. Williams, a native of Orlando. He wanted to tell us what a good job Harm did at the ceremony on Harmon Killebrew Day and to congratulate Harm for being a credit to the community and to the game. That's the kind of calls we always get about Harm."

Howie went on. "When I think back on those early days with Harm and now—what a difference there is. Then he was just a green kid; now I suppose he is as well known as any ball player in the world. But Harm hasn't changed as a person. Some stars are prima donnas. They expect to have people fall all over them. With all his stardom and success, he's just as humble as he was when he reported at seventeen. He's such a nice guy that people want to *do* things for him.

"I remember that during his early years with the team, Cookie Lavagetto, one of our coaches, was assigned to him as roommate. His job was to teach Harm everything he could about baseball. Harm proved to be a good student. Even today, now that he's on the top, he stays in his room while we're on the road and studies. There's never any worry about Harm staying in condition—he has no bad habits."

I couldn't refrain from interrupting and asked, "How do his teammates react to this? Do they think he's a prima donna?"

"On the contrary," Howie replied. "Harm is their leader in a silent way. They don't needle him. We used to call him 'long-haired Charlie' and kid him about how fast he could switch caps. No one in the world was as fast in switching from his batting helmet to his regular cap. But now the players seem to respect him too much to do even that. When something goes wrong, Harm doesn't yell or get aggressive."

"Doesn't he ever get angry?"

"Of course, he's human. But he never blows up. On occasion, when something is absolutely wrong, he speaks up in a quiet way and puts things right. He's always a good influence."

There was no point in prolonging the interview. I could perceive that Harmon Killebrew was also the "Big Guy" in Howie Fox's book, so I thanked the Twins Vice President and went back to watch the batting practice.

I had an appointment with Calvin R. Griffith, the Twins President, scheduled for the following morning; I looked forward to hearing how he felt about Killebrew. Perhaps the man who negotiates salary every year with Harmon would have a different slant.

During the interview, I became convinced that Calvin Griffith is a misunderstood man; the real man gets lost somewhere along the way when the news media presents his image to the public. As a result, some of the public visualize him as a shrewd, unfeeling, money-grabber. He has been called, "King Griffith," "Just a big kid"—and by other unsavory labels.

As we sat in his office in Orlando and chatted, his personality impressed me as being completely different from the one presented by his detractors. It was one of a sincere and friendly man. He was smartly dressed in a light blue chalk-striped suit with matching tie, and looked like the archetype of the successful businessman.

Calvin was a bit late for our appointment, and he apologized—explaining that he had been tied up at his hotel on a long-distance call involving league business.

I came right to the point. "I understand you've been taking a lot of flak since it was announced that you didn't give Harmon the $100,000 contract that everyone thought he deserved."

"That's right," Cal replied. "In fact, I've taken so much heat that Harm came into my office and said, 'I can't see you taking the rap for this, Cal. I'm going to tell the public about the details of my contract.' But I told Harm that he

Harmon, with Calvin Griffith, receiving one of his many trophies

didn't need to divulge anything. I've taken public criticism for years, and I'm used to it. Harm's happy with his contract, and that's all that matters to me."

Cal reflected a moment and then seemed to fumble for words as he said, "You know, I've had a struggle to get people to accept me ever since my uncle Clark Griffith died and I was made president of the Washington Senators. Uncle Clark was a great human being. He was a Hall-of-Famer and people liked everything he did. But me—people remembered me as the kid who used to bag peanuts at the ballpark. When I was made president they said I didn't have the ability or the experience to run the organization, and this constant harping on that theme has kept going even up to now."

"You must think quite a bit of Killebrew to take on some additional and unnecessary criticism about his salary."

"You can say that again," replied Cal. "Harm's still the same modest fellow that he was when he first came to us as a rookie. I remember once when he had a hot streak hitting homeruns when we were still in Washington. The Washington sportswriters, *Sports Illustrated, Life* and *Time,* and other national magazines all published pictures and stories about him. It worried me because I thought he might get the big-head. I called him into my office and had a long talk with him about guys getting inflated and losing the personality that was pleasing to the fans. I told him to keep a level head and not get conceited and ignore people. Harm said, 'Cal, don't worry about me. I had things like this happen when I played high school football, and it has never affected me.'

"Harm's kept this same philosophy through the years. He was an All-American boy then, and he's an All-American man now. Why, he's the most generous guy I know. Whenever parents of crippled children write in and want to bring them to the games, Harm will go and visit with the kids who are in wheelchairs all during the game. I get so many appreciative letters from fans regarding Harm. It's funny though, if he has a three or four day slump, then the same fans get on him.

"I make it a practice, when I have time, to see which of the ball players give autographs to the kids. I've seen Harm do it for as long as forty minutes. Tony Oliva is another great guy that way. But I see some of the other players walk away and completely ignore the kids."

As we concluded the interview, Calvin Griffith had left no doubt in my mind regarding his attitude toward Harmon. To him Harmon Killebrew is not only "The Big Guy," but even more than that he is the All-American man. I sensed that he felt a loyalty toward Harm that would never be shaken. And Calvin knows how to be loyal. When he was a youngster of seven, his Uncle, Clark Griffith, had Cal, whose last name was Robertson, and his sister Thelma leave their Montreal, Canada home and live with him. Clark Griffith did this to help the Robertson family as their father was ill. Calvin was reluctant to leave the family, but still set about to be as helpful as he could to his uncle. After their father died, Calvin and Thelma stayed with Clark Griffith, and although they were never legally adopted, they took his name. Later, the rest of the Robertson family, Jimmy, Sherry, Billy (all Vice-Presidents of the Twins), Mildred, and their late brother Bruce, moved to Washington. The Robertson family purchased a home and worked together to help support one another and be of help to Clark Griffith. They have all stayed close through the years. Mrs. Thelma Griffith Haynes is a Vice-President and Assistant Treasurer. Their sister Mildred is now Mrs. Joe Cronin. Joe is President of the American League. Otherwise, she would undoubtedly be working in the Twins organization.

Thelma, when talking about the family members holding key offices with the Twins, said, "They are not doing these jobs because they are relatives, but because they do their jobs well. We are all interested in baseball, and none of the family would think of doing anything to hurt the organization."

Calvin Griffith's statement that Harmon was an All-American man was a fitting climax to my research about Killebrew. I left Orlando convinced that he was the "Big Guy" of the Twins club, because everyone I had met from rookie players right up to the Twins President, Calvin Griffith, had told me so.

the killer

30

It was the final game of the season—a Thursday afternoon at Metropolitan Stadium. The Twins had already won the Western Division by nine games over their nearest rival, Oakland, and were looking forward to their play-off with Baltimore for the American League championship.

The opponents, the Chicago White Sox, had spent most of the season near the cellar. The teams were merely playing out the schedule, and you would assume that fan interest would have been at low ebb and attendance at the game sparse. But this was not so. Thousands of Minnesotans had jammed the stands, and the air was filled with tension. The reason? The Killer's fans had come to cheer their favorite in his attempt to hit his fiftieth homerun of the 1969 season.

Twice before, Killebrew had flirted with the fifty mark—forty-eight homeruns in 1962 and forty-nine in 1964. Surely, the third time would be the charm. Harmon was on a hot streak, having hit his forty-ninth homerun the day before. Pennant play pressure was off; fans were for him. So they settled back in their seats to await and savor the moment when Killebrew's fiftieth homer would crash past all retrievers.

But the White Sox pitcher had different ideas. He threw the ball neck-high and ankle-low, and sandwiched in an occasional ball-on-the-edge-of-the-strike-zone.

Harmon's wood kissed the ball early in the game, but the ball rose in high flight toward left field, coming down just inside the park.

Killebrew's final time at bat provided a moment of high suspense. As he started toward the batter's box, he took three practice swings, tapped the dirt from his spikes with his bat and stood at the plate like Goliath facing David with his slingshot. Lazar worked carefully, but to no avail. One pitch was a bit too good, and the Killer's mighty bat hit the ball with a crash. The tiny sphere rose in a majestic arc and soared through the blue sky toward the left center field fence. As the ball was in flight, 15,000 fans watched, transfixed. The religious prayed, the profane cursed, and the golfers used body English to help the ball go out. Just as everyone was set to celebrate that fiftieth homerun, fate intervened. It might have been a wisp of a breeze or an act of providence, but whatever the reason, the ball dropped from its lofty heights and came down just low enough that the White Sox outfielder could catch it—backed up against the fence. As Harmon turned from the plate and walked toward the dugout, he made a valiant effort to hide his disappointment.

The fans groaned as if in pain, and many filed toward the exits even though the game was far from over.

In the first half of the ninth, the White Sox got runners-on-base and threatened to overcome the Twins' one run lead and tie the game at six all. If they had, the Twins would have batted again in the last of the ninth, and Harmon who was due to bat, would have had another opportunity to try for that fiftieth homerun. With two out and Chicago runners in scoring position, the batter hit a slow roller in Killebrew's direction. This play is one of the most difficult for a third basemen to make because it's necessary to approach the ball at full speed, pick it up on the run, and throw to first, all in the same motion. Harmon pushed himself to the utmost, picked up the ball, and fired it to the first baseman just in time to beat the runner for the final out. By his own great effort he had closed the door on another chance to get his fiftieth homerun in 1969.

As I left the stadium at the end of the game, a pall of gloom seemed to hang over the fans. Men and women were shaking their heads with dismay, and I overheard comments such as "What tough luck for Harm."

I encountered Jerry Hanson, Minneapolis Realtor and a close friend of the Killebrews, who had disappointment written all over his face. He said, "We didn't get number fifty, did we?"

On the way home, I turned on the radio, and the first comment I heard was by Howard Vikan, popular WCCO broadcaster. "Harm didn't get number fifty today—darn. . . ." His tone was genuinely downcast.

For several days, Twin Cities sports fans who idolize Harmon, were discussing that elusive fiftieth homerun.

A few days later we were re-hashing the game with Harm, and I said, "Do you know if you hadn't made that tough play at third in the ninth inning you would have had another chance to get that fiftieth homerun. It was a difficult ball to get. If you had eased up a tiny bit, the runner would have been safe, the White Sox would have tied the score, and you would have come to the plate again in the ninth."

Harmon smiled and said, "Yes, I know." His tone closed the subject—conclusively. I should have been more discreet than to bring the matter up.

In the post-game interviews, Harmon made no excuses for failing to connect with his fiftieth homerun. He simply said, "I never saw so many good pitches as I had today. I suppose the problem was that I was getting too far under the ball on my swing."

One of the sportswriters brought up the fact that Harmon had indeed hit fifty homeruns during the '69 season because he had been robbed of one by an umpire's call in Boston. The ball had hit the screen and bounced back into the field. But, not having seen it, the umpire would not allow it. Killebrew preferred not to talk about the incident.

I had the opportunity of again discussing the final game of 1969, the following March when I encountered Danny Lazar, the White Sox pitcher, before a spring training game in Orlando. Lazar is an attractive and friendly young man and responded readily to my questions.

I said, "I remember that you pitched against Killebrew when he was trying for his fiftieth homerun during the final game of 1969. Do you recall how you felt at the time?"

Lazar smiled and replied, "I wasn't aware until after the game of all the implications. If I had been pitching in regular rotation, perhaps I would have been."

"Did you have a plan you followed in order to keep Killebrew from hitting one out?"

"No. I had no game plan. I wasn't pitching that well. I must say, though, that Harmon Killebrew looks like a hitter when he comes up. I've heard a lot about his self-control, and it may be that he is one of the players who takes out his aggressions in attacking the ball. I think this is good."

"How would you have felt if he had hit his fiftieth homerun off you?"

"If he hits it, he earns it. Whether it's number one or number fifty. He did hit a couple of good ones. One would have gone out, but it was too high and came down just inside the left centerfield fence."

My interview with Lazar gave me the impression that he is objective enough to admire the skills of his competitors.

Lazar's statement that "Killebrew looks like a hitter when he comes up," has been reinforced and elaborated on by other pitchers. In a report by Jack Zanger that appeared in *Sport* Magazine (June 1970) it was the consensus of top pitchers that Killebrew is the most feared long-ball slugger in the major leagues. When talking about Killebrew's prowess as a hitter, their feelings ranged from "respect, awe, and admiration to fear."

The pitchers were unanimous in their opinion that Killebrew has worked so hard at improving his hitting that he no longer has any obvious weaknesses at the plate. They also agreed that he is now "not only a feared slugger, but also an excellent all around hitter."

They all said that Killebrew is so strong that "he can make relatively poor contact and still hit the ball out."

Harmon is also known as a thinking hitter, and Sam McDowell, who tried to out-think him, related an experience which is typical of those of other pitchers. He said, "We were winning, luckily, when Harmon came up. I was throwing him nothing but fastballs and got behind on the count 3-1. I decided to fool him with a changeup. . . I hadn't thrown him any changeups in a long time. I think I had pitched four games against the Twins and faced him about twelve times without throwing him a changeup. So there was reason to think it would work. It didn't. He hit my changeup into the upper deck in left-field."

The pitchers' collective opinion of the best way to pitch to Killebrew is "to keep changing pitches, keep moving the ball around, pitch around him whenever possible, and above all—pray."

A few pitchers have taken to calling Killebrew the "The Fat Kid," but when pinned down they admit it is in jest, because "he's all muscle."

And finally, though he is a formidable enemy, all pitchers regard Harmon as a gentleman and a superb professional.

Ted Williams, who is considered one of the greatest hitters baseball has produced, rates Harmon Killebrew of the Twins with the all-time great hitters.

In an interview, June 17, 1970, with Sid Hartman of the Minneapolis Tribune, he said, "Harmon is a great homerun hitter, and all-around hitter. He knows when to try for a single or a homerun. And he is adept at getting either."

He said in addition, "I don't think Harmon has any one single weakness at the plate. A pitcher must constantly move the ball around and pitch him awful fine.

"He's a great hitter, first because of his strength, and second because of his intelligence."

Harmon's dedicated and studious approach to hitting is noticed by, and rubs off on, other team members. For example, he has Cesar Tovar the "Mighty Mite" of the Twins watching the strike zone more carefully. Harmon said, "I keep asking Cesar why he doesn't walk more. I hope he gets more this year than I do."

"Killie," said Tovar, flashing a grin, "plays with me and say why I no get more base on balls. He make me concentrate more now. You watch. Me catch Harmon."

Rick Renick gives Harmon credit for improving his hitting. "Harmon showed me how to smoothe out my swing and drilled the right technique into me so that I've continued to hit that way. It helped me out of a slump." Since then Rick has become the Twins' most consistent and potent pinch-hitter.

Much could be said about Killebrew's homerun hits. They are in fact works of art. Sometimes they soar majestically into orbit and then splash down in the most remote areas of the bleachers. On other occasions, they go out of the park like a blast from a howitzer. And in rare instances, they go just far enough to clear the fence, behaving as if they had been guided by a golfer sinking a six foot putt.

In most cases, when Killebrew connects squarely, the opposing outfielders don't even turn their heads to watch the ball in flight. They know in their hearts that nothing short of a Florida hurricane could alter its course.

Ken Berry of the Chicago White Sox says Harmon Killebrew hits a baseball harder than Baltimore's blond slugger, Boog Powell or Washington's giant, Frank Howard. After Harmon hit his second homerun of the game against Chicago on June 28, 1970, Berry said, "I had the ball in the webbing of my glove, but it just ripped my hand back and was gone."

Berry made this statement after hanging over the fence 410 feet away from home plate in an attempt to catch Killebrew's drive. Berry continued, "Frank Howard has hit two like that this year, that I've been able to hold on to, and Boog Powell one—but Killebrew's was going too hard."

Fan reaction to the homeruns is great. Killebrew is one of the primary reasons why more than a million spectators a year, for the last ten years, have crowded into Metropolitan Stadium. But the Killer doesn't always have to hit a homerun to excite the crowd. When he leaves the dugout and heads for home plate there is a murmur of excitement, and when the announcer says, "Now batting for the Twins, number three, Harmon Killebrew," voices cheer, hands clap, and feet stamp.

If Harmon swings at the ball and misses, an "ooooh!" slightly reminiscent of the shudder of a frightened child fills the air. And if he is given a deliberate base on balls, the opposing pitcher is roundly booed.

When he does hit a homerun, he will pause momentarily to watch the ball in flight, before circling the bases—meanwhile the crowd goes wild. Gray-haired ladies, prosperous looking business men, pulchritudinous peaches, potentates—youngsters of all ages jump to their feet and roar their approval.

Even if thousands of fans are stamping their approval or a dozen teammates are waiting to shake his hand, he still maintains his composure.

When asked once if he doesn't hear the crowd's applause, he said, "Sure, I'm aware of the roaring, but I can't pick out any specific thing that is said."

He has trained himself, as a professional, to take the crowd's reactions in stride, because he knows that the fans may cheer him for a homerun and then boo him for a misplay later in the game.

This happened May 31, 1970, in a game against the

Yankees. Harmon was cheered for a homerun in the third inning (a 417-foot blast), booed in the fifth when he couldn't score from third on a fly-ball to center field, and then cheered again when he won the game in the tenth inning with a 421-foot homerun.

It's an interesting study in crowd psychology to see people react when someone in the stands bellows forth and triggers their negative emotions.

Needless to say, sportscasters and sportswriters get a lot of mileage out of Killebrew's homeruns. Ever since his rookie days, his tape-measure blows have furnished pages of copy.

Typical of sportscasters' comments are the ones made by Halsey Hall, Twins announcer. When Killebrew won the Yankee game on May 31, 1970, with a tenth inning homerun, Halsey exploded with, "There's a high fly. It's going—going—gone. Holy Cow! What a way to win a game with a typical Killebrew homerun, slightly higher than the Foshay Tower (the tallest building in Minneapolis.)

"Wow! Bobby Mercer (Yankee center-fielder) ran a few steps after the ball and quit.

"Boy! Did the crowd go wild, and are they going home happy!"

At a 1970 game in Kansas City, Frank Buetel, another member of the Twins broadcasting team, said, "The bat is an impressive piece of lumber when Harmon's at the plate. When the Kansas City outfielders see him at bat they play way back in downtown Independence. That's down the road a piece. And the fans. They shudder every time Killebrew swings and misses."

Sportswriters have come up with such eye-catching headlines as:

"A Modern Babe Ruth. Killer can claim Title."
"5 Game-winners in hot Harmon start."
"Harmon smash hit upstages Howard."
"Killer loose—Pitchers Offer Reward."
"Twin HR 'Kills' Nats."

"Harmon Killebrew, Minnesota's Paul Bunyan of Baseball."

Harmon is often asked to list his most memorable homeruns. This is an almost impossible task, inasmuch as he has hit 470 at the time this is being written. He also hits them at the rate of one for every 12.99 trips to the plate; so the emphasis on which are most memorable is constantly shifting.

However, a few do stand out in his mind. I asked him if he could name the one that meant the most to him.

He thought a moment and said, "I suppose that the first one I hit after recovering from the rupture of my hamstring muscle meant the most to me—I knew then that I could still hit the ball out."

Harmon also mentioned the first homerun he hit after dislocating his left elbow. This one happened on September 28, 1965, against Wally Bunker of the Baltimore Orioles. He said, "It meant a lot to know I could still swing the bat the way I wanted to."

However, being the team man that he is, Harmon did not rate these homeruns as his most important. The ones that headed the list were those that contributed to team victories. These included a blast on July 11, 1965, at Metropolitan Stadium in Minneapolis which defeated the Yankees 6 to 5 and sent the Twins into the All-Star break with a five-game lead for the pennant. Notable was the 430 foot drive that he parked in Seat 9, Row 5, Section 34 of the upper deck in the left field pavilion at the Met. This homerun, made off Lew Burdette on June 3, 1967, led to the "retirement" of the seat, and it has been painted as a reminder of Killebrew's power.

Then there was the wallop which was the first ball to clear the left field roof in the Tiger Stadium in Detroit. This was hit off Jim Bunning on August 3, 1962.

One of his nine grand-slams was made July 18, 1962, against Jim Perry, then of Cleveland. The 440 foot blast led the Twins to a 14 to 3 win.

The homerun that enabled him to gain the lead and

go on to win the homerun title over Dick Stuart of the Boston Red Sox on September 21, 1963, was memorable. Stuart was leading the homerun race with forty-one to Killebrew's forty, when the teams met to play a doubleheader. Thousands of fans came out to see the two top sluggers. It was so close to the end of the season that it was possible that the winner of the homerun title would be decided that day.

Although his knee was bothering him, Harmon put on a great show. In his first trip to the plate, he hit one out to tie Stuart at forty-one each.

In the fifth inning, Killebrew walloped another to take the lead with forty-two; however, Stuart came back with his forty-second off the Twins' Lee Stange in the sixth.

Not to be outdone, Harmon hit number forty-three in the eighth and number forty-four in the second game of the doubleheader. Stuart, in the meantime, cooled off after his forty-second clout, and Harmon added number forty-five the next day to win the title.

No wonder Harmon remembers that day. Who wouldn't with four homers.

His first major league homerun hit was made from a pitch by Billy Hoeft of the Detroit Tigers on June 24, 1955. Harmon clobbered the ball and it landed in the twenty-fourth row of the left field bleachers—475 feet from home plate. Although the Senators lost the game 18 to 7, for their seventh straight defeat, Harmon's homeruns lifted their spirits, and Charley Dressen the manager was elated as he slapped Killebrew on the seat of the pants.

The homerun hit the day after the Killebrew's third daughter Erin was born, helped beat the White Sox 3 to 2 on May 2, 1965.

Harmon remembers two homeruns hit off Jim Bunning of the Detroit Tigers in Detroit on May 1, 1959. The second one won the game in ten innings, by a score of 4 to 3. These stand out because he regards Bunning so highly as a pitcher.

I haven't discussed them with Harmon, but he hit two

homeruns recently that I think he might add to his list of favorites.

One of them came on a Monday night June 15, 1970, in a game at the Met against the Washington Senators. It won the game after Frank Howard had put the Senators ahead with a two-run 389 foot blast in the first inning.

We had attended the game in a group. Our daughter Cherie and her husband, Robert Muirbrook, from Utah, wanted to see Harmon and Frank Howard in action. Elaine Killebrew suggested that they might like to have their pictures taken with Harmon and Frank. Harmon was kind enough to arrange it, and when we arrived at the Stadium before the game, he and Frank met us at the Twins dugout.

Frank Howard is really something else. Visualize a man who stands 6 feet 7 inches tall and is as sturdy as an oak tree (weight—close to 300 pounds) and you can understand why pitchers' hearts skip a beat when he comes to the plate. He looks like a menacing giant who could crush his opponents underfoot. Yet, close up, Frank Howard impresses you as being a very kind and sensitive man. He and Harmon asked me to pose for a snapshot between them, and there I was standing between the Gentle Giant and the Lovable Killer. I have relived the experience in my mind many times since. Where else in the world would you find two more superb athletes and gracious gentlemen?

Elaine Killebrew told me a story which illustrates the esteem in which Killebrew and Howard are held. In a Twins game with the Washington Senators, umpire Ed Runge threatened to kick Frank Howard out, and also called a third strike on Harmon that Killebrew felt was a ball. The next day Ed was umpiring at third base and Harmon said to him, "Ed, that was a bad pitch which you called a strike." Runge came back with, "Harmon, if I call a game where Frank Howard nearly gets kicked out and you argue about a third strike, how in the world will I be able to face my grandchildren and tell them you both were wrong. They'd disown me."

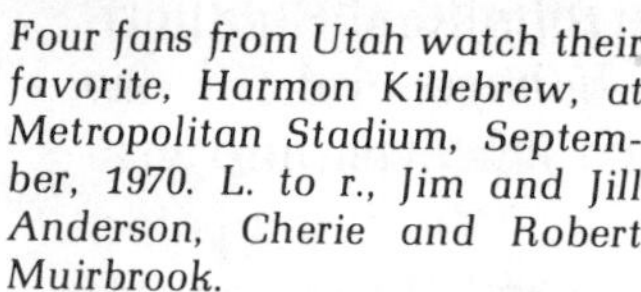

Four fans from Utah watch their favorite, Harmon Killebrew, at Metropolitan Stadium, September, 1970. L. to r., Jim and Jill Anderson, Cherie and Robert Muirbrook.

Robert L. Muirbrook, Ogden, Utah athlete and businessman traveled 1300 miles to meet his favorites Frank Howard of the Senators and Harmon Killebrew of the Twins at Metropolitan Stadium, September 1970.

An attractive fan (Cherie Muirbrook) from Utah poses with Harmon Killebrew and the Washington Senators' Frank Howard at Metropolitan Stadium, September 1970.

Incidentally, our son-in-law Bob Muirbrook intends to have the picture of him, standing between Killebrew and Howard, enlarged and hung on his office wall. He is in the dairy business and thinks the picture will help him sell more milk. It should. Cherie said it was the thrill of a lifetime for her to be photographed between the two superstars.

We sat next to Elaine Killebrew during the game and had the opportunity to observe her reactions to her husband's play. The Twins trailed until the seventh, and Harmon had fanned his previous time at bat. Elaine looked at me and said, "Harmon really felt down when he struck out."

Then with two on in the seventh inning, Killebrew's magic swing came back, and he sent a Joe Coleman forkball 427 feet into the deepest part of the center field stands to bring the game to its final score of 5 to 3 for the Twins. Pandemonium broke loose. People stamped, whistled, and screamed their lungs out. Amidst the din, I turned to look at Elaine. She was on her feet clapping wildly, and cheering at the top of her voice. Written on her face was an unmistakable look of pride which said, "That's *my* man!"

That was a beautiful night at Metropolitan Stadium. The deep blue sky provided a striking background for the emerald green grass of the playing field. The weather was perfect and a soft breeze cooled the air. We had visited with Harmon Killebrew and Frank Howard, both superb sportsmen; and the Twins had won an exciting game. I shall always remember it as a tremendous experience, but the picture that will appear most vividly in my mind as I reminisce in the years to come is that of Elaine Killebrew proudly cheering her husband.

The other homerun that Harmon might add to his hit-parade took place at Met Stadium on July 2, 1970. It was hit off Al Fitzmorris of the Kansas City Royals. At this time the American Legion, in a pre-game ceremony, honored all the players present who had played in their leagues. Harmon was given a huge trophy, and as an additional honor they flew in his former coach Jack Dailey. Jack, who is at present a principal in the Las Vegas school system, coached Harmon in American Legion and high school athletics at Payette, Idaho in 1952 and 1953. Jack was sharply dressed in a golden suit and tie, set off by an orange shirt. As he stood beside Harmon for his introduction, and 24,000 fans applauded, I could see both men beaming with happiness.

When we settled down to watch the game, I thought, "Wouldn't it be great if Killebrew could hit one out for his former coach who is seeing him play for the first time in 15 years."

In Harmon's first trip to the plate, in the second inning, he belted the first ball pitched to him 378 feet into the left field stands. I looked around and couldn't see where Jack Dailey was sitting, but could imagine his thoughts.

After the game, we had the opportunity to chat with Jack, his lovely wife Sidney who is an English teacher, and their blonde daughter Julie, before they flew back to Las Vegas. Jack, a tall, slender, well-muscled man who looks like a fighting Irishman said, "Standing beside Harm in front of that huge crowd was the thrill of a lifetime. Harmon is the greatest athlete I have ever coached. There were others with perhaps greater natural ability and more speed, but none of them had his dedication to the game. He was in on every play, whether it was football or baseball. And his consideration for others was something to behold."

"Writers seem to have made a point of labelling Harmon as slow," I said. "Do you feel that he was slow when you coached him?"

"Slow? He ran the 100 yard dash in 10.1 seconds. In one football game he ran back the opening kickoff 92 yards for a touchdown and later in the same game returned a punt 80 yards for a touchdown. No—he isn't slow.

"Harm had absolutely no physical weakness. He had both speed and power. In football he was a triple threat."

"Was he a good punter?"

"He only averaged about 46 yards."

"What kind of passer?"

"Well, his accurate passes made his receiver, Jimmy Davis, into an All-American end. He threw six touchdown passes in his final high school game while only playing three quarters.

"He was also the top basketball player on his high school team, and as a Legion baseball player he showed his power by hitting 17 homeruns in 23 games."

"People look upon Harmon as the silent leader of the Twins. Did he show leadership ability in high school?" I asked.

Jack grinned, "He didn't talk a lot, but the kids looked to him for leadership. I did get him to chatter along with the rest when he was playing in the infield.

"I remember one football game. I told him, before it started, to run it his way. Then I got nervous later and began to send in instructions. The guys would come back and say, 'Killebrew said you told *him* to run the game.' So I let him alone, and he won the game on his next call."

Casual observation revealed the mutual respect and affection Jack and Harmon still have for each other.

As Jack Dailey and his family left the airport to fly back to Las Vegas, Harmon's eyes were shining as he bade them godspeed with genuine affection in his voice.

One day, over a glass of cold apple juice, I asked Harm if he had ever called a homerun in advance as Babe Ruth did when he was batting against Charlie Root of the Chicago Cubs in 1932.

According to the story, Babe, who had taken an unmerciful riding during the game, quieted his detractors by pointing to the center field flagpole and immediately slugging the ball out of the park at that exact spot.

Harm shook his head, and then added, "I was lucky enough to hit a couple on May Day in 1964, after I'd told a boy in the hospital that I'd try to do that for him. His name was John Guiney, and he'd been in a New York hospital for three weeks recovering from burns. He was an altar boy and his robe caught fire while he was lighting some candles. They said he was a fan of mine; so I went to try and cheer him up. He was such a fine little boy, and just eight years old—the same age as our son, Cam. I gave him an autographed ball, and then he had me autograph his glove.

"His eyes sparkled when he told me, 'The doctors said I could watch you play on T.V. today.'

"For some reason I said, 'Maybe I'll hit a couple out for you.' I was lucky because I hit one off Ralph Terry in the first, and another off Steve Hamilton in the eighth.

"I don't know what made me tell John I'd hit a couple for him but it made me happy that I did."

Reporters crowd around Harmon, after he wins a game with a homerun, to try to get a story. But he is so modest that he usually minimizes his own contribution and points out what the other players did during the game.

A typical example of a Killebrew interview took place in Baltimore on May 3, 1970. With the Twins trailing 3 to 2 in the ninth and one on, Harmon won the game with a smash that landed on the roof of the Twins bullpen located in the right field of Memorial Stadium. Jim Palmer—pitching at the time—had allowed only three hits and had struck out eleven batters.

Just before the wallop, Frank Buetel had told Halsey Hall, "Harm has had a bad day so far. They can't hold him down too long."

As the ball went out, both sportscasters shrieked with delight, and Buetel said, "Harm has hit so many important homeruns that it's hard to describe them all. He hit another one today that won a ball game. We'll talk to him in a minute and find out what kind of pitch he hit."

Later, the interview went this way.

Buetel: Harm that was great! What kind of pitch did you hit out?

Harmon: Thanks Frank. I'm happy to see you. I hit a fast-ball going away. I was just trying to get Tony to third. I felt I hit it well, but high. I wasn't sure it was going out.

Buetel: You made two outstanding defensive plays today. How's your knee?

Harmon: It's coming along. I've been exercising and lifting weights every day to strengthen it.
This is an exciting team to play with, Frank. Tiant and Williams have strengthened our pitching staff and Alyea has been hitting in the clutches. We also should mention the great defensive play of Leo Cardenas.

Buetel: You're right, Harm. But you know, maybe at the end of the season, they'll look back and say "The game Killebrew won with a homerun on May 3rd made the difference." Thanks, Harm.

Before concluding this discussion of Killebrew's hitting it should be mentioned that he is a great hitter, not only because of his power, rhythm and natural ability, but also because he is an outstanding student of the art of hitting. From the dugout and in the on-deck circle he is constantly studying the opposing pitcher's every move. He observes little details in the pitcher's delivery, such as how he holds the ball for a fast-ball or cocks his wrist for a curve. He makes a mental note of the type of ball the pitcher throws in certain situations. He knows when to swing with power and when to try to place the ball for a hit. He knows how to handle a bat, swing smoothly, pull on inside pitches, and stroke on outside pitches. And every time he comes to the plate, he uses his great fund of knowledge to match wits with the opposing pitcher. He comes out well in the battle. As all pitchers say, "It's almost impossible to out-think Killebrew."

And above all, Harmon swings his bat for the good of the team—the final hallmark that stamps him as a great hitter.

The following summary of Killebrew's hitting accomplishments reprinted with permission from the Minnesota Twins 1970 Press-Radio-TV Guide, reveals his amazing record.

KILLEBREW, Harmon Clayton, Jr. 'Harm' **1B-3B No. 3**

Born June 29, 1936, in Payette, Idaho. Height: 5 ft., 11 in. Weight: 214 lbs. Bats and throws righthanded. Married. Lives in Ontario, Oregon.

The American League's 'Most Valuable Player', as well as the major leagues' homerun and rbi king, Harmon Killebrew reached the pinnacle of one of baseball's greatest careers in 1969. In leading the Twins to the circuit's West Division championship, Killebrew was accorded Most Valuable honors by the whopping margin of 294 votes of the Baseball Writers' Association to just 227 for runner-up Boog Powell of Baltimore . . . a fitting climax to the finest season of the modest Idaho slugger's eleven years as a major league regular. Eleven times an All-Star, and the last seven seasons in a row, Harm has led or tied for the A. L. homerun crown six different times, and has paced the loop in runs-batted-in on two occasions. He now ranks thirteenth among the all-time homerun hitters, fifth among active players, and could pass Frank Robinson (450), Stan Musial (475) and Lou Gehrig (493) in the coming season. In addition, by leading the league in bases-on-balls for the third time last season, Killebrew moved into the No. 21 position all-time in that category, and second only to the great Willie Mays among players still active. As a homer-hitter, only the legendary Babe Ruth hit 'em at a more frequent clip than Killebrew, the Babe averaging a homerun every 11.76 trips to the plate, while Harmon's rate is one for every 12.99 trips. Throughout his career, Killebrew has hit two or more homeruns in a game on 39 occasions. Dedicated and durable, Harmon was one of just three American League players to participate in every game last year . . . Oakland's Sal Bando and Boston's Carl Yastrzemski were the others.

Year	Club	G	AB	R	H	2B	3B	HR	RBI	BB	SO	SB	BA
1954	Washington	9	13	1	4	1	0	0	3	2	3	0	.308
1955	Washington	38	80	12	16	1	0	4	7	9	31	0	.200
1956	Charlotte	70	249	61	81	16	7	15	63	50	49	5	.325
	Washington	44	99	10	22	2	0	5	13	10	2	0	.222
1957	Chattanooga	142	519	90	145	30	7	29	101	70	123	2	.279
	Washington	9	31	4	9	2	0	2	5	2	8	0	.290
1958	Indianapolis	38	121	14	26	5	1	2	10	18	37	1	.215
	Chattanooga	86	299	58	92	17	1	17	54	60	68	4	.308
	Washington	13	31	2	6	0	0	0	2	0	12	0	.194
1959	Washington	153	546	98	132	20	2	42	105	90	116	3	.242
1960	Washington	124	442	84	122	19	1	31	80	71	106	1	.276
1961	Minnesota	150	541	94	156	20	7	46	122	107	109	1	.288
1962	Minnesota	155	552	85	134	21	1	48	126	106	142	1	.243
1963	Minnesota	142	515	88	133	18	0	45	96	72	105	0	.258
1964	Minnesota	158	577	95	156	11	1	49	111	93	135	0	.270
1965	Minnesota	113	401	78	108	16	1	25	75	72	69	0	.269
1966	Minnesota	162	569	89	160	27	1	39	110	103	98	0	.281
1967	Minnesota	163	547	105	147	24	1	44	113	131	111	1	.269
1968	Minnesota	100	295	40	62	7	2	17	40	70	70	0	.210
1969	Minnesota	162	555	106	153	20	2	49	140	145	84	8	.276
Major League Totals		1695	5794	991	1520	209	19	446	1148	1083	1201	15	.262

WORLD SERIES RECORD

Year	Club	G	AB	R	H	2b	3b	Hr	Rbi	BB	SO	SB	BA
1965	Minnesota	7	21	2	6	0	0	1	2	6	4	0	.286

ALL-STAR GAME RECORD

Year	Host	AB	R	H	2b	3b	Hr	Rbi	BB	SO	SB	BA
1959	Pittsburgh	3	0	0	0	0	0	0	0	1	0	.000
	Los Angeles	(Did Not Play)										
1961	San Francisco	2	1	1	0	0	1	1	0	0	0	.500
	Boston	(Did Not Play)										
1963	Cleveland	1	0	0	0	0	0	0	0	1	0	.000
1964	New York (NL)	4	1	3	0	0	0	1	0	0	0	.750
1965	Minnesota	3	1	1	0	0	1	2	2	1	0	.333
1966	St. Louis	1	0	1	0	0	0	0	0	0	0	1.000
1967	California	6	0	0	0	0	0	0	0	2	0	.000
1968	Houston	1	0	0	0	0	0	0	0	0	0	.000
1969	Washington	1	0	0	0	0	0	0	0	0	0	.000
All-Star Totals		22	3	6	0	0	2	4	2	5	0	.273

harmon's horde

31

Harmon Killebrew
U.S.A.
If you don't know where
he is, you ain't living.

A fan sent a letter addressed as above to Harmon Killebrew when he was playing for the Washington Senators. And the statement on the envelope "If you don't know where he is, you ain't living" represents, to a great degree, the attitude his fans have toward Killebrew. They look upon him as the ideal man, and the thousands of letters he receives contain either glowing compliments or requests for advice.

A few representative letters are printed below to show the kind of correspondence Harmon receives.

11618 Gravelly Lake Dr.
Tacoma, Wash 98499.
June 9, 1970

Dear Mr. Killebrew,

I was very glad to hear you won the M.V.P. I've read about you many times in both "Sport" magazine & "The Sporting News". I've also heard about how much of a "family man" you are. I was really surprised to see how in front of the NBC viewers you took enough time to say "Happy Birthday" to youre son. Thanks alot for youre time.

Youre fan,

John Winkler

P.S. Good Luck for the rest of the season.

DEAR HARMON KILLEBREW,

HOW ARE YOU DOING? YOUR MY FAVORITE PLAYER. I WISH YOU WERE NOT MARRIED, BECAUSE I LOVE YOU. CAN YOU SEND ME A AUTOGRAPHED PICTURE OF YOU? (PRETTY PLEASE ?????) I HAVE A BIG POSTER OF YOU IN MY ROOM. EVERY TIME I LOOK AT IT , I LOVE YOU MORE.

EVERY TIME I GO TO BED, I DREAM OF YOU HITTING A HOME RUN. I AM IN THE FIRST GRADE. I AM SIX YEARS OLD. MY TEACHER WAS MISS JORGENSEN, BUT SHE GOT MARRIED AND NOW SHE'S MRS. BLAKE.

WOULD YOU PLEASE WRITE ME A LETTER?????????????????

YOUR BIGGEST LITTLE FAN,
SHERRY FREADS
5523 LAYFAYETTE AVE.
OMAHA, NEBRASKA 68132

(P.S. MY BROTHER TYPED THIS FOR ME.)

Matt Leach
1840 Groselane
Sparks Nev
89431

Dear Harmon Killebrew,

I'm one of your fans. You might think I don't know you, but I do. I read about you, a lot. I glad you won the home run title last year, I want you to do it this year, too. But I'm most happy your Mormon, I am too. I want the Twins to have the world seires.

What good advice can you give a person who's played to years of Little League and wants to be a pro. I'm 9 years old. My first year I played SS, 2B My second year I played Cat, 1B and Pitcher.

Could I have an autographed picture of you. And posibly one of your team. If its asking to much don't bother to do it for me.

Rooting for you,
Matt Leach

Dear Mr. HARMON KiLLEBREW,

My Daddy Likes you very
much. HeLike the twins very
much. You are one of his
favorite players.

He allaways votes for you.
And my hold family Likes
you.
Love,
Laurie
Kerowein

This picture was
from the papper

↓

HARMON KILLEBREW
Third Base

July 2, 1970.

Dear Mr. Killbrew:
I think that your x
super, amazing, fantastick
plus best player in the
league. Could I please
have a autograph-pict-
ure of you so I could
prove that I wrote
to you and be admir-
ed by friends.

Yours Truly:

Mike Puffer

343 CHURCH ST STRATFORD ONT. CANADA.

Dear Mr, Kilabrue

I went to the baseball game last year.
You were up, and you strack out
Boy was I ever mad.
Will you give me your Pitcure or your atagrafe?
I am a 8 year old girl.

Love
Becky Holmes

P.S you are one of my best Players.

Becky Holmes
2432 15 ave so
Mpls Minn
55404

A ten year old boy wrote:

> Dear Harmon,
> My mother told me if I'd eat tuna fish sandwiches, I'll be a good hitter.
> Is this true?
>
> Respectfully,
> Bob Brown

Fans who don't write letters are equally enthusiastic in praising Harmon. For example, the phrase "Harmon's Horde," was coined by a group of Mormon missionaries who made a huge banner containing these words and displayed it at Metropolitan Stadium as they cheered for Killebrew.

Below are representative comments people have made about Harmon.

When I asked Halsey Hall, popular Twins sportscaster,

to give me his thumbnail description of Harmon Killebrew, his immediate reply was, "Harmon is simply a sweet and lovable guy. He is always courteous, totally selfless, and as far as his accomplishments are concerned, he would be just the same if he hit 105 homeruns a season or just 5 homeruns and batted .100. If he struck out four for four in a game, he'd still be an asset to the team.

"He is a fine family man and in addition he has endeared himself to the entire baseball world including his opponents, and the sportswriters. Because he's such a terrific homerun batter, he is called the 'Killer' by his opponents."

"Sweet" and "lovable" seem to be hardly the correct descriptive adjectives to hang on a man as muscular as Killebrew. Yet, as one reflects upon Halsey's words, they do make sense. Incidentally, Halsey Hall should know what he is talking about. Halsey has been associated with baseball for many years, knows the history of the game like the back of his hand, and has thousands of fans of his own. No one can say, "Holy cow! It's another homerun, ladies and gentlemen," just like Halsey does, and his colorful comments and genial personality have always contributed to baseball fans' enjoyment of the game.

I met a nationally-known sports photographer in Orlando, Florida, who reinforced Halsey's thinking. Don Wingfield, a tall, striking man who has made many pictures of the Washington Senators and at present is chief photographer for *Edited Sports Personalities*, said, "I remember Harmon when he first came to the Washington team. He was so modest I even had to show him how to pose with a bat so I could photograph him. Now that he is a superstar, he is still the same. He has never changed. He is always friendly. He talks with the rookies, and he is helpful to everyone. He's an inspiration, and he stands above the other players.

"It sounds corny to say I love a man, but I do. I love him."

John Sain, former pitching coach of the Twins described his feelings about Harmon:

> . . . Harmon Killebrew is a very close friend. He is a humble man and he is always considerate of people around him. He is the type of person that I would enjoy working with, if he should ever become a Manager. Harmon is also a person that I would like to influence my youngsters as they grow up.
>
> It is indeed a pleasure to know a person of Harmon's caliber in every respect. Needless to say, he is one of the greatest hitters in baseball.
>
> In regard to Mrs. Killebrew, she is an interesting, gracious lady and also a pleasure to know. . . .

Harmon's business associates also hold him in high esteem. A representative comment was made by Mr. T. C. Foreman, President of the Foreman and Clark men's clothing chain which operates stores in the Midwest states. Mr. Foreman's company has sponsored Harmon's pre-game WTCN-TV shows for several seasons; so he has had ample opportunity to observe Killebrew in business dealings.

"Of all the athletes we deal with, Harmon Killebrew is tops," Mr. Foreman said. "I've never heard him swear, never seen him take a drink; and he's so considerate that he never knocks those who do.

"He's even greater as a man than as an athlete, if that's possible. We've had business dealings a good many years, and he has always been helpful and never overbearing. He doesn't have his hand out for money, and he won't take a cent for making public appearances for us.

"And he is so considerate. I remember about four years ago, one of my sons was drafted into the army and he rented his home to Harmon and his family. Harmon and his wife Elaine and their five children and his sister-in-law lived there for five months. When they moved out the house was so clean and neat you wouldn't have known that anyone had lived there.

"I also remember the time when he dislocated his elbow. He was scheduled to appear in one of our stores the next day. Although he was in excruciating pain, he phoned that morning and apologized and said 'What can I do to make up for this? I'm sorry.'

"The man's an inspiration of exemplary living, and I

am sure some of his goodness has brushed off on his family, on the team, and on the community."

I got another businessman's reaction while giving a lecture on family life at a club. I mentioned that I was writing a book about Harmon Killebrew and his family. After the lecture, Bob Carl, who works for the Northwest National Life Insurance Company, said, "You know, our manager Buzz Wheeler is a great Harmon Killebrew fan. Buzz, who was a former All-American football player at Northwestern University, thinks there is no one like Killebrew. We employees always give Buzz a Christmas gift; so last Christmas we got one of the bats Harmon used during the season he was named Most Valuable. We made a walnut plaque with an inscribed metal plate and mounted the bat on it. When we presented the bat to Buzz he was almost overcome. He said, 'There is nothing else I can think of that would have given me greater pleasure.' "

Dave Yaeger, an executive for the Federal Cartridge Corporation and the 1970 world champion .410 gauge skeet shooting friend of the Killebrews, said, "You really get to know a man when you hunt and fish with him. At such times the real person comes through. My wife and I have spent some pleasant hours with Harm and Elaine in game farm hunting and target shooting, and we're crazy about them. They are both enthusiastic and skilled skeet shooters. (Dave gave them both some instruction.)

"Harm loves the outdoors and gets tremendous satisfaction from hunting and fishing. He hunts chukkars (a species of partridge) which are predominantly found in the western mountains. They are hunted by beating the brush at the bottom of the mountain, and as you flush them they fly higher up the slope. It's a strenuous activity.

"When you hunt and fish with people, you have a chance to see how they handle their frustrations. Harm obviously transforms his into useful activities. He has a great sense of humor; however, his humor is so dry and he keeps such a straight face that sometimes his jokes will finally dawn on you six weeks later. I've gradually

Harmon and Elaine Killebrew with their skeet shooting companion, world's champion, Dave Yaeger, 1968

learned, though, that he gets a little twinkle around his eyes when he's pulling your leg.

"His considerate nature and charming personality make him an ideal model for young people."

Harmon also has his share of female fans. Leah Finch, wife of Henry Finch (a Vice-President of General Mills), remarked, "Harmon is so nice and friendly. It's a joy to be with him." Henry added, "He's a great guy." Red Owl executive, Arthur F. Smith, and his wife Lois say, "Harmon and Elaine Killebrew are just tremendous people."

Betty Robertson, wife of Sherry A. Robertson, Twins Vice-President, told me, "Harmon is a gentleman who is a credit to the game of baseball, and a credit to life. He and his wife Elaine are wonderful family people.

"We knew him when he began his career as a sensational rookie. We've watched him grow through the years, and there isn't a thing he wouldn't do to help people and the game.

"I call myself the President of the 'Unofficial Harmon Killebrew Fan Club.' "

I asked a college coed—a baseball enthusiast—who her favorite player is. Her prompt reply was, "Harmon Killebrew."

"Why him?" I asked.

"I like Harmon because he is so natural. Grr! These players who put on airs make me sick," she replied.

The following comments by Bob Short, owner of the Washington Senators, are typical of Killebrew's fans. Bob visited the announcer's booth in a 1970 game in which the Twins defeated the Senators 4 to 2. When Harmon hit a homerun in the first inning, Bob exclaimed, "Wasn't that a beautiful homerun!" Later in the game Harmon hit a single to drive in two runs and win the game for the Twins. Short's comment was, "What a clutch player! What a tremendous man!" He later commented on Harmon's fine family.

Inasmuch as Harmon has suffered many injuries during his career, I thought it would be interesting to chat with the medical men who have treated him. I felt this would give me further criteria by which I might objectively measure his personality.

Leonard J. Michienzi, one of the Twins physicians, reported:

"Harmon is aware of the need for preventive medicine for his own personal care and that of his family. But when you prescribe something, he wants to know why and what for.

"He's completely cooperative. He's on time for his appointments and arranges his time to make it as convenient for you as possible. Although he's a very busy man, he has never cancelled an appointment. I wish all of the players were as considerate. Some of them don't care about putting you out—even some of the rookies.

"I'm just happy I know Harmon. It is one of the real pleasures of being the club physician. If I hadn't been religious before I met him, I think I would have become a Mormon because of his example."

Harvey O'Phelan, the other Twins physician, was also lavish in his praise of Harmon. He said, "Harmon cooperates in every way as a patient. With his recent hamstring rupture he had to undergo an intensive program of rehabilitation. His leg had to be treated carefully and gradually after the injury in order to strengthen it. During the winter months that followed the injury, Harmon had to run, exercise, and lift weights. He kept at it religiously in order to come back.

"As a physician I think one of the most wonderful things about Harmon is that whenever he has an injury, he has the gift of faith that he will get well again. I just couldn't say enough good about Harmon Killebrew.

"I think he is one of the finest gentlemen I've ever met. In fact, he's a super-gentleman."

The other member of the Twins medical staff is George "Doc" Lentz, the club trainer, who has watched over Harmon's health since his days as a rookie. Doc invited me into his training room in the clubhouse at Orlando, Florida. It is tucked away in a corner, and to reach it you pass long rows of hanging uniforms and clothes all grouped in neat order—like a regiment of troops standing for inspection. As I walked past them, two diverse thoughts flashed through my mind. What a thrill it would afford an ardent fan who could boast of touching all of the uniforms of his idols, and the tremendous task it would be to keep them all laundered.

Doc Lentz, who is a bit rotund and has an ever-present twinkle in his eyes, greeted me cheerfully and told me to make myself comfortable in the immaculate room where he administers to the players' ills. I could see at a glance that it was filled with up-to-date equipment. And it didn't take long to learn that Doc keeps abreast of the latest therapeutic techniques, and that he loves his job. He told me that he studied in pre-medical school for two years, becoming interested in osteology—the science of treating bones. Doc is highly respected in his field, and still maintains an associate professorship at George Washington University where he taught classes for trainers.

Then Doc started talking about Killebrew. He took off his Twins cap, brushed perspiration from his brow, looked at me intently, and said, "You know, I've taken care of

Harmon since the first day he reported to the old Washington Senators. He had been operated on for a high school football knee injury and the removal of some cartilage even before he joined us. And since he's joined us he's had several serious injuries. First, his knee had to be operated on again and a jagged piece of cartilage removed. Then he suffered a dislocated elbow. We put it in a balloon cast and straightened it out, and now it's as good as new."

"How about Harmon's hamstring rupture?" I asked. "Was that really his worst injury?"

"It's the worst injury I've ever treated," replied Doc. "When I first saw it, I thought he'd never play again. His whole leg was a mass of blue right down to the ankle."

"How do you treat such an injury? With whirlpool?"

"You have to be careful with whirlpool. So we often use ultra sound."

"Ultra sound?"

"Yes, it's this machine. It acts as a nerve stimulator and also as a healer."

I later read enough about this form of treatment to learn that hospitals make wide use of sound waves for physical therapy. And also that the waves are of such high frequency that humans can't hear them.

"Harm's one of our best patients . . ." Doc continued. "This last winter when he won Most Valuable he felt obligated to attend many banquets in his honor, so his problem knee suffered from lack of his usual conditioning routines. Another thing in his favor is that he doesn't drink or smoke, and he always keeps himself in good condition. He's instilled these ideals for physical fitness into the minds of his sons, Cameron and Kenny, and they both have great potential as athletes."

"You seem to have a pretty good opinion of Killebrew," I said.

"He's just like a son to me," Doc replied. "We've been close friends for years. I've seen fifty to a hundred kids waiting for his autograph, and he'll take time to sign for every one of them.

"And talk about self-control. If Harm gets mad his face may turn as white as a ghost, but he never says a word. If he doesn't like an umpire's call he'll look at him and then walk away.

"I've been in this game a long time, and I've never seen another athlete like him. A rookie will come to camp and the guys will say, 'There's another Killebrew.' But it never works out that way.

"I never expect to see another Harmon Killebrew. A man like him only comes along once in a lifetime."

a worthy hero

32

Eight thousand Boy Scout leaders gathered in the historic Mormon Tabernacle in Salt Lake City on February 9, 1970, at the invitation of the Great Salt Lake Council. These molders of boys, disturbed by contemporary attitudes toward moral behavior, had chosen as their convention theme the final words of the Scout Oath: "To Keep Myself Morally Straight."

To begin the convention, the thousands present rose to their feet and pledged allegiance to the flag. Then they united in singing The Star Spangled Banner. As the majestic words of the song rang throughout the vast expanse of the oval tabernacle, and the magnificent tones of the organ filled the air, one felt the strength of the American heritage and the dedication of the men present to the cause of the boys of America.

This feeling was reinforced by the prayer which followed:

> . . . Wash over us God, with your piney breeze and the moon's wee silver pool. Wash over us God with your wind and might and

leave us clean and cooled, not as a mere formality, but deeply and sincerely. Oh, God, we invoke thy blessing and thy divine touch and gesture upon this meeting, this coming together, this celebration. Thankful for the truth that a boy is as great as the dreams he dreams and as great as the love he bears, as great as the values he redeems, and the happiness he shares. A boy is as great as the truth he speaks, as great as the help he gives, as great as the destiny he seeks, as great as the life he lives. We lift our prayer and our word of invocation to thy glory and in the powerful living name of Jesus Christ our Lord. Amen."

The president of the Great Salt Lake Council, in his introductory remarks, noted the many civic and religious leaders who were in the audience, stating that Mr. and Mrs. Harmon Killebrew, as honored guests, were seated on the stand.

After the Silver Beaver awards were presented by Dr. George R. Hall, and the recipients were accorded tremendous applause, the president of the council said, "Now ladies and gentlemen we come to a highlight of our program, the introduction of Harmon Killebrew.

"Harmon was chosen to speak because he has become the idol of thousands of scouts throughout the country who send him large quantities of fan mail. He will be interviewed by Dr. Rex L. Campbell who has been the director of this entire production and sportscaster par excellence, Paul James—Sports Director of Radio and Television for KSL."

Paul James: "It is my great pleasure tonight to introduce one of the all-time great stars of major league baseball—a man who has been in the major leagues for thirteen and one-half years, one of the greatest homerun hitters of all time, one of the finest gentlemen in sports. One of my favorite of all-time players—Mr. Harmon Killebrew. Killebrew was the only major league player that was ever discovered by a United States Senator.

"Harmon Killebrew was born in Payette, Idaho, which is up near Boise, and he actually started playing baseball in the third grade.

"In high school he was a three star letterman; he was

the quarterback of the Payette High School football team, and in his last game, that was his greatest one, he accounted for 36 points.

"He played on the basketball team as a forward and was voted the 'Most Valuable Player' on a team that finished in last place.

"On the high school baseball team he played shortstop, third base, and pitcher. As a pitcher he gained an award for backing up third base the most times during the season. He was primarily known for his hitting, and he had a great fan who watched him up there in Idaho, United States Senator Herman Welker, who has since passed on.

"Senator Welker went back to Congress and told Clark Griffith about this amazing boy they had out there in Payette, Idaho. Mr. Griffith thought it was just another of those Senators' stories, but finally Clark decided to give a look at Harmon Killebrew, and in 1954 he was signed with the Washington Senators.

"Harmon has been primarily known as a third baseman. I don't think that most sports fans know that in his first assignment with the Senators he played second base.

"His first year with the Senators he hit .308. That's amazing, isn't it. He had three hits his very first ball game and only one for the rest of the season. He was four out of thirteen that season. He didn't play very much.

"Harmon saw a little more action the next year, and then the club decided to send him to the minors for more conditioning. They sent him first to Charlotte in the Atlantic league. Next he played at Chattanooga in the Southern Association. He also spent some time playing for Indianapolis in the American Association. After playing for these clubs, he was brought back to the Washington Senators. In 1961, the Senators' franchise was shifted to Minnesota. Since then Harmon has been known as the "Killer" with the Minnesota Twins.

"A year after signing in professional baseball, 1955, he married his high school sweetheart, Elaine Roberts, who is sitting here behind us. They have five children—two boys and three girls. Elaine says that Harmon's favorite food is ice cream, but she won't feed it to him. He's not overweight, actually; just sitting on his wallet makes him look that way. Harmon is not really wealthy from his playing; he tells me that he only owns three acres of land in Downtown Dallas.

"In 1968 in the All Star game, it looked like his career was over. He ruptured the hamstring muscle in his leg and sat out. He came back, and what a comeback! This last year he was named the Most Valuable Player in the American League. He was also named the Most Valuable Player by the *Sporting News,* and named the Comeback Player of the Year.

"When he has time he loves to hunt and to fish.

"I think the thing Harmon is most noted for is hitting. This past year he hit 49 homeruns. He has 446 major league homeruns, and he is 13th on the all time list of homerun hitters; still led by Babe Ruth. He is the only three-way hitter in baseball history—he hits left, right, and often. Twice he led the major leagues in stolen towels. I give you one of the great men in baseball, Harmon Killebrew.

Paul: Harmon, they have asked that we have you respond to some of the questions that the boys have submitted. First of all, tremendous homerun hitter, where do you get the power?

Harmon: Well, I should say probably that I get it from the food that my wife feeds me. I think this is a difficult thing to answer because there are many hitters built differently. I have seen small hitters hit the ball a mile out of the ballpark. I think, probably, a hitter gets his power from the forearms and a quick wrist."

Paul: It's not from the biceps but from the elbows down?

Harmon: "I think it's from the elbows down. I try to get everything into the swing that I can. Not being a real big fellow like Frank Howard of the Washington Senators, I need all the help I can get.

Paul: Who is the toughest pitcher you have ever faced?

Harmon: Believe me Paul, they are all tough. Every time you go out there in the major leagues, there's a tough pitcher on the mound or he wouldn't be in the major leagues. I think the toughest pitchers I have had the misfortune to bat against are Hoyt Wilhelm, and Stu Miller. Hoyt Wilhelm throws a knuckle ball that looks like a butterfly coming up to the plate and Stu Miller is not a pitcher who throws very fast but he has a real deceptive motion. These fellows probably gave me as much trouble as anybody.

Paul: As a youngster, did you have a hero in baseball or a team that you followed?

Harmon: Well, being a youngster from Idaho, I didn't have the opportunity to go to many major league ball games, and there was no TV then, but I used to listen to the game of the day every day on radio, and I think that I admired almost every athlete.

Paul: Any one in particular?

Harmon: One player that I have grown to think a lot of over the years is Ted Williams.

Paul: Harmon, when you were a boy did they have organized little leagues?

Harmon: No, we had what we called knothole baseball. I played in grade school, then knothole baseball, and I played about five years of American Legion baseball, 4 years in high school and then about a year of semi-pro ball.

Paul: What's your impression of little leagues? We hear a lot of comments about sometimes the parents put a lot of pressure on the little league players, and maybe the little leagues are more for the parents than for the boys.

Harmon: I think that could be true in some instances. But I think that the more boys we can get interested in baseball, the better; because if they're playing baseball they've got their minds on the game and not on other things. I think little league baseball is great if the parents don't interfere too much.

Paul: As a coach would you put all the emphasis on winning?

Harmon: I think I would put a great deal of emphasis on winning. I think this is probably very important. Just as in life, we need to try to excel and win, I think we should do this in sports also. But I do think that the boys should be given the opportunity to play at an early age, because if they don't, maybe they'll lose their desire.

Paul: Just recently they increased the major league schedule, and we're getting a lot of comment now about one sport overlapping the other. Are there too many games on the schedule in baseball, football, basketball?

Harmon: I think there are. I would like to see them shorten the season.

Paul: How about that, Elaine. Too many?

Harmon: She says, "about 150 too many." But actually, baseball is a great game, and when you play every day, if you're a player that plays every game, you've got to keep yourself in real top condition—so I think it's a difficult thing playing all those ball games. We play 162 games in the regular season, about 30 games in spring training, plus All-Star games, exhibition games, or nearly 200 ballgames, so by the end of the season you could be a little bit tired.

Paul: One of the youngsters wants to know, Harm, what you feel like when you're standing out there in the middle of the field, with the thousands of spectators watching?"

Harmon: A little shaky.

Paul: Even after thirteen and one-half years?

Harmon: I think every player, when he first goes on the field for every ball game, is a little nervous. I think if he wasn't, he wouldn't perform well. Actually, if there are 60,000 or 70,000 people in the stands, or more, you don't notice the comments from the fans as much as you might if there were just a few thousand people in the stands. I might add that it is a very humbling experience to be here tonight because I can remember the days in Washington when if maybe we'd turned the league upside down, maybe even won the pennant every year, we wouldn't have this many people in the stands.

Paul: Another of our young fellows would like to know whom you consider the greatest sportsman.

Harmon: There have been so many great sportsmen—ball players, (baseball, football, all sports) that I have admired, that I think it is a difficult thing to pick out one and say he's the greatest of all time, because certainly many players have their great attributes. I might admire a player not necessarily for the great success he's had in the game, but for the high standards and ideals that he sets in life.

Paul: If you had to choose all over again, would you still be a baseball player?

Harmon: I suppose so. Baseball has been good to me and my family. It has meant a lot of frustration and heartaches and certainly physical pain at times, but I think all that has made it all the sweeter to stay in the major leagues. I certainly have enjoyed it, and I suppose I would do it all over again if I had the chance.

(At this point Rex Campbell called upon Elaine Killebrew to stand up for just a minute so the audience could see her.)

Rex: Harmon, all of us in the Scouting Program are concerned about the moral condition of our nation. We hear preachers, commentators, newsmen, etc., tell us that we are degenerating morally. Do you feel that America is in sad shape as far as morals are concerned?

Harmon: I think it is probably true, Rex. I think that in the years ahead we've got to try to reverse that trend, and we've got to try to combat the many problems we have in our country today . . . drug problems, and others. But knowing the type of young people we have in our country, I'm sure that everything will turn out all right.

Rex: Although I know I am putting you on the spot, I think some unrehearsed questions and answers might go well and this is one that I didn't tell you I was going to ask you. What do you think it means when we say as scouts and scouters—as part of the oath—"keep myself morally straight?"

Harmon: I think this is truly one of the great things of scouting. I have two boys and I certainly would like to keep them involved in scouting and this is one of the things I like to stress to them and which I stress to all young people —to "keep themselves morally straight"—that if they'll do this, they'll not go too far off the beaten track in life. . . .

Paul: We've had a lot of changes in the last couple of years. We're starting a new decade with the 1970's. What is the greatest challenge?

Harmon: This is a difficult question to answer. I think that perhaps to stop the trend to the left, maybe, and try to get things straightened out morally. I think this would be one of the greatest challenges we have in the 70's.

Paul: Maybe a revision back to law and order?

Harmon: I think that would be a real good thing.

Paul: One thing that has amazed me over the past few years is the degree of change. Things are changing so rapidly that it becomes a challenge just to keep up with change itself. One other thing, if you would like to comment—we can go back to baseball again—who is responsible for your great interest in baseball?

Harmon: Not only in baseball, but in all athletics, the one person who was mainly responsible for getting me involved would be my father, who is no longer living. In his day he was a real fine athlete. He played football at James Milliken College in Illinois, and later played football under Earl "Greasy" Neal, a great football coach at West Virginia Wesleyan. My father encouraged me to play all sports and particularly baseball.

Paul: Harmon, in summing up here, is there some particular message you might like to leave with this group?

Harmon: Paul, I thank you for the kind words you gave me in the beginning, and as I mentioned, I think that this is really a humbling experience for me to be here tonight. I recently returned from a three week tour of the United States, and I couldn't help but remember the first time that I visited a lot of these cities.

I joined the old Washington Senators when I was seventeen years old and I can remember one writer referring to me as the 'fuzzy-cheeked, green-grass kid from the cow pastures of Idaho.' I guess I was probably green in those days, maybe a little bit fuzzy-cheeked, and maybe I had a little bit more hair. I hadn't been out of the state of Idaho too much when I joined the ball club in Chicago. I can still remember some of the older players helping me, loaning me equipment, and trying to help me learn all phases of the game of baseball—hitting, fielding, and also trying to give me a lot of help off the field. They were all trying to help. I think that all the managers, coaches, and players that I've come in contact with have had a great influence on my life, and I am certainly thankful to all of them.

I believe, today, that athletes have an obligation to the young people of this country to help them as much as possible and try to set a good example for them. We all know its' a tough world for young people to grow up in because of the many pressures and influences on them from all sides. And because they are more worldly than youngsters of a few decades ago, there are drug problems and many other things to be concerned with.

I know people are concerned about some of the young people today, but we have great young people in our country that no one really hears about. It's unfortunate that the more sensational things get into the newspapers, into the headlines, like a boy taking a trip on LSD, for instance. But things like a fellow receiving a Silver Beaver or an Eagle Scout award don't make the headlines, and they certainly should.

You people who work with youth are certainly to be commended. You do a great deal to shape the destiny of these people and the country that we live in. It's because of people like you, that I feel we will continue to be the greatest country on earth. We as parents, and you as leaders, have a great challenge in front of us—maybe bigger than ever before in the history of this country. In a day when there are so many outside influences on our youth which would seek to lower their moral standards, you help them to raise their standards and ideals and help them to prepare for the world of the future—help them to stay close to God and help them to walk upright before him.

In closing, I would like to tell you the story about a boy who went to his father one night while his father was sitting in an easy chair reading a newspaper. The boy went up to him and said, 'Dad will you help me put this puzzle together, it's a beautiful picture of the world.' His father said, 'Son, I've just come home from work, I'm tired. I would like to relax and read my newspaper. Why don't you go on and try to put it together yourself.'

The boy went away and a few minutes later came back and said he was still having trouble putting it together.

The father said, "Son, I told you I'm tired. Please go on and put it together, yourself."

He went away again but came back quickly and said to his father, "Look I put the map together."

His father replied, "That's wonderful. How did you do it so quickly?"

The boy answered, "I turned the puzzle over, and I noticed that there was a boy on the backside. I found out that if I put the boy together right the whole world was all right."

This is the way I feel. If we help our boys put themselves together right and guide them properly, the whole world will be all right.

After Harmon Killebrew's speech, folk music depicting stirring events in the history of our nation was presented by the Three D's, the popular trio composed of Dick Davis, Duane Hyatt, and Dennis Sorensen (who was ill and unable to be present)—recording artists for Capitol Records.

The meeting was concluded by the chairman who asked all present to rededicate themselves to the Scout Oath. And the following closing prayer for guidance in assisting the boys of America was spoken:

Oh, God, who by the light of the Holy Spirit, dost instruct the hearts of the faithful, grant that in the same spirit we may be truly wise and cherish what is right and good. Bless this organization, the Boy Scouts of America. Grant that the boys who are its members, may through its program, be closer to thee. And grant that men, more men, may realize more fully that work done for youth is a most important work that has a far reaching effect, not only on the individual, but also upon the future of the earth and of thy kingdom. In our efforts we need thy guidance. Direct all our actions with thy divine inspiration and further them with thy continual assistance so that all of our thoughts, words, and deeds may begin with thee and through thee be brought to a successful conclusion through Christ our Lord, Amen.

Baseball's good-will ambassadors to Viet Nam visiting with General Westmoreland, November, 1966

harmon's visit to viet nam

33

Following is Harmon's account of his memorable trip to Viet Nam in 1966.

We spiraled down through the dark sky like a corkscrew, and as we hovered over a small clearing a young boy emerged from the tangled brush of the jungle. Beside him stood a large dog—a magnificent specimen that made the GI look even smaller. We took them into our helicopter, and the boy sat down across from me. He noticed the name on my shirt and asked, "How did the Twins do this season?"

"We finished second," I replied.

He grinned and said, "I'm from Cleveland. How did they do?"

I told him, and then my curiosity got the better of me and I asked, "What in the world are you and your dog doing out here in this jungle?"

With a look of pride he said, "Butch here is a scout dog. We were out on a reconnaissance mission and we found a battalion of Viet-Cong. He stood and pointed them just like a bird-dog."

"How about that?" I replied.

We lapsed into silence. It was so noisy in the plane that it was difficult to talk. One reason was that one of the windows had been shot out. I looked at the GI again and thought to myself, "He looks so young—not a day over eighteen. What's he doing over here anyway?" Tom, the serviceman sitting across from me, was one of the reasons I had had to come to Viet Nam.

My mind went back to the All-Star game in July 1966. After it was over, the Commissioner of Baseball, General William Eckert, had asked me and five other fellows who were connected with baseball if we would make a trip to Viet Nam and talk to our servicemen there to let them know that we in baseball had not forgotten them. The others in the group were Mel Allen—the NBC announcer, Stan Musial—the great Cardinal ballplayer, Brooks Robinson—star third baseman of the Baltimore Orioles, and Hank Aaron—homerun slugger and Joe Torre—star catcher, both of the Atlanta Braves. We had all agreed to go because we thought it was a great idea. I suppose that none of us, at the time, had realized how young the fellows were (like Tom) whom we were supposed to cheer up.

We left from San Francisco on the first of November, and en route to Viet Nam stopped over in Hawaii, Guam, and Manila and then went on to Saigon.

Our trip was to be a quick one. Still, we were scheduled to visit nearly all of the bases, outposts, and hospitals in Viet Nam; so we went nearly everywhere by helicopter.

At this time in 1966, the United States had begun to use a much more mobile attack. They were moving infantry and artillery units around by helicopters with other air-support. This enabled them to move troops quickly into advance areas, and supply or lift them out as speedily as was necessary.

For safety reasons we travelled by helicopter, because we were in the position of not knowing just where our troops were. In fact, there were no fixed battle fronts when we were there. The Viet-Cong were entrenched in pockets throughout the area, so we had to be wary of enemy gunfire all the time we were going from one place to another.

Because of this, our helicopters would stay high and kind of corkscrew in for a landing and go out the same way. If this wasn't possible, the pilot would bring the 'copter in fast and close to the ground so we could get on top of the enemy and pass them before they'd realize where we were.

The trouble with riding in a helicopter is that you have a false sense of security. The aircraft can be hit by enemy gunfire without your knowing it.

I remember once when we flew in a C-123, a fixed-wing aircraft, and had landed at a helicopter base. The pilot motioned to us and said, "Would you like to see something?"

With curiosity we said, "What?"

"Look, and thank your lucky stars" he said, as he showed us a place where enemy bullet holes had damaged one of the wings.

This can happen because you can't hear any noise above the roar of the engine; consequently, unless you, yourself are hit, you don't even know you're being shot at. It frightens you even more when you learn that the Viet-Cong gather secretly and hide in the thick jungles surrounding the cities and villages when they are preparing to mount an offensive thrust.

However, one of the advantages of using helicopters was that it made it possible to contact GI's in remote jungle areas.

Our visiting group usually split up so we could meet more fellows. But I can remember one particular trip when Stan Musial, Brooks Robinson and I went together to a place out in the jungle. We dropped in by helicopter. There were only three American fellows stationed there and they said they hadn't seen anyone else for over five months. They were about ready to crack up. Maybe you know how it is when you meet another American in a foreign country.

You feel almost like he's your own brother. Well, these guys were really happy. They popped a running string of questions at us for two solid hours. They wanted to know everything from how all the ball teams were doing to the latest clothing styles in the United States.

We hated to leave them, but it came time to go. As we were getting ready to depart, I heard our two young pilots talking. One said, "We've overspun the propeller and it's working too bad to risk going out with it."

The other waved his hands and retorted, "Nuts! I can take it out of here."

To this Joe (the first one) replied, "Go ahead! Take it. But if you do, I'm not going with you."

I thought that if a pilot felt it was too risky to go out in the helicopter, I sure didn't want to go either. So we all talked it over, and the two pilots agreed to radio headquarters for another helicopter to get us out.

The jungle was so dense where we were that the soldiers lit smoke bombs so they could spot us from the air. Then another pilot came and took us out and sent back another helicopter to pick up the one that was out of order. They didn't dare leave it there because the Viet-Cong would have destroyed it, which would have meant a loss of about one-half million dollars.

Viet Nam is an interesting country. While we were on our trip, we saw all kinds of buildings and houses, as well as different styles of life. These ranged from modern to primitive. An example of the modern was Saigon. We met General Westmoreland there, and he impressed us as being a great leader. He thanked us for coming.

Saigon is a fairly up-to-date city. You could see that its architecture had been influenced by the French who had been there for years. There were many big stores and their prices were high. We were told that inflation had sent the price of certain items skyrocketing, and in addition a black market was flourishing.

It was hard to cross the streets because they were so crowded with bicycles and motor bikes. Everyone was riding them—from grandparents to small youngsters. The traffic (cars) was quite a bit lighter; and there were people of all descriptions.

Thousands of Viet-Cong infiltrators disguised as civilians have been active in cities of South Viet Nam; so it is difficult to know whether you are talking to an enemy or a friend. In fact, you can't even tell who the soldiers are because there is no standard uniform. Many of the people wear pajama-like outfits, or some kind of shirt or blouse with shorts or slacks.

It is quite common for a peasant to work on his farm during the day and join the fighting forces during the night without bothering to change clothes.

However, the regular North Vietnamese troops are a little easier to identify because they are usually dressed in khaki, and the members of their guerilla bands wear a kind of pajama outfit.

The contrast between the life style in Saigon and that of the peasants was great. Servicemen say that the average peasant's primary concern is to have a rice paddy and a water buffalo. Consequently, many of them give allegiance to the side which will provide them with food and protection.

We had an interesting experience seeing a unique family life style when we went to a Montagnaard village, made up of a tribe of Indians who live in the mountains. The whole family-clan lives in one hut. It would be like you and your wife and your children and their children and also your parents all living under one roof. It would be a three-ring circus, wouldn't it?

Well, the Montagnaards do it, and apparently with little tension. They just add on to the hut as their family grows larger and more room is needed. Their huts are long and are built on poles or posts. I suppose this is done to keep them out of the water and protect them from animals. Their chief foods seem to be bananas and rice.

The people in the village were friendly to Americans but not so friendly to the Vietnamese or Viet-Cong. We went there with a missionary who spoke their language.

Harmon talking with servicemen Rose and Curry in Viet Nam, 1966

Killebrew playing basketball with G.I.'s in Viet Nam, 1966

Meeting in the jungle with servicemen in Viet Nam, 1966

This helped them to become friendly toward us. They wanted to make us their blood brothers. The particular ceremony required was to drink both rice-wine and the blood of a chicken with them. We were all having a rough time not getting sick at the thought of it when the missionary got us off the hook by telling them we couldn't do it because we all had bad stomachs. I had to chuckle inwardly when I thought of my wife, Elaine, and how she would have reacted to the proposed ceremony. I could just hear her say, "Now look here. Don't you know that stuff isn't good for you!"

We had another eating experience which was much more pleasant when we went north to DaNang, and saw the Marine headquarters. Their commander, General Walt, invited us to his house for lunch and we enjoyed one of the nicest meals we had while in Viet Nam. The day after we left there, his house was bombed. Luckily, he was not injured, although he was shaken up.

Our visit took us to most of the remote outposts in Viet Nam. One reason for this was that larger groups of visitors, such as Bob Hope's shows, had to be confined to larger sites where it was possible to give them adequate protection.

Our visits took several different forms. When there were only a few fellows in the area, we would chat and get acquainted with them; however, in the places where there were larger concentrations of troops we would get the boys together for an assembly. Then we would show movies. One of a World Series game and some others, and after that we'd answer questions. If Mel Allen was along he would act as MC.

I'd like to say a little about the life of the GI's over there. It isn't easy. Some fellows get so lonely and frustrated that they are counting the hours until their tour of duty ends. There is constant danger. For example, when the fellows are out fighting in the jungles, they have to sleep with their rifles in their arms so they can be ready at any moment to protect themselves. It's easy to understand how tense this would make them. After we got back from the trip, I heard of one ex-serviceman whose wife divorced him because of the results of such experiences. It seems sad, but every time she even touched him when he was asleep at night, he sprang to his feet to protect himself. His months in Viet Nam of sleeping on constant alert had conditioned him so that with the slightest touch he would prepare to fight.

We went to many hospitals, and saw how heroic our boys are. A lot of them had suffered painful injuries from what they call "Pungy sticks." They would either fall into a hole lined with them or step on them. A fellow can unknowingly step on them and they will jab right through him.

I remember one man who had gone into a cave and had been bitten by snakes. They got him on the thumb and it had swollen up like a balloon.

The Viet Cong use snakes in several ways. One of the most deadly is to tie the snakes in caves before they vacate them, and then when our fellows come to check the cave, the snakes attack them.

Another serviceman had been bitten on the arm, and it was actually twice as big as the other arm. He said, "Don't worry, I'm okay. The doc checked the infection in time so I won't lose it. I'm itching to get back to my outfit."

We had to grit our teeth when we saw boys who had been shot up from their toes to the tops of their heads. Yet their spirits were high. Most of them were impatient with being in the hospital and wanted to get back into action with the men of their units. They'd say "I'm tired of lying around. Help me get out of here, and back to my outfit."

Our trip to Viet Nam took 18 days including going and coming. We all felt it was time well spent. Looking back I remember a lot of things:

The beauty of the Central Highlands and their cool mountain air.

The Mekong Delta, the heartland of South Viet Nam with rich rice paddies.

The friendliness of the people and some of their quaint customs.

The great job Stan Musial did on the tour. He was always joking and laughing—keeping everybody loose.

The times we stood in the chow line and ate with the fellows.

The beautiful and interesting pictures we took.

The sports facilities they had for the GI's. In some areas they had fine volley-ball and basketball courts.

How glad the GI's were to see someone from home. How happy they were to talk to us about baseball and other things.

However, the thing that impressed me most about the whole trip was the morale of the troops. It was just tremendous.

The following April our group was invited to the White House to report our observations to President Johnson. We waited over an hour for him, and when he came in he looked like he had been up all night. His suit was rumpled and his face haggard. You could see he was under great strain. He talked to us briefly, thanked us—and left.

my visit to baseball-minded japan

34

Harmon recounts his visit to Japan. . . .

Several years ago when the Detroit Tigers went to Japan to play a series of exhibition baseball games, their star homerun-hitter Rocky Colavito was unable to go. Consequently, the Japanese newspaper people who were sponsoring the tour requested that I take his place. I was quite disappointed when American League President, Joe Cronin, and Commissioner Ford Frick denied their request. I had heard a lot about organized baseball in Japan and the great enthusiasm the fans have for the sport.

My opportunity to see things first-hand in Japan finally came during November of 1969. At this time, some of the officials of Killebrew Enterprises, Incorporated went with Elaine and me to set up contracts with Japanese sporting goods houses and toy companies for the manufacture and sale of our products.

The others in our party were Vibert S. Kesler, Executive Vice-President of the company, and his wife Marilyn, Lynn Foster, patent attorney, and his wife Dorene.

We left Seattle by jet on Saturday, about 1:30 p.m. on November 15, and eleven hours later touched down in Tokyo. The flight was fast but rather confining. You really get to know your traveling companions when your accommodations are so crowded that you don't have enough space for a good-sized yawn.

I'd like to have you read some things from Vibert Kesler's journal. He kept a complete written account of our activities and has this to say about our arrival:

> We landed at about 9:00 p.m. on Sunday evening, November 16, at the Tokyo International Airport.
>
> The Japanese people are great baseball fans, and as they knew in advance about Harmon Killebrew's visit, we expected a crowd of people at the airport.
>
> They were there. But they were not Japanese. As flashbulbs went off and reporters crowded around Harmon, we were amazed that they spoke English without a trace of an accent. Then we discovered they were all Americans. Representatives from "Stars and Stripes," the United States serviceman's newspaper.
>
> Why no Japanese reporters? We soon found out. There was a riot going on and the airport had been sealed off to in-bound passengers. The leftist student organization was rioting in protest against Prime Minister Sato who was leaving for the United States to discuss with President Nixon the renewal of the Defense Treaty between the United States and Japan.
>
> Kent Nixon, sportswriter for "Stars and Stripes," obtained two taxicabs for us and we went to the Silk Center in Yokohama.
>
> After we were settled in the Silk Hotel, I contacted Mr. Karmen Kawamura of the Sanko Company. He was very apologetic because of his inability to meet us at the airport, and he proved to be a gracious host. He took us to lunch the next day and introduced us to a delectable dessert—Mandarin Oranges. We all liked them so well that thereafter we asked for them everywhere we went.
>
> During the afternoon of Monday, November 17, we went to Tokyo with Karmen for a press conference with Mr. Sadahura Oh, one of the Japanese people's baseball idols. The conference was held in the offices of the Nippon Television Network in Tokyo. Mr. Toru Shoruki, Vice President of the Nippon Television Network and owner of the Yomiuri Giants baseball team, was the coordinator of the conference. At this conference, Mr. Killebrew and Mr. Oh exchanged notes on their past year's performance. The comparison was interesting. Harmon had hit 49 homeruns and had 140 RBI's in 162 games and Mr. Oh hit 40 homeruns and had 120 RBI's in 142 games.
>
> The press took pictures of the two homerun kings as they used the Killebrew Power-Stride Batting Trainer.

I'd like to leave Mr. Kesler's notes now and tell what I learned about baseball in Japan.

The first baseball game was played in this fascinating country in 1873, under the guidance of an American teacher named Horace Wilson. The game soon spread across the country and was given impetus by periodic visits of American stars.

In 1913, John J. McGraw with Tris Speaker and Buck Weaver, first showed the Japanese people big-time American baseball.

Lefty O'Doul, Herb Hunter, Lou Gehrig, Mickey Cochrane and others made a tour of the country in 1931.

And in 1934, the immortal Babe Ruth had 100,000 spectators jamming Tokyo's Meiji Stadium to see him play. It began to rain during the game, and a polite fan immediately brought an umbrella out to Ruth who was on first base. Before the contest ended each of the players had one.

Today, everywhere you go, you find baseball teams. The enthusiasm is so great that when Casey Stengel paid a visit a few years ago, 500,000 people crowded the streets to watch him go by.

The little kids play ball "Yakyu" in the rice fields.

The factory workers keep baseball gloves in their lockers, and at lunchtime eat a hurried snack, so they will have time to play catch, "Ketchibaru."

An American who now lives in Tokyo told us a story illustrating how the Japanese people's interest in baseball seems to overshadow everything else. He said he and his family were taking a vacation trip on a luxury liner. As the ship cruised the ten miles along the sea coast they were enchanted by the scenic beauty of the shoreline. Pine-studded islands, shimmering white beaches and lovely landscapes dotted with the vivid colors of cherry and apricot blossoms captured their attention. They noticed that the other passengers, mostly Japanese, were ignoring the beauty around them and were crowded around the ship's television set.

The Americans walked over to see what important event was attracting the group. To their utter amazement, it was a high school baseball game.

In Japan, there are two major leagues that present baseball. The Central League and the Pacific League. The names of the teams are interesting.

The Central League includes the:

Yomiuri Giants
Kokutetsu Swallows
Chunichi Dragons
Hiroshima Carp
Taiyo Whales
Hanshin Tigers

In the Pacific League are the:

Nankai Hawks
Nishitetsu Lions
Toei Flyers
Daimai Orions
Hankyu Braves
Kintetsu Buffaloes

The major-league parks in Japan are beautiful, and baseball games are seen by well over ten million fans each year. At the stadiums, the white jacketed vendors sell:

softo drinku—Pepusi-coru—icu creamu—cold hot dogs—peanuts—popcorn—cracker jack.

The American influence also extends to their baseball terms.

They say:

Pray Barru!	—Play Ball!
Striku	—Strike
Outo	—Out
Safu	—Safe

Confucian ethics affect the players' conduct on the ball field. Before beginning the game, the members of the opposing teams line up, facing each other, and bow in unison. Sometimes, they go through ancient rites and toss a handful of salt for purification over home plate before the game starts.

If a player becomes involved in a rhubarb, after it is over, he will turn around, remove his cap, and bow from the waist facing the grandstand.

The spectators aren't always so polite. I hesitate to say

it, but sometimes the more rabid fans react more like some Americans do. According to those who told me about their conduct, they show their displeasure over a decision by tossing bottles and storming onto the field.

The baseball rules seem to favor the hitter over there. The strike zone is narrower and the pitching mound is higher. Mr. Oh said the pitchers have very good control and they take great pride in demonstrating their stamina. They like to throw as many pitches as they can, and if one of them gets knocked out of the game, he will continue pitching in the bullpen to show the crowd his great endurance.

Henry Borow, Psychologist at the University of Minnesota, who is a walking encyclopedia of baseball knowledge, has had considerable opportunity to observe baseball in Japan. From his experiences during two extended stays there as an educational consultant, he said:

"I witnessed a typical game in 1951 in the Korakuen Stadium in the Osaka area. Joe DiMaggio was appearing with a barnstorming team of American major league all-stars and the game was a sellout. The Japanese team scored first and there was tremendous crowd reaction. Later, the heavier hitting prowess of the sturdier Americans asserted itself and the crowd fell subdued. However, the fans still showed open admiration for, and interest in the hitting exploits of the visiting Americans.

The game was enlivened by the announcers as the Japanese sportcaster and the G.I. announcer (Japan was still under Allied occupation at the time) took turns butchering the names of Japanese and American players. For example, the Japanese announcer called George Strickland, American League player and coach, "STURICKO-RONDO."

"Never have I seen more intense interest in baseball than in Japan. The college baseball games often attract crowds of forty to fifty thousand. The cheering is deafening and the children present wear baseball caps with the college insignia on them."

Everything I learned about baseball in Japan was interesting, and I hope someday to play on an exhibition tour there.

I also should like to mention a few other interesting experiences we had—random observations made during our too brief visit to Japan.

Before going there, I read that Japan is now the number one competitor of the United States in the world's trade markets, and that the average Japanese worker is willing to save eighteen per cent of his take-home pay and by so doing help finance his nation's economic growth. I understand our savings rate is around six per cent. Of course we all know there is an increasing number of Japanese products on the market in America.

While visiting Japan, it was easy to see why their economy is booming. We saw one example on November 18, when we travelled to Nagoya on the fast train from Yokohama. Incidentally, the railroad train was spacious, clean, fast and comfortable.

In Nagoya, we visited a major sporting-goods wholesaler. The business was housed in a two-story warehouse-type-building on a main business street. The front of the building had a large, garage-type door which was left open during the day. It was a cold November day, but the employees were busily scurrying about the premises, filling orders. There were no security officers present, and it appeared as if the workers were completey trustworthy and intensely interested in what they were doing. We found the same situation in the Mitsua Tiger Company in Tokyo. Its manager is Mr. Teruo Nagochi, a very interesting person.

Tokyo is a beautiful city. It has many modern hotels and an efficient subway system. Wally Yonamine, an American citizen who lives in Japan got us three fine hotel rooms.

About the food in Japan—it is different and delicious. At one lunch, Karmen treated us to a Kobe Beef dinner. The steaks were out of this world—so tender you could cut them with a fork. The Kobe Beef gets its name from the Kobe area of Japan where cattle are raised. They say the animals are fed a ration of beer each day and also receive a daily massage when they are being fattened. No wonder their meat is so tender.

Vibert Kesler has an interesting account of another delicious meal we had. He wrote this in his journal:

> Mr. Nagochi suggested that we eat at a Tempura Teahouse which we reached through some back streets of Tokyo. Here we ate some typical Japanese food that tourists don't usually encounter.
>
> Tempura is a meal that is made up of several varieties of vegetables and fish that are dipped in a rice batter and fried in sesame seed oil. The Tempura was served to us as it was cooked, and it tasted delicious.
>
> While we were eating, the employees of the restaurant discovered that Harmon was an American baseball star, and within a few minutes everyone in the restaurant, employees and patrons, crowded around to get an autograph. After Mr. Killebrew had patiently written down his signature for everyone, the management of the restaurant served us a special Japanese delicacy as a reward. They handed us each a small board slab on which were four portions of steamed rice wrapped in seaweed topped by 1. raw tuna, 2. steamed shrimp, 3. a starfish paste, and 4. raw fish eggs.
>
> We were each given chopsticks and told that proper etiquette dictated that we pick up each separate piece of rice wrapped in seaweed and eat it and its topping in one bite.
>
> The steamed shrimp and raw tuna were tasty. But the starfish and raw eggs were, well, kind of slimy. A couple of times it looked like one or the other of us was pressing his gastronomic capacity too far and might have to make an abrupt departure from the table.

We met some hospitable and interesting people in our business contacts. One of them was Charlie Schlick, director of the Swiss Union Bank in Tokyo. Charlie was from Switzerland, had lived in Japan and Tokyo for seventeen years, and spoke fluent Japanese, English and German. He is a good friend of Hal Empey, a director of Harmon Killebrew International, Inc. He suggested the Bandai Toy Company as a good company to contact.

Mr. Naoharu Yamashima, president of the company and his son were very cordial when they discussed business arrangements for marketing our Power Stride with them.

We also had satisfying business conferences with Mr. Nagochi of the Mitsua Tiger Company. We also met with Wally Yonamine, the new manager of the Nagoya Tigers.

Harmon Killebrew explains his power-stride batting trainer to Mr. Naoharu Yamashima, president of Bandai Co. LTD, Tokyo, Japan, December 6, 1969

We took time out for some sight-seeing, and one interesting trip was to Nikko, the ancient palace and shrine of the Emperors. The shrine was open, which only happens once every fifty years. Elaine, Marilyn Kesler and I paid a fifty-cent entrance fee and climbed up many steps—it seemed like hundreds—to view a sacred pillar. The Fosters didn't make the trip, and Vibert Kesler refused to enter the shrine with us. He doesn't know what he missed. In another fifty years he can find out.

We found the people of Japan to be very clean, courteous, and industrious, and they dress attractively. Some dress in the traditional kimonos. The young people mostly wore western style clothing. And the businessmen dress very conservatively in dark suits with white shirts and black ties. The men seem to rule the households, and the women have little to say.

In their homes, they sit cross-legged on the floor to eat, yet they have modern appliances. They won't let outsiders see their bedrooms when they are not in use, and their sleeping mats are rolled up.

They are very serious about everything they do, even when they are just rehearsing for something.

Vibert Kesler has an incident in his notes which illustrates their complete dedication to everything they do.

"On Saturday morning November 22, I was awakened by a telephone call from Dorene Foster inquiring whether I had looked out the hotel window. I indicated to her that due to the early hour I had not yet taken the occasion to view the smog-bound horizon. She suggested that perhaps I ought to take a look anyway to determine our course of action. I opened my window, and, to my amazement, the street was filled with fire engines, and ladder trucks were extended to the uppermost floors of the hotel. Water from hoses was being profusely sprayed onto the hotel itself. I confirmed Dorene's concern that perhaps there was something afoot. I called Harmon, who groggy-eyed, leaned out the window and likewise became concerned. The switchboard to the hotel office was jammed, but finally I got through only to discover that it was a fire drill. We counted a total of 26 fire engines with hoses and men all over the street. Not having witnessed a fire drill previously, I have no way of judging the scope of a Tokyo drill compared with other cities. However, it was our impression that the drill was very thorough. Fortunately, everyone kept his cool and did not dash into the hallways in nightgowns or jump out of the window into a net. The fire drill lasted for some 45 minutes to an hour after we were awakened.

Our week in Japan was quite successful from a business standpoint, and a delightful experience with a different culture in a beautiful land. It was with reluctance that we left our many new friends.

We stopped briefly in Honolulu, on the way back and were met at the airport by Takema Arkawas and his brother who presented us with some orchid leis. The Touchdown Club in Honolulu invited us to be their guests and asked me to speak.

Some time, in the near future, we hope to return to Japan. It is indeed a land of hospitable and industrious people.

THE DAILY UNIVERSE, BYU

Harmon Killebrew receives the Exemplary Manhood Award presented by the 1970 freshman class of the Brigham Young University, Provo, Utah

harmon's philosophy of life

35

When Harmon Killebrew is standing at the plate, swinging his big bat, he is power personified. Although he is not short (5 feet, 11 inches) he is so well-muscled that at 214 pounds he looks stocky. His uniform seems to be struggling valiantly to contain his powerful body. The short sleeves of his baseball shirt reveal the league's most powerful biceps. His thick neck, broad shoulders, the tiniest suggestion of a waist, and sturdy legs all combine to present the picture of the powerful athlete that he is.

Off the field, in his business suit, he presents a different image. His well-tailored clothes hide his powerful frame so well that he appears to be an ordinary, trim, young business man.

But his image becomes impressive again when you have a face-to-face relationship with Harmon. For it is then you come to realize that he is a man of unusual personality. Set in his rugged, masculine face are clear blue eyes that survey you calmly and tend to twinkle when the conversation becomes humorous. His voice is warm and friendly, and his entire manner is one of interest in, and compassion for, his fellowman.

One senses that he is deeply spiritual and wonders just how this part of his personality developed. Then you gradually learn that his late father, Clay, whom he adored, and his mother Katherine, whom he loves with tender pride, brought him and the rest of their children up to be individuals of highest integrity, and also instilled within their hearts the love of God and the desire to serve their fellowman.

When Harmon reached his teens and was influenced by his peers, he was fortunate in having a group of clean-living athletic fellows to associate with. And of course the other influence which has helped develop his spiritual nature, and aided him in accomplishing his goals, has come from his wife, Elaine. Ever since he first met her, at the age of twelve, she has been a source of strength and inspiration to him. Their marriage has been blessed with five children, two sons and three daughters, and it is quite easy to perceive that the entire Killebrew family lives in an atmosphere of spiritual harmony.

Harmon's religious belief, as you know, plays an important role in his life. He has incorporated the teachings of the Church into his daily activities. In line with these teachings, he does not drink tea, coffee, or liquor, or use tobacco. He never uses profanity and starts to blush when the conversation becomes the least bit risque. He gives any available time he has to serving the Church and is in wide demand as a speaker for youth groups and their leaders.

He has complete faith in the power of the Priesthood. When he was fighting his way back to health after rupturing his hamstring muscle, he asked two priesthood holders to come and bless him. They responded to his request. Bishop Donald Nish and one of his counselors, Robert Wagstaff, gave him a blessing.

In recounting the incident he said, "After they finished

blessing me, I discarded my crutches and haven't used them since. . . ."

At the time he related this incident Harmon and Elaine were visiting in our home. To demonstrate his complete recovery from the ruptured hamstring muscle he sat in a chair and alternately extended each leg straight up until his foot was pointing directly at the ceiling. (Try this sometime, you fellows who have had no leg injuries. I tried it after Harmon left and found it practically impossible to accomplish.)

"You know," Harmon continued, "I have even greater flexibility in the leg that was injured than in the other one. It's funny how things happen. After I recovered enough to rejoin the team, I had an experience that really scared me. I had come out of the shower room and was wearing a terrycloth robe. Dave Boswell, who is always clowning, said I looked like a prize fighter and began fanning me with a towel. I went along with the horseplay and began to dance like a boxer. Suddenly I slipped and fell to the floor. I thought I'd re-injured the muscle, so I had Dr. O'Phelan check it. He said, 'Your fall didn't hurt your leg—it helped it. It tore loose some adhesions and as a result you should have greater flexibility in your leg.' "

We knew Harmon was thinking about his blessing when he told the story, but he didn't say so.

Harmon's religious philosophy is the guiding force in his life.

Regarding his role as a father he says, "I think a father should set a good example for his children and teach them a good philosophy of life. I also believe a father should teach his children to be dedicated to what they are trying to do and that working hard makes it all the more enjoyable when you succeed."

When asked his opinion of what role the Church should play in the individual's life, Harmon answered: "I think the Church should help us progress and live in such a way that we will have a good life here and after we leave this earth."

Because of Harmon's exemplary life, made outstanding by his religious and civic service and his tremendous professional accomplishments, he was named "The Man of the Year" by the Brigham Young University Associated Men Students and was presented a trophy symbolizing their annual "Exemplary Manhood Award" on March 10, 1970.

The award is presented each year to a man who has achieved success through his own courage and application, and whose life is considered a pattern for the BYU men to emulate. This is a high honor and in past years the award has gone to the late President David O. McKay of the LDS Church; Billy Casper, golf pro; Vernon Law, former ace pitcher for the Pittsburgh Pirates; former middleweight boxing champion Gene Fullmer; George Romney, Secretary of Housing and Urban Development; Art Linkletter, television personality; J. Willard Marriott, founder of the Hot Shoppes chain; Nathan Eldon Tanner, second counselor in the Church First Presidency, and Elder Marion D. Hanks, assistant to the Council of the Twelve." (Taken from "The Daily Universe" . . . May, 1970, a BYU publication.)

The unique campus life-style of the students of Brigham Young University gives added significance to their choice of a "man to emulate." The BYU catalogue spells out expected standards for both LDS and non-LDS students succinctly, and states: "The maintenance of standards of honor and integrity, of graciousness in personal behavior, of Christian ideals in everyday living, of a high standard of morality, and of complete abstinence from alcohol and tobacco is required of every student. The maintenance of standards as stated is applicable both on- and off-campus, at home or wherever the individual may be as long as he is in student status. Registration signifies a student's willingness to conform his life to these standards.

"Any pronouncements of disciplinary measures made by the President of the University becomes a part of these regulations. Violations may make the offender liable to suspension or expulsion from the University."

Apparently such rigid regulations do not deter serious college students from registering, which is affirmed by the fact that young people from all over the world are enrolling at BYU. The enrollment has reached 24,000 (the largest enrollment in a church-related university in the nation) and it has become necessary to put a ceiling on future attendance.

The BYU campus overlooks the city of Provo, Utah which is about 45 minutes south of Salt Lake City. Here hundreds of acres of land, occupied by attractive buildings and student facilities, are partially surrounded by a background of mountains of breathtaking beauty. The towering 12,000 foot Mount Timpanogos is the scenic focal point, and it casts a majestic aura over the entire landscape.

As one strolls among the lawns, flowers, and trees of the campus it is interesting to observe that the coeds' skirts hang to just above their knees and the fellows' hair does not hang—the standard is to keep it cut short. There are no protestors marching about, and the students seem to be happily and seriously engaged in pursuing their educational goals.

The BYU also has an outstanding athletic program, and students from every race and ethnic group in the world are invited to register and try out for their teams.

The Killebrews plan to send their sons, Cameron and Kenny—both promising athletes—to that school.

Perhaps the chief reason that the BYU has been able to maintain such standards of conduct on campus is the influence of its president, Ernest L. Wilkinson. Wilkinson has been described as "about the size of a bowling pin and just as hard." The former highly successful attorney has channeled his tremendous drive into making the BYU a leading school. With great promotional ability he has guided the university with an iron hand to international acclaim. A few years ago, he was laid low by illness, and after recovering and going back to work, he demonstrated his top physical condition to the students by doing 47 push-ups while 9000 of them packed in the field house cheering him on.

The expected standards of behavior that prevail at the BYU have brought favorable comments from educators far and wide.

This brief summary of behavioral patterns at the "Y" should help make it clear that the "Exemplary Manhood Award" given annually by the BYU Associated Men Students is based upon exacting standards of conduct.

In addition to this award, Harmon was also given the "David O. McKay Award for Athletic Excellence at a special banquet held on March ninth at Brigham Young University. Other athletes so honored at the banquet were Billy Casper, famous golf champion; Gene Fullmer, formerly middleweight boxing champion of the world; Vernon Law, former Pirate pitcher who won the Cy Young Award as the outstanding pitcher in the major leagues in 1960, and Jay Sylvester, world-record-holder in the discus throw. Each was presented with a plaque and a gold engraved pen and pencil set.

The Daily Universe for May, 1970 commented on Killebrew's Exemplary Manhood Award as follows: " 'Comeback' is a well-worn word around the Killebrew camp. Twice he faced serious threats to his baseball career—once when shipped to the minors while breaking in—another time when injury threatened to sideline him, but twice he rallied to play outstanding baseball.

"One thing that has led to his success is his versatility and willingness to play any position. He is the only major league player to have been selected to the all-star team at first base, third base and left field."

The day of the award, 9000 students crowded into the fieldhouse to see Killebrew honored, and an additional 4000 viewed the proceedings on closed circuit television.

President Ernest L. Wilkinson presided over the assembly and after brief welcoming remarks, turned over the introduction of Killebrew to Doug Whisenant. Harmon responded to the award with a brief speech—his philosophy of life, that of loving God and his fellowmen came through strong and clear. The proceedings went as follows.

President Wilkinson: "As part of Man's Week on Campus, the Freshman class sponsored last evening a David O. McKay Athletic Award Banquet. . . . Honored guests who were recognized for their great athletic achievements were Vernon Law . . . Jay Sylvester . . . Gene Fullmer . . . Billy Casper. . . . And Harmon Killebrew—whom we will especially honor today. All five are great champions, and all members of our Church.

"This morning, before we begin our regular devotional exercises, Doug Whisenant, Chairman of Man's Week, will present the Exemplary Award to Brother Killebrew. You will be interested to know that Billy Casper and Harmon Killebrew are converts to the Church."

Doug Whisenant: "This last year Harmon Killebrew was honored as the Most Valuable Player in the American League. He was also honored as Player of the Year. We feel it is our honor to present to him today the Exemplary Manhood Award of the Associated Men Students of Brigham Young University.

"Harmon Killebrew, for those who don't know, plays for the Minnesota Twins. This past summer, I had the opportunity to watch him play, and little did I know that I would have the privilege of presenting this award to him. He has a total of about 446 homeruns in the majors, 13 is a lucky number for him. For every 13 times at bat he hits a homerun. Thirteen is *unlucky* for a lot of pitchers, I understand.

"Harmon Killebrew, probably more importantly, is an outstanding father. He has five children, two sons and three daughters, and his wife tells me he is a wonderful husband. We feel it is a great privilege for us, the Associated Men Students of Brigham Young University, to give to Harmon Killebrew our Exemplary Manhood Award."

Harmon: "Thank you very much, and Doug, thank you for those kind words.

"I would first like to start by apologizing to the Freshman class for not being here last night for their athletic awards banquet. I feel very lucky that I was able to get off spring training for this occasion today, and I guess it would have been asking too much to get off yesterday. Elaine was telling President Wilkinson that I wasn't able to come home when a few of our babies were born, so I feel pretty lucky to be here this morning.

"I want to thank Ben Whitley for showing us around the campus this morning. That was a wonderful experience for us. My wife Elaine and Ken and Cam—our two sons, also had the privilege of touring campus and seeing the beauty here. I think the administration should be congratulated on the sanity that's here. It's really wonderful. Of course, I think you students should be congratulated for your lofty ideals. I hope that you will always keep them, and will never settle for anything less.

"Aside from the opportunity to come here to receive this award, about this time in spring training it's always nice to get a day off. We've been in spring training for about two weeks.

"I am thankful for the ability that God has given me to play baseball. If it weren't for that ability I doubt that I would be here this morning with you. I feel that baseball has taught me a great many lessons about life. Many athletes are taken in by the glitter of the lights and the headlines in the paper or the commentary on TV. The lights, headlines, and TV stop very quickly when you become a loser. One day you're on top, and the next day you're a has-been. I felt the need to find a better purpose in life. Sooner or later, every man asks himself, 'What is life all about? Who am I and why am I here?' These questions are answered in the Gospel of Jesus Christ. Many say God is dead. In my opinion, this is a false teaching. I believe in God and I believe that this belief provides a wonderful and new dimension to my life and gives me greater meaning in this life. Although I have never seen God, I regard him as the creator, but know not how he created this earth. This doesn't rob me of by belief.

"Thomas A. Edison, one of the greatest scientists that America has ever had, wrote in 1921, that we don't know the millionth part of one percent about anything. We don't know what water is. We don't know what light is. We don't know what enables us to keep our feet and stand up straight. We don't know what electricity is. We don't know what heat is. We don't know anything about magnetism. We have a lot of hypotheses about them, but that's all. But, we don't let our ignorance of these things deprive us of their use.

"We need always to keep in mind the wisdom and humility expressed by Thomas Edison in recognizing that there are many unanswered questions, and his wise counsel to us that ignorance about these things should not deprive us of their use. We may witness the creations of our Heavenly Father although we may not understand how they were made. But as Thomas Edison said, we would be remiss if our ignorance of these things would deprive us of our belief in God.

"As the Psalmist said, 'The heavens declare the glory of God; and the firmament sheweth his handywork.'

"We also should not let criticism stop us from working toward our goals. I've been playing baseball for a good many years, and over those years I guess I've had my share of hecklers in the stands. I remember one particular day in Minnesota, at the ballpark. A man was hollering at me all through the batting practice that day, and saying things that weren't too complimentary. After the batting practice, I went over to him and put out my hand and shook hands with him and introduced myself. After that, I think I had another fan.

"I understand BYU has had a few hecklers lately. To endure this requires courage. Men may pass many tests, but fail in one important one—that to bear trouble calmly. Injustice is often inflicted upon us by the meanness of others because of their ignorance and their prejudice. These difficulties must be surmounted with the loftiness of spirit that disdains revenge. More damaging than the hurts we suffer, is the wrong we do ourselves by nursing our resentments. This can destroy our good will, resulting in the loss of our serenity and poise. Magnanimity is a quality taught us by Jesus Christ, which lesson each of us needs to learn and exercise often in today's world.

"Disraeli spoke of magnanimity as follows: 'Life is too short to be little. There are too many worthwhile causes to serve, too many great books to read, too many lectures and musicals to be heard, too many trips to take, and too many friends and loved ones to help. There is too much to do to be little, grumbling over past painful experiences, brooding over injuries, conjuring up ways to get even, smarting over grievances that cannot wait until we sleep. Life is too short.'

"President Joseph Fielding Smith stated as follows: 'Christ's perfected philosophy teaches that it is better to suffer wrong than do wrong. . . . The life of Christ is certainly an example of this.'

"I can't tell you what a wonderful experience it is for me to be here this morning, to have my two boys and my wife with me. And I want to say to you people that I think this is one of the finest awards that I have ever received in and out of baseball, and it is one that I will always remember. Thank you very much."

The event was brought to a most appropriate close with a prayer of appreciation by Ben Whitley.

the killebrew family

36

When one meets the Killebrew children it becomes apparent that they come from a home in which they have been both loved and disciplined. Each one of them seems to possess a calm self-assurance as the result of feeling loved and the controlled behavior which comes from discipline.

Now don't misunderstand, these kids are not paragons of perfection. They have their own minds, are often mischievous, and have problems like all other young people. But unlike many others, the Killebrew children seem to have acquired two of the characteristics necessary for successful living; namely, consideration for others, and the ability to commit themselves to the task at hand.

I sensed the former quality in the two boys, Cameron and Kenny, at the time I met them during 1970 spring training in Florida. As we were sitting in their hotel room they answered my questions in such a natural and considerate manner, that I was amazed.

"Ken," I said, "What do you think about your dad

just getting his first homerun this far along in spring training?"

Ken lifted his ash blond head, looked at me with soft hazel eyes and replied, "He hasn't played much yet this year."

Quite a diplomatic answer from a fellow who was not quite twelve.

"Would you like to play pro ball when you get older?" I continued.

Ken shrugged his shoulders, "I don't know, yet."

"What about you, Cam?" I asked, as I turned to Kenny's older brother.

Cameron, who is two years older than Kenny, had a serious look in his blue eyes as he said, "I'd like to play pro ball if I'm good enough."

"What position?"

"Either shortstop or pitch."

Then modestly changing the subject Cam asked, "How do you like it down here in Orlando?"

Cam has the potential to play pro ball if I'm any judge of talent. From what I saw the following summer when I watched him play in the Edina Junior League, he can't miss.

I arrived after the game had started, and inasmuch as I had never seen Cam in a baseball uniform before, I thought it might be difficult to identify him as I didn't know which team he was playing for. However, as my eyes roamed over the diamond, I noticed that the fellow playing shortstop seemed to be dominating the game. Not in a boisterous way, but with intuitive and skillful moves that seemed to hold the entire defense together. His eyes were constantly on the ball and he was anticipating the coming play like a seasoned major league player. The shortstop was Cam. And his mannerisms were so much like his father's that it made me feel that I was seeing another Harmon Killebrew.

When he batted, Cam showed the same poise. The first time up he walked, stole second on the first pitch, and then dashed all the way home when the batter hit a slow infield roller.

On his second appearance at the plate he doubled in two runs, and then came all the way in when the batter bunted.

I spoke to the coach of Cam's team (The Edina First National Bank) after the game to solicit his opinion of Cam's ability. This friendly man, George Fonger, enjoys working with boys. He said, "It's uncanny the way the kid makes all the right moves. I know his dad is away a lot, and can't practice with him continually, so I must assume that Cam is a natural-born athlete."

Kenny also has natural athletic skills. I watched Harmon practicing with the two boys one afternoon on their back lawn. The boys took turns at the Killebrew batting trainer, and Kenny's booming drives matched those hit by Cam. Harmon fired the ball around to both of them, and their defensive skills were comparable to those of college athletes.

Although they are both athletic, the two boys have different personalities. Cam is quiet and serious like Harmon and is also a good student. Kenny is outgoing and full of mischief. Cam's modesty came out at one time when arrangements had been made to televise a program at his school that was to feature Harmon. When Cam heard about it, he said to Elaine, "Mom, you just don't know what this will do to me. I don't want the kids to think I'm trying to show off dad. Can't you get them to do it somewhere else?"

Elaine said it was with considerable difficulty that she finally got Cam to see that Harmon was just being recognized for his achievements and that the other kids at school would see it that way.

Neither of the boys will boast about their dad. And when they go to summer camps or play on various teams, their friends are often unaware that their father is Harmon Killebrew. Elaine said that at one summer camp the boys went for three days before the others learned their last name was Killebrew.

Kenny is as outgoing as Cam is shy. Harmon says

their younger son will do anything necessary to get a laugh such as falling down the stairs or tripping over a rug. One evening when we were visiting their home, he entertained us with magic tricks.

The three Killebrew girls are also much like their mother and father—natural, friendly, and charming. The oldest, eight-year-old Shawn, has ash-blonde hair and twinkling hazel eyes, and is full of fun and jokes. Her good humor came to the surface when she was recovering from chicken pox in Orlando. When she finally reached the stage at which her sores weren't tormenting her, she looked in the mirror, grinned, and said, "I look awful." Like the younger girls she adores her daddy and frequently climbs on his lap and puts her arms around him.

Shawn is also a perfectionist. I congratulated her once after she had done a clever devil dance at a church social. She listened to my comments, shook her head and said, "I spoiled it; I dropped my pitch fork once."

I suppose the personalities of the two younger girls, Kathryn and Erin, can best be portrayed by describing an incident that took place in Orlando, Florida. We were visiting in the Killebrew hotel suite, and tension and confusion were in the air. Shawn had been tortured for hours by the ugly pox that had broken out on her body, and Harmon and Elaine were almost beside themselves in their efforts to relieve her pain.

Dr. O'Phelan had paid a visit and had recommended a pediatrician who was going to make a house call and determine whether Shawn should be put into a hospital. Visits had been made to a pharmacy for drugs. Other necessary things such as family meals had been sandwiched in between the unceasing ministrations to Shawn. To make matters worse, the family was crowded in their two-bedroom suite making it impossible for anyone to get away from the general turmoil.

While enveloped in this atmosphere of tension, I happened to glance at Kathy and Erin. They both had on dainty pink nightgowns and were calmly stretched out on their backs in the middle of the floor watching television. They were completely engrossed in the program, and it was evident from their smiles that the surrounding tension was not affecting them. They seemed to have acquired the same ability to cope with pressure that their parents possess.

Like Cam and Kenny, the two younger girls have contrasting personalities.

Six-year-old Kathy has an active disposition and enjoys keeping busy. Her parents say she likes to help around the house and keep things neat. She also likes a challenge, and will hunt until she finds things that have been mislaid in the house. She is an excellent reader and likes to look up the meaning of big words. Her Killebrew self-assurance came out one day when she and my wife were walking around Lake Eola in Orlando. Kathy kept running around and darting near the edge of the lake so often that Elise became worried and said, "Kathy! Be careful! Don't go so close to the edge of the lake. You might fall in. I couldn't pull you out because I can't swim." "Well I can!" replied Kathy, promptly ending the conversation.

Kathy watches over Erin like a little mother. One sunny Florida day as she passed Elise, she was carrying Erin on her back down to the hotel swimming pool. "Erin's too heavy for you. Put her down," said Elise.

"Her feet hurt. I've got to carry her," said Kathy as she struggled on.

Erin, the baby of the Killebrew family, is another charmer. Her blonde hair is of a lighter shade than the ash blonde of the other children, and her blue eyes are also of lighter hue. She is as gregarious as a pitch man at a carnival. She also seems to possess unfailing good humor. When she caught the chicken pox from Shawn and the pox scattered themselves over her tiny body, one of the first things she did was come to me, loosen her robe, and say, "Do you want to see the spots on my back?"

Erin is quite a little actress and the other children will often complain, "Mom, Erin's trying to act cute again."

DON WINGFIELD

Harmon romping with his sons Cameron and Kenny

Harmon with his two sons at a father's and son's game, 1966

Like the other children she is proud of her dad in a modest way. She climbed up on my lap one day in Orlando and showed me the key to the city that had been presented to Harmon. Her comment was, "Isn't it pretty." In an effort to get her to boast about her dad, I said, "Your dad hit a homerun today. Isn't that something?"

"I know," she said with a grin.

The impressions I received of the Killebrew children while visiting with them in Florida made me feel that all of them possess personalities that show the results of careful parental guidance.

When one enters the Killebrew home and looks around, one senses another reason why Harmon and Elaine have been successful in rearing their children. The interior of the house is elegant, yet homey. Elaine has skillfully blended a mixture of deep reds and greens with lighter touches of gold—to fashion a living area that is delightful to the eye. In the dining space a wrought iron chandelier, which hangs from a beamed ceiling, adds an interesting touch to the setting. Glass doors connect the dining room with an expansive outdoor deck which overlooks a huge lawn-covered backyard. As you drink in the beauty of green grass and well placed shrubs all sheltered by a border of tall poplar trees, a unique sight attracts your attention. Right in the middle of the velvety lawn is a ball diamond. Base paths, a pitcher's mound and a batting box have been etched in the grass by youthful feet. These worn and bare areas in the lawn are symbolic of the Killebrew home. Although the beige and green rambler is stunningly attractive, you still see such touches of homeyness and realize that the home is designed to provide for the needs of all family members.

I might add that the Killebrew's other home in Ontario provides the same combination of elegance and homeyness. Its pale pink exterior is set off by a beautifully landscaped lot which is brightened with flowers in a great variety of colors. The entrance is decorated by a rustic lamppost from which hangs the Killebrew name and ad-

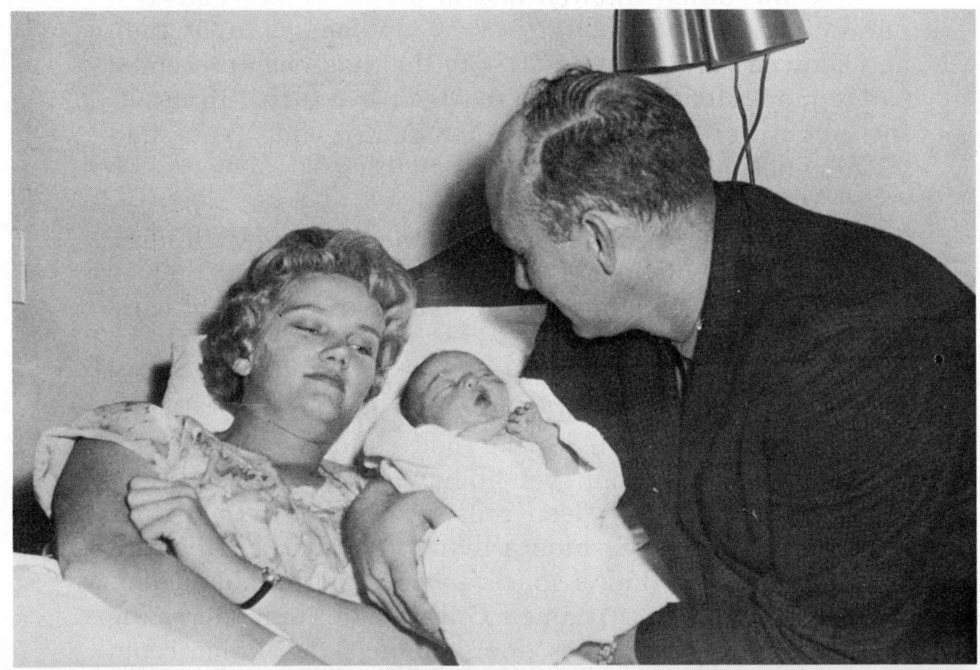

The birth of Shawn, the Killebrews first girl, February 18, 1962

Killebrew family

dress and a small bronze figure of a baseball player. Yet amidst all this beauty there is a much-used concrete basketball court—mute evidence that providing for the play of healthy children is more important to Harmon and Elaine than raising flowers.

As I sat comfortably on the large living room lounge which faces a fireplace that is adorned with huge trophies, I asked Harmon and Elaine their views on child rearing. The interview took place as follows:

Question: How do you see your role as parents? Do you think parents should give their children some guidelines for living or do you feel it is better to let them develop on their own?

Harmon: I have always felt it is important to set a good example for children. To do this a father must have a good philosophy of life and follow his convictions. I believe in God, and that He, as my Father, has sent me to this earth to grow and develop.

Elaine: I feel that I play roles as wife, mother, and as an individual. I feel that my role as a wife embraces taking good care of my husband and being an interesting companion to him. I like to be home when he is there, prepare nutritious meals for him, make our home a restful place for him and help him in any way I can. As a companion I want to give him plenty of affection. I also feel I should move with him from place to place as his profession requires. Although I sometimes resent making such a move, I'm happy after it's done.

I feel strongly about my role as a mother and I feel it is my duty to raise our children to be decent people. I also want to teach them the practices which lead to sound physical and mental health. There are many things I don't know, but when I learn something new that is helpful I try to use it constructively in all of our lives. Of course I believe in God as Harm does, and we are united in teaching our children that religious philosophy.

I have never felt frustrated in these roles. I have so many outlets and interesting things to do that life is always exciting to me as an individual.

Question: Elaine, you talked about good health. Do you have any special ways of meeting the nutritional needs of your family?

Elaine: Yes, I try to give Harm and the children balanced meals that will provide them with sufficient energy and not put on weight.

I serve them fresh fruits and vegetables as often as possible. Our favorite protein dishes are made from beef, fowl

Harmon snowmobiling with son Cameron in Utah, 1969.

Harmon and Elaine with their horses at their Ontario, Oregon home

and fish. We eat wholewheat bread and avoid all artificial sweeteners. We think honey is good, although it may pose problems for some people. For beverages we drink unsweetened fruit juices, with apple juice being a favorite. A lunch that we often take with us to ball games consists of sandwiches made of corned beef and pumpernickel bread and cold apple juice. For dessert we like fresh fruit, banana or date bread, or cookies, all baked with wholewheat flour and unrefined sugar.

Question: There are several current schools of thought regarding child discipline. What is your disciplinary approach? permissive, rigid, or what?

Harmon: One of the drawbacks of my occupation is that I'm gone so much that Elaine has to handle much of the discipline while I'm away. She phones to get my opinion of a disciplinary problem whenever possible, but sometimes she can't wait and has to handle the situation on the spot. Of course, I'm very thankful for her and the fine way she handles the family when I'm not there. When I'm home, I try to do things with the family as much as possible to make up for my periods of absence.

Elaine: With Harm away so much I feel it is my duty to maintain sound family discipline. I'm not the kind of mother who says, "Just wait. You're going to get it when your dad comes home." I don't think it would be fair to Harm to have to start disciplining the kids as soon as he gets home. So I take care of it right on the spot.

We are not permissive parents and we always try to keep our children under control wherever we go so they don't infringe upon other people's rights. We see parents who allow this, and we don't think it is right.

We spank our children occasionally. I may be wrong, but I believe a little bit of fear of a parent is good. I think this often deters children from engaging in undesirable practices.

There are some problems which require a family consultation—like the situation in our backyard. All the kids in the neighborhood have been playing ball on our back lawn. When I saw the grass it shook me up and we had a family consultation about it. Harm felt it was better for the kids to be playing ball in our yard than running loose somewhere.

After discussing all the facets of the situation, we agreed that the neighborhood kids would only be allowed to play ball there when our children were home and playing with them. We've already had a number of broken windows because the neighborhood kids have played in our yard while we were away.

I can see Harm's point. He feels as his father Clay did, that happy active boys are more important than grass.

But he also can see mine, that there is no sense in letting such activity ruin our property.

Question: How do you allocate family chores and work out your children's need for money? Do you give them allowances?

Harmon: Elaine can tell you more about arranging for family chores. As far as allowances go, we have really never had a set allowance for our children. We have tried to give them what they need, but never a large amount of money at one time or a specific sum each week or month. Possibly, our boys are old enough now that we might do this. But the girls still seem a little young to handle money.

Elaine: Our children have been very cooperative about receiving and spending money and doing chores. They all have chores to do and one that they all participate in is bringing in water. In our Ontario home all of our water comes from a pump and through a water softener. I don't like the softened water so the children take turns getting the water from the pump. During the winter they have contests to see who can get the water the fastest. I think Cam set a record of 40 seconds and he had to move like a whirlwind to do it.

They also have other chores. Kenny feeds the horses every day, and the girls get up in time to make their own beds each morning before they go to school.

I'm really proud of our children's cooperative attitude. Kathy seems to enjoy housework and keeps things straight, and Cam, as the oldest child, is setting a good example for the others. He has begun washing his own clothes and a couple of weeks ago the lawn needed mowing (it is huge) so Cam and I mowed it. He did a very conscientous job, so that evening I gave him two dollars. He handed it back to me and said, "No thanks, you don't need to do that." I didn't insist that he take it because I was happy he felt that way, so I told him, "Thank you, I appreciate it."

Question: There seems to be a lot of controversy nowadays regarding how and when you should talk to children about sex. How do you feel about sex education for children?

Elaine: I can speak for both of us about that because we agree completely on the approach. We think parents should discuss sex with their children and we've used natural opportunities to do so. We've always had dogs and our children have had the opportunity to see their puppies born.

One day quite by accident, Shawn who was seven at the time, saw some dogs breeding. I explained to her that it was a natural mating relationship. A short time later, one of the smaller girls saw the same situation and became quite concerned about it. Shawn put her at ease by saying, in a matter-of-fact way, "They're just breeding." When one of our boys was ten we took him with us when we bred our horses.

We don't believe in telling our children that a big bird

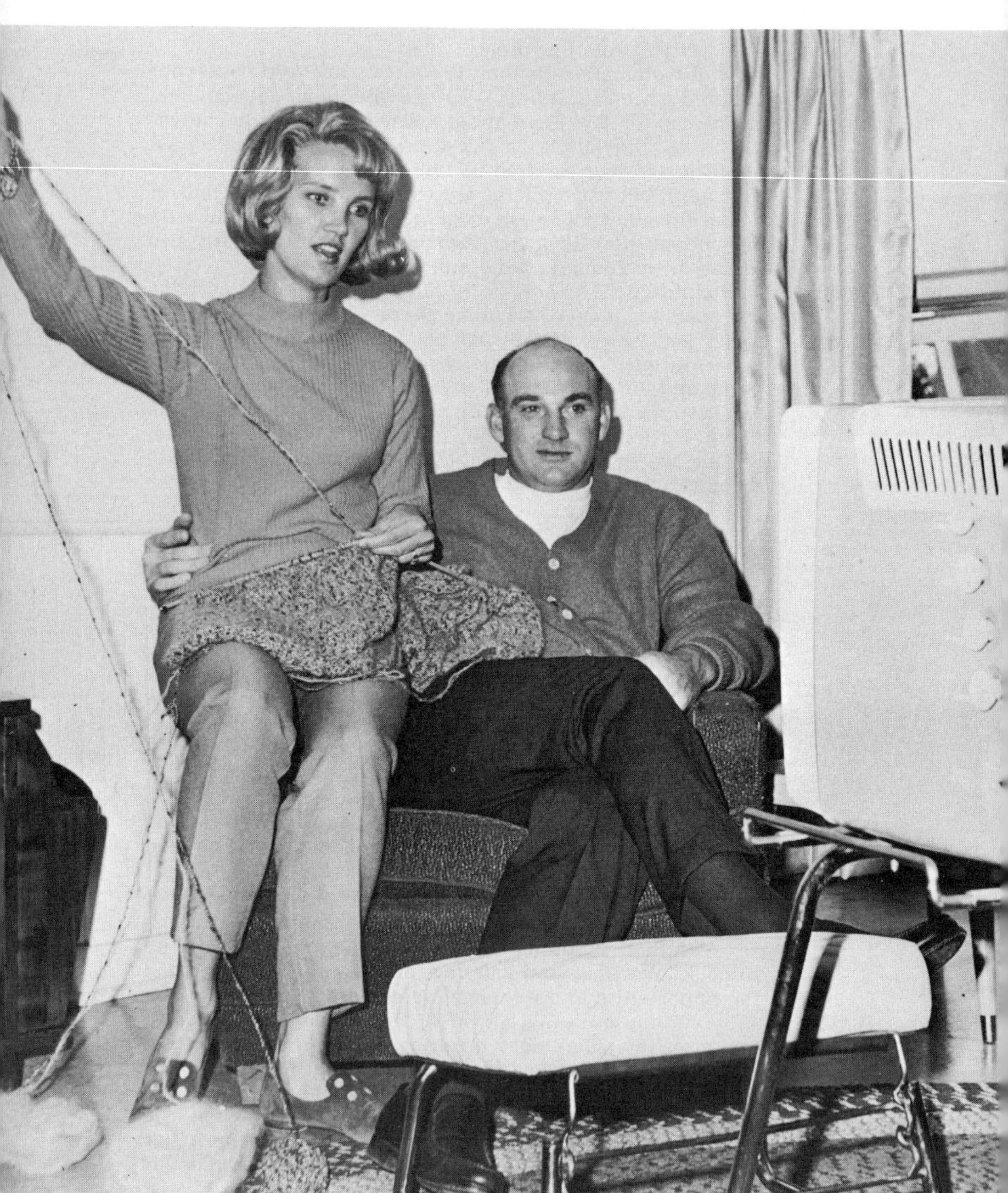

Harmon and Elaine watching the World Series at his brother Gene's home in Corvallis, Oregon

Elaine and Harmon with their handsome houseful back home in Oregon

brought them, so before our youngest child Erin was born we let the others place their hands on my body and feel her tiny kicks. And later, after she was delivered by Caesarean section, I let them see the scar from the incision.

We feel that girls should be prepared properly for the coming of the menstrual period and that boys should also understand this and their own growing up processes. Boys seem more reserved about discussing these things, but we have done it with the help of books.

You can see that we both believe that it is important to give children a sound and wholesome understanding of the place of sex in life.

Question: Do you have any special group activities or rituals that help draw you closer together as a family?

Harmon: We always have a special celebration on birthdays and if I am away at the time I phone to let them know I remember the occasion. We also all take turns in blessing the food before meals.

Elaine: We spend Thanksgiving, Christmas, and other special holidays with the children's grandparents and other relatives and we really appreciate being together.

Question: Do you think church activity helps unite a family?

Harmon: Since I have been converted to the church, I have felt a marked change in my life. Although I attended church with Elaine when we were in high school, it wasn't until I was baptized that I really understood the plan of life and how we should strive to work out our salvation. Now I want to live and help all our family live in such a way that we can be together forever. And it is my belief that we will be, if we keep God's commandments. We try to hold a family home night once a week as our church authorities suggest and on these nights we study and socialize together as a family.

Elaine: I think the church plays an important role in the life of a family. And it seems that our family activities revolve more around the church than anywhere else. The meetings and activities also give us all many opportunities to develop our talents.

I've been so happy since Harm joined the Church. I've always loved him dearly. And now that we have been sealed to each other in the temple and also have had the privilege of being sealed to our children my joy is complete. It is a great thrill to know that Harm and I and our children have the privilege, if we live worthily, of being together as a family forever. I know to do this that we must attend church regularly so that Harm and I can grow and develop together in our religion and reach the point where we can help our children understand and meet every challenge life offers. Harm met with the Mormon missionaries for a number of years before joining the church, but now that he has become a member he is faithful and dedicated.

Question: Do you have any frustrations to overcome in your family life?

Elaine: When Harmon is away a lot, I do get a bit down. But when he comes home he more than makes up for my previous loneliness. He's a real homebody. He plays with the children and although other husbands may hate me for saying this, he is great around the house. He helps keep the house clean, likes to take turns with the cooking, feeds the children and even changes diapers.

Harmon: I guess my frustrations come from being away so much. I don't enjoy the bright lights in big cities, and I can think of nothing more satisfying than being home with Elaine and the children.

Question: Do you have any specific plans for the future?

Elaine: Of course our primary goal is to help one another, as family members, to develop to full potential so we can better serve others. We feel this is our purpose for being; and I also hope that along the way some of Harm's calmness and patience will rub off on me.

Harmon: As long as Elaine is at my side, I don't worry about the future. She has inspired me and encouraged me in everything I've done. I suppose I'll play ball as long as I can, and then try to become established in business.

Elaine: Harm's just too modest. We both want him to continue playing baseball as long as he enjoys it. I feel personally that he could go on hitting homeruns forever, but running around the bases could become a problem. So we must be realistic. Ballplayers legs are usually the first part of them to give out and Harm has had some serious leg injuries. Harmon has some television shows now and I think he does an excellent job with them. He also would be good in public relations. He knows how to get people calmed down in a tense situation and how to help each side see the other's viewpoint. He is president of Killebrew Enterprises which manufactures the Killebrew Batting Trainer and other sports devices and games, and he is a partner in a wholesale drug company.

I'm not worried about our future, because I think Harm can do anything he wants to do.

Question: How about that, Harm?

Harmon: Elaine's really a good press agent, isn't she? I suppose our future will work out like things always have before. Elaine will encourage me and I'll just keep swinging.

The Killebrew family at Metropolitan Stadium, August, 1970

the future

The Minnesota Twins continued their winning ways during the rest of the 1970 season. Harmon played in the All-Star game and after the break, continued to pound out key hits.

September 9, 1970, was Bob Allison Tribute Day. At this time, Bob who has been a close and loyal friend to Harmon since their rookie days, announced his retirement.

Allison's feats as a player are legendary, his magnificent catch in the 1965 World Series being one of the greatest in baseball history. Throughout his entire career, Bob Allison retained his enthusiasm for the game and never let down, whether he was straining to catch an impossible fly, swinging for a hit or riding the bench.

Allison was presented with many gifts in the ceremony that night. Calvin Griffith gave him a luxurious, completely equipped motor home as a token of esteem.

Harmon represented the team in presenting Allison with a magnificent shotgun, case and gun cabinet. As the two friends stood in the pouring rain, Harmon wished

Bob luck in the future. I am sure that their many years as companions, as they struggled to succeed, will not be forgotten.

During the closing weeks of the season, Killebrew sustained a wrist injury that affected his timing at bat. But he refused to talk about it, and wouldn't use it as an excuse when his hitting fell off.

I met Doc Lentz in one of the stadium corridors about this time and asked him about Harmon.

He said, "Harm's overtired. He's worn out physically, but he's so conscientious he won't take a rest."

The 1970 Twins again captured the American League's Western Division pennant by about the same margin as in 1969. Rigney guided them through some trying periods and they finished strong.

Once again, they met the Baltimore Orioles, the Eastern Division's winners, in the playoffs. After Minnesota lost the first game, Harmon tried to rally the team in the second contest with a long homerun, but the breaks seemed to go against the Minnesotans, and the Orioles emerged victorious in the series. The Baltimore players later showed their strength by defeating the powerful Cincinnati Reds in the World Series.

At the end of the play-offs, Harmon and Elaine left for Ontario to rejoin their children.

What lies ahead in the future for Harmon Killebrew?

He is now recognized as one of the greatest right-handed hitters of all time. And in addition, is one of the most highly-respected individuals in the world of sports.

Bill Rigney made a statement that is representative of the thinking of Harmon's friends and associates. When Bill was asked at the end of his 1970 pennant-winning season if he planned to continue managing in the future, he said, "It depends a lot on what the 'Big Guy' does. If he's going to be around the next few years, I'd like to continue. Every manager should have the privilege of working with a Harmon Killebrew."

So, Harmon has won himself a place in the world of

baseball. It is highly possible that he can continue in some capacity associated with the game as long as he desires.

There also seems to be no doubt that someday, "The Big Guy," "The Killer" and to many the "nicest man in baseball," will be elected to the National Baseball Hall of Fame, in Cooperstown, New York.

But as is the way with men who dream, Harmon won't stop with these achievements. He has already become a popular television interviewer and has several profitable advertising contracts.

In August of 1970, Killebrew and his friends, Bob Allison and Dave Yaeger, led a group who purchased a nationally-known pharmaceutical firm to make it part of their World-wide Pharmaceutical Corporation.

And finally, he has Killebrew Incorporated based in Salt Lake City, which is concentrating on producing and distributing sports devices and toys. One of these products, the Killebrew Power Stride batting trainer, has been designed to help baseball players of all ages improve their batting techniques. At the time of this writing, it is being enthusiastically accepted throughout the nation.

Killebrew Inc., in Salt Lake City, bears the Killebrew stamp. The building that the company is housed in is clean, neat and well-designed. And the employees are the Killebrew-type—sincere, friendly, and committed to their jobs. Some of the key employees are Vibert Kesler, Executive Vice-President; Devere Watkins, Manager; Rudy Zander, Sales Director; and Rulon Dahl, Production Engineer. The company employs many students and young handicapped people. Service seems to play a major role in their philosophy.

When you talk to Harmon Killebrew about his various activities and interests, you learn very quickly that his family is the center of his life, and that his wife, Elaine, and his children are his most valued possessions.

Ray Looney, who was a teen-age companion of Harmon's, and as outstanding a pitcher as Killebrew was hitter on the Junior American Legion team which won the Idaho

State title in 1952, can attest to this. When I told Ray, who is a Trans World Airlines executive, that I was writing Harmon Killebrew's life story, he took time out from his busy schedule and sent me the following note:

"There was a certain 'something special' about the chemistry between these two. Whenever Harmon would see Elaine—in any situation or at any time, or under any circumstances—that was the end of any conversation with Harmon. He would immediately leave the group discussing a very important event, or game or whatever, and head straight for Elaine. His eyes would light up and a big smile would break out. You didn't even need to know that Elaine was in the area to know what those signs meant. I had never seen such a strong, romantic relationship between two people, and it was truly something to remember."

There is still "something special" between Harmon and Elaine Killebrew, and I have no doubt that in the years to come when Harmon dreams the impossible dream or reaches for an unreachable star, Elaine will always be at his side saying, "You can do it, Harm. You can do anything you want to do."

Index